WOMEN IN THE SKY

WOMEN IN THE SKY

Gender and Labor in the Making of Modern Korea

Hwasook Nam

ILR PRESS
AN IMPRINT OF CORNELL UNIVERSITY PRESS ITHACA AND LONDON

Copyright © 2021 by Cornell University

This publication was supported by the 2021 Korean Studies Grant Program of the Academy of Korean Studies (AKS-2021-P-010).

All rights reserved. Except for brief quotations in a review, this book, or parts thereof, must not be reproduced in any form without permission in writing from the publisher. For information, address Cornell University Press, Sage House, 512 East State Street, Ithaca, New York 14850. Visit our website at cornellpress.cornell.edu.

First published 2021 by Cornell University Press

Library of Congress Cataloging-in-Publication Data

Names: Nam, Hwasook, 1959– author.
Title: Women in the sky : gender and labor in the making of modern Korea / Hwasook Nam.
Description: Ithaca [New York] : ILR Press, an imprint of Cornell University Press, 2021. | Includes bibliographical references and index.
Identifiers: LCCN 2021002499 (print) | LCCN 2021002500 (ebook) | ISBN 9781501758263 (hardcover) | ISBN 9781501758270 (epub) | ISBN 9781501758287 (pdf)
Subjects: LCSH: Women in the labor movement—Korea—History—20th century. | Women in the labor movement—Korea (South)—History—20th century. | Women in the labor movement—Korea (South)—History—21st century. | Manufacturing industries—Korea—Employees. | Manufacturing industries—Korea (South)—Employees. | Women employees—Political aspects—Korea. | Women employees—Political aspects—Korea (South)
Classification: LCC HD6198 .N345 2021 (print) | LCC HD6198 (ebook) | DDC 331.4/780951909042—dc23
LC record available at https://lccn.loc.gov/2021002499
LC ebook record available at https://lccn.loc.gov/2021002500

To Chuck

Contents

Acknowledgments	ix
Note on Transliteration and Translation	xiii
Introduction	1
1. A "Woman-in-the-Sky": Female Workers on Strike in Colonial Pyongyang	12
2. Factory Women in the Socialist Imagination: The 1930s	39
3. Coping with Women Strikers: Nation, Class, and Gender under Colonial Rule	61
4. Factory Women in the Postwar Settlement: The 1950s	85
5. Women Workers in Industrializing Korea: From the 1960s to the 1980s	111
6. Female Strikers in Recent Decades and the Politics of Memory	151
Notes	189
Bibliography	249
Index	267

Acknowledgments

From the time I began my graduate study in history at the University of Washington (UW) in Seattle in the 1990s, my aspiration has been to write a book focusing on labor and gender to illuminate the turbulent twentieth-century history of Korea. In particular, I dreamed of composing a book in which women workers as protagonists guide readers through modern Korea's important historical moments and thereby facilitate a new way of seeing the country's political and economic history. This rather ambitious goal has shaped my academic career as a whole and defined my choice of research topics for the past two decades. I first studied male shipbuilding workers, writing a PhD dissertation on their activism, and I later published a book on the subject, first in English in 2009 and then in Korean translation in 2014. In subsequent years I continued to pursue research on various aspects of the history of the South Korean labor movement, looking into gender dynamics in particular, which resulted in several articles and book chapters on the subject. Over the years I accumulated many boxes of source materials on women worker activism through archival research, and I wrote versions of several draft chapters. But it was only after I opted to retire early from my teaching job in 2018 that I was finally able to devote my full time and attention to the book and compose the whole manuscript from beginning to end.

The high point of my research for the book and a major push toward completing it came in the spring of 2017, when I invited to Seattle two incredible female labor activists from Korea, Kim Jin-Sook and Hwang Yira, and organized a series of events around them. The support for their visit came from various entities, including the UW's Harry Bridges Center for Labor Studies, Department of History, and Center for Korea Studies. Support also came from the local Korean community and Seattle unionists. I had had previous contact with Kim, having first chronicled her central role in the democratization in the 1980s of the union at the Hanjin shipyard in Pusan, and later during several interviews I did with her in 2004 and 2006. But her Seattle visit offered me a precious chance to observe her, a key protagonist in this book, up close in public and private settings and talk with her at length. Kim Jin-Sook and her comrade Hwang Yira created many inspiring moments for event attendees, including myself, and the experience of watching them interacting with local unionists and Korean community people as well as students increased my resolve and sense of urgency to get on with this book project.

ACKNOWLEDGMENTS

A particular encounter with Kim Jin-Sook became seared into my memory and has affected the way I composed this book. During a workshop held on campus, Kim, who as a guest had been sitting in a corner of the room patiently listening to scholarly discussions, raised her hand and made a short but impactful observation. She said that while she could see that people were talking about her, she had no clue what the panelists, including me, were actually saying about her. I interpreted her comment as a protest arising from a deep suspicion toward highly educated elite intellectuals who, while professing sympathy to labor's causes, tend to work in a language that is difficult to access for workers like her. The memory of that moment has haunted me and forced me to continue asking who I am vis-à-vis Kim and other women workers whose lives and actions I discuss in the book. Mindful of the distance and complex power relations between intellectuals and workers in the South Korean labor movement, an issue broached in several chapters of the book, I have taken pains to contemplate my own perceptions and interpretations. I have also endeavored to make the book as readable as possible in the hope that Kim and Hwang, and other women workers, will one day read the book in Korean translation and express their own critical views of the book and its subjects.

I received help from numerous individuals and institutions during the many years this book was evolving. Teaching Korean and labor history, first at the University of Utah and then at the UW, afforded me the opportunity to advance my understanding of the issues covered in the book through innumerable helpful discussions with students and colleagues at those institutions. After joining the UW faculty in 2007, I received occasional support for this project from the UW's Department of History and Center for Korea Studies. Major financial support came in the form of a visiting professorship during the fall semester of 2011 from the Graduate School of East Asian Studies (GSEAS) of Yamaguchi University in Japan, at which time, while teaching labor history classes in English, I observed from afar the last leg of Kim Jin-Sook's historic crane-top sit-in. I thank the GSEAS and Professor Yokota Nobuko for hosting me and also arranging for me to give a public lecture at the university. That lecture represented my first attempt at linking Kim Jin-Sook and her 1930s predecessor, Kang Churyong, in the context of the unusual phenomenon of the high-altitude sit-in struggles South Korea was witnessing at the time. A year-long sabbatical leave from the UW during the 2015–16 academic year and a visiting professorship offered by the Department of History at Sungkyunkwan University in Seoul in the fall semester of 2015 allowed me to conduct more research at libraries and archives in Seoul and Daejeon. During that time, I benefited from the extensive collections on Korean social history at the Sungkyunkwan University Library, the Seoul National University Library, the National Library of Korea, the National Assembly Library, and the National

Archives of Korea. I am grateful to professors Ha Wonsoo and Chung Hyunback, my hosts at Sungkyunkwan, for that opportunity. I also benefited from the oral history and documentary collections held at the Labor History Institute of Sŏnggonghoe University and at the Korea Democracy Foundation.

Kim Keong-il of the Academy of Korean Studies kindly helped me digitally access the Sŏnggonghoe University oral history materials as well as colonial-period source materials, and Yi Sanggyŏng of KAIST University always offered ready answers to the many questions I peppered her with regarding colonial-period Korean literature and gender history. Women's historian Lee Namhee, then head of the Korean Women's Studies Institute, arranged for Kim Jin-Sook's special lecture for the Women's Studies Interdisciplinary Program at Seoul National University in September 2017 and shared the transcript of the lecture with me. I am grateful to these and many other scholars in Korea who have welcomed me into their research circles and made my research work in Korea an enriching and enjoyable experience. As always, outstanding holdings of Korean-language materials at the East Asia Library at the University of Washington and its offering of database access to source materials and publications in Korea have been indispensable for my research. I thank in particular the library's Korea librarian, Yi Hyokyoung, for all her support over the years.

Studying labor history alerted me to the important role Cornell University Press has played through publication of its many books on labor and gender, including studies of the South Korean labor movement. I am grateful to editors Frances Benson, Ellen Labbate, and Jennifer Savran Kelly for their encouragement, guidance, and support through the review and publication process. The book benefited greatly from the sharp comments and very useful suggestions offered by the two anonymous readers of the initial manuscript.

This book would not have reached completion without the enthusiastic and unwavering support of my compañero and fellow labor historian, Chuck Bergquist, who constantly reminded me of the importance of the stories I was working on and gave me editorial as well as moral support whenever I needed it. My family members and friends in Korea have continued to shower me with love and support through good times and bad. The respect for his "writer" mom conveyed by my son, Byungha, has boosted my morale and motivated me to produce a book I hope he too will enjoy reading. This book is a product of an ongoing collective labor of love by many people around me rather than an outcome of my own solitary labor, although all the shortcomings of the book, of course, are solely mine.

Note on Transliteration and Translation

Romanization of Korean and Japanese words and names follows the McCune-Reischauer and the Hepburn systems, respectively. I have made exceptions in the case of historical figures, place-names, or newspapers when alternative spellings in the English language are well known (e.g., Park Chung Hee, Chun Tae-il, Kim Jin-Sook, Pyongyang, Seoul, Dong-A ilbo). In such cases the pertinent transliteration is provided in parentheses following the first occurrence of the word. Korean and Japanese names of authors who publish primarily in their native language are ordered according to the East Asian convention of providing the given name following the surname (e.g., O Kiyŏng). All translation is my own unless otherwise noted.

WOMEN IN THE SKY

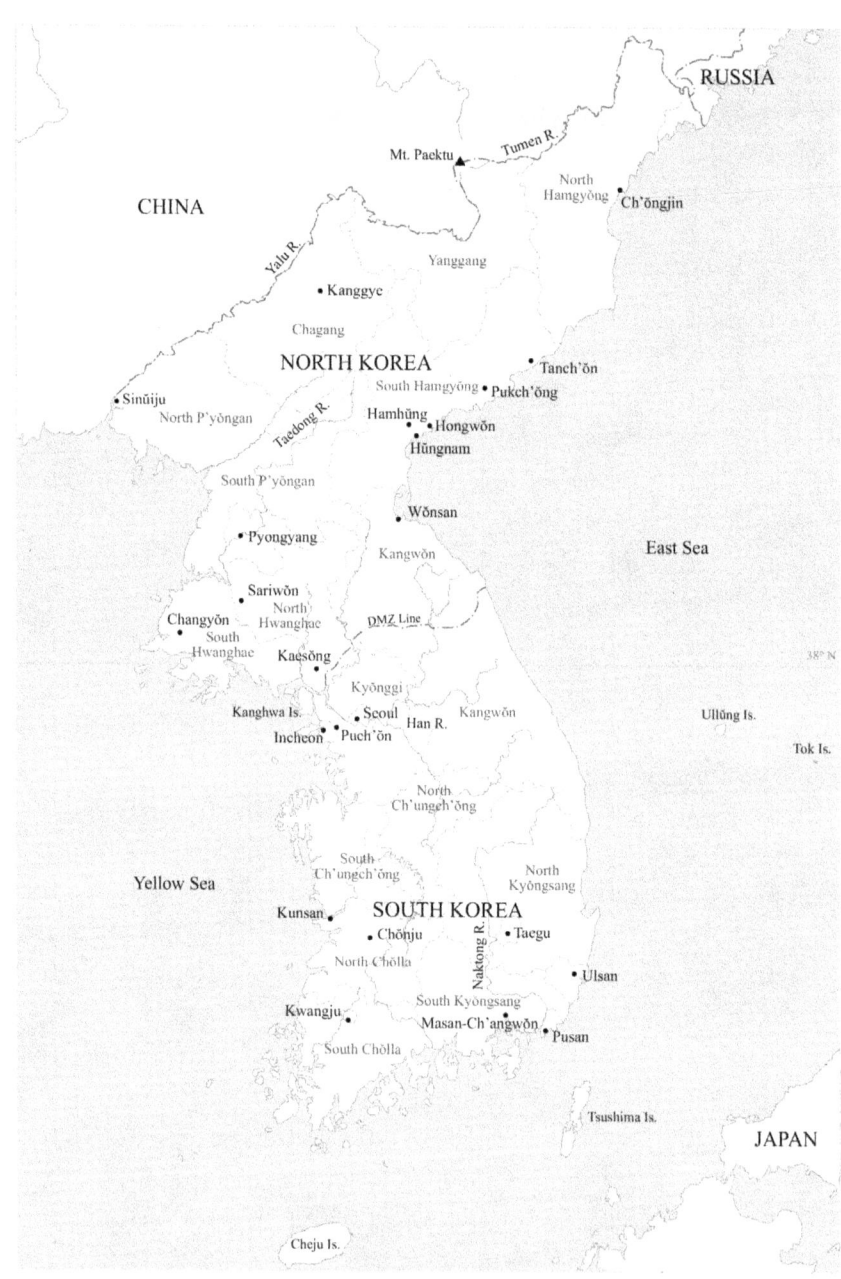

MAP 1. Korea, early twenty-first century

Introduction

"A Woman-in-the-Sky Suddenly Appeared," a major national newspaper in Korea reported on May 30, 1931, and the following day it featured prominently a black-and-white photo of the protagonist, a female rubber worker, perched on the roof of the historic Ŭlmiltae Pavilion in Pyongyang (P'yŏngyang).[1] The low resolution of the newspaper photograph made it hard to see the face of the woman, but the way she was squatting on the edge of the tile roof with her arms crossed signifies her firm resolution (see figure 1). Her traditional hairdo and the common working-class *hanbok* (Korean-style clothing), consisting of a white blouse and dark or black skirt, contrasts with the sartorial style of the two men whose heads are visible at the bottom of the photo. One man, who stands at the lower left corner facing the rooftop, is wearing a light-colored fedora-like hat with a round brim, a marker of a respectable bourgeois citizen at the time. Another man next to him is looking in the opposite direction, seemingly at a crowd, wearing a dark-colored army cap. Perhaps he is one of the forty policemen and firefighters sent to the scene. It was a strange juxtaposition that seems to capture a historic encounter between working-class Pyongyang and middle-class Pyongyang, one watched carefully by Japanese police and other colonial authorities in a modernizing Korea.

The news report accompanying this iconic photo highly praises the oratorical skills of this working-class woman. It describes how, facing a crowd of over seventy Pyongyang citizens congregated below, she passionately condemned the abuses of her factory's management and spoke of the wretched conditions of

FIGURE 1. Kang Churyong's sit-in on the Ŭlmiltae Pavilion in Pyongyang, *Dong-A ilbo* newspaper, May 31, 1931, p. 2. Courtesy of the Dong-A Ilbosa. The photo in the top left corner has the caption "P'yŏngwŏn Rubber *yŏjikkong* (female factory worker) sitting on top of the Ŭlmiltae." Below the photo, the headlines of the article read, "Employers' attitude stubborn / Striking workers all fired / Thirty or so *yŏjikkong* continue fasting / Breaking news on P'yŏngwŏn Rubber dispute." To the lower left of these headlines is another short report on Kang Churyong titled "Nine hours of staying in the air (*ch'egong*) / Dragged down."

factory life. The *Dong-A ilbo* correspondent recounts how she articulated the reasons why she and her fellow workers could not accept management-declared wage cuts at their factory, P'yŏngwŏn Rubber, explaining that it would lead to disastrous industry-wide wage cuts in the city and jeopardize the "lives of more than two thousand rubber workers." Her "memorable big speech" (*ilchang yŏnsŏl*) was so moving that a Protestant church elder, one Mr. Rim, who was in the crowd of spectators and heard her out, was in tears. Pyongyang's intellectuals marveled at how "eloquent" (*talbyŏn*) the working-class woman was in making the case for striking workers and emphasized the articulate nature of her speech. One intellectual applauded the high level of class consciousness he saw in her speech, and a poet wrote an emotional essay admiring her as a brave and strong-willed "female fighter."[2] Such was the initial impact of the "Woman-in-the-Sky," Kang Churyong.

This portrait of an intelligent and assertive factory woman making an eloquent and powerful speech literally looking down on middle-class citizens is jarring, because such an image contradicts the conventional trope of helpless, passive, and victimized factory girls in Korean society both then and now. Factory girls might scream and cry, or they might suffer in silence. Sometimes, the conventional narrative goes, these allegedly docile workers could be manipulated into militant actions by subversive forces taking advantage of their naivete and ignorance. Over the twentieth century, South Korean society became accustomed to this line of thinking about factory women despite the fact that women industrial workers time and time again showed a very high level of militancy against repressive labor control regimes, with or without union support. Once in a while articulate voices of some women workers, like the rubber worker Kang Churyong, pierced the veil of the media to reach the general public, and when that happened some perceptive people expressed astonishment and a sense of perplexity. But overall such disquieting moments did not last long.

The images most people in South Korea have conjured up when thinking about factory women, often called *yŏgong* (female factory operative), are nothing like the organic female intellectual figure Kang Churyong represents, even though ample, albeit scattered, evidence of articulate and militant women strikers exists in the historical record. By the 1970s, when the number of factory women grew markedly under the state's export-oriented industrialization drive, those images had actually worsened, and a derogatory term, *kongsuni* (I discuss this term in chapter 5), became a common way of referring to factory women. The neoliberal transformation of the last three decades worked to cheapen the worth of women's work and women workers even further (developments analyzed in chapter 6). This happened despite the active participation of women workers in the *minju* (democratic) labor movement and the anti-authoritarian democracy movement in the 1970s and 1980s. Why is that so? I argue that mainstream society's negation of women factory workers' worth as respectable members of the nation, its denial of their crucial contributions to both the economic development and the success in democratic resistance, is tied to the very nature of Korea's modern nation-building itself. In recent decades, on the brighter side, women workers themselves have increasingly been uttering their disappointment at mainstream narratives through oral history testimonies. And revisionist works highlighting women's achievements in the labor movement are slowly coming out in the study of Korean labor history. Kang Churyong, the memory of whose Ŭlmiltae sit-in was forgotten until very recently, is reemerging as a feminist class warrior in popular accounts in today's South Korea.

This book is an effort to understand the vast and persistent gap between the crucial roles women industrial workers played in the process of Korea's modernization and the development of its labor movement during the twentieth century and their continuing invisibility as key players in conventional social and historical narratives. A paucity of archival materials alone does not explain the invisibility imposed on them. It is true that women workers rarely had opportunities to have their words recorded, but archives are replete with records of their actions, albeit refracted through the perspectives of the media or the police in most cases. Women workers spoke through their actions and left traces of their thoughts in strike demands and fragmented utterances appearing in the contemporary media. Looking deeper, we can decipher how their actions were embedded in the political, economic, and social conditions of particular places and times and also see how their actions, in turn, generated transformative energy for democratic change. Understandings of the social milieu and the ethos of the time, if we grasp them, allow us to hear their voices more clearly and in a more historically informed way. The book focuses on the ways factory women gripped society's attention during certain critical moments in colonial and postcolonial Korean history and attempts to explain the conditions that have led to society's disremembering of their stories.

My interest in exploring the shifting social perceptions of yŏgong or factory women as well as new forms of consciousness emerging among them comes from a larger concern over the deep-seated and stubborn nature of social conservatism in South Korean society. Beneath the ultramodern and cosmopolitan lifestyle of today's South Korea, and despite the existence of strong progressive impulses manifested in vibrant political and social movements of a radical nature throughout the twentieth century, South Korea remains an intensely class- and gender-conscious society.

Unfortunately, the evolution of class and gender ideologies in the history of Korea's modernization in the twentieth century has not been well understood. As discussion at different points in the book makes clear, in the premodern period a hierarchical social system, rooted in a millennium-old hereditary slavery system and patriarchy, was upheld as a natural order. In that social milieu, nonagricultural manual labor, which smacked of slave labor, was despised as a marker of lower-class status. In addition, male superiority over females was an extremely important tenet in the organizing of society. New nationalist ideologies responding to the challenges of the era of imperialist contention that wreaked havoc in Korea at the turn of the twentieth century forced the Korean elite to accept working-class people, and even women, as essential components of the nation. While old habits of mind endured, the new era unleashed tremendous energy that allowed lower-class people and women to yearn for social recognition of their dignity and equal membership in society. This process of modernization and nation-building in Korea was hardly linear and clear-cut. Decades of colonial rule and fervent anticolonial resistance complicated class and gender politics in the first half of the twentieth century, and the collapse of the Japanese Empire in 1945 and postcolonial conditions of nation-building in South Korea under US hegemony and in the Cold War setting added more volatility to political, ideological, and social negotiations surrounding class and gender relations. In such a turbulent and fluid ideological and political landscape, how to define the place of laborers and women in society and the economy continued to be a knotty and weighty affair throughout the century.

The focus throughout the book on yŏgong, female industrial workers, is revealing because as lower-class women and as manual laborers, factory women, together with domestic service and sex industry workers, have historically been placed at the lowest rung of Korean society, receiving the brunt of both class and gender discrimination. Contemplating the evolving class and gender dynamics in the nation-building history of twentieth-century Korea through the lens of yŏgong and their struggle goes a long way toward understanding that history.

My interest in the subject of yŏgong goes back decades. A profound sense of injustice shook me in the late 1980s when, as a feminist researcher and former student activist, I encountered the soon-to-be-dominant discourse in the democracy movement. That discourse assigned only a minor place for the yŏgong who fought so gallantly and contributed so much to the democratic (minju) labor movement. This was a time right after the June Struggle of 1987 and the subsequent Great Workers' Struggle, when South Koreans began to demolish the military dictatorship and reclaim basic labor rights: the right to organize a union, to collectively bargain, and to conduct collective actions. Through the Great Workers' Struggle of July–September 1987, male workers, especially those in heavy industries, finally rose up in a massive wave of strikes. Ending a long period of male worker quiescence, they took the helm of the labor movement. As they celebrated the newly empowered union movement, both the activist and progressive scholarly communities turned their critical gaze on the shortcomings of the previous period of women-dominated labor struggle. And instead of recognizing and tackling rampant gender inequality on the shop floor and in the labor movement, as many women worker participants in the struggle expected, they criticized and downplayed women's contributions. Yet it was that very women-dominated labor movement that had provided the preconditions for the Great Workers' Struggle. Disregarding the conditions of these earlier struggles by women workers in female-dominated industries under authoritarian rule, critics were relentless in stressing the putative limitations of the female-led democratic labor movement of the 1970s. They argued that it suffered from an orientation toward economic struggle at the expense of a political struggle and from a lack of the physical power to effectively counter police and company violence. Women workers' sacrifice and accomplishments were thus often relegated to a prehistory before the beginning of a genuine, men-led labor movement.

Out of frustration at my inability to find a language or a frame of reference to formulate an effective counterargument against this unjust rendering of South Korean labor history, I decided to embark on the formal study of Korean labor history, moving away from my research focus on the Korean women's movement of the colonial period, on which I wrote my master's thesis. I wanted to understand how gender relations in the Korean social movements became the way they were. I had the good fortune of discovering a little-known and highly informative union archive at a shipyard in Pusan and subsequently wrote a book on shipbuilding union workers, titled *Building Ships, Building a Nation: Korea's Democratic Unionism under Park Chung Hee*. The story of these male workers showed me how critical it was to situate workers' story in the larger historical context of modernization in which labor, capital, the state, and the community tangled in complex and dynamic ways. I learned that South Korea's economic nation-building history was better told by bringing labor squarely into it. In that book on male shipbuilding workers, gender turned out to be a crucial category of analysis in understanding both economic development and labor resistance. I found that a particular state-capital-labor relationship nurtured by the developmental dictatorship allowed male workers to construct their subjectivities and claims to citizenship around their capacity to perform the role of a breadwinner man of the house. That role fostered their manly pride in being recognized as citizens. Fear of losing that status, as well as the desire to obtain it, often propelled male shipbuilding workers into resolute struggle.

Applying insights I gained from that study, in this book I focus on the labor activism of women workers and survey a much longer span of history, traversing colonial (1910–45) and postcolonial periods. I ask why women workers, despite their impressive and tenacious struggle since the 1920s, did not fare well in generating a widespread and enduring sense of empathy from society as a whole. I consider why women have been relegated to the periphery of the organized labor movement and why memories of women worker activism have, by and large, been downplayed or discounted even in otherwise progressive South Korean activist and academic accounts. I explore how the specific ways the state, businesses, and male workers constructed the industrial relations systems of the new South Korean republic in the early postcolonial decades generated the socioeconomic and political conditions under which certain gendered narratives of yŏgong and their struggle became firmly rooted in society. I also ask what it has meant for women workers to join the progressive endeavor to build a desirable modern society and nation-state when their struggle often resulted in underappreciation and forgetting.

Through this journey following women workers' footsteps, I believe, we begin to appreciate the lofty dreams they fashioned, and we witness the moments when conditions seemed to point to more democratic outcomes. We learn how women industrial workers were developing their capacity and agency, often pushing the boundaries of prescribed gender norms and jolting society as Kang Churyong did. If different kinds of gender and class relations had materialized and prevailed in Korea during the twentieth century, we can then ask what the nature and content of Korean democracy and Korean modernity would be today. If women workers' struggle added momentum to a continuing fight toward a better society, and if their sacrifices, albeit not commemorated, strengthened the undercurrents of democratic impulse in Korean society, how should we assess history writing that negates the historical significance of their contributions? As we witness the continuing social bias against factory women and working-class women in general, while at the same time we detect, albeit not in mainstream media, a strong countercurrent of labor feminism emerging among women workers, what does this situation tell us about South Korean society today?

The literature on Korean labor history has developed mightily since I began my study in the field in the late 1980s. And in this book I do not pretend to do full justice to the breadth and depth of the Korean labor movement and women's participation in it.[3] I do, however, attempt to point out relevant literature and suggest further readings as I go, while refraining from engaging historiographical issues unless they are directly connected to the story I tell. Also, because there are many studies in the Korean language, in particular on intellectual and social movement history and on individual actors and organizations, I try to give readers a sense of that literature, which is not widely known outside specialist circles in Korea. But to allow the story to flow smoothly for a broad general readership and not clog it with reviews of the academic literature, I have relegated details not crucial to the story line to the endnotes. Readers interested in particular issues can find more discussion and specific references there.

The book highlights several key moments in the history of the yŏgong struggle and explores them through the few yŏgong protagonists who left more documentary traces than most. In the colonial period the focal point is the early 1930s and the rubber shoe industry of Pyongyang in the north (chapters 1, 2, and 3), where workers like Kang Churyong produced simple rubber shoes called *komusin*. For postcolonial South Korean history I turn my gaze to the south and engage with textile strikes in the early 1950s in Pusan, the republic's second largest city and wartime capital (chapter 4), before exploring the female-led democratic (minju) union movement that blossomed in Seoul and surrounding areas in the 1970s and early 1980s (chapter 5). Shoe workers appear again as main actors in the last chapter (chapter 6), as it follows the fate of Pusan's footwear workers now producing sneakers for major global companies like Nike and Reebok.

In addition to these women workers, a key protagonist presented in the last chapter is a female welder, Kim Jin-Sook (Kim Chinsuk), whom I first encountered in my study of shipbuilding workers at the Korea Shipbuilding and Engineering Corporation (KSEC; now Hanjin Heavy Industries). Kim was a key leader of the shipyard workers' struggle to democratize their union in the 1980s.

The Hanjin Heavy Industries Union emerged as one of the strongest and most militant unions in the country by the 1990s, and Kim Jin-Sook was at the center of that union's struggles.[4] I wrote an article, published in 2009, on her continuing activism on behalf of Hanjin workers after the company dismissed her in 1986, and I emphasized the broadening of her concerns as she has embraced the cause of contingent workers, most of whom are women. Kim Jin-Sook shocked society with her 309-day high-altitude sit-in on top of a shipyard crane in Pusan in 2011, a feat that became a national sensation and engendered a surge of empathy from diverse segments of society.

Watching her on top of Crane no. 85, thirty-five meters above ground, from early January to November of that year, I often thought about Kang Churyong, whose image on the roof first caught my eye when I was studying colonial history at Seoul National University in the 1980s. Kim Jin-Sook rekindled my interest in Kang, and I began to investigate available archival collections to discover traces of Kang Churyong. Kim Jin-Sook shares many qualities with Kang Churyong, from her renowned oratorical skills and articulateness, to her creative deployment of tactics, to a readiness to sacrifice her life for fellow workers. Like Kang, Kim's actions and speeches stumped observers because she, an influential, respected, and charismatic leader and a rare case of a female metal worker, confronted society with a persona that was the clear opposite of the conventional female worker figure. A contemporary "woman-in-the-sky," her crane-top sit-in in a curious way stimulated a keen interest in Kang Churyong's Ŭlmiltae rooftop sit-in so many years ago, not only for me but also for other observers versed in the history of the colonial labor movement. As a result, after a long period of forgetting, new memories and appreciation of Kang Churyong are beginning to emerge in South Korean society today, as examined in the final chapter of the book.

The newly acquired visibility of Kang Churyong, however, is informed by a mix of political interests and yearnings that are different from those of the 1930s. To the surprise of people, including labor historians like myself, President Moon Jae-in (Mun Chaein) of South Korea called out Kang's name in his speech at the Liberation Day ceremony on August 15, 2018. In it he specifically emphasized women independence fighters and the responsibility of the nation to discover and commemorate them. In this passionate nationalist call to people to "make liberation complete" through active commemoration of forgotten activists, Moon portrayed Kang Churyong as an ardent nationalist fighter (*jisa*) who from the roof of the Ŭlmiltae Pavilion shouted out in favor of the causes of "women's liberation and workers' liberation" (*yŏsŏng haebang nodong haebang*). In examining the pathways of memory construction jump-started by Kim Jin-Sook's crane sit-in, the book closes by contemplating the political nature of memory and of history writing.

Let us now look briefly at some of the broader themes and issues explored in the book. Chapter 1 introduces Kang Churyong and the P'yŏngwŏn Rubber strike, of which she was one of the leaders, and situates Pyongyang's rubber industry and its workers in the larger context of colonial industrialization and the colonial labor movement. It also presents the contours of the bourgeois nationalist movement in Pyongyang and how the focal point of the strike, that is, the issue of proper wage levels for women workers, was intertwined with an emerging division among Pyongyang's nationalist elite. Chapter 2 examines Kang Churyong's association with the communist movement in the region, which at the time was concentrating its resources on the task of organizing industrial workers into revolutionary unions. A women's movement activist, Cho Yŏngok, served as a link between Kang and communist organizers. The chapter explores how the contemporary women's movement positioned itself toward women industrial workers and labor issues and surveys the rise of a new generation of educated "new women," some of whom were, like Cho Yŏngok, joining underground operations to organize women workers at rubber and textile factories. The surge of women worker militancy provoked intense interest not only from communist activists but also from radical writers who began to compose activist yŏgong characters in their literary works. The chapter ends with an exploration of some of these works, stories that portray rubber workers in particular. Chapter 3 reviews the ways the nationalist news media talked about yŏgong activists. This evidence hints at changing social perceptions of yŏgong and also highlights new forms of consciousness and subjectivity emerging among some yŏgong. The chapter then investigates the aftermath of the P'yŏngwŏn Rubber strike, especially a fascinating experiment of building a worker-owned factory. It ends with consideration of the question of how Kang Churyong was remembered.

Beginning with chapter 4 the book moves into the postcolonial period and to South Korean history. During the last decade of colonial rule, labor activism became almost impossible as the Japanese Empire rapidly turned the colony of Korea into a military supply base for its war effort, and a radical transformation of the economy and society followed. The formative experience during this period of modernization and resistance, including social movement experiences, continued to exert a heavy influence on postcolonial nation-building. The ideologies of labor-capital cooperation for the nation/empire enforced by the colonial government during wartime, on the one hand, and proposed by certain nationalist movement forces, on the other, shaped, to a significant degree, workers' own expectations and the direction of the anticommunist labor movement in South Korea in the postliberation decades. Chapter 4 examines the tempestuous 1950s centering on the momentous Chosŏn Spinning and Weaving (Chobang) dispute of 1951–52 in Pusan. The Chobang dispute helped create the momentum for a relatively progressive set of labor laws that passed the National Assembly in 1953. As in the Pyongyang rubber strikes of the early 1930s, women workers again performed a crucial role in the textile dispute and their role gained a certain degree of recognition and respect in 1950s Korea—unlike what happened in the following decades. The process and effect of the Chobang labor dispute, however, were quite different from those of the colonial rubber strikes. Postcolonial conditions of nation-building fostered a vastly different state-labor-capital relationship, in which organized labor controlled by men sought to consolidate male workers' rights and interests, a process that developed at the expense of women workers.

South Korea's developmental era, from the 1960s to the 1980s, is examined in chapter 5. It focuses on the effect of the industrial relations system that consolidated during the 1950s and 1960s and, in particular, the ways in which institutionalization of the male breadwinner model and family living wage discourse in the labor movement beginning in the 1960s enforced the continuing invisibility of yŏgong. The chapter then explores the ways in which women factory workers in the 1970s and 1980s built their grassroots organizational power and developed critical consciousness and practices regarding the gender discrimination they faced at work. The setting here is export-industry factories, including textile, wig, and electronics shops, in Seoul and the surrounding Kyŏnggi Province, although we occasionally visit Kwangju, the provincial capital of South Chŏlla Province. Radical intellectuals and students, like the socialists of the colonial era, recognized women workers' revolutionary potential, and another generation of students turned labor organizers emerged, forging a tension-ridden relationship of the so-called worker-student alliance (*nohak yŏndae*) and further complicating the politics of memory surrounding the 1970s labor movement.

The last chapter, chapter 6, steps into the post-1987, postdevelopmental period of democratization and neoliberal transformation in South Korea and considers the conditions that shaped the invisibility of yŏgong and the underappreciation of their contributions in the current organized labor movement and in the larger society. It features Pusan's female shoe workers' resistance to capital flight in the 1990s and assesses shifting gender politics in the union movement before and after the 1987 Great Workers' Struggle. The unresolved nature of the gender question reveals itself starkly in the case of woman welder Kim Jin-Sook in the changed neoliberal environment of the twenty-first century. During this period the progress that workers had achieved through massive strike waves in the 1980s and 1990s has eroded significantly under new management strategies aiming at reducing union power to cut costs and regain control on the shop floor. The process of irregularization of the workforce accelerated following the Asian financial crisis of 1997–98 and reached the unionized large-firm, heavy-industry regular male workers, engendering ferocious and long-lasting labor disputes.

Meanwhile, an apathy toward labor struggle has become widespread in society, as many South Koreans have lost interest in embracing industrial workers as an essential component of nation-building. Economic restructuring under neoliberal principles has relegated women workers disproportionately into contingent and precarious jobs, yet organized labor's attention has been fixated on what men have lost in the neoliberal transition.

The South Korean union movement, belatedly, began to address the escalating contingent worker problem by the early 2000s, but the question of manifested gender inequality in the restructuring process or the history of the entrenched labor market segregation by gender has not been seriously considered. Meanwhile, women contingent workers at the periphery of the organized labor movement have emerged as a leading force of resistance and their persistence and capacity to produce broad-based solidarity actions and creative cultural events have begun to generate social attention and empathy. The chapter traces this important new development centering on the story of Kim Jin-Sook, a rare case of a female heavy-industry labor organizer of national prominence who has increasingly moved toward a feminist position critical of gendered power relations in the organized labor movement. The book closes with an assessment of evolving memory work in today's South Korean society on yŏgong activism of the past hundred years. In protest of a general lack of appreciation of female workers' contributions to the labor and democracy struggle in Korea, veteran yŏgong activists of the democratic labor movement in recent years have begun to ask a fundamental question: "What if [female workers] had not been there [fighting] at that time?"[5] The stories this book tells of various groups of yŏgong activists, from Kang Churyong and rubber workers in the 1930s to Kim Jin-Sook and the female contingent workers on strike today, are informed by this poignant question. One hopes a retelling of history through the lens of the yŏgong struggle helps a broad audience see how shifting gender, class, and nationalist politics have molded the Korean society we know today and understand why it is vitally important to listen to women workers' voices.

1

A "WOMAN-IN-THE-SKY"
Female Workers on Strike in Colonial Pyongyang

In the early morning hours of May 29, 1931, a hundred or so Pyongyang citizens walking near the Ŭlmiltae Pavilion were surprised to find a woman squatting on top of the pavilion's roof, making a feverish speech. She said she would jump to her death if anybody brought a ladder to the roof. Ŭlmiltae, a popular site for morning walks for Pyongyang citizens, was perched on the edge of scenic Moran Peak on the northern shores of the Taedong River, which runs across the city of Pyongyang from northeast to southwest. The pavilion building where she sat was a little more than twenty-four feet above the ground on the front (southern) side, but the opposite (northern) side was built on a thirty-six-foot-high Koguryŏ-period stone embankment, a part of the Pyongyang fortress that followed steep mountain ridges to the north.[1] A morning walk through the Ŭlmiltae area was a popular activity for Pyongyang citizens and became part of nationalist programs for nurturing modern citizens through a healthy lifestyle.[2] For the purpose of grabbing the attention of the public, the roof of the Ŭlmiltae was thus a superb and creative choice for a protest. The woman's unprecedented tactic created a sensation among her astonished audience and attracted national news media attention to her and the strike that pushed her up on the roof.

She explained later how she had climbed up on the roof. She had purchased a roll of cotton cloth, tied a stone on one end of it, and hurled it above the roof until it caught. The Pyongyang police sent dozens of officers in three cars and brought in firefighters to find ways to make her come down. This unusual instance of a working-class woman taking a bold action in public and, moreover, making "eloquent" (*talbyŏn*) speeches on heavy-duty subjects such as solidarity of the proletariat (*musanja*) and the deplorable actions of employers caught media attention, and her story made national news the following day.[3] In the following weeks the *Dong-A ilbo* (Tonga ilbo; East Asia Daily), a major bourgeois nationalist Korean-language newspaper, reported almost daily on her and on the strike that propelled her to start the sensational high-altitude sit-in.[4] The paper also bequeathed to us the iconic photo of the woman, Kang Churyong, on the roof of the Ŭlmiltae Pavilion. A nationalist journal, *Tonggwang* (Eastern Light), published an interview with Kang in its July 1931 issue.[5] The author of the *Tonggwang* interview article, writing under the pen name Muhojŏngin ("A person of no-name house"), stated that Kang's speech during the sit-in showed "the [high] level of class consciousness of the Woman-in-the-Sky [*ch'ŏgongnyŏ*]." After she explained how the strike at her factory, P'yŏngwŏn Rubber, was in fact a pattern-setting battle that would affect the fate of two thousand rubber workers in Pyongyang, Kang told the crowd she would not come down unless the president of P'yŏngwŏn Rubber came to her and rescinded the wage cut order. If he refused to do so, she continued, "I would consider death as an honor, as a representative of the working masses (*kŭllo taejung*)."[6]

Newspapers tried to capture and sensationalize her unprecedented demonstration tactic by calling her "oksang yŏ(ja)" (a woman on the roof), or "Ŭlmiltae ŭi yŏin" (a woman of Ŭlmiltae), or "yŏ(ja) t'usa" (a female fighter).[7] Poet Kim Ch'angsul called Kang "Ŭlmiltae sang ŭi t'usa" (a fighter on the Ŭlmiltae) and "Sŏbu chŏnsŏn ŭi yŏt'usa" (a female fighter of the Western Front) who charted a "new tactic in *aji-p'ŭro*" (agitation-propaganda).[8] Some admired her as "yŏjangbu" (a female *changbu* [manly man]).[9] What became the defining moniker for her, however, was "ch'ŏgongnyŏ" (a woman-in-the-sky), a strange nickname initially given in a *Dong-A ilbo* article from May 30 in its sensational headline, "A Woman-in-the-Sky Suddenly Appeared on Pyongyang's Ŭlmiltae."

In this way a new type of female political actor was born. Conditions that allowed a factory woman to steer national attention had been in the making since the early 1920s. The labor movement in colonial Korea had developed into a mature stage by the early 1930s, and women workers actively participated in these developments. By the early 1930s socialist labor activism had grown in strength, and industrial workers were being called on to form the foundation of a revolution. By the time P'yŏngwŏn Rubber workers went on strike in May 1931, women workers, textile and rubber workers in particular, were already veterans of many brutal strikes. At the peak of this extraordinary wave of female worker militancy, Kang Churyong added a new tactic of high-altitude sit-in to the rich repertoire of resistance in the workers' arsenal and brilliantly succeeded in attracting the attention of the larger society. Equally important was the fact that a segment of elite society, forced by the reality of intensifying class conflict in a society seriously hit by the effects of worldwide depression, was ready to be drawn to her story. Kang sat on the roof of the Ŭlmiltae at a particular moment when the labor question was painfully touching a nerve in the Korean bourgeois nationalist movement. Of all the labor disputes in the country, rubber and knitwear workers' challenge in Pyongyang was especially agonizing to Pyongyang's business elite because the majority of factory owners in these industries were Koreans, and this local elite maintained deep ties to the region's Protestant nationalist movement. Kang Churyong's action was spotlighted in the national media in this context, and the stakes were high in terms of the legitimacy of the bourgeois Christian leadership of the city. How society responded to the cries of Pyongyang rubber workers at this politically critical juncture in colonial Korean history thus reveals both the potentials and the limitations of the bourgeois nationalist movement on questions of class and gender.

A socially active woman was not a novelty in Korea in the early 1930s. Colonial Korean media had carried "heated" debates on "New Woman" (*sinyŏsŏng*) figures since the 1920s, and stories of women actively engaging in social and political movements were not unfamiliar to Korean readers by the time Kang appeared on the roof of the Ŭlmiltae. By 1931 the women's movement had been a noticeable force in the Korean social and anticolonial movements for a decade. A women-only united-front organization, the Kŭnuhoe (Rose of Sharon Society), was jointly created by socialist and nonsocialist women activists in May 1927, as the sister organization of the national united-front organization Sin'ganhoe (New Korea Society, also established in 1927). The Kŭnuhoe had established over sixty chapters across the country and overseas, engaging thousands of members, by the time it collapsed in 1931 (see chapter 2).[10] The presence of women as active political agents was thus not a novel phenomenon by the late 1920s.[11] Kang's case, however, was especially jarring because she was not a typical "new woman" actor, conventionally understood as a product of modern education.[12] She was a rubber factory worker who lacked formal education, yet she was making the bold move of appearing in public and representing her fellow workers. Her public action of a solitary high-altitude sit-in was the first of its kind in Korean labor history and as such generated significant interest across society. At the end of 1931 *Chungang ilbo* recalled Kang's action as "a new record in the history of labor-capital relations in Korea."[13] Her action is today being acknowledged as the first instance of the mind-boggling phenomenon of widespread high-altitude sit-ins in the South Korean labor movement since the 1990s. This phenomenon has become a highly visible marker of the unresolved labor question and the continuing militancy of South Korean workers today, a question discussed in detail in chapter 6.

"A Woman-in-the-Sky Suddenly Appeared" in Pyongyang

The first report of Kang's Ŭlmiltae sit-in in *Dong-A ilbo* on May 30 that starts with the sensational headline, "On Pyongyang's Ŭlmiltae, A Woman-in-the-Sky Suddenly Appeared," ends with an observation that provides a clue to why Kang earned her nickname. It reads: "Juxtaposed to the Chimney Man [*yŏndol-nam*; *entotsu-otoko* in Japanese] in labor disputes in Japan, a woman factory worker in a Pyongyang labor dispute staying in the air on the roof of the Ŭlmiltae makes a very good comparison point [*hodaejo*]."[14] "Chimney Man" was the nickname originally given to Japanese labor activist Tanabe Kiyoshi, whose sensational high-altitude sit-in on a factory chimney the previous year during a strike at the Kawasaki factory of Fuji Gas Cotton Spinning had garnered much attention in Japan.[15] A labor dispute there over wage cuts and layoffs had hit an impasse, and on November 16, 1930, a young activist from the Japan Labor-Farmer Party climbed up a tall chimney and refused to come down. A train carrying the Shōwa emperor was scheduled to pass by the area on the 21st, and the police were fearful of the emperor seeing the red flag flown high on the chimney by Tanabe. Frantic negotiations ensued, mediated by the police and Labor and Farmer Party delegates, while thousands of onlookers on the ground watched the drama. In the end, thanks to Tanabe's attention-grabbing act, an agreement favorable to the workers was reached, and Tanabe came down from the chimney after 130 hours and 22 minutes.

Tanabe's feat was duly reported in Korean news media, and other "chimney man" events that followed during the early 1930s in Japan were also reported in the Korean press.[16] Considering the fact that the Japanese newspaper *Asahi shinbun*, which reported on Tanabe's chimney man incident closely, was widely circulating in colonial Korea, as were major Japanese magazines, including *Kaizō*, whose January 1931 issue featured an article titled "What Is Chimney Man?" it is certain that the term "chimney man" was well known among Korean news reporters by May 1931.[17] And at least one newspaper account called Kang "a chimney woman" (*yŏndol-nyŏ*) in a 1933 article reporting on her death.[18] But it was the term coined by *Dong-A ilbo*, "Woman-in-the-Sky," that was used much more often for Kang.

The strike at the P'yŏngwŏn Rubber factory started on May 17, provoked by the announcement of wage cuts.[19] Wages for rubber shoe workers in Pyongyang had already been lowered significantly in the previous year, in spite of a massive solidarity strike in the city by over 1,800 workers at ten rubber factories. Then in early 1931, management at P'yŏngwŏn Rubber, a small Korean-owned company employing forty-nine workers, spearheaded a new round of even deeper pay cuts from 4.5 chŏn (a chŏn is one one-hundredth of a Korean wŏn), 3.6 chŏn, and 2.7 chŏn per pair in different categories of rubber shoes to 4, 3, and 2 chŏn, respectively.[20] When the workers went on strike, the company began to hire new employees and fired all striking workers. Women workers then responded by organizing a hunger alliance (*tansik tongmaeng*) and occupied the factory on May 28. The "new tactic" of a factory sit-in was thwarted by the police, however, who evicted the strikers and began to patrol the factory grounds and arrest workers. Driven out of the factory by the police and watching fellow women workers crying, Kang Churyong later told Muhojŏngin, the interviewer from journal *Tonggwang*, that she contemplated committing suicide in protest but instead decided to perform a risky high-altitude sit-in on the Ŭlmiltae Pavilion. That way at least she could speak to her heart's content to the public about the injustices the company had inflicted on workers. Kang Churyong had lasted close to nine hours on the roof until about 8:40 a.m., when three firefighters snuck up from behind her and pushed her down into a net that had been installed underneath before the operation. Kang lost consciousness after the fall and was subsequently arrested on May 29. After her arrest, fifteen female workers again stormed the factory, but the police dispersed them a second time.[21]

After the initial shock of a public sit-in, Kang Churyong surprised the public once more by starting a hunger strike in the police station, which lasted seventy-six hours "without drinking even a single drop of water."[22] Women strikers participating in the hunger strike grew to more than thirty with support pouring in from factory workers in the area and several labor organizations.[23] But management remained adamant. Still, a group of thirty-plus workers continued to gather in front of the factory gate, and police were deployed there to prevent another worker "attack" on the factory. Kang Churyong was released on May 31, just before midnight, but the police arrested four other colleagues of Kang the next day. Those four also started a hunger strike, which lasted fifty-seven hours until they were released on June 3. The *Dong-A ilbo* news report of June 5 emphasized that the women "shocked society" by refusing to take "even a drop of water or a spoonful of rice" for so many hours.[24]

As the company brought in more strikebreakers, striking women workers set out to harass and discourage newly hired workers. Because striking workers waited outside the building, scab hires had difficulty moving in and out of the factory. At one point when newly hired workers tried to get away from the strikers by boarding a streetcar, more than a dozen women workers lay down on the tracks. When others attempted to get away in automobiles, women workers threw stones and, according to the Japanese-language newspaper *Chōsen shinbun*, even feces, at the cars that carried the new hires.[25] On one occasion a rock shattered a car window. Physical altercations between new hires and strikers occurred often, and at one point eight scab workers were captured and taken to the strike headquarters, where they had to "apologize" to strikers after receiving what one newspaper termed "various persuasions."[26] By June 4, thanks to these militant anti-scab tactics, the number of new hires working at the factory dropped from thirty-one to nineteen, and the following day workers rushed to the factory again, confronted the president of the company, and demanded, while leaving the issue of fired workers aside, that the company pay the new hires the original, pre-cut, wage rates if it wished to resolve the strike.

As soon as she was released from police custody, "far from being demoralized," Kang "immediately went back to the strike headquarters" and led the struggle from there, reported *Dong-A ilbo* on June 3. Kang Churyong's June 7 interview with the journal *Tonggwang* occurred in the midst of this tense and quickly unfolding situation, only a week after her release and three days before she would be arrested again. The day after the interview, the board of directors at P'yŏngwŏn Rubber met and made the decision to give up on the wage cut scheme and rehire twenty-seven of the striking workers while keeping twenty of the thirty-seven newly hired, which meant that twenty strikers would be sacrificed. This compromise was a response to mounting criticism of the company's strong-arm tactics. The great interest in the strike that Kang's high-altitude sit-in helped generate nationally put additional pressure on the company. In fact, the Pyongyang police, a colonial entity sensitive to a potential deterioration of the social order, summoned the head of the company on the day the board of directors met and criticized him, pointing out that initiating wage cuts and firing all strikers were not conducive to industrial peace.[27] The company's offer was also a response to striking workers' June 5 demand that scab workers should be paid at the original rates. But after the company offered its plan to revert back to original wage rates and to rehire some of the striking workers, the strikers refused the offer on the principle of allowing no "sacrifice" (job loss) among workers on strike. At this juncture, on June 10, the police, fearing that workers would "attack" the factory again, arrested Kang Churyong and another leader, Ch'oe Yongdŏk.[28] Kang and Ch'oe, called "the two leaders" of the strike by the *Chōsen shinbun* newspaper, began another hunger strike, which lasted fifty-four hours. The following day the police arrested another strike leader, Kim Ch'wisŏn. Losing these three "fighters" (*t'usadŭl*) was a big blow to workers, and the strike began to falter.[29]

The *Tonggwang* interviewer Muhojŏngin, whose real name was O Kiyŏng, interviewed Kang on June 7 at the strike headquarters in Sŏn'gyo-ri, near the P'yŏngwŏn Rubber factory.[30] "What kind of a person is this woman? What kind of life story does she have and what kind of environment shaped her?" were the questions the editors at *Tonggwang* asked O Kiyŏng to find answers to. Thanks to this interview, as well as other news reports on Kang, we know more about her life than about any other female labor leader of colonial Korea. That does not mean that actions of other women strike leaders were less impressive than Kang's. We already saw that Ch'oe Yongdŏk and Kim Ch'wisŏn were arrested together with Kang on June 10 and 11, and before that four strikers were arrested on June 1 and waged a fifty-seven-hour hunger strike in the police station. Those four women— O Yangdo (27 years old), Ri Inbong (31), Hwang Tosin (34), and Kim Ch'wisŏn (36)—were veterans of hunger strikes and also heroines of a lengthy, sympathetic article on women strikers (see chapter 3).[31] Hwang and Kim were senior to Kang, and Ri was probably the same age as Kang. Solidarity among these women workers was impressive. And although this chapter pivots around Kang's life and work, faint voices and images of other women are also present in Kang's story.

The *Tonggwang* interviewer describes his first impression of the Woman-in-the-Sky as follows: "Small eyes that beam out a powerful force, a nose that suggests sharpness of character, and eloquence in speech beyond my imagination— my first impression was that she was a person of considerable mental strength. But," he went on, "more than that, her past life surprised me as I listened to her. I could see that her [political] consciousness and her personality, which I would say is more upbeat than the average man, did not just happen to belong to her."[32] Although Kang Churyong is pretty much the only working-class woman activist of the colonial period whose name is being actively remembered today, there is no reason to regard Kang as a single exceptional figure in terms of commitment to labor's cause or bravery and leadership skills. As we know, other leaders at P'yŏngwŏn, including Ch'oe Yongdŏk and Kim Ch'wisŏn, fought side by side with Kang.[33] For that matter, these women strikers of P'yŏngwŏn were not unique figures in 1930s Korea, as news reports on the era's numerous and tenacious women worker strikes amply show. But what explains this consciousness and militant activism?

To begin to answer these questions we must detour a bit from the story of the strike at P'yŏngwŏn Rubber factory and explore the broader economic and social conditions of the city of Pyongyang in the early 1930s.

Pyongyang, Its Rubber Shoe Industry, and Its Workers

Rubber companies in colonial Korea produced mostly rubber shoes until wartime necessity propelled the production of military supplies, including tires, beginning in the late 1930s. Most rubber shoe companies were small- to medium-sized, owned by Koreans, and located in Pyongyang, Seoul, and Pusan. Large-scale Japanese investment in the sector was concentrated in Pusan.[34] The rubber shoe industry, together with the knitwear (mostly sock-making) industry, attracted Korean investment over the 1920s. Both of these industries did not require a great amount of capital investment, and production was very labor-intensive. Labor costs, especially in factories employing mostly women, remained low.[35] As rubber shoes became popular, demand for knitwear socks also increased. By 1927 Pyongyang factories produced more than 60 percent of the total sock production of Korea.[36] Among Korean-owned small- to medium-sized businesses in Pyongyang, rubber firms stood at the top in terms of capital investment. Compared to knitwear, rice polishing, or the liquor-making industries, the rubber shoe sector, due to mechanization of some production processes, required a relatively larger amount of capital investment, amounting to at least several tens of thousands of wŏn, and often multiple capitalists pooled their money to start a company.

The profit margin of the industry was very attractive to Korean businessmen in Pyongyang during the late 1920s, which led to overinvestment by the early 1930s when the market for rubber shoes appears to have reached a near saturation point.[37] Rubber shoes (*komusin*) first came onto the market in the mid-1910s as Japanese imports, and by 1923 already twelve domestic Korean rubber shoe companies were competing in this fast-growing market.[38] Before *komusin* were introduced, most Koreans wore homemade straw shoes (*chipsin*) or woven fiber shoes made of hemp, ramie, cloth, or paper (*samsin* or *mit'uri*) in everyday life, while the wealthy wore artisan-crafted and thus very expensive silk and leather shoes. On rainy days wooden shoes (*namaksin*) were also used, and people of *yangban* aristocratic status without sufficient means opted to wear *namaksin* even on nonrainy days in order to avoid the appearance of wearing lower-class shoes of *chipsin* or *samsin*.[39] With increased investment by Korean businessmen in rubber shoe factories, by the late 1920s *komusin* prices came down significantly, expanding the customer base and the popularity of rubber shoes further.[40]

The domestic demand for rubber shoes, especially in cities, was thus expanding rapidly in the 1920s, and the industry attracted native Korean investment especially in Seoul and Pyongyang. Since premodern times in Pyongyang and the northwest region generally, commercial activities had been more pronounced than in the middle and southern parts of the country. Diplomatic and trade routes between Chosŏn (the dynasty ruling Korea between 1392 and 1910) and China ran through the northwest, and the grip of Confucian culture, which had a strong anticommercial bias, was much weaker there than in regions further south. And by the early twentieth century the northwest region was producing many social reformers, Christian converts, and nationalist patriots. Pyongyang was thus a promising site of industrial development. It had relatively strong transportation networks and markets, the availability of cheap energy sources (coal deposits and hydroelectricity), access to ample water and raw materials for production, affordable wage levels, and land for factory construction.⁴¹ By the early 1930s Korean and Japanese authors writing about Pyongyang's economy, making a comparison to Japan, envisioned Pyongyang becoming the "Osaka of Chosŏn" or the "Kita (Northern) Kyushu of Chosŏn."⁴²

Pyongyang was also a major center of the bourgeois nationalist movement, where the "Movement to Promote Chosŏn Native Goods" started in June 1920, much earlier than the January 1923 launching of the movement in Seoul. And as the nickname the "Jerusalem of Chosŏn" shows, Pyongyang was also regarded as the center of the Protestant Christian religion in colonial Korea. In 1920 Pyongyang boasted 8,200 Protestant Christians (5,700 members of eight Presbyterian churches and 2,500 members of five Methodist churches), which was 15 percent of the city's Korean population of 54,643, while nationally Protestants accounted for less than 2 percent (323,574) of the Korean population of 16,916,078.⁴³ Pyongyang's industrial and commercial activities were dominated by the region's Christian elite, many of whom had been deeply involved in the nationalist movement that began in the early 1900s and had pursued educational and industrial/commercial activities as part of their nationalist endeavor.⁴⁴ From the early 1920s local Pyongyang notables began to actively invest in knitwear and rubber shoe factories, among other industries. Their business activities corresponded to the era's nationalist call to modernize Korean society and its economy to achieve the conditions for "civilization and enlightenment" and thus national independence. Korean capitalists sought to claim a moral leadership in society as the builders of the modern economic foundation for the Korean nation, and many businessmen participated in the bourgeois nationalist movement.⁴⁵ Pyongyang's Christian, mostly Protestant, businessmen, urban elite intellectuals, and nationalist activists—categories that often overlapped in the same person—were connected through a thick network of school, church, hometown, and other associations. In a 1930 magazine article titled "The Pyongyang I Saw after a Ten-Year Hiatus," Chu Yosŏp, an influential nationalist writer originally from Pyongyang, observed that "Christianity in Pyongyang is the monopoly of the bourgeois class above the middle-class level."⁴⁶ Of all the major commercial and industrial cities of colonial Korea, Pyongyang was distinctive in that the city's indigenous capital succeeded to a great extent in maintaining a space for itself in spite of the encroachment of Japanese interests.

The city was also a key base of the colonial Korean labor movement during the 1920s, and by the 1930s, as wartime rapid industrialization concentrated heavy-industry workers in the north, the Pyongyang area, together with the northeastern industrial centers of Wŏnsan, Hamhŭng, and Hŭngnam, became a crucible for a communist-led revolutionary labor movement. A contemporary newspaper account describes Pyongyang as a place famous for its "natural scenery, *naengmyŏn* [its cold noodle dish], Christianity, industries, labor disputes, and *kisaeng* [courtesans]."[47] The paternalistic relationship Korean businessmen often established with their workers, at least in rhetorical terms, and their willingness to join endeavors to create industrial worker organizations in the early 1920s at the dawn of Korean capitalist development reflected their "nationalist capitalist" (*minjok chabon'ga*) posture.[48] Their nationalist claims would face stiff challenges by the mid-1920s from the "socialist" movement and from many industrial workers, whose demands for better wages and humane treatment severely tested the capitalist argument that what was good for Korean companies was good for the Korean people. "Socialists" in the period's parlance meant radical nationalists of various ideological strains, the two main forces of which were communists (Marxist-Leninists) and anarchists.[49] Still, compared to other cities, Pyongyang was where Korean capitalists and the cultural nationalist movement they supported maintained a strong influence over society throughout the colonial period, despite the fierce challenges from an increasingly powerful labor movement backed by revolutionary nationalist forces.[50] Looking into the rubber shoe industry's labor-capital relations and nationalist politics surrounding it in Pyongyang therefore offers valuable insight into the vision and politics of the nationalist elite of colonial Korea and the northwestern wing of Christian nationalists in particular. Many of these Protestant intellectuals, activists, and businessmen fled the north and settled in the south in the postliberation years, heavily influencing the conservative nature of the nation-building process in South Korea.

Major centers of the rubber shoe industry in colonial Korea—Pyongyang, Seoul, and Pusan—were all located in big cities where demand for rubber shoes was highest. This demand was seasonal, peaking around the fall harvest season, probably because disposable income was more readily available to most people in a largely agricultural economy. According to testimony by a former rubber worker published in the official North Korean state newspaper *Rodong sinmun* (Labor News) in 1957, rubber factories were busy from the middle of lunar calendar July until the end of the year, while insufficient orders idled workers from lunar calendar January until July.[51] From the Tano festival (May 5 on the lunar calendar) until July, rubber workers employed in shoe-making jobs, who were mostly women, had almost no income, according to this worker. Relatively older, married women workers living in cities were deemed more appropriate for such cyclical employment than young factory girls recruited from the countryside, although in Pyongyang and Pusan recruitment of younger women from nearby counties may have been somewhat higher than in Seoul.⁵² Rubber and rice milling industries were characterized by seasonal employment and tended to hire married women, in contrast to the textile sector, which preferred young unmarried women who tended to be hired for a multiyear term and housed in dormitories to ensure effective control. The majority of women rubber workers were in their twenties or thirties, many of whom were married women with children.⁵³ A strict sexual division of labor prevailed at rubber factories, where women workers mostly performed the tasks of making the molds or assembling the soles, and male workers took charge of the rest of the processes, including the most technology-intensive work of running high-priced equipment.⁵⁴

Korean owners of rubber factories established an industry association early on, beginning in Seoul in June 1923. Those in Pyongyang and Pusan also created their own rubber industry associations in the late 1920s.⁵⁵ The strike wave of 1930–31 in rubber factories in Pyongyang was provoked when member factories in the city implemented uniform wage cuts, following a resolution passed by the All Korea Rubber Goods Manufacturers' Association. Most rubber strikes in the country from 1929 to the mid-1930s followed the same pattern. In other words, the rubber strikes of 1930 and 1931 represented a well-coordinated offensive by the Korean capitalists of Pyongyang aimed at Korean workers, which put moderate nationalists in a difficult spot, caught between the demands of working-class people and their bourgeois vision of nation-building through capitalist development.

According to the annual statistical data compiled by the colonial government, in 1930 there were 28,288 female factory workers in Korea, which amounted to 33.7 percent of the total factory workforce of 83,900 workers.⁵⁶ Among these women workers, a whopping 95 percent worked in the three most feminized industries: textiles, food, and chemicals.⁵⁷ The number of women employed in the chemical sector grew from 112 in 1921 to 19,777 in 1940, and in the late 1920s and early 1930s, the period when rubber strikes peaked, the rubber industry was the biggest employer of women in the chemical industry.⁵⁸

In 1930, when the historic Pyongyang rubber solidarity strike occurred, colonial government statistics put the number of rubber industry employees nationally at 5,320, which included 245 white-collar employees and technicians (244 men and 1 woman) and 4,971 manual workers (1,336 men and 3,635 women).⁵⁹ These numbers indicate that there were approximately 2,100 male and female rubber workers in Pyongyang during the "great strike" (*taep'aŏp*) of rubber workers in the city in 1930. Pyongyang rubber workers represented roughly 40 percent of the country's rubber workforce, and the 1,200 women rubber shoe workers of Pyongyang who participated in the strike that year represented 33 percent of total women rubber workers and 4.2 percent of the 28,288 women factory workers in the country.⁶⁰

Kang Churyong's life story fits these general characteristics of women rubber workers. Kang was born in a relatively well-off family in Kanggye, North P'yŏngan Province, and her birth year is estimated to be 1901, based on media reports of her age.[61] Her family migrated to Western Kando (Jiandao) in Manchuria when she was fourteen, because her father's "failure," according to Kang's testimony, wiped out the family's fortune. Her family farmed in Western Kando for "about seven years," and at age twenty, around 1920, Kang was married to a fifteen-year-old boy in T'onghwa County. Kang said she and her "lovely husband," Ch'oe Chŏnbin, maintained an affectionate relationship that was the envy of the whole village, but "a major change" in their life occurred about a year after their marriage when Ch'oe joined the Tongnip-tan (Independent Corps; printed as "XX-tan" due to censorship in Muhojŏngin's interview article), a guerrilla group led by the famous nationalist army leader known as Paek Kwangun, whose real name was Ch'ae Ch'an. Surprisingly, Kang joined her husband in guerrilla army life. As she put it, "Of course I, together with my husband, followed around the XX-tan, eating on the road and sleeping outdoors." After "six or seven months" of guerrilla band experience, she was sent back home by her husband, and "five, six months later" she was summoned to a village about twenty-five miles away from home to witness her husband's death. Thus, by about 1922 she became a young widow.

For some unidentified reason her in-laws accused her of being the cause of Ch'oe's death, and as a result Kang Churyong was incarcerated in a Chinese police station for a week. With no one helping her, she recalled, she "starved for the whole week." She wryly added, "Wouldn't you say that my three-day hunger strike this time around was a fairly easy affair after that [experience]?" She came back to Korea when she was twenty-four, and once home she "played the role of the son" of the family as the sole provider for her parents and a young brother.[62] The family moved to Pyongyang around 1926 or 1927, and Kang began working as a rubber worker in the city. She joined the Pyongyang Rubber Workers' Association, a coordinating body of employees at the city's rubber factories, "right before last year's strike occurred." That means she was a veteran of the 1930 Pyongyang "general strike" (ch'ongp'aŏp) of rubber workers.

The Historical Significance of Pyongyang Rubber Strikes

A crucial question emerged from the labor-capital conflict in Pyongyang's rubber industry in the early 1930s. It was a seemingly simple, yet loaded, question, on which employers and workers and also the nationalist media voiced strong opinions during the struggle: "What are fair wages for female factory workers in an era of depression?" Centered on this fundamental question, Pyongyang's rubber strikes of 1930–31 entangled Pyongyang's Korean elites, religious communities, various socialist movement groups, industrial workers, and colonial authorities in a momentous battle to settle on the desirable shape of class and gender relations. The processes and consequences of these strikes not only affected the lives and consciousness of the women participating in them; they also had a substantial impact on the subsequent political and ideological directions of Korea's various nationalist movements.

In colonial Korea's rubber industry sector, the proximity of multiple factories and the coordinated nature of management actions tended to generate solidarity strikes that involved many factories in the region. According to an authoritative study of the Korean colonial labor movement by sociologist and labor studies scholar Kim Kyŏngil, the rubber industry was one of those sectors where the "fiercest and most persistent labor movement" developed.[63] Most strikes were provoked by wage cuts, while other common demands included reinstatement of fired workers, removal of abusive supervisors, and abolition of the compulsory fine system, which was deeply loathed by workers.

The earliest rubber strike occurred in Seoul in February 1920 when more than a hundred rubber workers at two factories went out on strike. That was a time before labor organizations, including trade unions, actually came into existence in Korea.[64] Three years later another rubber workers' strike broke out in Seoul, and more than 150 workers at seven factories opposing wage cuts sustained the strike for a month.[65] During this 1923 strike, a "hunger alliance" (*asa tongmaeng*) launched by women workers provoked an outpouring of support from the larger society. Labor and socialist organizations (*sasang tanch'e*) sent investigative teams and convened public speech forums for them. News media coverage was sympathetic to workers, especially after they launched a hunger strike and sat in front of the factory. On the news of a hunger sit-in, which is said to be "the first case of *asa tongmaeng*" in Korea, a "sympathy corps" (*tongjŏngdan*) was organized to raise funds for striking workers, and the *Dong-A ilbo* newspaper came out with an editorial that was critical of the employers' stance. Favorable public opinion helped workers obtain a positive outcome to the strike. Pyongyang knitwear workers who went out on strike about a month later also succeeded in turning public opinion in their favor and thwarted employers' coordinated offensive aiming at wage reduction, which boosted the momentum of the labor movement in Pyongyang.[66] The 1923 Seoul rubber strike thus contains what would become the distinctive features of colonial period women workers' strikes: spontaneous, persistent, and militant struggle, which in turn generated wide support among labor and social movement organizations and prompted sympathetic coverage by the Korean-language media.

Over the 1920s numerous labor disputes occurred at rubber factories in Seoul, Pyongyang, and Pusan.[67] Strike actions began to intensify as the disastrous economic effect of the worldwide depression began to reverberate in colonial Korea. Between 1929 and 1931 Pyongyang saw ten strikes, including the 1930 solidarity strike, while Seoul had four and Pusan had three rubber strikes. The 1931 strike at the P'yŏngwŏn Rubber factory followed this wave of rubber strikes, and the city saw three more strikes later that year and ten more in 1933. Although tapering off after 1933, rubber strikes continued to occur until the end of the decade in these cities.[68] Among these rubber strikes, the twenty-three-day solidarity strike of all rubber workers of Pyongyang in August 1930 was the biggest clash between workers and Korean capitalists of the city.[69]

Lacking a competitive edge over powerful Japanese rubber businesses in colonial Korea, Korean rubber shoemakers tried to transfer the pain to workers through pay cuts and layoffs. The portion of wages in the total production cost in the rubber shoe sector was not high, and the prices and the availability of raw materials as well as market forces largely determined the success of the business.[70] In 1933 wages accounted for just 10 percent of the total production cost for rubber shoes.[71] Even though the possible savings from a wage squeeze were rather small, the Korean rubber shoemakers banded together and fought hard against striking workers to the extent that some colonial authorities eventually regarded their actions as problematic and intervened to soften their extremely hardline position.[72]

The 1930 Pyongyang rubber strike began when ninety-two women workers at Japanese-run Hisada Rubber factory struck, unsuccessfully, in May. Workers then decided to wait until July or August, the peak season in rubber shoe orders, before starting a joint action. While another strike, this time at Chŏngch'ang Rubber, was unfolding, the Pyongyang Rubber Industry Employers' Association declared industry-wide wage cuts averaging 10 percent, which prompted the Pyongyang Rubber Workers' Association to launch a coordinated general strike. By the morning of August 9, eighteen hundred workers from eleven factories, mostly Korean-owned, joined the strike, and workers set up a strike headquarters at the Pyongyang Labor Alliance office and convened a big rally, announcing their twenty demands. The decision by three hundred salaried technicians to side with the manual workers was a great boost to striking workers, mostly women, because without these male technicians' presence the companies were unable to run their factories as planned with newly hired *p'aŏp kkaegikkun* (strikebreakers).[73] Employers then began to vacillate, and they came up with a compromise agreement accommodating some of the workers' demands. At this critical juncture, however, the colonial police intervened and imposed a settlement package that rolled back the Korean employers' offer.

When factories resumed operation on August 23, more and more workers returned to work, beginning with the technicians. Strikers began to attack factories in waves, destroying machinery, and in some cases, they even cut telephone lines to disrupt police communication. This change of heart by male technicians, who had initially sided with the women workers but were persuaded by management to resume work, was noted by observers like reporter O Kiyŏng as one of the major reasons for the workers' defeat in the strike. As armed police patrolled the city, clashes between workers and the police continued for some time until the strike fizzled out by early September. Newspapers described the fierceness of the struggle in that summer using expressions like "a great scrimmage" (*taenant'u*), "a war of attrition," or "a murderous spirit that saturated the entire city" (*chŏnsi salgi ch'ungman*) of Pyongyang.[74]

The general rubber strike of Pyongyang was part of a surge of broader labor struggles in the era. The labor movement in Korea in the early 1930s gained stimulation and momentum from the Wŏnsan general strike of 1929, in which longshore and refinery workers in the major industrial cities of South Hamgyŏng Province spearheaded a massive general strike that lasted more than three months.[75] From January 23 until April, the region was engulfed in a warlike situation as the Japanese colonial government mobilized all its physical power, from the police to the Japanese imperial army, reservists, firefighters, and Japanese militia organizations, and unleashed the media under its control to battle and delegitimize striking Korean workers. The Wŏnsan general strike, although ending in failure, shook the colony and severely affected its economy by tying up the transportation network and galvanizing "socialist" movements in and around Korea.[76] Then a major strike in the same region at the Sinhŭng coal mine followed in May 1930, and in August Pyongyang rubber workers rose up on a massive scale. Contemporary observers dubbed the Wŏnsan general strike, the Sinhŭng coal mine strike, and the 1930 Pyongyang rubber strike the three biggest strikes of the period.[77] In Pyongyang between 1929 and 1931, at least twenty-nine strikes in diverse industries, including rubber, noodle making, brick making, textiles, knitwear, shoemaking, printing, and transportation, as well as electricians and retail and construction workers, erupted.[78] Thus, when women workers at P'yŏngwŏn Rubber decided to strike in May 1931, Pyongyang had been in the midst of a class war for some time, reflecting the nationwide upsurge of labor activism from 1929 to about 1933. The 1931 strike at P'yŏngwŏn Rubber was a continuation of the warlike clash in 1930 between capital and labor in Pyongyang. The stakes were high for both sides, and the colonial authorities were closely watching.

The Pyongyang rubber workers' strikes of 1930 and the P'yŏngwŏn Rubber strike of 1931 thus owed much to the growth of the Korean labor movement over the previous decade. Review of this history reveals what kinds of social movement forces were at work in these rubber strikes. The first national federation of workers in colonial Korea appeared in April 1920, with the name the Korean Workers Mutual Aid Association (Chosŏn Nodong Kongjehoe), which organized both industrial workers and tenant farmers, called "tenant workers" in the activist language of the day. Together with bourgeois nationalists, who began to pay attention to the industrial workforce as objects of enlightenment and mobilization, "socialists," especially anarchists, were instrumental in these early endeavors.[79] During the colonial period the term "socialism" (*sahoejuŭi*) was used to refer to a variety of leftist ideologies, including anarchism, Marxism, Christian socialism, social democracy, and even Marxism-Leninism, as a way to differentiate its "revolutionary" nationalist platform from that of bourgeois nationalism. The latter, which was usually called simply "nationalism" (*minjokchuŭi*), advocated a gradual, nonconfrontational way of working toward independence focusing on the transformation of the Korean nation through modern education and modern "cultural" changes.

As labor historian Kim Kyŏngil argues, activists upholding socialist ideologies, especially communists, began to dominate the labor movement by the mid-1920s, and "the role of the ideology of *minjokchuŭi* [nationalism] became relatively weak and limited" in the labor movement.[80] Nationally, by late 1922 or early 1923—although in some regions it was delayed to around 1924 or even later—"socialists" seized control of the Korean labor movement. Replicating this national trend, in Pyongyang nationalists and socialists jointly launched the Pyongyang Labor Alliance (P'yŏngyang Nodong Yŏnmaenghoe) in September 1922, but by February 1923 socialists took control of the alliance. The atmosphere in the mid-1920s was one in which, as Kim Kyŏngil puts it, "without the knowledge of socialism one's pretension as an intellectual did not go very far."[81] Among the major cities in colonial Korea, Pyongyang was a place where anarchism had a relatively stronger popular base, and anarchist organizations, including the Northwest Black Friends Society (Kwansŏ Hŭguhoe), had significant influence over trade unions in several industries, including Western shoemaking, carpentry, and the rubber industry.[82]

By the early 1930s Pyongyang rubber workers could thus count on the accumulated experiences and crisscrossing networks of activists, but they also found themselves at the cusp of a major change in state-capital-labor dynamics in the colonial period. Intensifying state repression was beginning to wipe out legal spaces for the trade union movement, and Korean communist activists began to shift toward "red" or "revolutionary" union activities in step with the changing Comintern strategies in Asia and worldwide (see chapter 2). Meanwhile, by the early 1930s Korean capitalists had learned to accept the patronage and the financial support offered by colonial authorities. For economic and political reasons, colonial authorities affirmed Korean businesses' coordinated offensives against labor. In this context rubber strikes in Pyongyang were destined to expose the contradiction inherent in the bourgeois nationalist position of local business leaders.

The Depression gave Korean capitalists additional ammunition to push for wage cuts, just as it did for their counterparts in Japan, even though they must have known that pay reductions when most workers were already living in dire poverty could provoke massive labor protests. As we have seen, Korean rubber factory owners made a collective decision to implement wage cuts, using the economic crisis as an excuse, and their argument asking for Korean people's sacrifice for the survival of "Korean" businesses was eagerly disseminated widely by news media like the newspaper *Dong-A ilbo*, owned by Kim Sŏngsu of the Kyŏngsŏng Spinning and Weaving company. Workers and leftist commentators countered these "nationalist" claims by pointing out that workers, who were members of the nation, had extreme difficulty surviving on reduced wages. The fact that in many cases management and stockholders were receiving high dividends and remuneration while claiming that their companies were faced with a pending crisis also strengthened the workers' and leftists' argument.[83] In the case of rubber strikes, the question boiled down to what would be an appropriate wage level for women workers in an era of depression, a question framed in the light of a shared Korean desire to build a modern nation. It was a heavily gendered question as well as a class question, and nothing less than national survival was at stake.

Women's Wages and the Korean Nationalist Elite

The biggest grievance of striking rubber workers throughout the colonial period was low wages and wage cuts. Yet colonial government statistics show that wages for women rubber workers tended to be relatively higher than those of other female-dominated sectors such as textiles. In 1930, before the effect of drastic wage cuts in the Depression era was felt in full force, adult female rubber workers' average daily wage was 0.81 wŏn (0.96 for men), while the average manufacturing wage in the same year was 0.61 wŏn (0.94 for men).[84] This number is deceptive, however, because the availability of work fluctuated by season, as explained earlier. According to a former worker, an average daily wage of one wŏn that an adult woman worker would make for a long day's work during busy months would in reality translate into an average daily wage of less than a third of one wŏn over the whole year.[85]

If there were no work orders, there was no income for female workers. Moreover, workers were subject to a harsh fine system that ate up a portion of their meager pay. For example, at the Hisada factory, whose strike in May 1930 was the precursor to the August solidarity strike of Pyongyang rubber workers, workers had to pay 0.05 wŏn on the first shoe that did not meet the standard, 0.10 wŏn on the second substandard shoe, and then a whopping 0.45 wŏn on the third.[86] The twenty demands workers presented in the 1930 strike included abolition of this abusive fine system as well as an elimination of fees for machine repair and tools. The dreaded system that imposed large fines on imperfect output was a key wage-lowering method utilized by managers in the industry.[87] With their meager pay, the aforementioned Pyongyang rubber worker claimed in 1959 that women rubber workers could not afford to "buy a pair of *komusin* for their own kids at home."[88] At the same time, he continued, the "maidens [*k'ŭnagidŭl*] of rubber factories" had to use their hard-earned money "to buy meat" to ply supervisors with, and some even had to perform unpaid laundry service for them. Those who refused to curry favor with supervisors risked dismissal or reduced piecework assignments.[89]

A key question in swaying public opinion during rubber strikes was whether wage cuts, as factory owners claimed, in an era of depression and rising foreign competition, represented a necessary measure for the survival of Korean-owned businesses in the city. Workers appealed to people's empathy regarding their abject conditions of poverty, increasingly a stark reality in Korea in the 1930s. A consistent strategy of moderate Korean language newspapers in this period, including the *Dong-A ilbo*, was to show sympathy toward the dire situation and poverty workers were experiencing on the one hand, yet on the other hand, to articulate employers' claim that wage reduction was an unavoidable measure. Mixed in with this basic narrative of pity versus hard economic reality was a "red" scare, and numerous and sensational news reports stoked it by relaying colonial authorities' announcements and views regarding subversive incidents and radical agitators who were allegedly lurking behind strikes.

In addition to these economic and political claims was a strong gender-based discourse that raised suspicions regarding women's earning power. One factory owner, when interviewed by a *Dong-A ilbo* reporter, put forward the argument that the wages of striking Pyongyang rubber workers had been "too high" for "women's wages." Another owner asked, "Well, a woman's wage goes over one wŏn a day, can you say that it is low?" The head of the P'yŏngwŏn Rubber, Cho Haik, argued that even though he felt "great sympathy toward workers," their wages "cannot be said to be low." A widely shared attitude toward women's wages was summarized by a businessman as follows: "Since a *yŏgong* has a man and she earns money on the side, it is no problem that her wage is low."[90] What these businessmen conveniently omitted was the fact that the seasonal nature of rubber work drastically reduced average annual wages for women and other workers. Also ignored was the common knowledge that many women workers, like Kang Churyong, were sole or crucial providers for their families. Individual news reports acknowledged women workers as playing the "role of a son" as in the case of Kang, but collectively media reports never challenged the conventional assumption that women's income was only supplemental to male breadwinner income. This was a gendered understanding of work and wages, which "nationalist capitalists" of the day had no reason to reconsider.

In his study of the Kyŏngsŏng Spinning and Weaving Company of the Kim family of Koch'ang in North Chŏlla Province, probably the most influential and well-known "nationalist capitalist" family of the era, historian Carter J. Eckert sheds important light on this issue. Eckert concludes that as Korean companies tried to expand their operations in the Depression era, utilizing the falling prices of capital goods and tantalizing prospect of future markets, "a cash flow crisis" occurred, creating the reason for the wage cuts. He argues in short that "corporate expansion, not corporate survival [was] the chief factor at work here."[91] This observation applies equally well to the case of Pyongyang's Korean-owned rubber businesses. At the Pyongyang rubber strikers' rally on August 10, 1930, a report of the joint investigation by the city's Labor Alliance, Youth Alliance, and Knitwear Workers' Union revealed that while using industrial rationalization as an excuse for wage reduction, rubber companies were still offering on average 20 percent dividends to their stockholders, a fact that infuriated workers.[92] Eruption of worker strikes at Korean-owned businesses created a serious predicament for the bourgeois nationalist camp. Nationalist news media like the *Dong-A ilbo* failed to directly confront the hard question of how nationalist capitalists should engage with worker demands to improve their livelihood and largely remained evasive on the labor question. Nevertheless, critical voices among bourgeois nationalists also surfaced from time to time in the pages of newspapers and periodicals. This bifurcation in the nationalist movement informed society's attitudes toward rubber strikes and Kang Churyong's high-altitude sit-in.

As we have seen, compared to other major industrial centers such as Seoul, Incheon, Pusan, and Taegu, Pyongyang was a place where the influence and legitimacy of Korean local capitalists and Christian nationalists remained solid throughout the colonial period. Their power in the local economy buttressed their dominance in society. The pioneers of rubber and knitwear factories in Pyongyang and most of the employers and managers of the two industries were Protestant Christians, and the strong networking capacity among Christians was one of the reasons for Korean capitalists' success in developing Korean-owned industries and deterring the encroachment of Japanese capital in the city.[93] Several of Pyongyang's rubber factory founders and managers had illustrious nationalist credentials since they had been persecuted by the Japanese colonial government in the Sinminhoe (New People's Association) incident of 1911.[94] That incident occurred soon after the annexation of Korea in 1910 when the Japanese colonial government fabricated a Korean plot to assassinate the first governor-general, Terauchi Masatake. The ensuing persecution of Korean nationalist activists aimed at establishing firm control over them, especially the most threatening secret society, the Sinminhoe, through harsh interrogation involving torture and imprisonment. In Pyongyang twenty-seven local notables were indicted and an additional eighty-four people were interrogated about the Sinminhoe case. Of 123 people indicted in the Sinminhoe incident, 116 were from North or South P'yŏngan Province. Ninety-one of them were Protestants, and fifty were engaged in commerce or industry, figures that illustrate the significance of the northwest region and Protestantism for the early nationalist movement of Korea.[95] Subsequently the Pyongyang business community, together with students, intellectuals, religious groups, and industrial workers, played a major role in the historic March First Movement of 1919 in the city.[96] The March First Movement was an epochal nationwide upheaval of Koreans demanding independence, and it produced a new "March First Movement" generation of committed independence activists. The nationalist eruption forced the Japanese to change their colonial strategies in Korea toward granting more room for bourgeois nationalists to conduct "cultural" activities. Kim Tongwŏn, whom we will encounter later as a powerful leader of Pyongyang's rubber industry, was one of the key nationalist leaders who supported the movement.

Church connections helped rubber factory founders put together a fairly large sum of investment capital—around 50,000 wŏn—for the machinery to start a factory. Church networks allowed them to reach out to merchants and landlords who were fellow believers. In turn, Pyongyang's Korean companies provided proselytizing opportunities for Protestant churches. The Christian connections of the rubber industry were well known. Myŏng Tŏksang, an influential nationalist activist of Pyongyang, claimed in his speech at a Pyongyang rubber workers' rally that "owners of Pyongyang rubber factories are in most cases Christians." And leftist writer Yi Chŏkhyo, who portrayed the 1930 Pyongyang rubber strike in his short story "Total Mobilization," describes the greedy leader among rubber factory owners who spearheaded the wage cuts in the name of "industrial rationalization" in the story as a "stalwart believer of Jesus Christ" (*ch'al-Yesu-jaengi*).[97]

The best study of the intellectual and political history of the Christian nationalist movement in colonial Korea is offered by historian Chang Kyusik, and below I introduce the gist of his arguments that are germane to our discussion here.[98] The Christian nationalist ideology that took root around the turn of the twentieth century was gradualist in nature and anchored in a social Darwinist understanding of the world. It sought to establish a free, civilized, capitalist, and Christian nation-state through self-strengthening efforts, especially in the areas of education and industry, while consciously staying away from the ideas of a citizen's revolution or armed resistance against imperialist aggression. The core mission of Christian nationalists was defined as the nurturing of "new people" (*sinmin*), and the name of the nationalist organization Sinminhoe, discussed earlier, reflects this core mission.[99]

The loss of sovereignty in 1910 had jeopardized the validity of the social Darwinist frame of thinking. After all, how could Koreans criticize the Japanese imperialist takeover of Korea when social Darwinism understands the stronger party's dominance over the weaker party as a natural process and a good thing for the human species? Some Korean Christian nationalists adopted socialist ideas. Some who refused to give up on the nationalist dream turned to an ultranationalist stance represented by the Taejonggyo movement, which began in 1909 and whose believers worshipped the nation's mythical progenitor Tan'gun as savior. Neither of the solutions was easily reconcilable with Christian beliefs, however. The most viable alternative for many Christians was to revise and repackage their "civilization and enlightenment" ideal, latching onto the belief that the world had begun a major transformation (*kaejo*) for the better after the disastrous World War I had revealed the bankruptcy of the existing world order. The new transformation would be led by the United States and its president, Woodrow Wilson, and in the civilized society of the future, not the "survival of the fittest" type of dog-eat-dog competition but justice, humanism (*indojuŭi*), democracy, and world peace would be the shared values. Although the euphoria over Wilsonian democracy was by 1922 replaced by a sense of disappointment and disillusionment after many observers witnessed the raw imperialist politics on display at the Washington (or Pacific) Conference (November 1921 to February 1922), Christian nationalist activists of Korea nevertheless clung to these humanist ideals. And the key strategies stemming from such a stance were that of appealing to the West by diplomatic means (*oegyoron*), a policy championed by Syngman Rhee (Yi Sŭngman), and that of self-strengthening (*sillyŏk yangsŏngnon*), which materialized in the various educational, economic, and social reform efforts of Christian nationalists over the 1920s and 1930s.

Within this general trend, two rival centers of the Protestant Christian nationalist movement emerged, one in the northwest with Pyongyang as the hub and the other in the central region with the capital Seoul at the center, each exhibiting somewhat different characteristics and trajectories. By 1925 the two groups had realigned themselves as the Suyang Tonguhoe (Society of Like-Minded Friends for Self-Cultivation) group based in the northwest, and the Hŭngŏp Kurakpu

(Club to Promote Industry) group based in Seoul.[100] Suyang Tonguhoe was not a religious organization per se, but most of the members were Protestant Christians and followers of An Ch'angho, who was in exile but continued to be the most influential leader of the northwestern Christian movement.[101] *Suyang* (self-cultivation) was the core concept of the bourgeois nationalist movement in the 1920s, and it was emphasized as the central mechanism through which the ideal subjectivity of the Korean people would be forged, especially that of the youth (*chŏngnyŏn*) who would take up the role of *t'usa* (warrior) for the movement.[102]

The humanism-based Christian nationalist ideology came under ferocious attack beginning in 1923 from socialist activists who questioned the viability of the pro-American, gradualist, self-strengthening–oriented program of the Christian-dominated nationalist movement and raised moral questions about the class interests embedded in some self-strengthening initiatives like the Movement to Promote Chosŏn Native Goods. As in China, a socialist "anti-religion" movement flared up in Korea and reached its peak in the mid-1920s, provoking some Christian activists to consider the possibility of embracing certain socialist ideas.[103] For example, Yi Taewi, who served as the secretary (*kansa*) of the Student Department of the YMCA from 1921 to January 1925 before he left to study in the United States, wrote many articles in the YMCA organ *Youth* (*Chŏngnyŏn*) contemplating ways to tackle the excesses of capitalism and reform the current social order by adopting select teachings from socialism. As workers constituted 80 to 90 percent of the world's population, he argued, a humanist reform of capitalism was needed in order to spread Jesus's Gospel to that population. By 1925 the work of Japanese Christian socialist Kagawa Toyohiko (1888–1960) started to circulate in Korea, and the principle of "love" (*ae*) he promoted gained popularity among some Christian students. In addition to Kagawa's idea that the progressive evolution of human beings resulted not out of cutthroat competition but from cooperation among people based on love, Peter Kropotkin's theory of mutual aid as the basis of human society's progress continued to exert influence among Korean activists, particularly anarchists but also Christian intellectuals.

Influenced by these ideas, some Christian thinkers like Yi Taewi delved into the issues of labor-capital conflict and social poverty from the perspective of Christian humanism, and their prescription was in essence a call for the spirit of labor-capital cooperation through capitalists' self-awakening to their social responsibilities and certain reforms of the economic order. Included among economic reform measures listed by Yi Taewi were profit-sharing for workers, unemployment and other labor insurances, acknowledgment of workers' rights to organize and to collectively bargain, and the establishment of collective farms, committees of small farmers, and producer cooperatives for farmers. These seemingly radical ideas, however, failed to take root in the Christian nationalist movement, nor did they materialize as actual programs. According to historian Chang, they represented no more than a "certain tendency."[104] Whether a mere tendency or a more substantial trend, it is important to note that the painful socialist attacks on Christian nationalism and a growing awareness that the poverty and social conflict that capitalist development brought about were tearing apart the fabric of society were pushing some Christian intellectuals, especially those associated with the Suyang Tonguhoe, toward a certain level of reformist thinking.

And in Pyongyang these reformist intellectuals were attempting to mediate between strikers and the larger society from their positions of influence, be it through the journal *Tonggwang* or the *Dong-A ilbo* newspaper or the united-front organization Sin'ganhoe. Interest in Kang Churyong by *Tonggwang*, which was the organ of Suyang Tonguhoe with Chu Yohan as editor, reflects this reformist tendency, and O Kiyŏng, the "Woman-in-the-Sky" interviewer, belonged to the reformist wing of the Suyang Tonguhoe. O worked as the special correspondent of the Pyongyang branch office of *Dong-A ilbo* from March 1928 to March 1936. According to Chang Kyusik, that branch office functioned as a base for Suyang Tonguhoe with key members working as branch heads or reporters.[105]

The late 1920s, when labor-capital clashes were heating up, was also a time when the national united-front organization Sin'ganhoe finally came into being after years of prolonged and heated struggle between the "nationalist" and the "socialist" camps, and women activists created the Kŭnuhoe, the women-only sister organization to Sin'ganhoe.[106] The period from the late 1920s to around 1931 was the most hopeful time in the Korean nationalist movement since the March First Movement of 1919. The Sin'ganhoe and the Kŭnuhoe were enthusiastically embraced by activists from a wide spectrum of groups across the country. Many local chapters of the two organizations were popping up, attracting local activists into their folds, and they began to assume leadership roles in the anticolonial movement. This united-front movement was the result of the development of ideological, youth, religious, women's, and farmers' organizations, and to a lesser degree labor associations, in the country during the 1920s.

The decision to join hands with "socialists," or radical nationalists, and launch the Sin'ganhoe was championed by the more reformist "left wing" forces among bourgeois nationalists, who opposed the more conciliatory political stance toward the Japanese colonial rule held by the "right wing" of the nationalist movement, which included the Dong-A Ilbo group.[107] The Suyang Tonguhoe was closely affiliated with the right-wing group, and thus the rise of the Sin'ganhoe movement created an internal split in the Suyang Tonguhoe. Reformists in the Suyang Tonguhoe, a vocal minority, called for moving beyond the concentrated focus on *suyang* (self-cultivation) for nurturing a core elite class, and they argued that the current situation demanded active participation in the political arena. An intense and prolonged internal discussion eventually led to the changing of the organization's name to Tonguhoe, deleting the word *suyang* from it and thereby signaling a willingness to engage in social and political matters.[108] And some Tonguhoe members, including Chu Yohan, the former head of the Pyongyang branch of the Dong-A Ilbo company, joined in an organizing endeavor for the Sin'ganhoe Pyongyang chapter in December 1927.[109] But key Tonguhoe leaders like Kim Tongwŏn and O Yunsŏn refused to join the Sin'ganhoe.[110]

In our story Cho Mansik and Kim Tongwŏn show the diverging trajectories of Pyongyang Christian nationalists in the second half of the colonial period. Kim Tongwŏn and Cho Mansik, together with O Yunsŏn, were called the "Three Elders" of the influential Sanjŏnghyŏn Church of Pyongyang and worked together on numerous nationalist projects of an educational and economic nature over the 1920s.[111] But by the late 1920s the paths of these elders began to diverge.

Kim Tongwŏn, a rubber company president himself, represented the interests of rubber factory owners and Korean businesses through and through. Kim, a Hosei University graduate, had been a local leader of the March First Movement and was respected as an ardent promoter of education in Pyongyang. He had been a teacher at the nationalist Taesŏng School and served as the head of the Pyongyang YMCA.[112] Kim, like many industrial pioneers of the day, wore many hats. He was a landlord, a merchant, a factory owner, a teacher, a cultural nationalist activist, and a church elder, and he initiated and led the Pyongyang Rubber Goods Manufacturers' Association. A core leader of the Suyang Tonguhoe and the Pyongyang business world, Kim was an important protagonist in the socially gripping drama of rubber strikes in Pyongyang. He did not join the Sin'ganhoe Pyongyang chapter when it was organized in December 1927 with Cho Mansik as president.

Cho Mansik led the Christian nationalist movement in the northwestern (*sŏbuk*) region, which included North P'yŏngan, South P'yŏngan, and Hwanghae Provinces.[113] Cho was the son of a merchant who rose to be the "king without a crown" of the Pyongyang Christian movement through his work at the Pyongyang YMCA and the Pyongyang Society for the Promotion of Chosŏn Native Goods, as well as his involvement in various initiatives to found and run educational institutions.[114] Cho was known for his leading-by-example teaching method, frugal and diligent everyday practices, and promotion of the use of goods made by Korean businesses, small and large, to foster autonomous national economic development, which earned him another sobriquet, "the Gandhi of Chosŏn." Unlike many right-wing nationalists of the day, Cho Mansik maintained an uncompromising stance against the colonial power, and he tirelessly worked to achieve unity in the Christian social movement.[115] He seriously considered socialist social policy ideas while adamantly opposing materialist and antitheist elements, a stance that provoked criticism from conservatives that he might be a Christian socialist.[116] It was therefore not surprising that Cho decided to lead the Sin'ganhoe movement in Pyongyang by serving as its president.

The particular economic, political, and religious alignments among Pyongyang Koreans meant that the series of rubber strikes in Pyongyang in the early 1930s struck a particularly painful nerve among the city's Christian cultural nationalist elite. They exposed for the whole country to see the contradictions in Pyongyang's labor-capital relations that pitched Korean workers against allegedly nationalist Korean employers. The critical voices we hear from the nationalist media that challenged the dubious claims of Pyongyang capitalists reflect this sense of crisis among nationalists and reveal the anxiety felt by reformers in the Christian nationalist movement. Reporter O Kiyŏng's articles on the Pyongyang rubber strikes in *Dong-A ilbo* and the magazine *Pyŏlgŏn'gon* provide good examples of the nationalist reformist critique of the time.[117] In these articles, O sharply criticized rubber factory owners' claims that wage reduction was necessary for the survival of Korean factories during the time of recession and rising competition from foreign producers. He reported on an interview with a factory owner who stated, "Compared to the time in the past when [stockholders] received 70 percent, 80 percent, or 100 percent dividends, today's 20 percent dividend might be small," but he said, "Even without the wage cuts, it is possible to get a 20 percent dividend," thus vouching for the reporter's conclusion that "the wage reduction was not fair."[118] Voices like O's, however, were not sufficient to create enough momentum in the nationalist movement to address labor issues head on.

As the head of the Pyongyang Sin'ganhoe chapter, Cho Mansik, to his credit, tried to mediate between Pyongyang's rubber factory employers and striking workers.[119] He engaged the city's most influential Christian business leaders, including O Yunsŏn and Kim Pyŏngyŏn, in this effort. O was one of the "Three Elders" and a key leader of the Pyongyang YMCA, the Suyang Tonguhoe, the Society for the Promotion of Chosŏn Native Goods, and the Pyongyang Chamber of Commerce and Industry. Kim was the executive director of the Pyongyang Chamber of Commerce and Industry. But overall their attempts at mediation did not sit well with workers.[120] Criticism of the inability of the Pyongyang Sin'ganhoe chapter to intervene on behalf of workers in the 1930 Pyongyang rubber strike was severe. Activists criticized the Pyongyang chapter's effort as "half-hearted" (*sogŭkchŏk*) and the Sin'ganhoe headquarters in Seoul registered its protest.[121] Left-wing commentators in unison raised their criticism against the Pyongyang Sin'ganhoe chapter.[122]

The Pyongyang Kŭnuhoe chapter was even less engaged with the city's women strikers than its Sin'gan counterpart.[123] The Pyongyang Kŭnu chapter was especially known for the power of the "nationalist" (nonsocialist) group within its ranks led by Cho Sinsŏng, a major Christian and nationalist activist and educator of the era known for her anticommunist stance.[124] The chapter mostly focused on practical programs geared toward "enlightenment" of the female masses, and there is no record of the chapter ever coming out in support of any of the numerous strikes by women workers in the city.[125]

While the Kŭnuhoe Pyongyang chapter was busy running "practical" programs for working-class women while avoiding direct support of women worker activism, at least one Kŭnuhoe member was deeply involved in the labor movement during the time of the P'yŏngwŏn Rubber strike. *Dong-A ilbo* broke a sensational news story on June 13, 1931, about Kang Churyong's affiliation with a communist "red union" cell, and more tantalizing news followed over the course of July and August, although authorities did not release the details of the so-called Pyongyang red union incident until March 1933, when the pretrial phase of interrogation was finally over (see chapter 2).[126] The person who connected Kang Churyong with communist activists coming to town to organize workers into "revolutionary unions" was Cho Yŏngok, a twenty-year-old member of the Kŭnuhoe.[127] The involvement of a Kŭnuhoe member in a "red union" organizing effort among women rubber workers in Pyongyang contrasts sharply with the general indifference of local Sin'gan and Kŭnu chapters toward worker activism, and it also points to the fluid and dynamic ideological environment of Pyongyang in the early 1930s. The communist red union movement was spreading from industrial cities of South Hamgyŏng Province to Pyongyang, and rubber worker Kang Churyong was walking right into the center of a storm from which she would suffer dearly.

Kang's "red" connection unexpectedly provided a convenient way to explain away the unusual deed of a working-class woman in her Ŭlmiltae high-altitude sit-in and added an activist aura to her name above and beyond ordinary women strikers. As we have seen, the colonial police, throughout the history of the labor movement in Japan's Korea colony, were eager to blame "behind-the-scenes" (*paehu*) agitators as the cause behind workers'—especially women workers'—struggle. And colonial news media routinely copied, without critical engagement, police announcements about *paehu* agitation. Kang's arrest as a cell member of a communist underground organization likely had the effect of alleviating the pressure on the local nationalist capitalist leaders to answer women workers' cry for basic livelihood and made it easier for them to deflect heavy criticisms of their decision to disrupt industrial peace by severe cuts in already low wages. A gendered frame of ignorant, uneducated, and feeble-minded working-class women being manipulated by devious outside forces, like the "red" *paehu* or "the hand behind the black curtain" (*hŭkmak ŭi son*), was a powerful weapon for the Korean nationalist bourgeoisie. It was also a typical ploy employed by companies and the authorities in many subsequent strikes by women workers in twentieth-century South Korea. Was Kang Churyong a communist, or was she manipulated by communists? Were there many women activists like communist female labor organizer Cho Yŏngok, or was she an exceptional figure? We explore the socialist connections of the Pyongyang rubber strikes in the next chapter.

2

FACTORY WOMEN IN THE SOCIALIST IMAGINATION

The 1930s

Korea was at a crucial juncture in history in the early 1930s as deepening economic depression and changing Japanese colonial policies generated diverse sets of opportunities and hardships for different groups of Koreans. The peak of the colonial Korean labor movement between 1929 and 1933 corresponded to the beginning phase of ever-tightening state control over subversive anticolonial and leftist forces in Korea as Japan embarked on the disastrous fifteen-year war phase of its imperialist history. A discourse of *paehu* (literally meaning "behind the back"), which held that behind-the-scenes maneuvering by subversive forces was provoking women's struggle, emerged as the dominant mainstream discourse in this period and eclipsed merits of women workers' demands for better wages and working conditions. At the same time Kang's connection to the communist movement, when revealed, led unfortunately to the premature and abrupt ending of her career as an activist. It is thus important to inquire more deeply into the so-called *paehu* agitators' activities and explore how her encounter with communists may have shaped the actions and subjectivities of Kang and her colleagues.[1]

Kang Churyong and the "Red Union" Movement

The underground communist group that recruited Kang Churyong in order to gain access to rubber workers in Pyongyang was led by Chŏng Talhŏn. Chŏng was a well-known communist activist who hailed from Hŭngwŏn in South Hamgyŏng Province, which lies east of South P'yŏngan Province whose provincial seat was Pyongyang.[2] He became an activist as a student at Yonsei University (then Yŏnhŭi Chŏnmun) in Seoul and joined the Korean Communist Party in 1926. He fled the country in May 1926 to avoid a massive police roundup of communists. At that time communists, together with other groups of nationalists, were secretly preparing mass demonstrations in the country, in what came to be called the June 10 *Manse* [Long Live!] movement of 1926.[3] In the USSR Chŏng was admitted to the Communist University of the Toilers of the East (Tongbang Noryŏkcha Kongsan Taehak) in Moscow, run by the Comintern (Communist International, also known as the Third International; 1919–43), and studied at the school for four years. He was one of more than 150 Koreans trained at the university, which instituted for them a "Korean Department."[4] On graduation Chŏng Talhŏn was dispatched to Korea by the Profintern (the Red International of Labor Unions). The Comintern set up the Profintern in 1921 to coordinate communist work in labor movements around the world, and the Profintern convened a congress of Asia-Pacific leftist trade unions in May 1927 in Hankou, China. That congress led to the establishment of the Secretariat of the Pan-Pacific Trade Unions (Pŏm T'aep'yŏngyang Nodong Chohap, known as T'aero) based in Shanghai. The Profintern and the T'aero Secretariat began to actively intervene in the labor movements of the region, sending out activists, providing funding, and issuing directives that exerted a powerful influence over activists on the ground.[5] The central task entrusted to Korean communists, including Chŏng Talhŏn, was to expedite the "revolutionary" or "red" (*chŏksaek*) union movement in the colony, which would serve as the foundation for the future Communist Party of Korea.[6]

Chŏng snuck into Korea in late 1930 and began to work in the Hamhŭng-Hŭngnam area in South Hamgyŏng Province. This was a rapidly developing heavy-industry zone and also Chŏng's native region. Chŏng Talhŏn's main goal was to organize male heavy-industry workers at the Korea Nitrogen Fertilizer Company (Chōsen Chisso) in Hŭngnam, a branch company of the Japan Nitrogen Fertilizer Company (Nihon Chisso). Chōsen Chisso, founded in 1927, was by far the largest Japanese investment in manufacturing in the colony.[7] It thus attracted an intensive communist organizing effort. Chŏng proved to be a competent organizer. Together with Chu Yŏngha and other local activists, he successfully organized secret cells in Chōsen Chisso and by the end of 1930 launched a "research bureau" that coordinated education and propaganda work among various work sites.[8] Chŏng's group linked up with another T'aero organizer, Kim Hoban, and in February 1931 they created the Hamhŭng Industrial Union Committee, which established departments devoted to organizing carpentry, chemical, metal, and railroad workers. Soon South Hamgyŏng Province developed into a bustling center of red union organizing, from which activists were sent out to other cities, including Seoul, Incheon, Pusan, and Pyongyang. T'aero organizer Yi Chuha was assigned to target Pyongyang, and Chŏng Talhŏn also came to Pyongyang with the same purpose.[9] The red union movement led by T'aero activists in the Hamhŭng-Hŭngnam area, however, collapsed when the police rounded up somewhere between one hundred and five hundred participants (the estimates vary) in mid-1931. Even before the mass arrests, though, organizers sent to other cities do not seem to have accomplished all that much.

Pyongyang, however, was an exception, and Chŏng Talhŏn's effort there quickly yielded fruit. After establishing prior communication with local labor activists, Chŏng arrived in the city on February 4, 1931. Disguised as a day laborer, he set out to recruit trustworthy workers and local activists into his expanding organization. Pae Sŭngnyong and Ch'oe Yŏngok, both hosiery workers, and a female activist, Cho Yŏngok, were early recruits, who then connected Chŏng with workers they knew through various organizational connections. At that time Chŏng was 33 years old in Korean counting, two years older than Kang Churyong, and Pae was 25, Ch'oe was 28, and Cho Yŏngok was 21. Once several workers were sworn into the movement, a three-person *yach'eik'a* party cell, also known as a *pan*, was established at the factory level. Once several *pan* units were formed, a red union local would be the next step, which would eventually grow into an "industrial union." By May Chŏng Talhŏn's group was setting out to organize three embryonic "industrial unions" in the transportation, textile, and chemical (rubber) sectors, with a "regional council" as a coordinating body.[10] Also organized at that time were electrical and tobacco workers.

It was Cho Yŏngok, a young Kŭnuhoe member, who recruited rubber workers into Chŏng's red union movement. Cho was from nearby Chŏngju County, and, according to court documents, when she was a student at Pyongyang Women's Higher-Normal School she "already harbored leftist thoughts, attended the events of labor organizations, and befriended labor activists in Pyongyang," including Pae Sŭngnyong. Because poverty drove her to give up on the schooling, the prosecutor in charge of her case speculated, she regarded "the current social system as absurd [*pulhamni*] and was burning with maledictory [*chŏju*] thinking against the capitalist class." With Pae Sŭngnyong's introduction in mid-February, Cho met Chŏng Talhŏn and agreed to work for the cause of the revolutionary union movement. Chŏng asked her to locate "militant elements" among rubber workers and create secret cells in each factory. Cho suggested Kang Churyong and Ch'oe Yongdŏk as promising candidates. After dropping out of school Cho Yŏngok had worked as secretary (*sŏgi*) of the Pyongyang chapter of the Kŭnuhoe, and through her Kŭnuhoe work and also through her connection to labor activists

Cho knew many women rubber workers. A few days later Chŏng asked Cho to take a personal letter to Kang Churyong, and Cho obliged.[11]

The main method Chŏng used in training worker recruits before assigning them leadership roles was to share with them the written material he himself prepared. The court documents on his case, which was dubbed the "Incident of the Plan to Organize an All-Korea Red Union" (Chŏn Chosŏn Chŏksaek Nodong Chohap chojik kyehoek sakŏn), describe the contents of several of these political documents. Titles included "An Evaluation of the Past Pyongyang Labor Movement and Current Tasks of Vanguard Fighters," "General Thesis on the Organizational Matters Regarding Red Trade Unions," and "Several Things a Worker Must Know." Chŏng usually made three copies of each set of materials and gave a copy to each key member for study. Each member then was supposed to circulate the document to workers he or she was in charge of training. It was through this mechanism that Kang Churyong began to learn about the communist red union movement sometime in March 1931.[12]

In mid-March Cho Yŏngok succeeded in organizing a cell at P'yŏngwŏn Rubber with Kang Churyong as the head and Chŏng Okchin and Ko Tosil as members. She also organized a cell at Chŏngch'ang Rubber with Yi Yugam as head and Kim Tusil and Yi Susil as members. The name of another leader of the P'yŏngwŏn strike, Ch'oe Yongdŏk, was mentioned initially by Cho as one of the potential recruits at P'yŏngwŏn, and Chŏng's letter to Kang Churyong was titled "To two comrades, Kang and Ch'oe," according to court documents. But Cho seems to have failed to recruit Ch'oe Yongdŏk, who was apparently not part of the cell at P'yŏngwŏn. Afterward documents flew from Cho to Kang Churyong and Yi Yugam, and then to other cell members. In this explanation by colonial authorities it is noteworthy that basic literacy among these women workers was assumed without question. There is no mentioning in court documents of illiteracy as an obstacle to this type of political education.

Chŏng Talhŏn was very much interested in organizing the rubber industry, partly because of the previous year's general strike among rubber workers in Pyongyang, which was highly acclaimed among communist activists both in Korea and abroad and confirmed the importance of this sector in the Pyongyang labor movement. His attention to the sector was also a result of his past work in organizing chemical workers in Chōsen Chisso before coming to Pyongyang. Just before his arrest in May, while he was busy launching three so-called industrial unions, he opted to take charge of the chemical industry union himself. Chŏng asked Cho Yŏngok to arrange a meeting with Kang, and in early April Kang Churyong had a secret face-to-face meeting with Chŏng.[13] It seems that Chŏng had high hopes for Kang Churyong, who was, according to the court documents, "already a leftist element," although court documents are mute on how Kang might have acquired this "leftist" political consciousness.

As we have seen, the P'yŏngwŏn Rubber strike began on May 18, 1931, about a month or so after Kang met Chŏng Talhŏn, and at most two and a half months after Kang Churyong was connected with Chŏng's group through Cho Yŏngok. It is not clear if Kang and other cell members had coordinated their struggle with Cho Yŏngok and Chŏng Talhŏn between May 18 and the roundup of Chŏng's group on May 28. By the time Kang went up on the roof of the Ŭlmiltae Pavilion, however, Chŏng was already in police custody. When her connection to the Chŏng Talhŏn group came to light, Kang Churyong was waging her second hunger strike in police custody. (She was arrested the second time on June 10, together with Ch'oe Yongdŏk.)[14]

News reports and court documents never doubted that Chŏng was the *paehu* of Kang Churyong and other P'yŏngwŏn strikers. *Dong-A ilbo*, after reiterating the story of Chŏng Talhŏn group's recruitment of Pyongyang workers, reported that at the P'yŏngwŏn factory, Chŏng's group's work generated "the actions of more than a dozen fragile female factory workers" (see figure 2).[15] This conventional narrative, premised on women workers' lack of intellectual ability, expunges from view the evidence that the court documents inadvertently brings out, namely, that Kang was already a "leftist element" and regarded as a "militant" worker. We know that Kang Churyong was a veteran of the 1930 Pyongyang rubber strike, and that women rubber workers in this period waged strikes without any known connection to communist union organizers. But the persistent activities of T'aero organizers, following Chŏng's arrest, in support of strikers at P'yŏngwŏn Rubber and at other factories in the area certainly intensified the concerns of colonial authorities about the subversive *paehu* behind rubber workers' actions.[16]

In the end, after languishing in jail for close to three years, on May 8, 1934, Cho Yŏngok and six other members of the Chŏng Talhŏn group received prison sentences of two years and six months each and were released from jail. Chŏng himself was sentenced to six years and served until 1938. Kang Churyong's fate was different.

The activities of the Chŏng Talhŏn group were part of a surge of the Korean red union movement in the 1930s, a surge concentrated in the northern part of Korea, especially the South and North Hamgyŏng Provinces. A distinctive characteristic of this red union movement was that it was an international and transnational endeavor in which Korean and Japanese activists fought side by side in the name of international solidarity, linked to communist parties and institutions of Japan, China, and the Soviet Union and moving in and out of national and ethnic boundaries. The Korean labor movement in the 1930s was thus in many cases

FIGURE 2. Report on the Pyongyang red union incident, *Dong-A ilbo*, March 25, 1933 (evening edition), 2. Courtesy of the Dong-A Ilbosa. The top right shows mug shots of activists charged in the case (*top*, Chŏng Talhŏn; *third from bottom on left*, Cho Yŏngok). The photos below show the two who died in custody (*top*, Kang Churyong). Headings beside the group photos read, "Two years of agony in pendency / Pretrial investigation ends for the Pyongyang red union incident / Two died, eight brought to trial / Life of the secret organization just 24 days." (The case of one activist was separated from the group.) Left of the main report are two reports detailing the group's activities. The first set of headings reads, "With a mission from the international party / Transformed existing unions / Fled in relation to the June 10 *Manse* incident / Chŏng Talhŏn's path of activism." On its left, the second set of headings reads, "Incited electrical workers / Planned power stoppage / Manipulated strikes at individual factories / Distributed a large quantity of flyers." Above Kang's photo is a report on her life and deeds with the title, "Nine hours on the Ŭlmiltae / Persevered in fasting for three days / One who fell ill and died during pretrial investigation / The life story of Kang Churyong."

a biethnic or multiethnic endeavor. Many Japanese activists participated in red union organizing efforts or strikes in Korea in solidarity with Korean workers.[17] This international nature of the movement and the forging of thick solidarity networks among Korean and Japanese activists continued for a decade or so until intensifying wartime control diminished the spaces for communist activities in the colony as well as in the metropole by the late 1930s.[18] When Kang Churyong went up onto the roof of the Ŭlmiltae Pavilion in May 1931, Korean activists were just beginning to open up a new era of this transnational socialist movement, focusing on the revolutionary task of reaching out to and organizing industrial workers to establish a strong mass base.

Kang was sitting at the center of this growing web of international connections and knowledge circulation in East Asia, and more and more men and women, mostly young people, would step into the whirlwind of revolutionary struggle over the tumultuous decade of the 1930s. There is no direct evidence that shows that Kang Churyong was aware of the "chimney man" incidents in Japan when she tied a stone at the end of a roll of cotton cloth and threw it onto the roof of the Ŭlmiltae. We do not have records of her intellectual journey and reading habits, except for small clues in court documents that depict her as a criminal who read revolutionary propaganda pieces written by Chŏng Talhŏn and taught the content to other workers in her cell group. Considering her avid interest in the labor movement at least since the time of the 1930 Pyongyang rubber strike, it is likely that she followed news of strikes in both Korea and Japan to some extent. Whether Kang Churyong knew about Japanese "chimney men" or not, the Korean media did and quickly came up with her rather romantic name, a "woman-in-the-sky."

Socialist Women Encounter Yŏgong

In the story of Kang Churyong's advance into the dangerous revolutionary movement, another woman activist, Cho Yŏngok, demands particular attention. She was the only female member among the otherwise all-male local organizers who connected work site cells with top leaders like Chŏng Talhŏn or Yi Chuha. Her case is especially intriguing because through her we can get a glimpse into the life of a new generation of highly educated (given the era's standards) "new women" activists. Unless they were nationally known figures and worked in Seoul, we rarely meet such women in historical records. This new generation of socialist women emerged with a distinctive path to activism. In this section I turn to this new generation of young women activists who chose socialist dreams over the bourgeois nationalist or Christian visions for women's liberation, discussed below. Doing so will help us better situate the lives of Kang Churyong, her colleagues, and Cho Yŏngok in the larger context of the women's movement and revolutionary struggles in 1930s Korea.

To better understand Korean socialist women, we must first examine the evolution in Korea of the category of "new women" (*sinyŏsŏng* or *sinyŏja*) to which they belonged. The appearance of "new women" and the "modern girls" (*modŏn kkŏl*) was a global phenomenon.[19] Yet the way they were discussed and deployed in Korea was somewhat different from the parallel process in Japan.[20] Compared to the situation in Japan, in colonial Korea the economic basis that could support the life choices of a "new woman" or a "modern girl" in areas of education, employment, and consumption was not sufficiently developed.[21] Consequently, the number of women participating in knowledge production and social movements remained very small, and, as sociologist Kim Sujin argues, debates on the "new women" and "modern girls" were monopolized by male intellectuals who almost completely controlled magazine production and news media at the time. This means that in Korea the figures of "new women" and "modern girls" mainly functioned as "an object of nationalist scrutiny," and debates on them were more about the desirable nature of modernity and the anticolonial modern subject than about women's issues and gender questions per se.[22] In this process women's own voices and a feminist agenda were marginalized.

In the nationalist envisioning that thus resulted, the desirable role of the "new women" subjects was defined as that of the rescuers of the female masses, dubbed the "old-style women" (kuyŏsŏng), and a broad consensus was formed on that mission in the women's movement of the era. If that is the case, on the perceptional map of the "new women" projected by male intellectuals and accepted by women activists, what place was available for yŏgong, women factory workers? Were factory women deemed modern enough to be the subject of modern transformation, or were they viewed mainly as daughters of tenant farmers who were fresh from the countryside and therefore still closer to the "old-style women" recipients of the rescue mission? This question has rarely been raised in studies of colonial Korean gender history because studies that look at both elite "new women" and working-class women are not many.[23]

Examining the relationship between the "new women" and yŏgong is meaningful because by juxtaposing the two groups and social perceptions of them, we can reveal hidden layers and elements in the gendered construction of both categories. We can start with a simple question: were yŏgong viewed as "new women"? The dominant categories of new women—sinyŏsŏng, the modern girl, and the good wife—must have been hard to apply to women industrial workers because most of them did not have opportunities for formal education, which was an important, albeit not a conclusive, qualification for the modern womanhood, and a yŏgong could not easily afford being a consumer of modern goods or a stay-at-home housewife. Some factory women, especially younger women, with a modicum of financial resources from their earnings ventured out into the city when possible, emulating the glamor of "modern girl" lifestyle. Historian Yun Chŏngnan shows that in the 1920s, when factory jobs first became available in substantial numbers for women in Korea, factory work was often positively featured in news media as an example of clean, modern, exciting jobs for women.[24] But in the contemporary media, factory women were not called "modern girls" or even factory "girls" (kkŏl).

Women's studies scholar T'ae Hyesuk argues that factory women in colonial Korea were not called *kkŏl*, even though the term was used for women in service jobs such as "bus *kkŏl*" and "department *kkŏl*" or for politically conscious women such as "Marx *kkŏl*," because the English word "girl" not only had a strong association with male sexual desire toward women but also conjured up images of modern urban space where the women, while working, were exposed to the public's gaze.[25] It might have been that, although factory women worked at a definitely modern space, the factory, and also were constantly exposed to sexual harassment and seduction by male supervisors and coworkers, the factory was, unlike a bus or a department store, a space closed to the outsider's gaze, and thus their existence had less chance of invoking sexual fantasies from male intellectuals like bus girls, department store sales girls, or elevator girls did. For whatever reasons, factory women in colonial Korea were called yŏgong (female factory operative) or yŏjikkong (female factory employee) and not "factory *kkŏl*," but the fact that colloquially they were also called *k'ŭnagi* (maidens) and the crude jokes that circulated widely about their sexually loose behavior complicate the picture (see chapter 3). Clearly their morality was put under suspicion, and they were hardly immune to the sexualized gaze of society. But the process of sexualizing the figure of yŏgong apparently worked differently from that for "modern girls."

Arguably the "new woman" status became the aspiration for many young women in colonial Korea and thus worked as an important comparative point in the development of yŏgong subjectivities. If so, the question of whether women factory workers qualified as "new women" must have crossed the minds of "new women" activists and the yŏgong they met. Socialist feminist activist Chŏng Ch'ilsŏng uttered the most direct statement on the matter in her 1926 essay in the newspaper *Chosun ilbo* and another short essay in the January 1932 issue of *Tonggwang*, the journal that carried Kang Churyong's interview about half a year prior. In her *Tonggwang* article, "Women Workers Who Gaze at the Future" (Amnal ŭl parabonŭn puin nodongja), she argued forcefully that the "genuine new women" were women workers found "in the black coal and chimneys of tobacco, spinning, and textile factories" and they, not those fashionable new women who "got to study faraway in the United States, thanks to Jesus" or those who "after graduating from a good school were happy to become a concubine" of a wealthy man, were the ones who "would signal the noble new life of the future." Chŏng Ch'ilsŏng was a famous *sasang kisaeng*, a top-class courtesan who transformed herself into a political activist. She came from a working-class background and was a leading socialist voice in the Kŭnuhoe movement, in which she championed the task of organizing women workers and farming women.[26] Two other essays of hers, one in the inaugural issue of *Kŭnu* (May 1929), the organ of the Kŭnuhoe, and another in the January 1931 issue of the leftist journal *Pip'an* (Criticism), also emphasized the cause of working-class women.

It is not easy to speculate how yŏgong viewed "new women" activists because we do not have written sources to rely on to tease out their thoughts. We have an account of a young yŏgong of the Kyŏngsŏng Spinning and Weaving Company, a company that had just gone through an eight-day strike from late May to early June 1928. She made a critical remark about the elite women activists gathered at the national meeting of the Kŭnuhoe in July 1928. A factory worker, she criticized Kŭnuhoe representatives gathered at the meeting for their lack of "strategy and tactics for fighting on behalf of ten million [working-class] women," and she predicted that the organization would remain a mere "[social] club" unless it actively engaged militant "working women" (*nodong puin*). She urged them to "take off that glamorous attire, break the perfume bottle, remove the gold watch, and go among the working women!"[27] The essay reflects, more than anything else, the viewpoint of the journal editors, that is, leftist male intellectuals, preaching on what they viewed as lacking in the women's movement. Even so, we can see from the episode that it was possible by 1928 that some yŏgong were already critically examining the rescuer-rescued relationship between "new women" activists and themselves.

The gulf between elite "new women" activists and the women "masses" was a serious issue theoretically and practically in the women's movement in colonial Korea. Awareness of class cleavages among women sharpened over the 1920s as socialist ideas spread in Korea and the pace of industrialization picked up, producing a small but visible class of industrial workers and also attention-grabbing labor disputes. Some new women activists began to embrace socialist feminist ideas and criticize the limitations they saw in the liberal feminist agenda, which they felt only served the needs and interests of bourgeois women. Many new women activists, including Hŏ Chŏngsuk, Yi Hyŏn'gyŏng, and Hwang Sindŏk, studied at Japanese universities and interacted with Japanese feminists, while some embraced socialism and socialist feminism in China or in the Soviet Union.[28] In particular, Yamakawa Kikue, one of the most important theorists of Japanese socialist feminism and a founder of Japan's first socialist women's organization, the Red Wave Society (Sekirankai), exerted significant influence on Korean women activists who studied in Japan, including Chŏng Ch'ilsŏng, Yi Hyŏn'gyŏng, and Hwang Sindŏk.[29] Socialist feminism with its direct engagement with the class question and a coherent and revolutionary vision for women's liberation appealed to many women activists in colonial Korea. It offered "an alternative path to women's liberation" to a liberal feminist position, which was centered on "women's education, economic independence, and sexual autonomy" and thus vulnerable to charges of "cultural elitism."[30]

Beginning with the Korean Women's League (Chosŏn Yŏsŏng Tonguhoe; 1924–27), the first socialist women's organization launched in May 1924 by a small group of first-generation socialist women activists, including Pak Wŏnhŭi (1899–1928), Chŏng Chongmyŏng (1896–?), Chŏng Ch'ilsŏng (1908–?), Chu

Sejuk (1901–?), and Hŏ Chŏngsuk (1902–1991), the socialist women's movement grew briskly in the 1920s. Although the number of women authors and the size of female readership remained small, which led to a near monopoly in colonial Korea of male intellectuals on virtually every issue, including women's issues, some socialist feminist women were able to articulate their thoughts in pages of newspapers and periodicals. In addition to Chŏng Ch'ilsŏng, mentioned above, Hwang Sindŏk, Hŏ Chŏngsuk, and Yi Hyŏn'gyŏng were important voices, articulating socialist perspectives on the women question.[31] These women leaders formed the core leadership group of the socialist wing of the Kŭnuhoe movement. The Kŭnuhoe movement in the late 1920s and the early 1930s was the culmination of this development.[32] And Cho Yŏngok stood on this development in the Korean women's movement when in 1931 she joined the Chŏng Talhŏn group and set out to organize Pyongyang's rubber workers.

The united-front movement of Kŭnuhoe lasted from 1927 to 1931, and by 1930 the Kŭnuhoe boasted sixty-four chapters, including three abroad (two in Japan and one in Manchuria).[33] The women-only association offered a chance for women activists to overcome the split between the bourgeois nationalist and the socialist camps and plan joint operations. It was possible because for some time a shared understanding was developing among women activists that in order to reach out to the female "masses," it would be essential to combine the strength of socialists in urban areas and the influence of nonsocialist feminists, mostly of Christian and Chŏndogyo (Religion of the Heavenly Way) ilk, among rural and religious women. As expected in a united-front movement, various groups with different ideas on women's liberation intermingled in the Kŭnuhoe, and the official platform of the organization tended to coalesce around a basic common denominator, which was the "enlightenment" (*kyemong*) of non-elite women. The "Declaration of the Kŭnuhoe," published in *Kŭnu*, delineates this enlightenment-centered agenda succinctly. It claims that Korean women suffer from "feudal remnants and modern contradictions" and that in the struggle against these two problems there would not be major differences among all Korean women, except for those belonging to the reactionary group.[34] Hŏ Chŏngsuk, for her part, declared early on, in an essay published in *Chosun ilbo* on January 3, 1926, titled "A New Year and the Women's Movement: Pioneers Must Work Harder for Self-Cultivation" ("Sinnyŏn kwa yŏsŏng undong: Sŏn'gakcha nŭn suyang e tŏuk noryŏk"), that "women, regardless of which class they belong to, occupy a common status" as women. And in a substantial essay that followed the declaration in journal *Kŭnu*, titled "The Historical Status and Current Task of the Kŭnuhoe Movement" ("Kŭnuhoe undong ŭi yŏksajŏk chiwi wa tangmyŏn immu"), Hŏ emphasized the "feudal fetters" that oppressed Korean women in general. According to her assessment, both the "objective and subjective conditions of women" in Korea called for "a separate women-only organization," that is, an organization that would struggle "against discrimination based on gender" and pursue the "women's enlightenment movement."[35] The "objectives" (*Kangnyŏng*) of the Kŭnuhoe at its founding were set in the broadest possible terms: to work for the unity of Korean women, and for the improvement of the status of Korean women.[36]

The question for the socialist women in the Kŭnuhoe movement, like Cho Yŏngok and Chŏng Ch'ilsŏng, was how to reconcile this umbrella doctrine of "enlightenment" with their socialist feminist agenda centered on organizing women industrial workers and rural women. Chŏng Ch'ilsŏng, the chair of the Central Steering Committee in 1929, represented the view of socialist members in the journal *Kŭnu* by arguing that "proletarian women draw no benefit from modernity, rather suffering from an increasing misery that turns from bad to worse with all those developments."[37] Chŏng Ch'ilsŏng was not a lone voice in the Kŭnuhoe in emphasizing the need to be attentive to the class issue. Some socialists in the Kŭnuhoe, especially the Tokyo chapter members, wanted to push to the fore the task of organizing among women industrial workers, and many action programs, statements, and agendas of the Kŭnuhoe and some of its local chapters reflected members' commitment to the labor question, by including issues of gender-based wage discrimination, maternal leave, prohibition of dangerous and nighttime work for women and youth workers, daycare provisions, and preparation of labor-related statistics.[38]

The socialist leadership overall dominated the Kŭnuhoe movement until about 1930, when the Christian nationalist wing, led by Cho Sinsŏng of the Pyongyang chapter, took over the helm. The main locus of strength in Kŭnuhoe activism among socialists lay among the urban female student population, and by 1930 key socialist leaders, including Hŏ Chŏngsuk, had been arrested and removed from their leadership positions as a result of their involvement in the student movement. By early 1930 Pak Wŏnhŭi was dead, Yi Hyŏn'gyŏng was in exile, and Hŏ Chŏngsuk was in jail. Cho Sinsŏng, the champion of the Christian conservatives in the women's movement and a staunch anticommunist, became the new chair of the steering committee in 1930, and one of the changes she implemented was the dismantling of the labor and farmers' department (Nonongbu), which the Chŏng Ch'ilsŏng leadership had established in 1929.

Even so, some local chapters, especially where socialist influence was strong, vigorously pursued the agenda of organizing industrial workers and rural women. Some of these chapters suffered from the arrest of officials and police raids on offices because of their support of striking women workers. The Hongwŏn chapter in South Hamgyŏng Province, for example, discussed establishing a labor department and sent a negotiator to intervene in a local labor dispute, and members of the nearby Pukchŏng chapter aided women strikers at Katakura Spinning in their effort to block scab workers, which resulted in three of the chapter's officials being arrested. In South Kyŏngsang Province, the Tongnae chapter raised the issue of "equal labor, equal pay" and resolved to escalate efforts to organize women workers, and the nearby Pusan chapter established a labor department that tried to organize women workers into a union. Out of its sixty-four chapters, as of 1930 at least one chapter, the Kyŏngdong chapter in Seoul, was actually created by organizing women workers, and the majority of the chapter membership in Kunsan, a southwestern port city, was composed of female laborers.[39] And the Tokyo and Kyoto chapters in Japan had strong affiliations with trade union "women's bureaus" or other women industrial worker organizations.

Overall, however, Kŭnuhoe's inroads into the labor movement remained limited and sporadic. Among several thousand women who joined Kŭnuhoe, the proportion of women industrial workers remained much less than 10 percent.[40] It was, however, a meaningful development that women industrial workers and middle-class "new women" members were beginning to work together at many chapters. Through the Kŭnuhoe movement bourgeois nationalist and socialist activists joined hands to work for the female population as a whole, albeit for a short duration, but also yŏgong and "new women" activists had a chance to get connected. By early 1929 some Kŭnu chapters, including the Kunsan, Pyongyang, Nanam, and Tokyo chapters, had fifteen or more female workers as members.

Students Turned Activist Women in the Labor Movement

When Kŭnuhoe socialists like Cho Yŏngok stepped into the red union movement, they encountered a particular kind of socialist gender discourse that put great emphasis on the task of stimulating class consciousness in women workers. They operated under the hegemony of the communist movement and affirmed the priority of class revolution and national liberation as prerequisites for achieving a genuine women's liberation for all classes of women. Women's awakening as autonomous subjects had to be reimagined within the framework of revolutionary mobilization of workers for class revolution. In the 1930s a new generation of young women emerged, who abandoned their chances at a comfortable life as elite "new women" and chose a difficult and dangerous life as revolutionary worker-organizers. If we use the 1980s activist jargon from South Korea, these young women belonged to the first generation of the *hakch'ul* (*haksaeng undong ch'ulsin*, meaning "from the student movement"), students turned labor organizers. The experiences and ethos of these activists in the colonial labor movement are not well understood.

One way to gain a better understanding of the historic encounter between "new women" activists like Cho Yŏngok and yŏgong activists like Kang Churyong is to look at how contemporary communist ideologues defined the position and historical roles of women factory workers. A useful source for examining the evolving leftist discourse on female industrial workers is the organ of the Pan-Pacific Trade Union (T'aero) Secretariat, *T'aep'yŏngyang rodongja* (*Pacific Workers*). The T'aero Secretariat issued the influential "October Letter" of 1931, which served as a crucial guideline for red union organizing in Korea, and T'aero-affiliated union organizers, including Chŏng Talhŏn, persisted in mounting revolutionary endeavors among workers. One result of these efforts was the imprisonment of thousands in four major T'aero incidents that occurred in the early 1930s.[41] Fortunately, most of the issues of the Korean-language version of *Pacific Workers* between 1930 and 1932 are available for scrutiny.[42] Many commentators wrote about the status of the Korean labor movement in the journal and pointed to women workers' militant struggle as a major development in the movement. Several articles, including Ch'ae Rin's 1930 article and Paektusan's 1931 article, highlighted the Pyongyang rubber strikes.[43]

A pronounced feature in *Pacific Workers* articles on yŏgong activism was an inordinate focus on the collective, that is, the Korean industrial workers as a whole, and a steady refusal to see individual heroes among women workers. The focus of both Paektusan's and Ch'ae Rin's articles was squarely on the collective, called *nodongja* (workers), and the strike leadership as a whole, not on an individual, regardless of his or her contribution. In fact, the subject of the movement, factory workers, was often not defined particularly as "women" workers even when yŏgong strikes were being discussed. Class-conscious women workers were often referred to as "revolutionary elements" (*hyŏngmyŏngjŏk punja*).[44] These articles also did not use the term "female fighter" (*yŏt'usa*) for women strikers as contemporary nationalist news media did. Even in a piece assessing and celebrating the P'yŏngwŏn Rubber strike, the author writing under the pen name Paektusan (Whitehead Mountain) called Kang Churyong simply "yŏgong Kang Churyong."[45] These practices were in stark contrast to the way contemporary nationalist newspapers foregrounded the gender of rubber strikers and constructed an image of a respectable *yŏgong t'usa* (female worker fighter) figure.

Looking through the pages of *Pacific Workers*, it becomes apparent that there existed a big gulf in perceptions and cultures between communist organizers and women workers. Differing views on women strikers' tactic of the hunger strike provide one salient example. While praising "resolute" (*pijang*), "bitter" (*t'ongnyŏl*), and "gallant" (*changnyŏl*) struggle by striking workers, as was conventional in socialist writings on worker struggle, Paektusan criticizes the tactic of the hunger strike as "suicidal and passive" and as a move tantamount to "disarmament" in war because it damaged the "frail" body of the strikers who needed physical strength to fight.[46] This seems to have been a widely shared opinion among Korean communists. Pak Hŏnyŏng, a key communist leader and future head of the South Korean Workers' Party after Korea's liberation, expressed essentially the same view in a 1932 report criticizing the "passive types of struggle such as hunger struggle" among women workers. A Korean representative at a Profintern meeting in December 1931 voiced the same concern.[47] Instead of "achieving its class-based demands by militantly fighting," Paektusan claims, the tactic of hunger strike "resorts to pleading [aeso] to the humanistic sentiment of pity of the bourgeoisie."[48] But fasting as a tactic was geared toward exhibiting workers' firm resolution and courage and thus gaining the moral high ground vis-à-vis management, and not simply a public display of helplessness aimed at generating pity from the bourgeoisie as communist intellectuals saw it. It is intriguing that communists denied the power of women workers' desperate yet socially effective hunger strike tactic. One wonders what P'yŏngwŏn workers would have said to this criticism that they were hurting their "frail" female body by protest-fasting and that their "humanistic pleas" were demeaning.

Female red union activists likely encountered contradictions and tensions stemming from the still pervasive patriarchal gender culture in the communist movement when they tried to bridge the gap between male leaders and factory women. There is a growing literature on the numerous and eventually failed efforts to rebuild the Communist Party in Korea during the 1930s, all of which involved red union organizing as a core part of the program.[49] We know that many activists, male and female, in the 1930s organized communist cells and study groups at the factory level, but not much is known about their experiences in those organizations. Studies of the legendary Yi Chaeyu group by labor historians Kim Kyŏngil and An Chaesŏng, together with literary scholar Yi Sanggyŏng's study of leftist women writers, add some depth to our understanding of the lives of several female students turned labor organizers during this period.[50] Their findings help us contextualize the relationship between Cho Yŏngok and Kang Churyong in the milieu of the era's communist labor organizing effort. Prior to becoming factory worker-organizers, the personal backgrounds and occupational experiences of the radical women featured in the existing studies were diverse. For most, however, the experience of joining school socialist study groups, called the "RS" (reading societies) in activist jargon, constituted a major turning point in their lives. Organizing student demonstrations and campus strikes as student leaders also had a fundamental impact on these young women, nudging them toward the life of revolutionary organizers. The student movement represented one of the most vital sectors of radical activism during the 1930s, and teachers played an important role by nurturing a new generation of committed activists, both men and women.

Young people (chŏngnyŏn) were a major target of communist organizing along with industrial workers and tenant farmers in this period. Student strikes and anticolonial demonstrations by politically awakened students were numerous in the late 1920s and early 1930s. The most important of these were the Kwangju

Student Movement of 1929 and the Seoul Female Student Movement of 1930. The latter was also called the Kŭnuhoe incident due to the heavy involvement of Kŭnuhoe socialist women in it.[51] The Sin'ganhoe and the Kŭnuhoe, especially the socialist elements in them, actively supported this anticolonial student activism and suffered police repression as a result.

Many schools in the 1930s had RS organizations, and some of the veterans of RS training and student strikes transitioned into red union organizing, now mentoring workers using the same small-study-group method of consciousness-raising they learned in student activism.[52] During the first half of the 1930s, colonial police records show, more than 1,759 activists were arrested in seventy-plus cases of red union incidents, and most of these arrested activists were young people twenty-five years of age or younger.[53] Among them were many graduates of higher-normal (secondary) schools, both male and female. Among women's schools located in Seoul, Tongdŏk Girls Higher-Normal School, a school established by the native Ch'ŏndogyo order, and Methodist Ewha Girls Higher-Normal were famous as the cradle of socialist women activists in the 1930s. Tongdŏk produced many famous radical women activists, including Yi Sun'gŭm, Pak Chinhong, Yi Chonghŭi, and Yi Kyŏngsŏn. Yi Sun'gŭm and Yi Kyŏngsŏn, encountering socialist literature at school and plunging into the red union movement after leaving school, show a typical path through which a young Korean female revolutionary was born in this era.[54] Yi Kyŏngsŏn worked at a factory in the East Gate area of Seoul. Yi Sun'gŭm worked at a textile factory in the Yŏngdŭngp'o industrial area of Seoul and organized several cells before being arrested. Yi Chonghŭi worked with rubber shoe workers in Seoul, leading a 1933 strike at Pyŏlp'yo Rubber in Seoul and intervening in strikes at Seoul Rubber and the Seoul factory of Chongyŏn Spinning (Kanebō) in 1933.[55]

Among women labor organizers of the colonial period, the most famous was probably Pak Chinhong. Pak was expelled from Tongdŏk as the ringleader of a student strike and became a full-time worker-organizer at rubber and textile factories in Seoul, including Taech'ang Textile, Taech'ang Rubber, and Chosŏn Cotton. She joined the Kyŏngsŏng RS Association, a secret organization that helped students launch campus strikes as well as endeavored to organize workers in Seoul. The association helped organize student strikes at more than ten schools in Seoul, including a major strike at Tongdŏk in June 1931.[56] In the RS Association Pak was put in charge of organizing rubber workers and operated at Taejŏng Rubber and Uri Rubber factories.[57] Of all these female students turned labor activists, Hŏ Kyun's case draws our attention in particular because she, like Cho Yŏngok in Pyongyang, was a radical woman who was a Kŭnuhoe member. Hŏ was a key official of the Kyŏngdong chapter in Seoul, which, as mentioned earlier, was a chapter created by organizing female workers.[58] Hŏ Kyun resembles

Cho Yŏngok also in that she dropped out of school due to financial difficulties and subsequently became a labor organizer. Hŏ worked at rubber and textile factories, including Seoul Rubber and Taeryuk Rubber. After liberation, Hŏ Kyun became the head of the women's bureau at the leftist Chŏnp'yŏng (National Council of Korean Labor Unions), the highest position held by a woman in that powerful national umbrella organization of labor.[59]

This general pattern of development for young radical women in 1930s Korea applies to the Cho Yŏngok–Kang Churyong duo. From the cases of Hŏ Kyun and many others, we can see that rubber and textile factories had become a central target of communist organizing efforts, a situation that made the role of young women organizers who could approach yŏgong at the factory level very important to the movement. The full scope of red union organizing at factories in Korea is unknowable because the evidence we have shows only the prosecuted cases, and there might have been many undetected efforts. Even so, police and court documents confirm that red unions were active at many rubber and textile mills in the 1930s, despite all-out anticommunist propaganda and brutal repression by the colonial authorities, including murderous torture techniques and harsh prison conditions that resulted in the deaths of many activists.[60] Not only "new women" activists who received formal modern education came to factories as organizers, but also a significant number of organizers with worker backgrounds, like Kang Churyong, were emerging from the ranks of yŏgong. Another example is "Chobang [Chosŏn Spinning and Weaving] yŏgong Pak Sunhŭi" listed as one of the twenty-four male and fifteen female activists prosecuted in a major red union incident in Pusan in October 1934.[61] And of the approximately one hundred workers participating in the Yi Chaeyu group's red union organizing activities in Seoul in 1933, many were textile and rubber factory yŏgong. Yu Sunhŭi, a militant factory worker and a member of the Yi Chaeyu group, led a strike at Shōwa Spinning in 1933 and afterward worked as an organizer at the Yŏngdŭngp'o factory of Kyŏngsŏng Spinning and Weaving (Kyŏngbang) and also at Chosŏn Silk. In addition to professional organizers coming from outside, four or five, or in some cases as many as ten, workers joined communist cells at several textile and rubber factories in Seoul, including Kyŏngbang, Chosŏn Silk, Katakura Spinning, Chongyŏn Spinning, Tongmyŏng Rubber, Seoul Rubber, Kyŏngsŏng Rubber, Koryŏ Rubber, and Chungang Rubber.[62]

This brief survey indicates that not a few "new women" labor activists existed in 1930s Korea, and some yŏgong were transforming themselves into labor activists as well. The relationship between Kang Churyong and Cho Yŏngok were being replicated in and around many rubber and textile mills in the early 1930s. The distance between these two groups of women in terms of their socioeconomic backgrounds does not seem to have been vast, especially in the cases of "new women" from poor families like Hŏ Kyun or Cho Yŏngok.

Little has been uncovered about the day-to-day experiences of these women activists at factories, especially their interactions with their male activist colleagues and with other workers. The thorny issue of the so-called housekeeper role assigned to young radical women, in which they were expected to perform a range of caring labor, including cooking and cleaning, for a senior male colleague in hiding as well as providing a cover for him, hints at a prevalent and abusive sexist culture among the revolutionaries of the era, which must have troubled these women deeply.[63] That sexist culture was also revealed in the mainstream media's sensationalization of the pursuit of free or "red love" by some socialist women.[64] As activities of radical women became visible in a society where conservative gender norms were deeply entrenched, the Korean media had a field day associating them with "red love" and churning out "scandals" involving their alleged promiscuity.[65] In this culture of sensational reporting on radical women, there was a tendency in media coverage to turn female labor organizers' revolutionary endeavors into a salacious story of foolhardy women, a story that also suggested by extension the allegedly immoral nature of socialist activism. It is thus hard to find in media reports clues to the questions of how these women revolutionaries negotiated difficult gendered social settings and how they were able to forge cross-class bonds among women despite those formidable problems.

Information on women labor activists who operated in provincial cities or small towns, like Pyongyang's Cho Yŏngok, are harder to unearth than stories of those who were involved in major Seoul-based communist group activities, which, albeit fragmented, have found their place in historical accounts. Under these circumstances the proletarian literature, produced in the 1930s by leftist writers, can offer us some help in our attempt to imagine the lives of female organizers in the labor movement. The theme of an intellectual vanguard moving into the masses and trying out consciousness-raising schemes, be they aimed at industrial workers or poor farmers, appears frequently in this literature, a subject we turn to next.

The Literary Represen[tation of] Yŏgong Activists

Famous leftist novelists of the day, i[ncluding] [H]an Sŏrya, Kim Namchŏn, Yu Chino, Ri Kiyŏ[ng, ...], present female factory worker characters in [their work, and some settings involve] rubber factory workers.[66] Women rubber workers, especially after the Pyongyang strikes of 1930 and 1931, appear frequently in contemporary leftist literature. Among these Kim Namchŏn's two short stories, "Factory Fraternity" ("Konguhoe," 1932) and "Factory Newspaper" ("Kongjang sinmun," 1931), are set at a "P'yŏnghwa rubber factory," and Yi Chŏkhyo's "General Mobilization" ("Ch'ongdongwŏn," 1931) depicts the 1930 Pyongyang rubber strike.[67] Literary scholar Samuel Perry points out that, according to the records of the colonial publication police, Kim Namchŏn and other leftist writers actively supported the 1930 Pyongyang rubber strike. Kim was said to have tried to inspire workers by "singing poems and reading out stories" for them.[68]

Through the literary images of rubber workers we can get a glimpse of how contemporary leftist intellectuals imagined revolutionary red union organizing and the intellectual and worker activists involved in it. The short stories "Factory Fraternity" and "Factory Newspaper" depict male and female workers endeavoring to organize a union together, but male workers are firmly in the leadership role. In its fictionalized portrayal of the 1930 Pyongyang rubber strike, "General Mobilization" presents a powerful rubber yŏgong character named Okchŏng, who emerges as a passionate and articulate leader of the strike. This was perhaps a nod to the well-known fact of yŏgong militancy in the 1930 strike.[69] When her union president husband betrays two thousand strikers after receiving bribe money from a "ch'al-Yesu-jaengi" (stalwart believer of Jesus Christ) factory owner (a character perhaps modeled after the influential Presbyterian leader and rubber factory owner Kim Tongwŏn), Okchŏng comes out publicly against her husband, who in turn accuses her of disobeying him and subsequently murders her.

Some works go further and touch on the delicate and tension-ridden relationship between workers and intellectual activists who come to the factory to "enlighten" them, and in great detail portray the process through which a yŏgong character comes to attain self-consciousness as an autonomous individual and develops revolutionary political consciousness. Ri Kiyŏng's Wŏlhŭi (1929), Song Yŏng's O Suhyang (1931), and Kang Kyŏngae's The Human Predicament (1934) are examples of these more insightful works.

O Suhyang is interesting because it depicts the process of a working-class heroine, O Suhyang, who becomes a kisaeng entertainer to support her family after graduating from elementary school. She gradually gains political consciousness through a male activist customer turned lover and then by joining a "XX [the name is censored by the colonial authorities] chapter" on her own.[70] It is reasonable to read the censored name of the organization as "Kŭnu." This conjecture is based on the discussion of the dissolution of the organization among women activists Suhyang meets after quitting her kisaeng job and joining the "XX chapter." Women characters argue that women should join a "women's department" of a farmers' association or a trade union organized by industry, instead of maintaining a women-only organization, which, if captured by "bourgeois women," could actually "obstruct" organizing effort among rural women, factory women, and unemployed women. Suhyang embraces this argument and soon volunteers to infiltrate a silk reeling company to organize yŏgong in another locale, a task she brilliantly accomplishes by the end of the novel when her fellow women workers erupt in a strike. Through her involvement in the labor movement, Suhyang, who initially was timid and insecure about her abilities, grows to become an autonomous human being. In the last scene Suhyang charges forward, confronting management "as if she were a mad lioness."[71] This idealized portrayal of a successful consciousness-raising operation by a vanguard activist from outside is intriguing because of Suhyang's gender and her non-elite, lower-class, *kisaeng* courtesan background. It is also interesting because her transformation into a capable labor organizer was mentored by presidents of two Kŭnu chapters.

Pak Sŭngguk's "Restart" ("Chae ch'ulbal," 1931) is set in an industrial city where thousands of workers labor in steel, rubber, and silk reeling factories.[72] It features a group of activists discussing conditions and strategies for social movements and a member of the local union, the head of the Sin'ganhoe chapter, and a Kŭnuhoe official show up as visitors. In the end four protagonists, one each from a youth association, a labor union, the Sin'ganhoe chapter, and the Kŭnuhoe chapter (who is called "female comrade Suni"), make a decision to "change courses" and become workers. Soon the first steel union in the country emerges in the area, and industrial unions in silk reeling and rubber manufacturing follow. Eventually a general strike erupts, which lasts three months. From the prominence of Kŭnu members in these stories we can speculate that the linkages between Kŭnu local chapters and red union organizing might have been stronger and denser than the extant evidence, including in the case of Cho Yŏngok, allows us to see.

Of all the colonial period fictional works that feature yŏgong characters, Kang Kyŏngae's full-length novel *The Human Predicament* (*In'gan munje*, 1934) gives us the most developed and memorable yŏgong activist figures.[73] The story follows two rural girls, Sŏnbi and Kannan, who, after suffering the miseries of poverty and sexual violence in their home village, end up at a textile mill and grow into committed worker activists. The socialist male intellectual figure of the novel, Sinch'ŏl, is an ambiguous character who "idly vacillates between fatuous romance and a shaky political commitment."[74] Meanwhile the working-class village lad Ch'ŏtchae, who loves Sŏnbi, matures in the end into a stalwart revolutionary. Socialist women writers in colonial Korea appear much more sensitive to the power dynamics between male intellectuals and women workers than their male counterparts. Literary scholar Sunyoung Park notes the significance of Kang

Kyŏngae's novels as "paradigmatic of the broader production of 1930s socialist women writers" and argues that "once read in the context of contemporary Korean culture, many works by socialist women writers can be seen to perform a genuinely feminist function" of critiquing socialist patriarchy.[75] Through the yŏgong characters of Sŏnbi and Kannan and the male revolutionary characters of Sinch'ŏl and Ch'ŏtchae, *The Human Predicament* earnestly tackles the gender question as well as the class question. It reveals "a tension between the class-oriented ideology of socialism" and the emerging "gendered critical subjectivity" among politically conscious yŏgong and female writers like Kang Kyŏngae.[76]

Kang Kyŏngae, born in 1906, was about five years younger than Kang Churyong. She grew up in poverty, aspired to become a "new woman," and succeeded in getting a formal education through sheer toughness of character. She attended Sungŭi Girls' School in Pyongyang, from which, like many socialist women of the period, she was expelled after leading a student strike in 1922. Afterward she studied at Tongdŏk Girls' Higher-Normal School in Seoul for about a year, then lived in northern Manchuria for two years around 1927 to 1928, and after returning to her hometown Changyŏn, she joined the Kŭnuhoe chapter there and served as its General Affairs Department chief.[77] Changyŏn, in Hwanghae Province, is located between Pyongyang and Seoul. While she was an active member of the Kŭnuhoe in Changyŏn, it is likely that Kang paid keen attention to the many strikes by women workers that happened in the northwest during 1930 and 1931. A rubber factory activist is portrayed in her poem "Replying to Older Brother's Letter" ("Opppa ŭi p'yŏnji hoedap"), published in the December 1931 issue of *Sinyŏsŏng* (New Women), not long after the P'yŏngwŏn Rubber strike ended. In a letter to her older brother who has been arrested, a rubber yŏgong heroine proudly reports:

> Brother! But this sister
> is a fool no more who stupidly cries forever
> Now she works in a factory making *komusin* pretty well
> Dear brother, look at this upper arm!
> It has become stronger and healthier than yours
> . . .
>
> In street after street flyers are flying in the wind
> Oh, dear brother! Do you know this? Do you not know?
> Brother! Please share the joy with me, as this sister
> sticks out her chest, which had stayed recoiled shyly,
> standing as a leader of a great many comrades of mine
> with her face flushed red XX [censored] against the factory owner.[78]

The 1930s red union movement in colonial Korea produced many memorable struggles by workers, and it is impressive that many women workers were squarely at the center of this highly dangerous underground anti-imperial class struggle. The 1931 P'yŏngwŏn Rubber strike that produced many unforgettable scenes, not only Kang Churyong's dazzling high-altitude sit-in on the Ŭlmiltae Pavilion but also desperate hunger strikes, the shocking "attacks" on the factory, and the dramatic street demonstrations, was a representative case that shows the level of yŏgong activism and their assertiveness. From the roof of the Ŭlmiltae, Kang Churyong expressed confidence in her level of knowledge, which, as she put it, she had acquired "through learning" (*nae ka paewasŏ anŭn kŏt*).[79] New subjectivities of factory women activists, now armed with the "knowledge of liberation" gained through hard work and engagement in labor activism and proud of that knowledge, were emerging in the colonial and socialist modern landscape of Korea.[80] More than male writers, socialist women writers seem to have sensed the feminist and proletarian spirit of this new breed of working-class women. This aspect of the colonial revolutionary movement, which affected the very sense of self-worth of individuals, helps explain why women workers like Kang Churyong so fearlessly embraced the dangerous life of a labor activist.

How did the larger society then react to the emergence of these new yŏgong activists? The next chapter takes up this question and details the risks and costs of the newly acquired consciousness of these young female activists. A discussion of the aftermath of the P'yŏngwŏn Rubber strike, including the launching of a worker-owned factory and what we know about Kang Churyong's fate, follows.

3

COPING WITH WOMEN STRIKERS
Nation, Class, and Gender under Colonial Rule

In the previous two chapters we followed the stories of Kang Churyong and other women rubber workers of Pyongyang and their relationships with that city's business elite, nationalists, and socialist activists. Zooming out one step further, we can now explore the larger society's relationship with Kang Churyong and her fellow women strikers.

Knowledge producers and social movement activists of colonial Korea tried to fix yŏgong identity and narrate their miseries and potentials in particular ways. At the same time voices and actions of women workers themselves pointed to a new kind of yŏgong subjectivity that was developing in tension with mainstream discourses about them. In 1930 the number of female factory workers mentioned in colonial government statistics on the industrial workforce—only the number of employees at factories that hired five or more workers on a regular basis were counted—was rather small, not quite reaching thirty thousand in a population of about twenty million people.[1] Most people living in that period did not have a chance to visit a factory to see yŏgong working, and what they knew about the yŏgong's living conditions mostly came through news media reports or representations in literary works. Unlike working-class people in urban areas, who often encountered yŏgong in their everyday lives, for middle-class Koreans and elite opinion makers the yŏgong was an unfamiliar figure. Except for some rare occasions in which women strikers were interviewed by a reporter or an individual yŏgong's viewpoints were solicited by a magazine, factory women's voices were seldom heard.

Considering the paucity of documentation revealing factory women's own perspectives, we can access the question of how yŏgong were perceived by society and by women themselves from two angles. First, examining representations of yŏgong figures through contemporary news media and magazines, as well as literary works and political literature, offers us a way to apprehend evolving discourses on the yŏgong question among elite opinion makers and activists, who swayed mainstream perceptions of yŏgong to a large extent. Second, we can read actions and strike demands of women workers carefully to find clues to the ways yŏgong positioned themselves socially and politically in the larger society. The forces that produced and steered gendered perceptions of factory women over time included not only the colonial Korean media and social movement circles but also women workers themselves. Some women, now armed with activist or class consciousness, affected the ways the media and society conceived yŏgong. Women workers' resistance often exceeded the boundaries of conventional gender norms and images of yŏgong. And although the bourgeois nationalist media and vanguard activists tried to define and mold the figure of yŏgong and their activism, there existed clear limits to their efforts as women oftentimes defied and destabilized elite viewpoints by acting out their own agenda. The second section of this chapter probes emergent activist self-identity of women workers and listens to their voices.

While being mindful of this mutually constitutive process in which new images and discourses of yŏgong emerged, we can also discern signs of emergent pro-labor ideas and understandings among a segment of the nationalist elite who were willing to grapple with the labor question yŏgong strikers so persistently raised. The chapter's third section explores the short-lived rubber workers' cooperatives movement in Pyongyang in the context of the fluid and tense ideological terrain of the time. The movement represented the high point of hope and goodwill between Pyongyang's working-class residents and the city's elite leadership. The final section of the chapter then traces the fading memories of Kang Churyong and militant rubber yŏgong strikes as labor radicalism dissipated after the early 1930s under the repressive fascist regime of the final ten years of colonial rule.

Media Representation of Women Worker Activists

How did mainstream Korean society in the colonial period narrate and define yŏgong, a novel category of working women, the majority of whom were of lower-class background and from rural tenant families? What was at stake in the representation of yŏgong and their struggle? This section explores these questions using Kang Churyong's case based on information mostly culled from contemporary media source materials. A particular focus is placed on the difficulties the nationalist media seems to have faced in covering news of militant female factory workers. Confronted with the jarring presence of yŏgong in large numbers, many of whom did not shy away from violent actions and routinely violated established gender and class norms, what kinds of rhetorical strategies did media commentators use to contain the odd and threatening presence of yŏgong activists within the confines of conventional gender narratives?

Collectively, women factory workers were most often referred to as yŏjikkong (female factory employee) or yŏgong in the newspapers and magazines of the era. It is relatively easy to examine media usage of these terms. I assembled a large sample of their usage in newspapers and magazines, mainly using the National Institute of Korean History's online Korean History Database, which contains a vast amount of digitized colonial period documents and periodicals, including the *Dong-A ilbo*.[2] Searches of the database using keywords "yŏjikkong" and "yŏgong" yielded thousands of entries.[3] If we limit the scope of the search to a narrower period between 1929 and 1933, which saw numerous large-scale strikes by women workers including the two Pyongyang rubber strikes under discussion, several hundred entries show up, mostly from newspaper and magazine articles.[4] Popular magazines of the day, including *Tonggwang* (Eastern Light), *Samchŏlli* (Three Thousand *Li*), and *Pyŏlgŏn'gon* (Another World), provide several dozen entries, including interviews, recollections, and literary works. To complement this database, I also included entries from a twelve-volume collection of newspaper articles on social movements categorized by region, which offers news articles from the era's other major newspapers, including the *Chosun ilbo*, the *Chungang ilbo* (later, *Chosŏn chungang ilbo*), the *Sidae ilbo*, and the *Maeil sinbo*, in addition to the *Dong-A ilbo*.[5] Reflecting the nature of the archives used, this sample overall is tilted toward major bourgeois nationalist publications like the *Dong-A ilbo*, while leftist voices are scarcely represented, although a small number of items that seem to have been penned by leftist writers are captured in it. Nevertheless, for our purpose of gauging mainstream media representation of women factory workers and their activism, this sample seems sufficient.

A survey of yŏgong/yŏjikkong entries in this sample confirms the strength of the basic paternalistic frame of mind in which respectable men expressed pity at the poverty and suffering of young women and warned about the potential corruption of these allegedly innocent and ignorant factory girls. At the same time, however, we can also sense uneasiness and discomfiture in the language the media reports used. By the 1930s, reports describing horrible working conditions at factories where women workers toiled became numerous in newspapers and magazines as well as in literary works portraying labor issues. This is in contrast to the previous decade in which generally more positive portrayals of modern factory life were more readily found.[6] In conventional newspaper narratives, women workers were primarily situated in relation to their family and family livelihood rather than being considered as workers per se. Categories mobilized to define middle- and upper-class women of the period, such as the "new woman," the "modern girl," or the "wise mother, good wife" figure, seldom found their ways into the talk about yŏgong. Women factory workers were said to endure enormous hardship to make a pittance for their family's survival. Their sacrifice for the family was considered laudable, albeit pathetic. By foregrounding women's roles as family members, whether daughter, daughter-in-law, wife, or mother, women's public work in a morally dubious modern space called the "factory" (kongjang) was made acceptable and in some cases even respectable, especially for married women shouldering the burden of family livelihood. Pervasive social anxieties about women factory workers, who supposedly inhabit a dangerous public space full of possibilities for sexual harassment, rape, and lax sexual morality, were diluted in these accounts through the image of poor women sacrificing for the family. And women workers in turn utilized the woman-sacrificing-for-the-family narrative to claim respect and dignity for themselves. An example of this is when Kang Churyong spoke of her stint as a rubber shoe worker. With pride she told her story of stepping into the "role of a son" as the main "breadwinner" ("pappŏri rŭl hamyŏnsŏ") providing for her parents and a younger brother.[7]

News articles on women workers on strike are replete with emotive language that is meant to evoke predictable yet powerful images of the harrowing existence of women factory workers and thus help produce empathy in readers. Common adjectives used to describe scenes of women's protest, for example, included "wretched" (chŏch'amhan), "ghastly" (ch'amhokhan), "tear-inducing" (nunmul kyŏun), and "pitiable" (pulssanghan). But if the discourse of "misery" and family survival, and the paternalistic attitude toward working-class people framed the bourgeois nationalist narrative about female factory workers, the militant activism of these workers and their tendency to use violence required some rhetorical engineering in order to reconcile this aggressiveness of women strikers within the paternalistic discourse. Especially when female factory workers were, as Sŏ Hyŏngsil shows, widely believed to be "docile" and "patient" and therefore useful as a source of cheap labor, their militancy required a more complex narrative strategy to deal with it and fit it into the conventional social map of gender and class hierarchies.[8]

Three noteworthy aspects of media portrayal of women worker militancy at the time of the Pyongyang rubber strikes of 1930 and 1931 emerge from this examination of media coverage. The first is a sense that something unusual has happened. Oftentimes during a large-scale strike, women workers stormed the factory, smashed the machinery, harassed *kkaegikkun* (strikebreakers), and demonstrated noisily in the street. During the 1930 rubber workers' general strike in Pyongyang, more than two thousand male and female workers attacked factories more than ten different times. A *Dong-A ilbo* article penned by O Kiyŏng describes them as follows: "Like angry bulls who got out of harness, male and female workers darted out to perform violent acts attacking the factory."[9] In newspaper coverage of labor disputes of the late 1920s, readers were already exposed to assertive and militant actions of women strikers. And by the time of the Pyongyang rubber strikes of 1930 and 1931, this image of militant women strikers who did not shy away from violent tactics came to be displayed on a massive scale for the national audience, destabilizing the conventional frame of reference of miserable, helpless, and obedient yŏgong.[10] Police reaction to women workers' militant behavior was often described in news reports using expressions like being "thrown into confusion," "flustered," or "perturbed" (*tanghwang* or *ch'anghwang mangjo*).[11] These words began to be used in relation to social conflict cases in the late 1920s, mostly in the reports of thought crimes, industrial and rural disputes, and student activism. In such accounts it was often government authorities or company or school officials who revealed the sense of being flustered or perturbed. In relation to yŏgong strikes *Dong-A ilbo* first used such expressions in December 1928 when reporting on a textile strike, and the usage—almost exclusively in relation to women's strikes, not men's—continued until about 1935.[12] This focus on the imagined discomfiture of the authorities—the company and the police—facing yŏgong militancy seems also to reflect reporters' own sense of being at a loss when confronted with the wildly aggressive behavior of working-class women.

A second interesting and noticeable aspect of media responses to the Pyongyang rubber strikes is a fixation on the hunger strikes by women workers. Elite society and the police were depicted as baffled especially when factory women protested resolutely through fasting. A poet wrote in the journal *Tonggwang*: "[Kang Churyong] risked death and began a total fasting with determination. An unbelievable seventy-eight-hour fast! . . . Those wretches [*nomdŭl*] [holding her] must have been fearful and in shock. They therefore had no other way but to release her."[13] In fact, Kang Churyong was released because the maximum number of days stipulated for police custody without filing a formal charge were up, but the poet and newspaper reports depicted the situation as if her release had been the result of her unusually long hunger strike.[14] On June 10, 1931, *Chosun ilbo* printed a moving photograph of P'yŏngwŏn women workers participating in a "hunger alliance," which showed them lying on the floor, weakened from fasting. Hunger strike was a frequently adopted tactic of strikers, both women and men, in this period in Korea, and it was not uncommon in Japanese labor disputes either. As early as 1923 female rubber workers in Seoul pioneered an *asa tongmaeng* (starving-to-death alliance). In the case of the P'yŏngwŏn Rubber strike of 1931, about two dozen women workers organized an *asa tongmaeng* and relentlessly deployed the hunger strike tactic to demonstrate their resolve to the larger society and pressure it to act on the dispute. On June 5, 1931, *Dong-A ilbo* reported on four women workers who walked out of a police station after a fifty-seven-hour hunger protest there. I quote the article at length to convey the tone of the narrative.

> Four striking women workers, who surprised the world by not drinking a drop of water and not eating a spoonful of rice since they were arrested by the Pyongyang police on the first [of June], were freed from the police station around 5:30 p.m. on the third.
>
> After fasting for a long time in jail in the summer heat, they went out the door of the police station but were unable to control their legs and tumbled after walking a few steps. [They then got up] and fell down again. The comrades [*tongji*] who had anxiously been awaiting their release [outside the station], therefore, had to carry them on their backs. Without taking time to drink a mouthful of water they went to the P'yŏngwŏn factory, where newly hired laborers were at work. On spotting the new hires who, after finishing their shift, were about to get in [the company-provided] automobile to return home, those four women workers, who were until then unable to move their bodies, suddenly gained strength and lunged toward the new workers, blocking them from getting in the automobile. The new workers then tried to ride a tram, but the four and more than ten of their comrades lay down on the tram track, blocking the tram from moving away. The conductor of the tram had no way to proceed and kicked the new workers off the tram. . . .
>
> The four yŏgong reached the factory gate in the pouring rain and pleaded for [the management] to open the gate, but it was to no avail. Because they were all very weakened and had been suffering through cold rain on top of [their prolonged] excitement, two of the four, O Yangdo (27 years old) and Ri Inbong (31 years old), ended up passing out in front of the factory gate and became unconscious.
>
> . . .
>
> Meanwhile the other two yŏgong, 34-year-old Hwang Tosin and 36-year-old Kim Ch'wisŏn, fainted in the street while heading toward the strike headquarters in Sŏn'gyo-ri. . . . More than two hundred workers from the nearby Kukche Rubber and Kŭmgang Rubber factories

were coming out after their shifts, and, on witnessing this scene, more than one hundred young female workers [among them] suddenly sat down in the street and began to cry out loud.

As the two yŏgong in hunger strike lay on the ground unconscious, and next to them more than one hundred young female workers wailed in unison, a heartbreaking sight was created on that rainy evening street, and the number of people coming over to see them surpassed three hundred.

The reason hunger strikes gained so much attention in this period may have been related to the fact that starvation was a real problem in a society hard hit by depression. Desperate levels of poverty and horrendous living conditions among working-class Koreans, both in urban and rural areas, were major subjects of concern socially and politically. The year 1931 was one of the worst in terms of economic hardship for working-class people in Korea as the disastrous global effect of the 1929 US stock market crash rippled through the world economy.[15] The fact that rubber workers were often married women with children, rather than unmarried young girls, may have increased sympathy toward them even further.[16] The image of poor women, especially mothers, refusing to eat and risking starvation in protest must have been a disturbing one indeed, especially because of the irony in the story that women who labor to feed their families are choosing starvation on purpose.

There seem to be, however, other reasons behind the media's preoccupation with fasting by women strikers. Narrating the hunger strike through the image of a "heartbreaking sight" on a "rainy evening street," instead of dwelling on how surprisingly strong-willed and brave women workers seemed, would have an effect of transforming a militant and radical struggle by women factory workers, one bursting out of the existing nationalist frame of explanation, into a much more manageable story of miserable, helpless underclass people in need of society's sympathy. The *Dong-A ilbo* article I have quoted at length tells the strike story as a story about *women*, downplaying the central issue of class conflict between Korean-owned businesses and Korean workers in Pyongyang. Through this seemingly humanist approach and an all-too-familiar tearjerker narrative style, nationalist newspapers turned the serious question of women workers' challenge to the colonial capitalist order into a story of poor women crying out about human miseries and skillfully evaded both the labor question and the gender question.

Still, the cause women workers upheld—a guarantee of basic humanity and family livelihood befitting members of the nation—was something that could not be dismissed as frivolous or unjustifiable. As a result, certain pressure on the nationalist media to balance the legitimacy and bottom line of the local national bourgeoisie, on the one hand, and the merits of workers' claims, on the other, was inescapable. As historian O Miil argues, the Christian capitalist elite of colonial Korea pursued a well-defined strategy of anchoring their legitimacy in society in their pioneering and essential role in the task of economic modernization of Korea.[17] Their actions would thus be good for the whole nation, including the masses. But the relatively low level of capitalist economic development in Korea in the early 1930s and the increasingly competitive economic environment of the Depression era did not leave much room for the bourgeois nationalist pretensions of the capitalist elite. This crisis in their claim of moral leadership must have been disconcerting and embarrassing to sincere nationalist observers and activists. The excessively emotional language used in *Dong-A ilbo* reports on yŏgong strikes perhaps corresponded to the depth of emotional distress the nationalist elite were experiencing.[18]

Overall, in the wailing women stories that touched sympathetic emotive chords, in combination with the *paehu* red scare stories that triggered fear, bourgeois nationalist media seem to have found an effective formula to deradicalize women workers' mounting challenges to the nationalist version of economic modernization. But the chasm between the discourse of pathetic poor women in need of paternalistic help and the reality of aggressive women fighters charging like "angry bulls" was not easy to suture. Thus, the last noteworthy aspect of the narrative strategy the nationalist media employed was to exalt Kang Churyong and, to a much lesser degree, other female strike leaders as exceptional figures that proved the norm. The effect was to skirt the unsettling reality of yŏgong militancy and create a safe distance between these exceptional individuals and ordinary yŏgong workers. On at least four occasions Kang Churyong was called *yŏt'usa*, "female fighter" (sometimes similar terms like *yŏryu t'usa* or *yŏja t'usa* were used).[19] The term *yŏt'usa* was used in the colonial period media only in a small number of cases.[20] Among them I have so far located only three instances in which an individual yŏgong was honored with the term *yŏt'usa*, and Kang Churyong was one of them.[21] In addition to the case of Kang as *yŏt'usa*, I have found one occasion in which the yŏgong trio of Kang Churyong–Ch'oe Yongdŏk–Kim Ch'wisŏn was collectively referred to as generic "fighters" (*t'usadŭl*) who stood in the front line of the P'yŏngwŏn strike, the loss of whom by police arrest made the strike headquarters "permeated with an awful desolateness."[22]

While the Korean media rarely used the *yŏt'usa* title for Korean women, famous women activists were more often called *yŏgŏl, yŏjangbu,* or *yŏryu hohyŏp,* all meaning the female version of a man of strength and bravery.[23] Kang was once called *yŏjangbu* by *Dong-A ilbo*.[24] When addressing individual women worthy of respect, the media frequently called her *yŏsa* (Madame).[25] It is interesting that the media used this term of respect, which was usually reserved for high-status, married women, for Kang Churyong and another leader of the P'yŏngwŏn strike, Kim Ch'wisŏn.[26] The use of this honorable title *yŏsa* for women factory workers is jarring not only because of status discrepancies between the title and the person but also because the term *yŏsa* implies adulthood, which went against the conventional infantile image of yŏgong. Thus, the usage represents a quite striking change in attitudes toward female manual laborers when we consider the Korean aversion, stressed earlier, to nonagricultural manual labor, thanks to a centuries-long slavery system. In the early 1930s, only several decades after the abolition of slavery in 1894, status consciousness was still very strong in society, as was the Confucian patriarchal gender ideology.

This radical change in the perception of some working-class women's agency and capacity in the media seems to have been possible because the majority of women rubber workers were older, married women from local communities. In the rubber industry, as discussed earlier, the pattern of employment was different from that in the textile industry. Textile workers tended to be younger, single women from rural areas, and they were often understood as poor tenants' daughters. This is the explanation offered by women's studies scholar Sŏ Hyŏngsil, who compared rubber workers and silk-reeling workers in order to understand the conditions for militant collective actions of married rubber workers. She found that married women workers in the rubber industry appear to have been "somewhat freer from social norms that prescribed obedience and femininity."[27]

Still, rubber workers were no exception to a collective image of factory "girls" who were prone to sexual degeneration and thus in need of firm paternalistic control. Women rubber workers were commonly called *komu kongjang k'ŭnagi* (rubber factory maidens), a term that often conjured up images of promiscuity and vulnerability to sexual exploitation. A popular folk song titled "Komu kongjang k'ŭnagi" supposedly circulated in society in the 1930s.[28] The lyric goes in part,

> From morning till night while fastening shoes together, squatting,
> the maiden's breasts thump often.
> For a maiden with a pretty face gets many more pairs
> a flirtatious smile for the manager, coquetry as seed capital.
> The rubber factory maiden's serge skirt
> they say it's a gift from the Honorable Manager.

While the image of docile and pathetic "factory girl" continued to undergird social perceptions of the ordinary yŏgong, it seems that the nationalist media began to produce an alternative image of yŏgong for certain yŏgong activist figures. A few exceptional persons among them were even deemed to deserve a certain level of respect as *yŏsa* or *yŏt'usa* because she proved her worth by exhibiting leadership skills, mental toughness, and capacity to articulate her thoughts, all much-touted traits of modern personhood in bourgeois nationalist thinking. *T'usa* (fighter or warrior) was a term chosen in Protestant nationalist movement circles in Korea to refer to the ideal subjectivity of Christian activists, those who exhibited utmost dedication and spirit of sacrifice in the cause of creating a Christian modern society. In a letter to fellow Koreans in the United States, written in 1929, An Ch'angho, the leader of the Suyang Tonguhoe and a towering figure in the Christian nationalist movement, across the country but especially in the northwest region, exhorted, "To implement a revolution, more than anything else we need to nurture *t'usa*."[29] The imagery of Korean people, especially the youth, maturing into confident and committed modern *t'usa* was therefore not the sole property of socialist movements at the time, and it appears that this reformist yearning for the emergence of *t'usa* among the masses began to seep into the nationalist media's portrayal of factory women strikers.

Unfortunately, this experimentation with a new *yŏsa* yŏgong or yŏgong *t'usa* imagery was short-lived. By the late 1930s the kind of militant strikes by women workers that produced Kang Churyong as a nationally known figure became impossible under wartime conditions. As we have seen, the communist red union movement that persisted underground developed a different image of a desirable yŏgong fighter persona that highlighted her dedication to class struggle and her location in society not as an individual but as part of a collective, the proletariat.

In the end, when the dust all settled, factory owners came out the winners of the fiery multiyear class struggle in the rubber industry. Although Kang's P'yŏngwŏn factory had to retreat from its plan of wage cuts in June 1931, management at Sech'ang Rubber, also in Pyongyang, defeated a strike by two hundred workers in late July. That struggle also involved a hunger strike by seven workers, including a breastfeeding mother and a pregnant woman.[30] In mid-August all twelve rubber factories in Pyongyang, with the exception of the Mutual Aid Cooperative created by workers and discussed here in a later section, began to implement deep wage cuts, finally fulfilling the original plan that local rubber businesses had wished to deploy in early 1930.[31]

New Yŏgong Subjectivities and Agency

Except for an uncommon opportunity like Kang Churyong's interview, we cannot hear women workers' voices directly. Scholars have tried to tease out traces of women worker subjectivities by looking into their actions. Women rubber strikers showed, from a 1923 strike in Seoul to a 1935 strike in Pusan, very high levels of determination, militancy, organizational skills, and ability to articulate their messages to the media. The P'yŏngwŏn strike we have examined at length provides one of the best examples. Women textile strikers were also well known for their militancy.[32] The intensity with which women workers fought in labor disputes, the pride they repeatedly exhibited in the process of negotiations with management, and leadership roles they played at local levels all speak volumes about their subjectivity as autonomous modern individuals.

When we start from this new reality of women workers on the ground, we can sense a clear disjuncture between their world and the perceptions of male socialist ideologues around them, who saw yŏgong as lacking sufficient political consciousness and in need of vanguard guidance. Factory women and socialist women organizers in colonial Korea had to maneuver through a narrow and tension-ridden gendered terrain in order to express their agency and voice. Communist journals like *Pacific Workers* and contemporary leftist novels written by male intellectuals reveal the typical understanding of Korean male radicals regarding factory women and their potential as allies. In the 1933 issue of leftist magazine *Pip'an*, for example, a male commentator with the pseudonym Pyŏngch'ŏl lamented the alleged shortcomings of women workers as "being docile in character, lacking sufficiently rebellious spirit, and obeying whatever orders come out from factory owners or managers."[33]

The discourse of miserable factory girls suffering inhumane oppression and in desperate need of help was starkly represented by Hosoi Wakizō's book *The Pitiful History of Female Factory Workers* (*Jokō aishi*; *Yŏgong aesa* in Korean), published in July 1925 in Japan. According to Japanese historian Vera Mackie, *Pitiful History* was influential in consolidating "the convention of writing about women workers as objects of pity and compassion" in Japan.[34] The colonial censorship office immediately banned the book, as well as a host of others presenting socialist and socialist feminist ideas, but *Pitiful History* apparently circulated in Korea among labor activists. A reference to the book as one of the texts read by workers appears in Song Yŏng's novel *O Suhyang*, published in 1931. The *Pitiful History* discourse seems to have been pervasive in leftist imaginings of factory women's ordeals in Korea while at the same time seamlessly backing up the paternalistic bourgeois nationalist view of the misery of working-class women.

A good example of the sway of this "pity" discourse is the controversy surrounding the tactic of the hunger strike, which the nationalist media much sensationalized and communists maligned as a wrongheaded tactic that damaged the "fragile" bodies of women workers. How, then, did women workers themselves talk about the experience of hunger strike? Kang Churyong's statement in her *Tonggwang* interview gives us a clue. As we have seen earlier, referencing her three-day hunger strike at the police station, Kang calmly told the interviewer that after her experience at a Chinese police station in Manchuria, in which she had to "starve for the whole week" because nobody was extending a helping hand to her, a three-day hunger strike was "a fairly easy affair."[35]

This connection between a female rubber worker's activist subjectivity and her Manchurian experiences, which included participation in an armed guerrilla movement, reveals a possible new dimension in understanding female subjectivities of the 1920s and the 1930s in Korea. Especially in the northern regions, where rapid industrialization and the proximity to China and the Soviet Union exposed residents early on to foreign and modern ideas and practices and also nurtured radical activism and vigorous "revolutionary" organizing among workers and farmers, it is possible to imagine the emergence of a new breed of women with an expansive perceptive horizon, which included not just "new women" types but also working-class women like Kang Churyong. Kang had seen the larger world, fought in an anti-imperial war, and suffered much. It is plausible to imagine her attaining an autonomous sense of self as well as political consciousness through her life's journey from northern Korea to Manchuria and back. Life experiences in Manchuria from age fourteen to twenty-four (approximately from 1914 to 1924) meant unavoidable encounters with the politics surrounding migration and anti-imperial movements. It meant brutal counterinsurgency campaigns executed by the Japanese, ethnic tensions among Chinese, Korean, and Japanese residents, and the reality of widespread poverty and human deprivation. How such experiences may have affected women's subjectivity in colonial Korea is a question that is beginning to be asked in the field of Korean literature. A case in point is the study of Kang Kyŏngae, a Korean woman writer who spent two years as a teacher in northern Manchuria in the late 1920s, witnessing anticolonial struggles there and embracing socialist ideas. She later migrated to Kando (Jiandao) in mid-1931 with her husband and wrote most of her literary works there before she became gravely ill and returned to her hometown, Changyŏn, in 1939.[36] I believe Kang Churyong might be another good example of a woman whose personal growth owed much to what life in Manchuria taught her. I believe it is likely that Kang had begun to acquire political consciousness long before her entanglement with the red union movement on the eve of the P'yŏngwŏn Rubber strike.

According to Kang Churyong's testimony in *Tonggwang*, after coming back to Korea at age twenty-four, she first lived in Sariwŏn, a town south of Pyongyang, for about a year, and when the P'yŏngwŏn strike happened in 1931, it was her fifth year living and working in Pyongyang. Pyongyang in the late 1920s and early 1930s was a place bustling with active social movements. She joined the Pyongyang Rubber Workers' Association right before the 1930 strike and went through the bitter general strike of the city's rubber shoe workers that year as a member of the workers' association. That "great strike" of 1930, as we have seen, was unprecedented in terms of the militancy and the audacity exhibited by women workers. Workers not only stormed factories many times but also clashed with police forces in the street, and in one case hundreds of workers, including at least 150 women, "barged into" (*torip*) the police station in protest, demanding the release of a jailed labor activist.[37] It thus seems likely that Kang was radicalized before she was connected to the Chŏng Talhŏn group. If that was not the case, it might be that her actual encounter with the communist movement through Cho Yŏngok and Chŏng Talhŏn worked as a catalyst that propelled her to set aside her breadwinner role and plunge into labor activism. In any case, by 1931 Kang Churyong was linked to an emerging international circle of communist labor activists who followed the directives from the Comintern and the Profintern, their spirit lifted by the Comintern vision of an imminent worldwide revolutionary wave. It is quite possible that she read some issues of communist propaganda journals such as *Pacific Workers* or at least learned the gist of red union strategies and tactics promoted there.[38]

Whatever route she had taken in her development into a labor activist, it is clear that when she was making a passionate speech on the roof of the Ŭlmiltae Pavilion, Kang was aware of the significance of her deed. In the rooftop speech she was also capable of deploying socialist language to justify her cause. From the rooftop Kang stated,

> We don't regard the wage cuts that we, forty-nine members of the strike corps, received as a be-all-end-all. It is because this [wage cut] will eventually lead to wage cuts for twenty-three hundred rubber workers of Pyongyang that we oppose it with all our might as if our lives hung on it. I would not regret if my own body perishes if I could prevent the flesh of my twenty-three hundred comrades from being whittled away. Of the things that I know through learning, the most important one is that for the people [*taejung*] it is an honorable thing to [abridged by censors], and that is the most important knowledge that I possess. That is why I resolved to risk death and came up onto this roof. I will not come down unless the president of P'yŏngwŏn Rubber comes here and cancels [his] declaration of wage cuts. If he insists on not retracting the wage cut order, I would consider death as an honor, as a representative of the working mass [*kŭllo taejung*] who are [abridged by censors] by the capitalists.[39]

One can sense her confidence and pride in her own knowledge—"the things that I know through learning." As a working-class woman who did not have the opportunity to receive formal school education, the knowledge she had acquired through her engagement with the labor movement, including an encounter with a robust international communist movement, as well as that obtained through her life's other journeys, must have meant a lot to her and fortified her courage and activist persona.

Another notable statement Kang Churyong made in her passionate speech was about her willingness to risk death—"I would not regret if my own body perishes"—which seems to have been more than mere rhetoric. Kang Churyong allegedly left a letter addressed to her father dated May 28 (she went up onto the roof of the Ŭlmiltae about 1:00 a.m. on May 29), which conveys her determination to fight to the end to win the strike. In the letter published in the May 31, 1931, issue of *Chosun ilbo*, she told her father, "This unfilial daughter might see you again if my wish comes true. Otherwise I will see you later in the nether land." In her interview for the journal *Tonggwang* she recalled that her original reaction to the eviction from the factory that night was "to die" as a way of protest, but, worrying about the possibility that people would gossip about her death as a widow's suicide caused by some indecent affairs, she made a rope out of the cotton cloth she had bought as a means of suicide and climbed up onto the Ŭlmiltae roof. We often see this expression of intense commitment to the point of a willingness to die among many communist activists of the era. This was true of the radical women activists Yi Sun'gŭm and Pak Chinhong we met in chapter 2. Yi and Pak time and again sought to reconnect with the underground movement on their release from prison, clearly knowing that their choice could lead to another round of imprisonment and torture, or even death.[40]

Was Kang's attitude toward life and death also based on faith in communist tenets and the inevitable victory of "revolution" in Korea? Perhaps, but given the short time she had been associated with the red union movement, it seems more likely that her determination and emotional attachment to the fortunes of her fellow workers stemmed from diverse sources in her life experiences, including the injustices she witnessed in the rubber strikes in Pyongyang, feelings of solidarity with fellow women workers, and what she came to know through various opportunities for "learning," including underground socialist training. Whatever paths she had taken to get there, by the time she made her memorable rooftop speech, Kang Churyong was talking as a confident leader of fellow women workers and was sure of her purpose in life as such.

Kang Churyong did not represent an exceptional case of a class-conscious, resolute, and assertive yŏgong either. For example, women strikers at Chōsen Spinning and Weaving (Chosŏn Pangjik or Chobang; Chōbō in Japanese) in Pusan declared the following during their strike in January 1930: "People often say that women are all stupid and ignorant know-nothings and weak beings, and those of us factory women [yŏgong] are particularly looked down upon as nonhumans, but after we launched the strike we can say that the strong power of solidarity of us factory women startled the company executives. Until [the company] accepts our two most important demands, we will continue to fight without bending a bit."⁴¹ In some cases, striking women workers in the 1930s were voicing gender-specific grievances. For example, during the April 1930 strike at Yamajū (Sansip) Silk Reeling in Pyongyang, six hundred women workers demanded the company "ban [sexual] jokes by male workers."⁴² Sometimes female workers opted to establish a strike headquarters of their own, separate from male leadership, as in the cases of the 1930 Pyongyang rubber strike and the Pusan Chōbō strike of the same year.⁴³

Kang's link to the red union movement, when revealed, did not seem to have made her fellow workers turn their backs on her. The news of Kang's involvement in a red union broke out while she was already in police custody (Kang had been arrested a second time on June 10 together with Ch'oe Yongdŏk and was in the middle of another hunger strike in jail). The revelation came as a result of a police roundup of the T'aero group led by Chŏng Talhŏn in Pyongyang. Kang was kept behind bars after her connection to the Chŏng Talhŏn group was revealed, and her release only occurred in June of the following year when she became gravely ill.⁴⁴ Her poverty-stricken family and friends were unable to provide much medical treatment, and she died in a slum area of Pyongyang on August 13, 1932. Newspapers reported her death as a "death in prison" (*oksa*) following the convention of reporting on activist deaths caused by sufferings in jail. It is unknowable if she regretted getting associated with the Chŏng Talhŏn group as she went through harsh interrogation and a year-long imprisonment. Available evidence also does not reveal if her association with the red union movement negatively affected the workers' hand in the negotiation process that wrapped up the strike. What is clear is the fact that her comrades did not walk away from her despite sensational news reports on the communist *paehu* of the strike. Kim Ch'wisŏn and Ch'oe Yongdŏk, who as coleaders of the strike suffered police arrest together with Kang, stood by Kang Churyong. Ch'oe and several others took charge of supporting Kang's family in dire poverty, and Kim Ch'wisŏn, who found employment at a rubber factory in Seoul, sent part of her meager income of 0.50 wŏn a day to support Kang in prison.⁴⁵ "Over a hundred male and female comrades" gathered to perform a funeral rite for her, after which she was buried in the Sŏjang-ri cemetery.⁴⁶

The "Peace" Rubber Factory

The P'yŏngwŏn Rubber strike ended with a modicum of success in that it blocked wage cuts, albeit only temporarily, and *Dong-A ilbo* defined the outcome as "the victory of workers."⁴⁷ But twenty yŏgong, including leaders Kang Churyong,

Ch'oe Yongdŏk, and Kim Ch'wisŏn, lost their jobs, and Kang remained in jail. The next step taken by fired women workers revealingly shows the complex mix of ideological currents present in early 1930s Pyongyang. Led by Ch'oe Yongdŏk, fired workers joined hands with the local elite, who were described in the media as local notables, in a progressive experiment to form a worker-owned factory. The local elite participants included businessmen, professionals such as news reporters and lawyers, and social movement activists. This move had a precursor in the launching of the Mutual Aid (Kongje) Rubber factory as a workers' production cooperative in the aftermath of the 1930 Pyongyang rubber workers' general strike, an initiative described more fully below. The fact that the idea of launching a worker-owned factory was embraced by some elite leaders and that they actually made substantial financial commitments to that reformist idea reveal that the warlike strike events of 1930 and 1931 had indeed stirred up Pyongyang society. That development also suggests that the surprising images of militant and often violent women workers had perhaps begun to crack the conventional class and gender notions of ignorant and passive yŏgong. To fully understand this decision to try a worker-owned factory cooperative as a solution to labor-capital conflict, we need to first survey the changes in the Christian nationalist movement and in the anarchist movement in late 1920s and early 1930s Pyongyang. Knowledge of the evolving strategies and programs of these social movement circles in the city will bring this unusual story of the "Peace" rubber factory into sharper focus.

We saw in chapter 1 how the ideologies and practices of the Korean Christian nationalist movement changed in response to escalating class conflict and intensifying socialist critiques of bourgeois nationalism in the late 1920s and into the 1930s.[48] In the first half of the 1930s the gravity of the rising labor-capital conflict led to an ultimately unsuccessful call in the Korean nationalist media, including the *Dong-A ilbo*, the *Chosun ilbo*, and the *Chosŏn chungang ilbo*, to extend to the colony the labor legislation that had already been implemented in the metropole.[49] This reformist call to respond to the real problems of class polarization and poverty was, as in Japan, based on the belief that the interests of labor and capital ultimately converged in a capitalist society through rising productivity.[50] But Christian reformers like Yi Taewi, who sincerely grappled with the labor question to find nationalist solutions to it, were in the small minority.

Meanwhile, by the late 1920s the larger Christian nationalist movement was making a conscious turn toward the countryside as its primary field of action, turning away from the urban labor question. Of the population in Korea, 80 percent was engaged in farming at the time, and the deteriorating economic situation in the countryside was demanding action not only from conscientious activists but also from the colonial government. As historian Albert L. Park's recent study

Building a Heaven on Earth shows, faith-based social movements of the Korean religion Chŏndogyo, the Presbyterian Church, and the YMCA invested heavily in rural campaigns beginning in the mid-1920s. The Dong-A Ilbo company launched an energetic *kwinong* (returning to the countryside) campaign targeting the student population as core actors in the late 1920s. This shift in the bourgeois nationalist movement toward the countryside and rural problems was an effort to move beyond the focus on individual cultivation of the self (*suyang*) and tackle social problems caused by capitalist modernization. It was also in large measure a response to socialist challenges. The Dong-A Ilbo group and religious nationalist movements poured their resources into rural campaigns in an effort to redefine and galvanize nationalist youth by creating a new dynamic image of young men returning to countryside to serve the needs of the nation. The hope was that nationalist youth would emerge as leaders of the rural enlightenment movement and combat the powerful discourse of socialist youth.[51] The countryside was also an arena ripe with radical activism, and by the early 1930s communists were also trying to organize farmers into "red" farmers' unions. All in all, the enlightenment discourse and self-strengthening programs of the religious nationalist movements found more fertile soil in rural areas than in factories.

With bourgeois nationalists' turn to the countryside, the cooperative movement (*hyŏptong chohap undong*), the Danish model in particular, gained considerable attention beginning in the mid-1920s. Park argues that Protestant social movement activists, as well as their Chŏndogyo counterparts, attempted to develop "an ethical form of capitalism" in rural communities by applying a Danish-style cooperative system that promoted a communal form of labor, the cultivation of personality, and mutual love.[52] Various kinds of cooperatives were organized in the countryside, including credit unions, consumer cooperatives, and producers' cooperatives, although by the mid-1930s most of these efforts were absorbed into the rural revitalization campaign the colonial government launched in 1932.[53] A key leader of the cooperative movement, Ham Sanghun, estimated that as of 1931 at least two hundred consumer cooperatives and "not a few" production cooperatives existed in the country.[54] The Sin'ganhoe made the active support of the rural cooperative movement part of its action plan.[55]

These developments in the bourgeois nationalist movement in the late 1920s and early 1930s meant that by 1931 the idea of organizing a cooperative as a promising solution to social problems caused by capitalism was a familiar and popular one for nationalists in the northwest, and perhaps for Pyongyang rubber workers too. Chŏndogyo, YMCA, and Presbyterian rural social movements were all very active in the north. Although most of these cooperatives were constructed in rural areas, Pyongyang was the hub of the northwest cooperative movement, and in April 1931 Christian activists in the region formed a coordinating umbrella institution providing various services and education to member cooperatives in South and North P'yŏngan and Hwanghae Provinces, with Cho Mansik as its director (*isa*).⁵⁶ The Christian Rural Research Association (Kidokkyo Nongch'on Yŏn'guhoe) under Cho Mansik's influence developed a Christian socialist movement platform over the 1930s, the twin pillars of which were Christism or "the ideology of the cross" (*Kidokchuŭi*) and a movement to build utopian "Jesus Villages" (*Yesuch'on*), which would be anchored by rural churches and the cooperative movement.⁵⁷

As noted above, veterans of the 1930 Pyongyang rubber strike launched a worker-owned factory named Mutual Aid (Kongje) Rubber in 1930, and fired P'yŏngwŏn workers launched a production cooperative named Peace (P'yŏnghwa) Rubber in 1931 with the help of local luminaries. Contemporary Japanese-language newspapers described Mutual Aid Rubber as *kongsan* (meaning "communist" or "collectively produced") or *kongyŏng* ("collectively managed") factory.⁵⁸ The word *kongsan* here is intriguing, as is the name "Mutual Aid," because it makes us wonder if the choice of words reflected a heavy involvement of local anarchists in the endeavor.

As noted in chapter 1, Pyongyang was known for the strength of its anarchist movement as well as that of the Christian nationalist movement. The fact that in Pyongyang anarchists had established a strong base in the 1920s and that anarcho-syndicalism became a major current among Pyongyang anarchists toward the end of the decade increased the possibility of cross-class cooperation between elite nationalists and radical anarchists of Pyongyang.⁵⁹ According to historian Yi Horyong, who has extensively studied Korean anarchist activism during the colonial period, anarchism, first introduced in Korea in the 1880s, began to gain traction after World War I and the Russian Revolution, and rapidly spread after the March First Movement of 1919. It played a crucial role in the Korean socialist movement during the 1920s and 1930s in competition with the Marxist-Leninist, or communist, movement, which became dominant in the socialist movement scene by the mid-1920s.⁶⁰ In the Korean anarchist movement, as noted earlier, anarcho-communism, centered on Peter Kropotkin's mutual aid theory, was preeminent throughout the colonial period, but anarcho-syndicalism continued to exert influence as well. The country's first labor organization, the Chosŏn Nodong Kongjehoe, established in 1920, already exhibited strong anarchist tendencies, and many anarchists continuously participated in the trade union movement throughout the 1920s and 1930s.

Anarcho-communists and anarcho-syndicalists differed in the strategy of revolution, especially the place and role of the trade union movement. Anarcho-syndicalists prioritized the labor movement and trade unions as the basis for a social revolution. Through trade unions workers would learn to establish democratic structures and self-management of production, following an "economic direct action" strategy.⁶¹ Anarcho-communists, on the other hand, were suspicious of heavy anarchist involvement in organized class struggle by industrial workers. For them the labor movement constituted just one sector among many in the larger revolutionary movement. According to Yi Horyong, anarcho-syndicalism began to form a major current in the Korean anarchist movement from the end of the 1920s.⁶² Despite the strong tradition of anarcho-communism in the Korean anarchist movement, it was in a way imperative for anarchists to tackle the labor question by turning to anarcho-syndicalism, especially in the industrialized northern region of Korea, and by doing so they could counter the aggressive work of their archrival, the communists, among industrial workers.

Anarchist intervention in the labor movement accelerated beginning in the mid-1920s. Northern industrial towns such as Wŏnsan, Hamhŭng, and Tanchŏn in South Hamgyŏng Province and Pyongyang in the northwest were where the anarcho-syndicalist labor movement was most active.⁶³ In Pyongyang, by the mid-1920s, anarchists had a strong presence in the unions of carpentry workers, Western shoemaking workers, rubber workers, and casual laborers.⁶⁴ The most important anarchist organization that emerged in colonial Korea in the late 1920s to early 1930s was the Northwest Black Friends Society (Kwansŏ Hŭguhoe) located in Pyongyang. The society was organized in December 1927 to compete against the Sin'ganhoe Pyongyang chapter.⁶⁵ The Northwest Black Friends Society demonstrated its leadership position in the Korean anarchist movement by embarking on an ambitious campaign to hold the first ever national convention of Korean anarchists in late 1929.⁶⁶ By then anarcho-syndicalists had substantial power in the organization, and its anarcho-syndicalist members began to actively engage the labor struggle in Pyongyang, including rubber strikes.⁶⁷

Anarcho-syndicalists were adamantly against the "centralist and authoritarian" communist method of labor organizing performed by "professional activists"; they upheld instead the principle of "free association" (*chayu yŏnhapchuŭi*). Opposing red union–type organizing initiated by outside agitators and opposing as well an emphasis on political struggle, anarcho-syndicalists preferred economic direct action by workers in the form of boycotts, industrial sabotage, and strikes. They also promoted worker-centered institution building, including "work bureaus" (*chagŏppu*) and "industrial cooperatives" (*sanŏp chohap*), as a way to develop worker capacity.⁶⁸ These institutions were viewed as stepping-stones toward the anarchist dream of achieving the "socialization of the institutions of production" and a fair distribution of profit. Anarcho-syndicalists were heavily involved in the establishment of the work bureaus of the Pyongyang Western Shoemakers' Union and the Pyongyang Carpentry Workers' Union, and also in the initiatives of women rubber workers like the Mutual Aid Rubber and the Peace Rubber factories.⁶⁹

The primary momentum for the Mutual Aid Rubber factory, built in the aftermath of the 1930 Pyongyang rubber strike, came from the local business world.[70] Factory manager U Chesun took the lead, and lawyer Kim Chigŏn, newspaper reporter Ch'oe Yunok, and influential local figures like Hwang Yŏn and Kim Insu joined in. Kim Chigŏn was chosen to serve as the factory manager. This operation had a large paid-in capital of 100,000 wŏn, out of which each worker bought stocks, in installments if necessary, at ten wŏn per share. In this "factory of workers" (*chikkong ŭi kongjang*) the laborers and conscientious businessmen would work together as equal shareholders, and promote the condition of better treatment, an eight-hour workday (in three shifts), and better wages for workers through the "rationalization of labor" and "equalization of profit." *Dong-A ilbo* articles likely penned by O Kiyŏng praised the factory as "the crystallization of laborers' blood and sweat" and "an epochal outcome of a labor-capital conflict." When Pyongyang's rubber factory owners again conspired to lower wages in August 1931, Mutual Aid Rubber was, as mentioned earlier, the only company that kept the existing wage levels.[71]

The idea of establishing a worker-owned factory like Mutual Aid Rubber had begun to circulate soon after the end of the P'yŏngwŏn Rubber strike and in the midst of another rubber strike, this time at Sech'ang Rubber.[72] The Peace Rubber factory was launched in October with a rather modest paid-in capital of 20,000 wŏn.[73] Public opinion in general seems to have been favorable to the endeavor, and *Dong-A ilbo* eagerly followed its progress.[74] From news accounts we can make an informed guess that nationalist elites and anarchists again joined hands in establishing Peace Rubber, like they did in the previous year's Mutual Aid Rubber case. A *Chungang ilbo* report, while noting the support of "local notables," mentions Sŭng Togyŏng, a founding member of the Northwest Black Friends Society, as one of the key people who took the lead in creating the factory.[75]

Korean anarchists viewed bourgeois nationalists as representatives of the capitalist class and saw the united-front movement endorsed by communists and left-wing nationalists as a serious threat to the growth of working-class people's capacity. One wonders, then, what made anarchists, long virulently against bourgeois nationalists and the capitalist system, cooperate with the nationalists in this case. Yi Horyong argues that by the early 1930s Pyongyang's anarcho-syndicalists had drastically changed their attitudes toward nationalists and were open to the idea of cooperation with them, igniting strong criticism from anarcho-communists in the movement.[76] We do not know why and how, but it is clear that Pyongyang anarchists moved toward a joint endeavor with nationalists in creating worker-owned factories. Perhaps it was a function of their chosen strategy of building production cooperatives and work bureaus, which required a certain collaboration with local capitalists. It is also likely that the deepening anticommunist sentiments among anarchists helped seal an anticommunist alliance with bourgeois nationalists, an alignment that continued into the postcolonial years in South Korea.[77]

The communists, for their part, were vehemently against the idea of "industrial cooperatives" in general and the experiments by Pyongyang rubber workers in particular. Ch'ae Rin, in his scathing article criticizing Mutual Aid Rubber in the April–May 1931 issue of *Pacific Workers*, claimed that it was nothing but a time-worn capitalist tactic to "numb the class spirit" of workers and to "extinguish once and for all the desire for struggle against the capitalist system."[78] The slogan of "equalization of the distribution of profit" might sound "very beautiful," he warned, but workers who barely managed to invest one share of ten wŏn were in essence deceived and further exploited by "sixty gentlemen," who put up two-thirds of the paid-in capital of 100,000 wŏn. Workers were being swept up by false promises that were "impossible" to realize under the capitalist economic system, he lamented. Korean communists at the time, before the knowledge of the Comintern's turn to the anti-fascist popular-front strategy at its seventh convention in 1935 spread among them, were bent on fighting against "reformist" elements in the labor and social movements, following the directives of the Comintern and the Profintern.[79]

These communist warnings notwithstanding, Ch'oe Yongdŏk and other fired P'yŏngwŏn workers joined forces with local businessmen and well-meaning investors as well as anarchists and busied themselves through that summer and fall to start up a factory. Each share was set at twenty wŏn this time, and a worker fired from the P'yŏngwŏn factory would be employed at the new factory if she purchased five or more shares.[80] The trust shown by participating workers toward the local nationalist elite and also the sympathetic public opinion to this seemingly radical human-faced capitalist solution suggest the lingering legitimacy of the local bourgeoisie and its paternalistic labor relations culture. The presence of reformist Christian nationalist activists and their rhetoric of social reform and labor-capital cooperation probably helped the organizers of the factory win the trust of yŏgong. *Dong-A ilbo*, which had run many favorable reports on Mutual Aid Rubber before, praised Peace Rubber in its editorial on January 7, 1932, as "an institution that is the crystalized blood of working people" ("kŭllo minjung ŭi hyŏlmaengch'e"). Workers also seem to have believed in this possibility of a humanistic capitalist development, and they did their utmost to buy shares to participate in the endeavor. Peace Rubber, according to a *Dong-A ilbo* article, was a factory workers built "by selling their hair and their thatched-roof houses."[81] Be it anarchist dream, reformist nationalist dream, or workers' dream, an inspiring vision of an alternative capitalist system in which workers as "co-owners" of the factory would prove that extreme exploitation was unnecessary for business success seems to have been alive in Pyongyang in 1931.

This lofty dream, however, soon collapsed under the weight of reality. The company became embroiled in internal disputes of a financial nature and reached a point of near bankruptcy by the end of the following year.[82] The Mutual Aid Rubber begotten by the 1930 rubber strike fared a bit better, lasting about four years, although the radical ideas behind the cooperative, including that of giving equal representation to stockholders regardless of the amount of their stock, faded out early on.[83] This dream of a worker-run model factory, however, did not die with the failures of these two rubber cooperatives. It first resurfaced after the liberation at Chobang, and again in the dream of Seoul's sweatshop garment industry worker Chun Tae-il (Chŏn T'aeil).

Remembering Kang Churyong

While enthusiasm for the worker-run rubber factory was running high, Kang Churyong was suffering a long pretrial detention in jail. (It was a routine practice for colonial authorities in Korea to keep defendants in jail for a prolonged period of time in the name of "pretrial investigation" [*yesim*].) Kang was one of the rare cases of a female political prisoner from a worker background. Terrible prison conditions, compounded by the injuries and deleterious health effects of interrogation and torture sessions, killed numerous anticolonial activists under Japanese rule. As noted earlier, Kang died in August 1932, soon after her temporary release from jail. Her premature and tragic death eerily resembles the tragedy that befell the Japanese "chimney man" Tanabe, whose body was found on February 14, 1933, at a park in Yokohama. *Akahata* (Red Flag), the Japanese Communist Party organ, reported that he was picked up by the police in January and murdered during torture.[84]

With Kang's death, an incredible woman activist perished tragically, destroyed by the anticommunist persecution of the Japanese colonial government. Did anyone remember her after her funeral? Kang Churyong's name disappeared from media coverage after a flurry of reports in March 1933 on pretrial findings of the Pyongyang red union incident and subsequent reporting on the outcome of the trial.[85] In one of those news reports her photo appeared along with those of other prosecuted members of the group (see figure 2), and her life story, including her tragic "death in prison," was described in some detail. The fading of Kang Churyong's memory was partly because of the drastically changed political and social environments in Korea. Beginning in the mid-1930s the Japanese Empire, including its Korea colony, entered into a period of "total war" mobilization and ruthless anticommunist persecution, and a strict censorship regime ensued. The fact that her feat did not occur in Seoul, the center of politics, likely did not help her remain in the national memory.

In the northwestern region, however, Kang Churyong's high-altitude sit-in and tragic death seem to have been remembered and lamented by socialist activists for some time. For example, one censored article for a children's magazine in Ŭiju, north of Pyongyang, counts "Auntie Kang Churyong's prison death" as one of the most tragic and unjust events of the year 1932.[86] It is interesting that Kang was positioned as an "auntie" (*sungmo*) to young readers in the familial imagination of socialist activists. In the Pyongyang area in particular there is evidence that her memory was kept alive among local rubber workers and residents. Historian Song Chiyŏng, in his authoritative article on the 1930 Pyongyang rubber strike, published in 1959 in North Korea, states: "The name of [Kang], respected by Pyongyang rubber factory workers" at the time of his writing, was "widely known among the people."[87] Perhaps Kang's name continued to be included in people's memories because the two Pyongyang rubber strikes that shook the local society to its core became part of the legendary tale of the colonial Korean labor movement.

In postliberation North Korea, the fact that Pyongyang, the capital of North Korea, was the location of the two rubber strikes made those strikes especially valuable as a powerful piece of evidence that connects the triumph of the communist movement in the north and the persistent and heroic struggles in support of it by the working masses. The trajectory of Kang's memory in North Korean labor history narratives still awaits study, but it is clear that she was celebrated at least until the end of the 1950s. An article in the August 1959 issue of the magazine *Chosŏn nyŏsŏng* (Korean Women), published in North Korea, portrays Kang to women readers as an exemplary communist warrior who waged a heroic struggle and sacrificed her life for the revolution. It is interesting to see that the overarching image of this story is Kang standing up on the roof of Ŭlmiltae with a "red flag" in her hand. In a way that image collapses her story with the original chimney man Tanabe's story of menacingly flying a red flag on top of a tall chimney. The author of the article states that her arm was "spiritedly stretched outward with the flag firmly in her hand," thus clearly demonstrating her strong will. She continued to make speeches against capitalist greed, the author goes on, sometimes "vigorously raising the red flag" and sometimes "pointing toward the [nearby] Pubyŏk Pavilion with the red flag." The author calls Kang "a precious daughter of our working class," a "patriotic martyr" who "showed the spirit of the working class on the roof of Ŭlmiltae waving the red flag."[88]

Kang Churyong and other women workers who bravely fought in strikes or joined the red union movement in the 1930s signaled the rise of a modern and self-conscious factory woman subjectivity, and we see awareness of this new yŏgong subjectivity in contemporary literature produced by leftist writers like Kang Kyŏngae, whose poem, "Replying to Older Brother's Letter" ("Opppa ŭi p'yŏnji hoedap"), appeared in chapter 2. Perceptive observers of working-class life like Kang Kyŏngae recognized and celebrated the emergence of a new breed of class-conscious yŏgong workers armed with self-awareness as modern individuals and ready to show their spirit of resistance. Did the memories of their presence endure through the dark years of the late colonial period and the tumultuous and violent politics of the postwar decades in South Korea? Did militant yŏgong of the colonial rubber and textile strikes reemerge in the postcolonial labor movement in the south, and did they get to claim their legitimate place in the union movement and in society?

In the following chapters we follow the largely unsung and paradoxical history of female worker struggle in South Korea in the decades since the liberation (chapter 4) and during South Korea's developmental era (chapter 5). At the end of this story we meet Kang Churyong again when a 2011 crane-top sit-in by another remarkable woman worker activist, Kim Jin-Sook, stimulated an unexpected rediscovery and flourishing of Kang Churyong's memory in South Korea in the new century (chapter 6). In South Korea, remembrance of Kang Churyong was much slower in coming than in North Korea, but when it came it was more complex and more attuned to the challenges facing women industrial workers. Between the time of Kang Churyong and that of Kim Jin-Sook, women workers continuously registered their resistance to the class and gender hierarchies they faced at work sites and in society, and their actions to a large extent shaped the contours and nature of the South Korean labor movement. The following three chapters examine the complex politics surrounding yŏgong activism in postcolonial South Korea and explore the reasons behind the particular ways South Korean society has remembered women workers' contributions to the country's great strides in achieving both economic development and democracy.

4

FACTORY WOMEN IN THE POSTWAR SETTLEMENT

The 1950s

In December 1951, when the Korean War (1950–53) was raging in the middle section of the Korean Peninsula, an unusual and rather strange struggle involving workers, the police, and management was happening at the Pusan factory of Chosŏn Spinning and Weaving (Chosŏn Pangjik; Chobang). The struggle was about wall posters (*pyŏkpo*) that read "Down with Despot Kang Ilmae!" The trade union at the factory originally posted the slogan against company president Kang on walls in the factory, but the North Pusan police, claiming that the posters "contaminated the building," arrested the union president and five other union officials.[1] Workers then hung a line inside the building and attached posters on the line instead of the walls, until the police pressured them to remove the signs for "aesthetic reasons." A large vertical cotton banner some sixty-five feet long with the same slogan on it then appeared draped from the top of the tallest chimney at the factory, about 130 feet high. Photographs of the banner and news about it made the headlines of the local media. The banner was also removed, and a social section reporter at the *Pusan ilbo* (Pusan Daily) whose reporting exhibited sympathy toward striking workers had to leave the paper under political pressure mounted by Kang Ilmae, according to a 1972 recollection by An Chongu, the union president at Chobang at the time of the struggle. The union did not give up and this time hung a similar banner from the second-floor office window of its upper-level union, the Pusan Regional Federation of Trade Unions, which stood in front of city hall in downtown Pusan. Again, the banner was taken down by the police.

The next step workers took was quite creative and eventually successful. They printed the slogan on cotton cloth (*kwangmok*), the main product of the factory, and sewed it on their clothes. Many clashes erupted between workers and policemen who tried to catch them and tear off the slogan cloth. Then workers, using a tin sheet, mimeographed the slogan on the back of their work clothes. The back side of the ubiquitous "white blouse" (*chŏgori*) that women workers wore prominently displayed the slogan in black ink. The police had to let it go this time. Union president An Chongu, whose firing on December 15 prompted the "wall poster struggle," recalled that even an office girl working in the company president's office wore her white blouse with the slogan printed on the back. Kang Ilmae, he went on, was "flabbergasted" when she turned her back to leave the office after pouring tea for him. According to An, people talked about how Kang Ilmae developed a phobia after repeatedly facing the "Down with Despot Kang Ilmae" slogan popping up everywhere, and he became fatally ill from heart disease. The company faltered despite the management's eventual victory over the union, and Kang never recovered from his illness and died before the April Revolution of 1960. To be sure, this is a "good-triumphs-over-evil" story that circulated among workers, but the existence of such a story attests to the emotional depth and fierceness of worker protest in the winter of 1951–52 at Chobang.

The menace of the "white blouse" did not stop there. A thousand Chobang women workers demonstrated in front of the National Assembly's temporary wartime location in Pusan in January 1952, and later 1,300 women workers demonstrated in the streets of Pusan. The authoritative labor history account *The History of the Korean Labor Movement* describes the Chobang dispute as "a conflict that resembled a [nineteenth-century] popular rebellion" (*millan*).[2] The labor dispute at Chobang has been regarded as one of the most important labor struggles of the 1950s, and it is considered the key labor dispute that prompted the National Assembly to pass the nation's first set of labor bills in 1953. These labor laws have framed the labor-management relations system of South Korea until now, despite many revisions.[3] Historian Nakao Michiko, whose 1989 master's thesis is the first and only monograph on the Chobang dispute, situates the dispute at the "starting line" of the South Korean labor-relations system in particular and of the South Korean political system as a whole.[4] But if the 1951–52 Chobang dispute was a "rebellion," it was largely a rebellion of yŏgong, female factory workers. Following a decade of inactivity during the dark, final phase of Japanese colonial rule, female industrial worker militancy resurged in the post-liberation period. Striking women workers would only gain such visibility and attention in society when yŏgong again came to the fore of the labor movement in the 1970s.

The joy of liberation from Japan in August 1945 was soon replaced by the dismay at the physical division of the country at the Thirty-Eighth Parallel and the occupation by two competing world powers, the USSR in the north and the United States in the south. As the south plunged into civil war–like conflicts between Soviet-aligned leftist forces and pro-American rightist forces, the labor movement became one of the most important venues where this epic and brutal left-right battle played out. The Korean War was the culmination of domestic and global tensions and conflicts brewing throughout the 1940s within and around Korea. In the end, in the south soon-to-be-dictator Syngman Rhee (Yi Sŭngman) and anticommunist forces won out in this struggle, in large measure thanks to unflinching support by the US occupation (1945–48) determined to establish an anticommunist client state. The following decade of the 1950s was thus a crucial formative period in the history of the Republic of Korea (South Korea, established in 1948). It is bookended by the epic turmoil Koreans went through during the long 1940s, on the one hand, and the earnest beginning of capitalist economic nation-building under the military man and nation-builder Park Chung Hee (Pak Chŏnghŭi) in the 1960s, on the other. The 1950s was a transitional period in which various ideas and practices constructed during the colonial period, including class and gender ideologies, continued to exert great influence in politics and society, all the while adapting to the new reality of Cold War geopolitics.

It was during the tumultuous 1950s in South Korea that a version of anticommunist liberal democracy based on an affirmation of capitalist economic principles took shape and gradually gained hegemonic status. In the field of industrial relations, diverse ideas and initiatives of "labor-capital cooperation" (*noja hyŏpcho*) of the late 1940s and early 1950s that critiqued excesses of capitalist practices slowly gave way to an endorsement of a capitalist labor-control regime. Understanding this formative era of the new republic is crucial because what happened during this period still shapes South Korean politics and society in large measure today. This chapter explores how industrial workers, yŏgong in particular, fared in this turbulent period of the late 1940s and early 1950s. Focusing on the Chobang case, it examines the political and social conditions in postliberation Korea that made possible both women workers' spirited struggle and male unionists' appreciation of yŏgong activism and militancy.

The Long History of Labor Activism at Chobang

The union at Chobang's Pusan factory at the time of the 1951–52 labor dispute was a staunchly anticommunist one. It was also a militant union ready to fight for workers' interests despite the immense pressure from the dictatorial regime of Syngman Rhee. The journey that thousands of Chobang workers had taken to build such an activist union was eventful and violent, spanning three long decades. Chosŏn Spinning and Weaving was established with Japanese capital in 1917 and began operation at its Pusan factory in 1922. An affiliate of the Mitsui *zaibatsu* (Japanese business conglomerate), the company over time diversified into multiple areas of business, including knitwear, real estate, and oil, and expanded its operation to other cities in Korea and also in Manchuria.[5] Until Japanese companies Tōyōbō (Tongyang Pangjŏk), Kanebō (Chongyŏn Pangjŏk), and Dai-Nipponbō (Tae-Ilbon Pangjŏk) set up textile factories in Korea around 1935, Chobang (Chōbō) was the biggest cotton textile company in Korea. It remained very profitable throughout the colonial period and into the early 1950s.

Chobang workers built a proud history of labor activism beginning in the 1920s. As soon as operations began in March 1922, five hundred workers struck for two days demanding wage increases and work-hour reduction, and a series of one- or two-day disputes followed in April, June, and July of that year, all without the presence of a trade union. Another massive labor dispute involving seventeen hundred workers shook the company in August of the following year, albeit without much success.[6] The best-known strike at Chobang in the colonial period happened in January 1930, several months before the 1930 Pyongyang rubber workers' general strike we examined in earlier chapters.

Like Pyongyang rubber company owners, Chobang management used the worldwide economic depression as an excuse for wage cuts in 1930, even though the company was not suffering much at the time. More than two thousand workers, presenting twelve demands, conducted a well-organized and resolute protest for more than ten days. Their demands included, in addition to those for wage increases and an eight-hour workday, the abolition of the resented fine system and ethnic discrimination, installation of a promotion system for manual workers, and the improvement of the quality of food in the company dining hall.[7] At the time of the 1930 strike, Chobang had 2,675 employees, composed of 109 white-collar employees (all Japanese) and 2,566 manual workers (all Korean).[8] Among Korean workers, eighteen hundred were women, constituting the great majority, as was common in the textile industry of the time. Women workers fought aggressively in the strike, like their rubber-worker colleagues in Pyongyang. Support poured in from other labor and social movement organizations, and radical leaflets popped up, alarming the police. Even some Japanese employees came out in support by starting a sympathy strike and distributing pro-labor fliers. The police arrested many members of the Pusan chapter of the Sin'ganhoe and local youth and social movement groups on the suspicion that they were controlling the striking workers from behind as *paehu* (behind-the-scenes agitators). Not only the Sin'ganhoe Pusan chapter but also the Kŭnuhoe Pusan chapter, which, as noted in chapter 2, pursued a plan to organize women workers in the city into a union, actively supported striking Chobang women.[9]

The January 1930 Chobang strike ended in worker defeat following joint repression by Japanese management and the police, and many female and male workers were fired. But worker activism at Chobang continued. In October of that year another strike plan was thwarted, and in 1933 Chobang workers were able to launch a strike despite heavy surveillance. Not a few Chobang yŏgong leaders were arrested by the Pusan police in the early 1930s in relation to Chobang strikes or because of their involvement in underground communist incidents.[10] Little is known about these Chobang women, although further research into police and court records may reveal a fuller picture of their activities and backgrounds. In chapter 2 we saw that a "Chobang yŏgong Pak Sunhŭi" was one of the twenty-four male and fifteen female activists prosecuted in 1934 in Pusan in relation to a major red union incident.[11]

The Chobang strike of 1930 was part of the upsurge in radical activism in the early 1930s, and it shared many characteristics with other contemporary strikes like Pyongyang rubber strikes, which were affected by the communist red union movement. In early 1930s Pusan rubber workers were as active as textile workers. In 1933, for example, Pusan saw, in addition to a Chobang strike, a month-long strike at Yulchŏn Rubber in April, a thirty-six-day strike of 360 Marufuto (Hwandae) Rubber workers in July, and a twenty-five-day solidarity strike of seven hundred rubber workers from seven companies in October. The October rubber strike demonstrated women workers' capacity clearly because women from multiple factories carefully planned the strike for some time and did not back down for several weeks despite brutal violence committed by company-hired thugs, dismissals by the company, and arrests by the police.[12]

While sharing similar characteristics, differences between the Chobang strikes and Pyongyang's rubber strikes are clearly noticeable. The core of the strike leadership at Chobang was formed by members of the "Chungnakhoe" (Association for the Happiness of the Multitude), a friendship organization that male workers established at the factory in November 1929 with 112 members.[13] This male-dominated leadership at Chobang contrasted with the Pyongyang rubber strikes, which were effectively led by women workers. Women workers at Chobang were also mostly young women recruited from the countryside and housed in dormitories, unlike rubber workers, many of whom were older and married. And the fact that Chobang was a large factory owned by Japanese while Pyongyang rubber factories were small- to medium-sized businesses owned and run by Koreans affected the ways the state, the business community, and the society at large responded to workers on strike.

During the 1930 Chobang strike, contemporary newspaper accounts mostly focused on male leadership and outside agitators, although, according to historian Pak Chaehwa, in many ways women "practically led the strike."[14] Women conducted hunger strikes and passionate demonstrations and clashed with the police. Like P'yŏngwŏn Rubber strikers, Chobang women textile workers established a separate "women's strike headquarters" when the company fired core women leaders.[15] Thus, Chobang textile workers and Pyongyang rubber strikers exhibited both militancy and autonomy, but contemporary media coverage of yŏgong activism showed subtle differences. *Dong-A ilbo* articles and editorials on strikes at Chobang voiced sympathy for women workers suffering from hard-to-endure working conditions, often deploying the usual discourse of "fragile" yŏgong crying out "pathetically."[16] Unlike in the case of the P'yŏngwŏn Rubber strike, however, they did not show much appreciation of women's agency and leadership capacity. Paradoxically, while repeatedly reporting on the aggressive nature of the struggle waged by Chobang women workers and relaying, albeit occasionally, defiant statements by yŏgong strikers, *Dong-A ilbo* published an editorial that without reservation defined yŏgong as poor women "devoid of the spirit of resistance" (*mujŏhangjŏk*), thus reverting to typical victim imagery.[17] No woman was called *yŏsa* (Madame) in association with the Chobang strikes, and no memorable female figures like Kang Churyong emerged in media representation. Meanwhile, many news stories detailed the names and activities of male leaders and communist *paehu* agitators. The Chobang case, compared to Pyongyang rubber strikes, was a more straightforward story to report on as the battle was between Japanese capital and Korean workers, and male leaders were the public face of the strike.

By the late 1930s, as "total war" mobilization policies began to engulf the colony, trade union activism became virtually impossible except for sporadic red union activities, most of which were short-lived given severe police surveillance.[18] In Japan, wartime reformulation of labor relations policies took the form of the "Industrial Patriotic" (*Sangyō hōkoku*, or *Sanpō*) movement.[19] There, by 1940, a government-led Sanpō labor front replaced trade unions, and unions had to "voluntarily" dissolve themselves. In the new patriotic units organized at work sites under a "New Order for Labor," both employees and employers were called to serve the empire's production needs as "dedicated workers" (*kinrōsha* in Japanese; *kŭlloja* in Korean) who, in consultation with each other, performed "dedicated labor" (*kinrō*) for the emperor.[20] Some of these Sanpō policies and practices as well as wartime labor mobilization laws spread quickly into Korea (in contrast, the 1916 Factory Law of Japan was never applied to the Korea colony).

The Movement for General Mobilization of the National Spirit (Kungmin chŏngsin ch'ongdongwŏn undong) was launched in Korea in 1938, a year later than in Japan, and from provinces down to the village level "patriotic units" (aegukpan) were organized.

Like their Japanese counterparts, Korean workers were organized into patriotic units at work and subjected to the same ideological inculcation centered on the ideas of "dedicated labor" and labor-management cooperation as in Japan, although Korea did not see the organization of an umbrella Sanpō association as the coordinating body.[21] As the war expanded Korea gained a new significance in the Japanese Empire as the supply base for the war effort on the Asian continent. Korean men and women were subject to state-controlled labor mobilization into domestic and overseas work sites, and certain groups of young men began to be conscripted into the military.[22] This was the time the colonial government deployed extreme measures for assimilation, including attempts to ban the use of the Korean language in public spaces and to force Koreans to adopt Japanese-style family names and the Japanese Shinto religion. From the colonial authorities' perspective, it was by then deemed urgent to make loyal Japanese out of colonized people who would work in the factories and fight as soldiers. In 1943, following the Sanpō practices in Japan, military-type organizations of platoons, companies, and battalions were created at work sites in Korea with workers and managers as members, all called on to serve the Japanese emperor as "industrial warriors" (sanŏp chŏnsa) performing their honorable duty as "children" of the emperor. Beginning in 1944, "current-employee conscription" began, turning hundreds of thousands of workers at key factories into conscripted laborers prohibited from leaving their jobs.[23]

We do not know much about how the Sanpō campaign unfolded at large-scale key factories like Chobang, or how workers responded to colonial labor mobilization policies. And no study so far has investigated the critical question of how the colonial state's wartime gender discourse that exalted women's role as the "mother of the military nation" (kun'guk ŭi ŏmŏni) guarding the home front affected women industrial workers. How this wartime labor discourse specifically tailored the meaning of "dedicated labor" for factory women's consumption remains an open question. In the absence of protective labor legislation, did workplace patriotic units develop measures to protect the health of yŏgong, future mothers and wives of the nation? While there is a growing literature on evolving labor-capital relations in this final decade of colonial rule, gender is seldom deployed as a category of analysis in these studies.[24] One way to fathom what it meant to live through wartime mobilization as workers, however, is to observe what happened at large factories following the Japanese surrender. Two developments that occurred at Chobang that were also replicated at many other factories in Korea are important to consider for our story. They show a persistent undercurrent of radical and militant activism among workers despite the intense wartime ideological inculcation of labor-capital cooperation, and they suggest the potential radicalizing effect of wartime labor practices.

The first of these postwar developments was the spectacular rise of a leftist national trade union federation, the Chŏnp'yŏng, in the immediate postliberation years. Following liberation, workers immediately organized trade unions, which gathered under the National Council of Korean Labor Unions (Chosŏn Nodong Chohap Chŏn'guk P'yŏngŭihoe or Chŏnp'yŏng), established in November 1945. Chŏnp'yŏng, which initially claimed the whole Korean Peninsula, including both the northern and the southern zones, under its jurisdiction, grew into a formidable institution that boasted, by February 1946, 574,479 members in sixteen industrial unions, 235 locals, and 1,676 sub-locals (*punhoe*).[25] Many in the Chŏnp'yŏng leadership had connections to the 1930s red union movement. One example is the case of Hŏ Kyun, a 1930s female labor organizer we met in chapter 2. She became the head of the Women's Bureau in the national headquarters of the Chŏnp'yŏng. In the immediate postliberation years, the legitimacy of leftist activists, who had persisted in underground resistance and, unlike many bourgeois nationalists, refused to collaborate with the colonial government, easily overwhelmed right-wing forces. A clearly left-leaning ideological landscape in the country during that time was reflected in industrial workers' strong allegiance to Chŏnp'yŏng.[26]

The second development was a spontaneous wave of what came to be called the "factory self-management movement" (*kongjang chaju kwalli undong*) that swept through the manufacturing sector in the south. It was a product of a particular historical juncture. As Japanese employers and managers fled Korea, leaving behind what were called the *kwisok chaesan* (formerly Japanese-owned assets that reverted to the government of Korea), workers were left to deal with the power vacuum and disruption in production. Workers at many factories responded by claiming their capacity and right to manage production themselves.[27] Statistics are flimsy, but one account puts the number of "factory management committees" at 728 and the number of involved workers at 88,000 as of early November 1945, three months after liberation.[28] These committees varied in nature depending on who was in control, and in cases where workers rather than management personnel led the movement, the United States Army Military Government in Korea (USAMGIK) swiftly responded with repression. Workers claimed that they were the legitimate owners of such factories, which had been built by their labor, and that they could run the factory much better than so-called managers sent by the USAMGIK. These radical claims and the strong moral overtone their narratives carried point to one possible effect of the late colonial experience of the Sanpō labor control regime. It is plausible that, at least at large companies, workers learned to imagine themselves as equal partners with managers and that they developed a sense of mission and pride as workers performing noble, patriotic labor for the nation.

Women workers participated actively in the Chŏnp'yŏng-led union movement and in the self-management movement. Out of a total of 170 labor disputes in 1946, the textile industry's portion was the largest with forty-three cases involving 10,232 workers. The statistics for the year 1947 were similar.[29] At its founding, the Chŏnp'yŏng textile industrial union had 15,340 members in ninety-six sub-locals, and as of February 1946 women members accounted for about 25 percent of the Chŏnp'yŏng membership of 574,475.[30]

A Chŏnp'yŏng union sub-local emerged at Chobang's Pusan factory. As one of the biggest and most profitable factories in the US occupation zone, the factory was a prime target of both leftist and rightist labor organizing. We do not know much about the Chŏnp'yŏng-affiliated Chobang sub-local, except for the fact that it participated in Chŏnp'yŏng-organized general strikes of March 1947 and February 1948.[31] The sub-local seems to have persisted in its allegiance to Chŏnp'yŏng through 1947, despite unforgiving anticommunist persecution by the US occupation government and violent attacks by right-wing youth and labor groups. In the February 7 general strike of 1948, Chŏnp'yŏng claimed a massive turnout for the strike, including textile workers at Tongyang, Chongyŏn, Taehan, and Chobang factories.[32] More than three thousand Chobang workers, most of them women, participated in the general strike, which was called for an explicitly political purpose: to protest the United Nations' decision to conduct a south-only general election in May. But following that strike the Chŏnp'yŏng movement largely collapsed.

While little is known about the workings of the Chŏnp'yŏng sub-local at the Chobang factory in Pusan, we do know Chobang workers organized a factory management committee a little more than a month after liberation, in late September 1945. The committee set out to restore and stabilize production. Workers guarded equipment and materials from theft and put remaining Japanese personnel under surveillance. The committee platform emphasized its "contribution to the genuine nation-building project" and the "unity" of all employees based on the principle of "rooting out the slave-like and exploitative class system."[33]

The fact that Chobang had become a key base of the leftist Chŏnp'yŏng movement made the factory a major target of the counterattack by right-wing forces. The right-wing national labor organization, the Taehan Noch'ong (Federation of Korean Trade Unions), sent its militants to Chobang to take over the union and purge Chŏnp'yŏng unionists.[34] Those activists included many from right-wing youth groups like the infamous Northwest Youth Corps. An Chongu, one such

Taehan Nochʼong activist, recalled the process of takeover in detail in his two-part recollection of the Chobang dispute introduced earlier.[35] An Chongu was a seasoned anti-Chŏnpʼyŏng crusader who had already busted a Chŏnpʼyŏng-affiliated union at a small shipbuilding ironworks company in the Yŏngdo district of Pusan. This was a time when a Chŏnpʼyŏng union at Chosŏn Heavy Industries (later renamed Korea Shipbuilding and Engineering Corporation or KSEC; currently Hanjin Heavy Industries), a major shipyard in Yŏngdo, was going through the same brutal red purges at the hands of Taehan Nochʼong activists. An gathered six hundred right-wing activists and founded a Taehan Nochʼong–affiliated union at Chobang on November 17, 1947, and started a war against Chŏnpʼyŏng unionists. A violent battle between the union and the incoming youth movement–affiliated Taehan Nochʼong forces ensued, paralleling developments at the KSEC shipyard. An recalled how at one point thirty to forty former Chŏnpʼyŏng unionists stormed the factory and bloody hand-to-hand combat erupted. In some cases threats of "spraying potassium cyanide" and various other methods were used to force Chŏnpʼyŏng leaders to resign from the company.[36] Through this violent process the Taehan Nochʼong took over Chobang and other key factories and shipyards in Pusan, a city in which until 1947 "left-wing forces were so powerful" that it had been impossible even to "hang up a Taehan Nochʼong signboard" at its office.[37] Many hundreds of Chŏnpʼyŏng unionists in the area were then corralled into local chapters of the government-created Anticommunist Alliance (Kungmin Podo Yŏnmaeng; literally, the Alliance to Protect and Guide Dutiful Nationals) for reeducation and surveillance. Many of these alliance members in the country became victims of massacres at the hands of the police and military forces fleeing from the invading North Korean army after the start of the Korean War in June 1950.[38]

Among many Chobang yŏgong, allegiance to the Chŏnpʼyŏng had been strong. A key official of the Taehan Nochʼong Chobang sub-local, Yi Sangok, recalled that in a Taehan Nochʼong attack on the Pusan City Office of the South Korean Workers' Party (Nam Chosŏn Nodongdang, a coalition party led by communists), a party membership roster was discovered, and it included more than seventy Chobang workers' names, most of whom were yŏgong.[39] We do not know what befell these workers after their names were revealed. What is clear is that Chobang workers bounced back from these horrifying and tragic experiences of the red purges and rose up for a determined collective struggle in the winter of 1951–52.

While the violent purge of Chŏnpʼyŏng was going on in the late 1940s, "managers" (*kwalliin*; also called "directors" or "presidents") of the factory, appointed by the US occupation government, rotated in and out at Chobang. Chŏng Hojong, who had chaired the factory management committee organized right after liberation, stepped in as the fourth manager/president in April 1948 and continued in that role in the new republic of South Korea until Kang Ilmae replaced him in September 1951. Chŏng was a highly regarded and respected textile technician known to have installed Chobang's textile machinery himself. He seems to have enjoyed strong support from employees both as the chair of the factory management committee and as the manager/president. Chŏng was a Chobang man who had worked at the factory since graduating from the Tokyo Industrial College in 1932.[40] He must have been familiar with stories of Chobang strikes during that decade, whether he himself was a strike participant or not.

Under Chŏng's leadership Chobang reduced work hours by adding a third shift, increased the workforce from around four thousand to 6,800, and improved pay and benefits for workers. In spite of this new expenditure for workers, Chobang made a handsome profit of eight billion wŏn in 1950. Chŏng and the Pusan factory's union sub-local president, Chang Chaebong, were on good terms, and together they were talking with Kim Chit'ae, a prominent local businessman and a national assemblyman, about a plan to jointly purchase the factory when the government put it on the market.[41] An investigative report of the Chobang incident, officially presented to the National Assembly during the labor dispute, noted that Chobang employees, "because they had worked at the company for more than twenty or thirty years," possessed "a strong sense of attachment to Chobang as their own [company]." The report said that a movement to make it genuinely theirs had been "brewing up into the surface ceaselessly."[42]

Chobang, the largest spinning and weaving company in operation in South Korea at the time and one of the rare profitable businesses in the midst of the Korean War, as of 1951 employed 7,300 workers at its Pusan factory and another factory in Taegu, a city 110 kilometers north of Pusan. Of these employees, 6,300 or 86 percent were female. Chobang workers were raising money to prepare a sales deposit for the purchase of the company. They were also hoping to receive some shares of stock as a "reward stock" (*kongnoju*) for their long-term contribution to the company. The newly passed law on the disposal of *kwisok* (vested) assets affirmed that "preference" should be put on "those with special connections to the company [*yŏn'goja*] *and employees*" (italics added), and thus there was a good chance that the management-union team at Chobang would get the company and turn it into a worker-owned enterprise.[43]

The Law on the Disposition of Vested Properties had gone through bitter debates in the National Assembly in late 1949. Chŏn Chinhan, a national assemblyman and the head of the Taehan Noch'ong, argued that the methods of disposing the vested properties should reflect neither capitalism nor socialism, but the spirit of the constitution, which prescribed a state under which "there is no class confrontation and all the people cooperate with each other." He successfully pushed through an amendment to the bill to include an "employee union" among the parties who would receive priority in sale.[44] President Rhee, who sided with those who wanted to uphold strict capitalist principles, used his veto power to override Chŏn's position, and in the end the word "employee union" was modified to "employees."[45] Still, the law opened the door for employees to dream of becoming the owners of the company for which they had toiled for many years. In many ways, the dream of purchasing the company that Chobang workers and managers pursued in 1951 was a continuation of the ideals expressed in the self-management movement of workers, which flared up in the postliberation years. It also resonated strongly with the experiments of Pyongyang's women rubber workers in creating worker-owned production cooperatives.

The seemingly radical ideological position of Chŏn Chinhan and the anticommunist labor ideology of the right-wing Taehan Noch'ong he led in the late 1940s and early 1950s need some explanation here. As I argued in a previous study, the late 1940s and early 1950s, following liberation, was a time before capitalist ideology fully took hold in South Korea. It was a time when there were still questions about the concept of the inalienable right to private property and the crucial importance of guarding managerial prerogatives—the right of management to control personnel matters, including hiring, firing, and disciplining, as well as financial decision-making.[46] The economic articles of the founding Constitution of South Korea, promulgated in 1948, point to the still-lingering radicalism of the period.[47] The famous Article 18 of the constitution guaranteed workers' right even to share profits (*iik kyunjŏmkwŏn*) at privately owned companies. It was a dynamic and unsettled time when diverse strains of ideologies comingled and competed for hegemony in a historical setting that would eventually be determined largely by US hegemony and the solidifying Cold War conflict in the region.

The intense ideological inculcation of the late colonial period during the militaristic Sanpō mobilization campaign, as seen earlier, familiarized Koreans with the ideas of labor-capital cooperation, anticommunist patriotism, and the nobleness of "dedicated labor" performed by "industrial warriors." The refrain of the official song of the Taehan Noch'ong (1948–60) offers a good example of how familiar these ideas had become to Korean workers: "We are industrial warriors / united like steel / to construct this country."[48]

Fascist tendencies and assumptions that some returning nationalist fighters from China brought with them complicated this already complex ideological terrain further. Among those who absorbed fascist ideas working with the Kuomindang of China or through contacts with German and Japanese philosophers, the most influential figures were Yi Pŏmsŏk, a nationalist hero who led military resistance against the Japanese in China, and An Hosang, a philosopher trained in Germany. Yi, with the support of the US occupation, created a youth organization, the Chosŏn Minjok Chŏngnyŏndan (National Youth Corps or Chokchŏng), which ran a sophisticated training program for young people, nurturing a significant number of Chokchŏng-line activists. Chokchŏng, the well-known slogan of which was "The nation is supreme, and the state is supreme," advocated a noncapitalist path to nation-building.⁴⁹ Chokchŏng soon emerged as an important center of the right-wing youth movement, which also joined in the anti-Chŏnp'yŏng battle.⁵⁰ An Hosang, a nationalist who received a doctoral degree at Jena University in Germany, was a key ideologue behind the pseudofascist *ilminjuŭi* (one people-ism) ideology that provided the ideological basis for Syngman Rhee's rule in the early 1950s. The political ideology of *ilminjuŭi* called for unity among Koreans, opposing divisions along lines of social status, regional background, and sex, and criticized both capitalist and socialist solutions.⁵¹ We can gauge the influence of fascism-influenced thinkers like Yi and An in the late 1940s and early 1950s by the fact that Yi became Rhee's first prime minister and the defense minister in 1948, and An served as Rhee's first minister of education.

Many bourgeois nationalist reformers found employment in the USAMGIK. In particular, voices of Christian intellectuals who studied in the United States during the colonial period exerted strong influence in shaping the nation-building process in the postliberation south, and many of them were from the two P'yŏngan provinces and had ties to An Ch'angho's Hŭngsadan movement.⁵² They included Christian reformers whom we met earlier, like Yi Taewi, who had advocated labor-capital cooperation since the colonial period, and Cho Pyŏngok, who was a leader of the reformist wing of the Suyang Tonghuoe (see chapter 1).⁵³ Yi Taewi served as the head of the Labor Bureau of the USAMGIK and advocated for pro-labor legislation based on the view that labor's bargaining power needed to be strengthened to achieve a balanced relationship between labor and capital. O Kiyŏng, the former *Dong-A ilbo* reporter, and a few other bourgeois reformers chose to be in the "middle-of-the-roader" group in the raging left-and-right conflict of the day and advocated left-right cooperation to overcome the pressures of the Cold War and prevent the grim possibility of a permanent division of the country.⁵⁴ In contrast to O, Kim Tongwŏn, the leader of Pyongyang's Christian businessmen, prioritized an anticommunist agenda and supported the creation of the south-only republic, the position of mainstream bourgeois nationalists. He served as an advisor to the US Army military governor.

More broadly, there existed a strong and widely shared consensus in the immediate postliberation period that equality should be a central principle for organizing a new society, a consensus carried over from the colonial period. During the 1930s exiled independence fighters tried to reconcile bourgeois nationalist and socialist agendas to forge a united front against imperial Japan and in the process developed a consensus platform that acknowledged the urgency of the class problem. This evolving consensus became fully articulated in the 1941 document of the Provisional Government of Korea, titled "Principles for the Founding of the State" ("Kŏn'guk kangnyŏng"), which elucidated a "democratic republic" and an "equal society" as the core organizing principles of the future Korean state.[55] Later, the Constitution of South Korea closely followed this platform. In addition to the idea of building a "democratic republic," this consensus pivoted on the concept of *kyun* or *kyundŭng* (equality), often elucidated as the "Principle of Three Equalities" (*Samgyunjuŭi*). It promised political equality (*kyunkwŏn*), economic equality (*kyunbu*), and educational equality (*kyunhak*) to all Koreans regardless of class, sex, or religious affiliation. These values would be realized through universal suffrage and a parliamentary system, the nationalization of land and "large production facilities," and mandatory education, which would allow an "equal life" (*kyundŭng saenghwal*) for the people. The constitution, influenced by the prevailing consensus on the *kyun* principle, thus envisioned an alternative form of democracy and economy that transcended both capitalism and socialism. The unity among Koreans would be feasible, in the *kyun*-based imagination, because all Koreans, except for a handful of pro-Japanese collaborators, belonged to the oppressed class vis-à-vis the oppressor class of Japanese.

This ideology of equality or *kyun* exerted significant influence in politics and society in the postliberation south, and key political groups that led the effort to create the right-wing union federation, the Taehan Noch'ong, operated under the influence of this ideology. In particular, nationalist An Chaehong's Kungmindang (peoples' party) group was instrumental in the founding of the anticommunist Taehan Noch'ong and crafting its platform and ideology.[56] The overwhelming national consensus on the need for land reform and the unusual articles in the constitution guaranteeing labor rights and also workers' right to profit sharing reflected this widely shared belief in the principle of "equality."

In addition to these reformist nationalists who approached the labor question from the principle of *kyun*, a group of anarcho-syndicalists also actively participated in the founding of Taehan Noch'ong and played a central role in its early activism. Anarchists began to cooperate with bourgeois nationalists in the 1930s, and despite their more radical anti-capitalist vision for nation-building, they were eager to join the fight against communist-influenced Chŏnp'yŏng power by allying with the right-wing Taehan Noch'ong labor movement.

Chŏn Chinhan and other committed Taehan Noch'ong activists seem to have absorbed these multiple layers of ideologies seeking labor-capital cooperation to formulate their own version of *kyun*-based labor ideology that was, unlike its colonial-period versions, now more strongly anticommunist.[57] To fight against the popularity of Chŏnp'yŏng, which championed the class interests of industrial workers, a strongly anticommunist yet sufficiently pro-labor ideology that promoted labor-capital cooperation was a must. Based on the assumption that Korea had not yet reached a high level of capitalist development and therefore class conflict was not inevitable, these thinkers argued that protecting workers' rights and interests would be the best way to avoid class struggle that would debilitate the national economy. For them organized labor should be strengthened to engage industrial workers and bring them into the mission of anticommunist nation-building. Under Chŏn's leadership the Taehan Noch'ong claimed to "strive for the reconstruction of the national economy and the construction of a *kyundŭng* [equalized] society in which '*manmin kongsaeng*' [all the people living in harmony] would be realized."[58]

The core promise and attraction of Taehan Noch'ong's ideology of labor-capital cooperation for workers was this potentially radical idea of accepting industrial workers as full-fledged citizens of the new republic. This democratic ideal of equal citizenship for manual laborers, albeit only after violently purging communists or alleged communist sympathizers from the ranks of organized labor, was what drove some anticommunist unionists of the 1950s and 1960s into spirited labor activism.[59] In the formulation of workers as patriotic citizens entrusted with the mission of building the economy and fighting against communism, however, the category of "workers" (*nodongja*) or "dedicated laborers" (*kŭlloja*) was imagined as male. Numerous statements and documents of the Taehan Noch'ong are mute on women workers' place in the category.

This ideology of labor-capital cooperation lost its staying power, however, as the communist threat subsided and labor conflict increased.[60] The Chobang labor dispute in the winter of 1951–52 had the effect of starkly revealing the contradictions inherent in anticommunist organized labor's dream of pursuing workers' interests through labor-capital cooperation.[61] And in subsequent years the political atmosphere of the country changed drastically. Conforming to US pressure, by 1954 Rhee had clarified his commitment to a US-style capitalist development and a US-style democracy, and purged Yi Pŏmsŏk's Chokch'ŏng group. *Ilminjuŭi* propaganda receded, and to cap off this process, a constitutional revision in 1954 removed some articles that went against capitalist tenets in that founding document of the republic.[62]

"Our Female Comrades" in White Blouse and Black Skirt: The Chobang Textile Dispute of 1951–1952

Chobang workers were pulled directly into this momentous political turmoil of the early 1950s. Because of the size and profitability of the company, Chobang was one of the most attractive and closely watched cases among the "vested [*kwisok*] properties" disposed of by the government, and it was regarded as a major "source of [political] funds" by politicians, including President Rhee.[63] It was, as all participants—politicians, state officials, and labor leaders—were well aware, a major battle site at which to settle what kind of economic and political order the new Republic of Korea would pursue.

In a sense the chain of events that led to the strike began when, out of the blue, on March 16, 1951, the dreadful Counterintelligence Corps (T'ŭngmudae or CIC) of the army showed up at Chobang and arrested several top managers, including company president Chŏng Hojong, as well as union president Chang Chaebong. Businessman Kim Chit'ae was also arrested. Charged with treason, they were then sent to a military tribunal (South Korea was under martial law at the time). Chŏng and Chang were dismissed from the company soon after the arrest, and the much-anticipated sale of the company was suspended. The charge was that under Chŏng's leadership Chobang recycled cotton linters (*nangmyŏn*) by mixing them into new batches of cotton in order to produce more cloth from the limited supply of raw material, resulting in inferior quality cotton textile goods for military consumption, which, according to the CIC, constituted a treasonous act. Such mixing was in fact a customary practice allowed by the Ministry of Commerce and Industry (MCI), but the CIC claimed that the Chobang executives and the union president conspired to save cotton to produce extra cotton cloth to sell internally to employees, thus attempting to accumulate funds to purchase the company.[64] A ludicrous charge was added in the indictment of key Chobang defendants, including Chŏng, Chang, and Kim, that they had aided the South Korean Workers' Party and even organized a preparation committee to welcome the "puppet army" of North Korea.[65] Kim Chit'ae was eventually exonerated in appellate court, and everyone was freed on probation. But by fabricating the so-called Nangmyŏn incident the Rhee government was able to get rid of the most viable bidder group for the company and suspend the sale. In July the Rhee government fired Chŏng, and on September 5 it sent in Kang Ilmae, a confidante of Rhee, as the new president.

Kang, who had no prior experience in the textile industry, showed up at the factory with dozens of policemen and armed young men who arrived in more than ten vehicles. On arrival Kang hired 120 new employees, including sixty-seven white-collar employees (*sawŏn*), and harassed existing employees to make them quit. He also dismissed twenty skilled workers who were sixty or older and had twenty or more years of seniority at the factory, and he stopped the payment of cotton cloth to workers, which angered workers greatly.[66] The MCI had designated 5.5 percent of the cotton cloth produced at the factory to be used for worker welfare, on the condition that a certain production quota was met. This practice acknowledged the serious problem of hyperinflation on workers' livelihood; inflation rates in the postliberation years and early years of the Rhee regime were astounding.[67] In such a situation, for Chobang workers and for workers at other factories, payment in goods such as cloth or grain was in many cases more important than the actual cash wage. Payment in kind represented a core element in the welfare practices at large companies. Such payments were supposed to show the company's commitment to worker livelihood, and during the war they had been understood as a reward to "production warriors" who kept the factory running twenty-four hours a day in two shifts to churn out military supplies.[68] It was this move by Kang in particular, together with the firing of employees without cause, that seems to have antagonized workers the most.

As president of the company Kang Ilmae performed a caretaker role for Rhee, who wanted to secure Chobang on his side at a time when the lucrative company could fall into the hands of businessmen like Kim Chit'ae, whom Rhee suspected of being a key figure in an anti-Rhee group in the National Assembly.[69] Thus the immediate reason to send in Kang and remove Chŏng and Kim Chit'ae was to secure a crucial source of secret political funds. But there were two additional, and equally or even more significant, reasons for Rhee's takeover of Chobang. In order to counter the power of the second National Assembly (1950–54) under the control of opposition parties and progressive assemblymen who opposed Rhee's plan to revise the constitution to allow direct presidential elections, Rhee had decided to create a party of his own.[70] For that crucial political work, Chobang would serve as a major platform for recruiting and mobilizing workers into the fold of the new party. Another reason was more fundamental and ideological. The sale of Chobang to a coalition of managers and workers would set a powerful precedent in the struggle over ownership and managerial rights at companies taken over from the Japanese—this at a time when the memories of the workers' self-management movement were threateningly fresh.[71] If the scheduled sale of Chobang had continued, there was a strong possibility that Chobang would end up as a production cooperative–style business run jointly by workers and management. As he did after purchasing Chosŏn Silk in March, Kim Chit'ae was said to have created a plan to set aside one-third of the stock for the employees' share.[72]

Kang Ilmae also attempted to intervene in a crucial union election through bribery and violent threats against core unionists. A key union leader, Yi Sangok, was ordered to move to Chobang's Taegu factory two days before the election, but he attended the assembly of representatives with luggage in hand. His speech and vote were important in thwarting Kang's scheme as Pak Chŏngt'ae, the candidate supported by workers, beat his opponent by just one vote.[73] After refusing to negotiate with the newly elected union leadership, in mid-December Kang fired key union leaders Han Sŭngnyong and An Chongu. Workers' wrath at Kang's dismissal of longtime employees and union leaders and at his "despotic" behavior of cursing at and beating up workers exploded into a resolute collective action soon after.[74] The "wall poster battles" described at the beginning of this chapter began to unfold, and Kang responded by bringing in police forces and thugs. Then on Christmas Day Kang fired the union's president, Pak Chŏngt'ae, and the vice president, Yi Sangok, with the wall poster struggle as an excuse. Another firing of seven unionists followed soon after.

The Taehan Noch'ong under Chŏn Chinhan's leadership came out in support of the fight of the Chobang Pusan factory union (officially a "sub-local" of the larger Chobang union "local") early in the conflict. Chŏn Chinhan came to the factory to persuade Kang Ilmae to negotiate with the workers on December 14, but Kang Ilmae behaved disrespectfully toward Chŏn and sub-local unionists. He went so far as to pull out a pistol and threaten the unionists with it. Under Chŏn Chinhan, Taehan Noch'ong created a "Task Force for the Chobang Dispute," but surprisingly, an anti-Chŏn faction in the Taehan Noch'ong aligned itself with Kang and publicly denounced the actions of the Chobang sub-local and Chŏn in late December.[75] Thus, the Chobang dispute became embroiled in a long-running internal power struggle within the Taehan Noch'ong, which in turn became tangled with national party politics. Chŏn Chinhan, unlike the anti-Chŏn group, was weary of turning the Taehan Noch'ong into a tool for mobilizing the popular vote for Rhee. Considering this far-reaching political alignment, the Chobang dispute was destined to become a hard-fought national-level struggle.

During the dispute Kang Ilmae mobilized the police and CIC soldiers through his close ties to the Rhee regime and used organized squads of hooligans to intimidate and subjugate workers with violence. Kang created a company union that forcefully took over the union office. In response, the slogan "Down with Despot Kang Ilmae" gained widespread and emotional support from workers, hundreds of whom were battered by Kang's people. On January 21, 1952, more than a thousand women workers from Chobang demonstrated in front of the National Assembly, shouting the slogan, "Down with President Kang Ilmae!" Several hundred policemen wielding batons struck workers indiscriminately, and the mounted police barged into the midst of marchers creating, in An Chongu's words, "hellish scenes" ("abigyuhwan"). It was not easy for the mounted police to deal with these women workers either. A *Dong-A ilbo* column reported on a textile yŏgong at the scene who pulled the tail of a police horse to block its moving. That afternoon thirteen hundred women workers left the factory and marched through the streets of Pusan. They returned to the factory and surrounded the president's office, shouting, "Down with Kang Ilmae!" and clashed with the police and thugs mobilized by the company union.[76]

Workers' desperate public actions and perseverance defying of violent repression aroused widespread public interest in the labor dispute. The National Assembly organized an investigation committee, and the MCI suspended Kang and an executive director, giving workers hope. But on January 31, a police roundup of union leaders and activist workers commenced, and the MCI reinstated Kang "in the name of maintaining the order of corporate management."[77] Kang returned to the factory again accompanied by policemen, including mounted policemen and plainclothes detectives. Three women workers—Kim Samdŏk (age 22), Yi Oesŏn (age 22), and Kim Okcha (age 21)—were detained and indicted, together with two male workers and the president and vice president of the Chobang sub-local, on the charge of committing acts of violence.[78] On February 27 the Chobang Task Force under Chŏn Chinhan at last decided to call a strike that was to commence on March 3. This was not an easy decision because the country was still at war and under martial law. The "Declaration for a Strike at Chobang" raised a crucial question, saying, "If Kang Ilmae's action is something permitted in a democratic country, then we cannot but harbor doubts about such democracy." The declaration emphasized that the Chobang strike represented a "nationwide struggle" aimed at "protecting the human rights of our workers and securing the democratic and free trade union movement."[79] Meanwhile, on February 29 the National Assembly, after listening to the report from its investigation committee, voted ninety-three to zero to approve a resolution calling for the dismissal of President Kang by the MCI and the suspension of the strike by the Taehan Noch'ong. In respect of the National Assembly resolution, on March 1 Taehan Noch'ong suspended the strike scheduled to occur two days later.

But the Rhee government did not waver from its support of Kang Ilmae. The national political situation was getting extremely tense after Rhee's constitutional amendment for direct presidential elections was voted down by the National Assembly on January 18, 1952. Rhee's amendment was defeated by a telling margin: 143 votes against versus 13 votes for. In addition to attacking Chobang unionists, Kang's hooligan squad was mobilized in pro-Rhee demonstrations against national assemblymen who had cast "no" votes. Hundreds of workers were arrested by the police, and violence against pro-strike unionists became a daily affair. But the union held steady and support was pouring in from other unions. Some Chobang workers in frustration were writing letters to the task force in blood, pleading with them to allow a strike.[80] Finally, on March 11 Chŏn Chinhan went to the National Assembly and announced that a strike would begin at 8:00 a.m. the following day because the government was refusing to honor the National Assembly's resolution and repressing the union with force. It was at this point that Yi Oesŏn and other women workers pulled off a secret mission of uniting thousands of workers behind a work stoppage that would start the following morning.

After a decision was made on March 10 to launch a strike in two days, women workers spearheaded the secret preparation work, organizing communication networks and disseminating a secret code to workers of both the day and night shifts, avoiding the probing eyes of detectives and managers. The code that would signal the execution of the strike was set as a yŏgong making rounds on the shop floor "wearing a white blouse and a black skirt and holding a handkerchief in her hand."[81] By then all union officials were either arrested or fired and prohibited from coming near the factory, which was surrounded by armed police forces. Plainclothes detectives were stationed at strategic locations inside the factory. Kang Ilmae and the police assumed that they had effectively demolished the union's command structure and thus the strike would not be possible. At 8:00 a.m. on March 12, the time when day and night shifts crossed, however, six thousand workers, defying Rhee's stern warnings and the terrifying atmosphere of martial law, all at once poured out toward the factory gate, clashing with the police. In his recollection, An Chongu, the dismissed union president and the founder of the Taehan Noch'ong union at Chobang, praised the role of Yi Oesŏn and other women workers who "methodically and swiftly" performed the difficult task of organizing a strike in just one day.[82] These women apparently enjoyed great support from rank-and-file workers at the factory. Even in the company's estimation, some 81 percent of the day-shift workers joined the strike.[83] The iron gates of the factory fell as workers' bodies slammed against them, and the ten or so trucks the police installed as a barricade to block the main gate proved useless as women workers stormed the trucks, dragging out the policemen manning them, pinching and biting.[84] The police fired warning shots, and the vicinity of the factory became a virtual war zone. An Chongu nostalgically recalled, "Neither thugs nor batons, neither gun shots nor buttstock could block workers who pressed on like gigantic angry waves." He felt that the "souls" of six thousand workers were "united with a burning sense of solidarity as if saying 'death cannot block us.'"[85]

That day's strike was, in An's view, "a success beyond expectation," regardless of the end result. Dozens of workers and union leaders were arrested and suffered harsh treatment in custody, and Kang announced that anyone not returning to work within twenty-four hours would be fired. Even so, about 85 percent of night-shift workers stayed out that night. To the workers' dismay, however, Chŏn Chinhan buckled under Rhee's pressure and called off the strike after just one day, and the strike quickly collapsed.

The casualty numbers of this defeat were very high. According to An Chongu, about a thousand male and female employees were "dragged away like dogs" and detained by the police, among whom about six hundred suffered injuries. Twenty-six bureau chiefs and section chiefs, the core management personnel who opposed Kang Ilmae, were fired, and more than six hundred workers, many of them yŏgong, were dismissed. Following this mass firing, An recalled, "employees who slammed down their resignation letters and quit because they could not endure [the injustices committed] reached over five hundred."[86] The defeat was sweeping. The company union stayed, Chŏn Chinhan was kicked out from the presidency of the Taehan Noch'ong by President Rhee, and many fired women workers, according to the official history of the organized labor movement, "fell to the bottom of society," meaning they had to turn to prostitution for survival.[87]

Kang Ilmae was eventually able to purchase Chobang in 1955 at a price far below the government appraisal price.[88] Intermittent struggle by dismissed Chobang workers continued in the late 1950s and flared up after the April Revolution of 1960. But a dream of a producer cooperative based on labor-management cooperation was quashed.[89] The once highly profitable company, however, struggled financially. During the dispute the company fired key personnel, including Chŏng Hojong, as well as many skilled workers, a loss that weakened the company's technical base. And Kang Ilmae's heyday at Chobang did not last long. He died in 1959, and Chobang was sold to Chŏng Chaeho of Samho Textile, which proceeded to neglect necessary capital investment while extracting large-scale political funds from the company.[90] Eventually the bankrupted company was turned over to the city of Pusan in 1968, and the city razed the factory for urban development.

Legacies of the Chobang Strike

By crushing the Chobang strike, the pro-capitalist position supported by Syngman Rhee achieved a decisive victory. Rhee was able to push through his constitutional revision in July 1952 and won the direct presidential election on August 5. The Taehan Noch'ong was reduced to a shell of its former self, and from that time on it obediently towed the line as a tool of the Rhee regime in charge of mobilizing industrial workers in support of the government.[91]

In the early 1950s the new Republic of Korea was at a crossroads in terms of how to define the nature of its economic system and the role of the trade union movement in it. Blocking the worker purchase of Chobang, one of the most important vested properties, despite strong union support represented a crucial first step in postcolonial and post–Korean War economic planning leading to orthodox capitalist development. In that context we can understand the steadfast position taken by the MCI and Rhee in support of Kang Ilmae, despite the fact that Kang was an extremely problematic figure for any person with common sense.

The Chobang dispute was thus a colossal struggle and a fundamental turning point, and women workers played a central role in it. It was large-scale strikes by textile, mining, and dock workers beginning in late 1951 as the war came to stalemate that generated momentum for pivotal discussions on industrial democracy and led to a consensus on the urgency of labor legislation. In a previous study I showed how this labor unrest propelled an energetic legislative drive for labor laws.[92] Here it is important to stress the direct role that the Chobang dispute played in this momentous national political and legal process and the power of rank-and-file yŏgong activism that sustained the yearlong process of struggle.[93] Spearheading the passing of progressive versions of these labor laws was Chŏn Chinhan, who won an assembly by-election in the Yŏngdo district of Pusan, held in the midst of the Chobang dispute in February 1952. Although twenty-three candidates, including many well-known politicians, crowded that election campaign, Chŏn won by a landslide partly because of the voluntary electoral work performed by thousands of Chobang workers and their family members who covered the district "house by house." Women workers took turns, and each day five hundred volunteers went out, "visiting each household twice or three times, pleading with tears that 'electing Mr. Chŏn Chinhan and sending him to the National Assembly is the only way to save us,'" according to An Chongu.[94]

Through the labor laws promulgated in 1953—the Labor Union Act, the Labor Disputes Adjustment Act, the Labor Committee Act, and the Labor Standards Act—the trade union movement secured its legitimacy as partner in industrial life. Through them workers secured rights to organize unions freely, bargain collectively, and engage in collective actions. Through the laws, these rights, already recognized in the constitution, gained strong legal protection, although in reality the enforcement of the laws turned out to be spotty at best. Companies were obliged to bargain with unions by law, and discrimination against unionists because of union membership or intervention in union activities became punishable as unfair labor practices. The Labor Standards Act required companies to offer a high level of labor protections. This forging of political consensus on a very advanced level of industrial democracy was possible because of a decades-long history of union activism in Korea, including the Chŏnp'yŏng movement of previous years. Chŏnp'yŏng propagated socialist dreams among workers and the wider society and helped shape industrial relations practices through aggressive collective actions.[95] But a more immediate stimulus for labor legislation came from militant strikes, of which the Chobang strike was the most publicized and influential one. Even in defeat Chobang workers achieved much.

In these ways Chobang's women workers earned the respect of male unionists as "women comrades" (*yŏdongji*). This phrase was used by Kim Chuhong, the president of the National Railway Workers' Union, who took the side of the Chŏn Chinhan group in the Taehan Noch'ong during the Chobang dispute. In his June 1953 declaration (*kyŏngmun*), which assailed his rival faction as "labor aristocrats" and "political brokers," Kim asserted that those "labor aristocrats" were more responsible than Kang Ilmae in "making innocent and pure-minded *women comrades* of ours [*uri ŭi yŏdongji*] roam about the world of prostitution" by allowing Kang to snatch good jobs from Chobang women workers.[96] *Yŏdongji* or "women comrades" was a term that reflected a certain recognition of women's autonomous facility as activists and a respect for their role in the labor movement. That a high-ranking union official like Kim was ready to call Chobang women *tongji* and that union president An Chongu heaped high praise on yŏgong leadership show that Chobang women workers' capacity for struggle impressed contemporary labor leaders, if not the larger society.

This kind of recognition and respect for women strikers largely disappeared after the Chobang strike, however, both in the labor movement and in contemporary media. It would not reappear in force until the 1970s. Even in the Chobang dispute it is noticeable that women's voices were rather mute in media coverage, compared to those of women in the rubber strikes of the 1930s in Pyongyang, despite the important role they played. We only glimpse the level of yŏgong's agency and capacity through male leaders' recollections, through haunting images of "women comrades" in white blouses and black skirts making rounds on the shop floor to organize a strike or menacing Kang Ilmae with their persistent and militant struggle. And even these traces largely vanished as time went by. It is thus ironic that women workers became invisible in industrial relations following the passage of the labor laws, to which they contributed so much.

Another intriguing part of Kim's declaration, which provides clues to Chobang yŏgong's agency, needs some explanation. Kim lamented the fate of "women comrades" falling into the world of prostitution, and, as we have seen, the official history book of the Federation of Korean Trade Unions (Han'guk Noch'ong, a successor to the Taehan Noch'ong, established in August 1961) echoes Kim's declaration by recording that many fired Chobang women "fell to the bottom of society." Apparently, the narrow distance between factory jobs and sex work was well understood by those who produced this memory.[97] In early 1950s South Korea the Chobang jobs were highly coveted given the high unemployment and hyperinflation, and especially for women, equivalent jobs were hard to come by. And before the 1960s the South Korean economy was still based heavily in agriculture, with manufacturing accounting for only 6 to 10 percent of GNP, while agriculture accounted for 44 to 48 percent between 1953 and 1958.[98] In 1952, out of 4,300 work sites in the country that had five or more employees, only 240 sites employed two hundred or more workers, and 147,446 workers were fortunate enough to be employed there.[99] In 1957, after the economy had somewhat recovered from the devastation of the war, there were 136,230 manufacturing workers at companies hiring five or more employees in South Korea, and among them 49,141 were employed in the textile industry (11,499 men and 37,642 women), which was the leading manufacturing sector in the 1950s. The six thousand Chobang textile yŏgong in the early 1950s thus represented the cream of the crop among gainfully employed women, the vast majority of whom worked at smaller companies or as housemaids, street vendors, service workers, or farmhands.[100] Obviously Chobang yŏgong dismissed in large numbers in 1952 had great difficulties finding comparable employment in wartime Pusan.

Thanks to the work of historian Yi Hŭiyŏng, who studied women worker subjectivities through oral history testimonies of yŏgong who worked at Chŏnnam Spinning and Weaving (Chŏnnam Pangjik; Chŏnbang) in Kwangju in the 1950s, we have a clearer idea of the social position yŏgong occupied in that period. She noticed a particular discourse on factory women in the 1950s and calls it a discourse of "factory [kongjang] kasinae" or "textile-industry [chŏngbang] k'ŭnaegi" (both kasinae and k'ŭnaegi mean maidens). At the time millions of casualties from the war deprived many households of male breadwinners and pushed women to look for gainful employment outside the home. Factory jobs, which paid regular wages for women, were scarce, and interviewees recalled how stiff the competition to enter the textile factory was. Gaining admission to it was, in one interviewee's words, "like passing the university entrance exam in today's sense."[101] Reflecting the dominant Confucian gender ideology of the time, which proscribed women's proper place in the domestic realm, kongjang kasinae discourse of the 1950s showed a deep suspicion of young women working in factories and a strong desire to socially control them.[102] It was, however, different from the yŏgong discourse of the 1960s and 1970s, Yi argues, in that the latter was much more clearly colored by attitudes of social discrimination and exclusion against women manual workers. Unlike the yŏgong discourse during the era of rapid industrialization, the "factory maiden" discourse of the 1950s contained a feeling of envy toward their good fortune and a certain degree of respect for risk-taking actions of good daughters as they ventured out into a dangerous world for the sake of a family's livelihood. Again, a family frame of understanding made yŏgong's existence tolerable and even respectable.

Considering the scarcity of stable factory jobs for women, it is quite something that Chobang women workers persevered for months on the front line of industrial battle, and that must have added to male leaders' admiration of women's "death cannot block us" attitude. From their actions we can imagine the kind of pride and self-awareness these women possessed as an elite group of working women waging a battle of grave historical significance. We do not know how much these Chobang women were aware of the proud history of labor activism at Chobang during the colonial period and in the immediate postliberation period, but it is likely that memories of prior yŏgong struggle culturally conditioned male unionists to see yŏgong as their "comrades."[103]

At the same time, it was also clear that the 1951–52 Chobang dispute was led by male leadership at both the sub-local and national levels. In postcolonial South Korea, unlike during the colonial period, a government-sanctioned national trade union federation—Taehan Noch'ong—functioned as the sole representative of industrial workers vis-à-vis the government. From women's perspective, an important consequence of progress in the institutionalization and empowerment of organized labor was that women's role became diminished to that of rank-and-file foot soldiers. The Chŏnp'yŏng movement with all its organizational prowess had already showed this tendency. In labor disputes that garnered national attention like the Chobang case, male Taehan Noch'ong leaders were clearly in charge, and the media focused its attention on them, regardless of the fact that women provided actual combat power. Strikes at female-dominated sites were no longer portrayed as "*yŏgong* strikes." Contributions by women workers were duly noted by male union leaders, but female voices tend to be mute in the extant documentary evidence.

In the 1930s bourgeois nationalist media and intellectuals noticed the desperate calls of women workers, who were viewed as constituents of the future Korean nation, in theory at least. And women's militancy was appreciatively recorded. The communist red union ideologues and activists of the period highly regarded women workers' power as strikers and tried to tap into their potential to act as good proletarian foot soldiers fighting for a revolution. In the 1950s arrangement, the new nation-state recognized and institutionalized the trade union movement, but men monopolized union leadership at national, regional, and local work site levels, and women workers were marginalized.

In the next chapter we examine how the ongoing institutionalization of the trade union movement during the 1950s and 1960s and the accompanying consolidation of the male breadwinner model in industrial relations sealed women workers' marginal status in industrial life and in the larger society and how women workers fought back and reemerged as the core force of the new militant unionism by the 1970s.

5

WOMEN WORKERS IN INDUSTRIALIZING KOREA

From the 1960s to the 1980s

After the Chobang strike ended in 1952 and the industrial relations system was institutionalized following the passage of the labor laws in 1953, it became rare in the remainder of the 1950s and most of the 1960s to see collective struggle by factory women capture national attention.[1] The yŏgong question, together with the visibility of factory women as important social actors, rapidly receded from public conscience as the organized labor movement, led by men, established its control over industrial relations negotiations. When female industrial workers reappeared in the newspapers as militant subjects of labor struggle, it was at female-dominated, largely export-oriented, textile and electronics industries in the 1970s. By that time economic, social, and political conditions were much different from those of the 1950s.

As we saw in the previous chapter, the 1950s was an unsettled time ideologically, socially, and culturally as various social groups fought to have their interests integrated into the emerging social and economic order of the new republic. The ethos of South Korea's developmental era of the 1960s and 1970s, in contrast, was quite different from that of the war-torn 1950s. The 1960s began with the hopeful episode of the April Revolution of 1960, which toppled the dictatorial Rhee regime and fundamentally changed South Korean society by demonstrating the transformative capacity of struggle by broad coalitions of people. That event established the legitimacy of a broad-based struggle for democracy. The euphoria over witnessing democracy unexpectedly blossoming in Korea, however, was soon replaced by the harsh reality of living under another dictator, this time in the form of an anticommunist military dictatorship launched by General Park Chung Hee following his successful military coup d'état on May 16, 1961. Park, *the* nation-builder of South Korea, as he came to be known, was not a simple dictator. Skillfully appropriating common desires and aspirations of the population, both those of elites and non-elites, he electrified the nation with the promise of "overcoming poverty" and "modernizing the fatherland." Park oversaw an era of remarkable rapid economic growth in the 1960s and 1970s that fundamentally reshaped society and state-society relations.

Organized labor, as we have seen, had secured a fairly advanced industrial relations system in the 1953 labor legislations—a process in which women factory workers played an important role. Now in the 1960s organized workers began to push for the realization of what they called *saenghwalgŭp*, a "livelihood" or "living" wage that would allow not only individual workers but also their wives and children to live decently. In effect, these wage offensives by unions under the umbrella of the government-sanctioned Federation of Korean Trade Unions (Han'guk Nodong Chohap Ch'ongyŏnmaeng, or Han'guk Noch'ong; hereafter FKTU) sought realization of the male breadwinner worker ideal. The continuing institutionalization of labor and employment relations under the Park government's export-driven developmental strategy thus generated a deeply gendered system of mobilizing and rewarding workers for developmental tasks. In the newly streamlined sexual division of labor, women industrial workers were channeled into export industries as the prime source of cheap, disposable labor, and were controlled by the male-dominated trade union system, which simply did not see the structural discrimination against women workers as a problem.

The Park government's export drive centered on the labor-intensive and female-dominated industries of textiles, wig and shoe manufacturing, and electronics. It triggered a surge of migration from the countryside to cities and a rapid increase in the number of female factory workers. Alienated from the leadership of the unions under the FKTU, women worker resistance nevertheless did not abate. By the late 1960s yŏgong-led labor disputes began to break out in large numbers, which in turn brought out harsh repression by the state and tightening control of militant rank-and-file workers by the FKTU. Industrial unions of the FKTU, over the late 1960s and early 1970s, caved in under state pressure and began to actively aid management in the effort to quell worker resistance.

At the same time the Park Chung Hee period (1961–79) engendered a powerful democracy movement that rediscovered the importance of engaging the non-elite population. Called the movement of *minjung* (people), this "people's" movement championed democratization and social transformation against the all-powerful authoritarian state. Progressive intellectuals and student activists, like the communist organizers of the 1930s, started to pay attention to labor issues beginning in the late 1960s, a process that rapidly accelerated after 1970.

The dual process of a massive economic mobilization of yŏgong, on the one hand, and the development of a new "democratic" (*minju*) union movement among them buttressed by a new labor-intellectual alliance, on the other, begot a complex gender politics regarding working women and generated competing and conflicting images and perceptions of South Korean women industrial workers. The larger society saw the rise of a derogatory slang term for yŏgong, *kongsuni* (factory girl), that defined yŏgong as lower-class, uneducated, and thus socially unworthy young women whose exposure to the factory environment made them unfeminine and made their morality suspect. This occurred despite government propaganda that praised women factory workers as patriotic "industrial warriors." At the same time, women workers and progressive intellectuals who participated in the minju labor movement developed, by the late 1970s, a polar opposite image of *yŏgong t'usa* (factory women fighters), militant and politically conscious yŏgong who were, like Kang Churyong before them, trailblazers in the new militant union movement. Yet the politics of yŏgong democracy fighters were also deeply gendered.

I begin the chapter by examining the effort by male industrial workers to secure their place in the new republic by claiming their entitlement to a living wage, a goal that fulfilled their status ideal as breadwinner citizens and heads of the household, but which proved to be problematic for women workers. The second section of the chapter examines the conditions that allowed the suicide and martyrdom of a male garment worker, Chun Tae-il, to become the foundational memory for the minju labor movement, while an equally authentic protest suicide in 1962 of a "Miss Kim," a textile labor activist, failed to ignite social interest and fell into oblivion. The section explores how women workers, despite the exclusionary tendencies against women in the union movement under the FKTU, continued to develop their gendered class consciousness and militant activism, largely through small group organizing activities. Those stories of awakening and empowerment among women workers themselves complicate the mainstream narrative of the minju labor movement that highlights Chun Tae-il's martyrdom as the beginning and the ensuing worker-student alliance as the central mechanism for the movement's success. The chapter's last section continues this focus on the bottom-up development of women workers' autonomous and democratic union activism, showcasing select cases of minju union activism of the 1970s and early 1980s that exhibited a new level of gender consciousness. Although they were pushed to the margins in union politics initially, in the 1970s and early 1980s women workers in the minju union movement again established themselves as significant actors in the labor and democracy movements, and it was on such women that often violent labor repression measures of state authorities and management became concentrated.

The Male Breadwinner Ideal and Women's Wages

The 1950s started with a period of intense national crisis that shook society to its core. In addition to millions of refugees from the north who came across the Thirty-Eighth Parallel before and during the Korean War, the vast majority of the southern population was also uprooted by the war, which engulfed the whole country except for a small area in the southeast stretching from Taegu to Pusan, dubbed the "Pusan Perimeter." As families were thrown into cutthroat competition for survival, centuries-old Confucian social norms began to weaken, including deeply entrenched status and clan consciousness. Although official statistics vary, the war produced, in addition to millions of casualties, more than 300,000 war widows.[2] In the aftermath of the war, many intellectuals and much of the media became obsessed with the debilitating impact of Western culture, especially American GI culture, on Korean women. Unlike men, who were encouraged to adopt cultural trappings of the West, women were pressured to continue to perform the role of repository of cultural authenticity for the Korean nation. Social customs rooted in patriarchy were slow to change, yet the wartime and postwar reality pushed unprecedented numbers of women into the marketplace, factories, construction sites, and various kinds of service work, some of which bordered on prostitution.

Reacting to the expanding scope of women's activities in society and women's increasing power and voice over family finances, men sharpened their vigilance over transgressive behaviors of womenfolk that could destabilize patriarchal gender norms. This was the time a best-selling novel turned film, *Madame Freedom* (*Chayu puin*, 1956, directed by Han Hyŏngmo), became a box office phenomenon.[3] It was a morality tale about a middle-class woman who allegedly ignored her feminine duty in pursuit of frivolous Western culture. In the end she comes to the painful realization that her adventuresome spirit ruined her life. The authorial character in the novel *Madame Freedom* candidly reveals his view by saying, "When [women] confuse freedom and license and social order could get harmed by that, we might have to strictly control the womenfolk [*anangnedŭl*] until each woman comes to her senses, even if that means we have to ignore democracy for the time being."[4] Male fear of women who pursued "freedom" indicates a certain empowerment of women in the family and conspicuous changes in women's subjectivities in postwar South Korea, a situation that made men's capacity to fulfill breadwinner responsibilities that much more important to men's sense of masculine prowess and self-worth.

By the time industrial workers in South Korea secured constitutional and legal guarantees of basic labor rights in the early 1950s, organized labor, represented by the Taehan Nochʻong, was a shadow of its former self. It had already lost its original vision and autonomy, and its leadership was mired in corruption charges and factional strife. Nevertheless, as labor historian Kim Chun's study of the National Railway Workers' Union (Chŏnʼguk Chʻŏlto Nodong Chohap, or Chʻŏllo) shows, a kind of patron-client relationship between the regime and the Taehan Nochʻong allowed segments of organized labor to successfully utilize the legal framework provided by labor laws to their members' benefit.[5] Especially workers at large government-managed enterprises, including railway, electric power, and banking sector workers, as well as unionized workers at large private companies, benefited from this new scheme of industrial democracy. By the late 1950s unions at those sites had learned to effectively wield their legally guaranteed labor rights to their advantage. In addition to Kim's study, my own study of the union at the Korea Shipbuilding and Engineering Corporation (KSEC), South Korea's largest shipyard during the 1950s and 1960s, confirms this empowering development in the union movement, at least in certain male-dominated industrial settings.[6]

The National Railway Workers' Union had been a key leader of the South Korean trade union movement since the inception of Taehan Nochʻong, and in the 1960s that union and the KSEC shipbuilding union were among the most advanced and powerful unions in the country. These two male-dominated unions are also unique in that, in an uncommon move for unions in South Korea before the 1970s, they preserved an abundance of union materials for posterity to study.[7] What is conspicuous in the activities and records of these two unions is the fact that union leaders, government representatives, managerial personnel, and even police detectives exhibited an attitude of mutual recognition and respect as negotiating partners in the newly established industrial relations system. What was being negotiated through their men-to-men talks was in essence the question of how unionized (male) workers should be treated in industrial life. For these workers it was a matter not just of securing livelihood but of being acknowledged in their full membership in the republic, a membership that vouched for their manliness. Contention in industrial strife was not only about pay and benefit issues. As KSEC union documents clearly show, it was often about the principle of equality between management and unionists at the negotiation table and about various workplace issues involving the question of who should be in control.[8]

While male workers at certain unionized sites in the late 1950s and 1960s often successfully made claims to what they saw as their legitimate share of the economic pie through the legally sanctioned trade union system, the same cannot be said for women workers. Regardless of their position on the question of class and capitalism, in postliberation South Korea almost all visionaries and politicians of the new republic shared a staunchly patriarchal understanding that pivoted around the sanctity of the family, which was supposed to be headed by the husband-head of the household whose breadwinner role was to be buttressed and protected. Capitalism—at least some tenets of it—was challenged by some, but patriarchal culture and institutions were never seriously questioned. As sociologist Ham Inhŭi argues, in defining labor rights in the Constitution and in labor laws, the norm was the adult male worker citizen, and women's labor outside the home was understood as occurring only under exceptional circumstances.[9] Once male workers secured the legitimacy of the trade union movement in the new polity and thereby consolidated, at least in principle, male industrial workers' place in society as full citizens, the appreciation for yŏgong militancy waned. Women workers were marginalized even in women-dominated sectors like the textile industry. The national industrial union of the textile sector, whose leadership was monopolized by men, remained one of the weakest and most corrupt industrial unions from the 1950s through the 1970s, when rank-and-file women workers finally revolted against it.[10]

In this way the institutionalization of industrial democracy in the 1950s proceeded in a manner that reaffirmed the hegemonic patriarchal culture of the larger society. The patriarchal consensus between organized labor and management in this period mirrors the dominant policy discourse on women-related matters in the larger society, which was centered on the notion of protecting and controlling *punyŏ*, a term referring to women positioned in relation to family as wives and daughters. Sociologist Hwang Chŏngmi sees the late 1940s and 1950s as the time when a particular gender discourse of framing women as *punyŏ* was consolidated.[11] *Punyŏ* in the postwar years were approached primarily as the target of rescue missions and social control, on the one hand, and of enlightenment campaigns aiming at nurturing modern mothers and wives, on the other. Hwang concludes that in the framework of *punyŏ* it was hard to acknowledge women as individual "citizens" or "workers." The relationship between the state and women was mediated by the family, and women who stepped outside of the normative family realm and proscribed feminine roles were viewed as lower-class *punyŏ*, potentially dangerous to the health and morality of the society. From the perspective of the male elite and state planners, "protecting" and strictly controlling these potentially dangerous women thus became an urgent task and the focus of government's gender policies, and that policy consensus endured in subsequent decades.

In industrial life, true to this shared patriarchal understanding, women workers were defined primarily as members of working-class families, not as "workers" pure and simple, regardless of the obvious fact, reported in mainstream media, that many women workers were in fact breadwinners.[12] And just like the family power structure that positioned women as dependents of their male head of the household, be it their husbands or their sons as dictated in the nation's civil law, it was deemed natural that yŏgong were represented and controlled by the male leadership of their union.

While such familial understanding of women workers prevailed, it was hard to push forward women's specific needs as part of the union agenda or raise the thorny issue of pervasive sexual violence on the shop floor. On this point past union practices did not show much difference either. Although the communist labor movement in the colonial period paid pro forma attention to women's special demands, and Chŏnp'yŏng's platform in the immediate postliberation years elaborated on them, in actual strikes women's issues seldom took central stage even when women workers constituted the majority of strikers.[13] And the issue of gender equity in the union movement itself never bubbled up to the surface.

The new industrial relations system consolidated by the mid-1950s inherited practices of a gender-segregated labor market and a sexual division of labor from the colonial times, although the ethnic tensions and ethnic discrimination of the Japanese colonial era were now gone. During the colonial period, as we saw in the case of colonial rubber industry, women workers were channeled into certain lower paid, female-dominated industries and jobs as a disposable temporary workforce while male workers monopolized better paid, more secure jobs with opportunities for promotion and career employment. The wartime Sanpō ("industrial patriotic") mobilization campaigns, while introducing meaningful changes in the way companies treated manual workers in order to induce their "dedicated labor," seem to have mounted little challenge to the gendered nature of workplace hierarchy.

As revealed in chapter 4, one of the enduring legacies of Sanpō experiments in colonial Korea, in addition to workers' heightened sense of their worth as an equal partner to management engaged in patriotic industrial service for the nation, was the entrenchment of certain wage practices, especially a seniority-based pay scheme in male-dominated sectors and the notion of wages sufficient to provide for family livelihood. In Japan, as historian Andrew Gordon has shown, the Sanpō experiment of the late 1930s and early 1940s encouraged active discussions among the elite—government officials, business managers, and labor specialists—on proper wage schemes that would induce hard labor from the workforce and reduce labor conflict, and over time a new wage structure that put greater weight on workers' livelihood needs took root in key industrial sectors. This "living" or "livelihood" (*seikatsu* in Japanese, *saenghwal* in Korean) wage rewarded and favored senior, skilled men as age and seniority functioned as the best proxy for life-cycle needs of workers, who were understood as male heads of the household.[14] Thus the Sanpō movement in Japan introduced fundamental changes in the wage structure away from output- or job-based pay and toward the family livelihood needs of workers, although actual practices were restricted largely to the provision of "family allowances." Japanese workers adopted the vocabulary of the need-based, living wage through the Sanpō experience, and the demand for a living wage became the central thrust of wage offensives in post-surrender Japan.[15]

The "living wage" concept had a long history in the West and stood on the patriarchal assumption that an individual male worker should be allowed to build a bourgeois family and match the ideal of a manly man/citizen by earning a wage sufficient to keep a wife and children at home. In the case of Western countries, a sizable literature exists that delves into the gender and political implications of the family living wage ideal.[16] Hilary Land, for example, examines various arguments for and against the policies of family wage and family allowance in nineteenth- and early twentieth-century Great Britain. She shows how, despite feminist voices, the debates on wages, interconnected with various issues of social welfare and tax systems, were informed to a great extent by conservative gender notions and the prevailing assumption that it was not normal for women workers to work after marriage. The topic of women's wages also received much attention in this Western literature, work that illuminates the patriarchal bases of maintaining lower wages for women.[17]

Historical conditions behind the emergence of the livelihood wage concept in Japan differed from those of Western countries, although both the Western and Japanese concepts were based on the male breadwinner worker model. Within the sizable literature on industrial wages in Japan, the connection between the wartime Sanpō experiment and the postwar living-wage demands of unions has been explored by some scholars, including historians Andrew Gordon and Laura E. Hein and economist Saguchi Kazurō. Saguchi argues that the idea of a need-based wage system or living wages gained strength under wartime government wage control measures as it was deemed important to provide economic stability to the emperor's "industrial warriors." According to his study, in practice the idea was often institutionalized in the form of "family allowances," and almost all the "industrial" and "transportation" companies with more than a thousand employees offered family allowances by July 1942.[18] Hein's study of Japanese energy industry workers and Gordon's study on the evolution of Japanese labor relations show the conditions and context for the emergence of an influential wage formula, called the "Densan wage structure," in late 1946, which quickly became the model in the wage negotiations of Japanese organized labor.[19] This innovative wage system was successfully pushed through in a major labor dispute by Densan (Nihon Denki Sangyō Rōdō Kumiai, or Japanese Electric Power Industry Labor Federation) and firmly established the principle that wages should be linked to workers' livelihood needs. And both Gordon and Hein note the direct linkage between the Densan wage plan and the wartime bureaucratic proposals for a livelihood wage system.[20] Although managers by the early 1950s were able to erode the power of the Japanese union movement and the influence of the Densan wage system, reasserting the firm's profitability and productivity as key factors in wage determination, some early postwar gains, including the significant weight given to individual attributes of age and experience in calculating wages, endured.[21]

The process through which the concept of the living wage became hegemonic in the union movement in Korea has not been fully studied. The trajectory of the concept in Korea is more difficult to follow since Korea, coming out of decades of Japanese colonial rule, was subjected to an intense US effort to remold the country into its own image, which included areas of economic planning and labor relations. What is clear is that in postliberation Korea the vocabulary of the "livelihood wage" in union demands and a wage structure prioritizing individual attributes of seniority and age had already become well established in the industrial scene, at male-dominated companies in particular. Korean managers had an extremely difficult time in their efforts to "rationalize" the deep-rooted seniority-based wage culture during the 1960s. This rising consensus of the need-based, "livelihood wage" ideal in Korea needs some explanation because such a wage scheme had serious consequences for the ways women's wages were understood.

The similarities between the wage cultures of Japan and South Korea after World War II point to the shared wartime Sanpō experiences. Again, the question is how significant the wartime discussions and practices of a livelihood wage were in shaping Korean workers' expectations and managerial practices. Sociologist Sin Wŏnch'ŏl cautions against the conventional assumption of a full-scale deployment of the Sanpō movement in the Korea colony and emphasizes that the campaign in Korea, unlike in Japan, was mostly forced on the society from the top down, led by the police and the colonial government. Yet his study reveals a significant degree of ideological inculcation at workplaces during wartime, despite his assertion that its effect on Koreans was "very limited."[22] The case study by sociologist Lim Chai Sung (Im Ch'aesŏng) of Sanpō practices at the government-owned Korean Railway shows the significant extent to which the Sanpō ideology of labor-management cooperation for the emperor was practiced at the company. The Korean Railway was one of the militarily essential workplaces that implemented wartime labor control measures systematically. "Patriotic units" on the shop floor at Korean Railway discussed ways to improve work on a regular basis, replicating a key Sanpō practice of Japan.[23] Wartime labor control in Korea was extended even to worker households in some cases, according to Lim's study, which reveals the extensive scope of ideological inculcation at the time.[24]

As Sin Wŏnch'ŏl argues, despite sweet talk about honorable work and equal partnership between workers and managers in the "holy" war, it is reasonable to estimate that the colonial government and companies in Korea, mostly of Japanese capital, were disinclined to offer substantial material incentives to workers, especially Korean workers who were ethnically discriminated against. Even so, considering the intensity and the scope of the propaganda campaign, which permeated the whole society down to the village and household level for at least seven years beginning in 1938, and taking into account the fact that colonial authorities demanded not passive but "voluntary" and active expression of loyalty from each individual in everyday life during this *Kōminka undō* (movement to create imperial subjects) period, it is hard to imagine that total-war imperial discourses did not have considerable influence. This seems to be especially true of aspects that were actually appealing to workers like the nobility of workers' patriotic mission and a need-based wage as reward, which seem to have left indelible marks in the perceptions of affected workers and the language they used. At least at some large and strategically important heavy-industry factories and mines in Korea, where Korean and Japanese employees worked side by side, that seems to be the case.[25]

Scholars who have examined the wage structure in the 1950s and 1960s of large South Korean firms all highlight a pronounced characteristic of assigning a very strong weight to seniority in wage calculations.[26] Labor scholar T'ak Hŭijun sees, albeit without direct historical inquiry, that tendency as a remnant of colonial experiences that had to be rooted out. According to him, not only at large companies but even at small- and medium-sized companies the tendency for a seniority-based wage system was "extremely strong," and youth and women workers suffered as a result. Sin Wŏnch'ŏl's study shows how difficult it was for companies with a well-established seniority-based wage culture to introduce job-based pay under government initiatives in the 1960s.[27] Economist Hwang Ŭinam, in his detailed analysis of South Korean wage structures and policies, notes the long history of family allowances in Korea, which, according to him, largely evolved to supplement deficiencies in the wage levels of breadwinner male workers.[28]

Workers in postliberation South Korea phrased their wage demands in terms of livelihood needs all along.[29] But union documents and contemporary news reports reveal that it was in the mid-1960s that "Secure the Livelihood Wage" became the core slogan in labor disputes led by major national unions. Until 1972 union struggles for raises were steered by national industrial unions, not the FKTU headquarters, whose role was restricted to collecting basic data and providing policy-related support.[30] The highlighting of the livelihood wage demand in union offensives began with the National Railway Workers' Union in a struggle that started in October 1963, and in January 1964 the Communication Workers' Union and the Monopoly (tobacco and ginseng) Workers' Union joined in the struggle.[31] The Chemical Workers' Union formed a task force for the struggle to secure the "minimum livelihood wage" in January 1964. And the KSEC shipbuilding union launched a struggle in April 1965 under the slogan of "Secure the Minimum Livelihood Wage!"[32]

It is not clear how the term "livelihood wage" (*saenghwalgŭp* or *saenghwal imgŭm*) became a common slogan of major union offensives at this particular point in time. In addition to the legacy of the wartime industrial practices we examined earlier, a possible path of transmission of the living wage ideal was through contacts with the international union movement. Taehan Noch'ong was a founding member of the International Confederation of Free Trade Unions (ICFTU), established in 1949, and it actively participated in union diplomacy. Korean unionists were also exposed to the discourse of the International Labor Organization (ILO), which in the process of preparing for an Asian conference in 1947 circulated its recommendation of instituting "living wages or a minimum wage system that could secure an appropriate level of livelihood."[33] The US government actively supported and promoted exchanges between South Korean and US unions during the 1960s, including student exchanges and visits by US labor specialists to the FKTU.[34] Another source of inspiration for the living wage–centered offensive might have come from the Japanese union movement, but not much is known about the nature and extent of exchanges between South Korean and Japanese unions before the Korea-Japan Normalization Treaty of 1965. The FKTU unions sent delegates to meetings and seminars of international labor organizations, including those held at Tokyo, even before the 1965 treaty, as evidenced by FKTU's annual activity reports.[35] Industrial unions of South Korea and Japan began to forge active relationships after the 1965 treaty, but it is also possible that even before the treaty Korean unionists closely followed, through union diplomacy and media reports, developments in the Japanese labor scene, including the Densan wage system.

A more immediate stimulus for the mid-1960s union offensive may have been the wage-cutting efforts of the Park Chung Hee government, which passed the

Wage Control Law for Employees of the Government-Managed Enterprises in September 1961 to streamline wage systems at large enterprises under its control. This law effectively reduced wages for 47,500 employees, mostly better paid male workers in mining, electric power, transportation, banking, shipbuilding, chemical, and metal industries, and provoked a concerted, long-term, and eventually successful struggle to repeal the law by the FKTU.[36] It was a rare large-scale mobilization of major unions against the Park government, and that multiyear struggle had the effect of stirring up union activism at many affected sites. Labor's livelihood-wage offensive that began in late 1963 and lasted throughout the remainder of the decade seems to have been connected to this struggle between the state and the nation's top unions.

Regardless of the specific route of dissemination, South Korean unionists clearly embraced the concept of the "livelihood wage," and when they were ready to hoist it as the central demand by the mid-1960s, the living wage ideal had the power to galvanize widespread support by workers in male-dominated, unionized sectors like the railways and the shipbuilding industry. To back up their claim of regular raises, unions in the 1960s routinely attached series of statistical data, produced by the government or the Bank of Korea or obtained through union surveys, to their official demands to the company. Included in these data sets, geared toward proving the deficiency of current wages to meet the material needs of breadwinner workers, were national wholesale and retail price indices, price data on major daily necessities, and union surveys of average monthly cost of living in member households, whose average size during the 1960s was between five and six.

Thus, by the mid-1960s the idea of setting wages in tune with the needs of male breadwinner workers became strongly established in the South Korean trade union movement and this wage discourse of organized labor, standing on the male breadwinner model, had an effect of obscuring the issue of rampant wage discrimination by gender. A major business newspaper, *Maeil kyŏngje* (Daily Economics), explained to its readers in 1968 that the "livelihood wage"–type Korean wage system paid more wages to male workers because they were "by custom responsible for the livelihood of the family."[37] An emotional statement by railway unionists during the 1963–64 struggle to achieve the livelihood wage, addressed to "brothers and sisters of the railway," laid the logic bare by lamenting the "loss of face by heads of the household" that had resulted from workers' failure to secure the livelihood wage.[38] When the normative industrial worker was imagined as male, despite an inclusive gesture of mentioning "sisters," and when the male-centered discussion of wages was never challenged, the below-subsistence-level wages of women workers, who were often breadwinners, received marginal attention at best in the union movement.

The FKTU, while championing the family living wage ideal, avoided confronting the unsettling question of how women workers would fit into the framework of the livelihood wage demand. The national textile union, whose members were mostly female workers, attempted during the 1960s to move toward sector-wide wage negotiations, sorted into cotton spinning and weaving, silk reeling, and synthetic textile sectors, and to its credit began a discussion of what should be the basis of wage demands in the textile industry. Its conclusion was that a minimum cost of living (ch'oejŏ saenggyebi) should be the basis of wage demands, and with intellectual specialists' help the union in 1969 was able to present its calculation of a minimum cost of living for the first time.[39] That year the national textile union launched a major offensive to alleviate the troubling situation of extremely low wages among its women worker members, understood as the cause of increasing resistance from them.[40] In the union's justification of a 28.5 percent raise, the familiar discourse of securing family livelihood was, understandably, missing. We do not have studies analyzing gendered discourses of wage demands by unions of female-dominated industries. But it seems that discussions of women's wages were more closely associated with the issue of the minimum wage (ch'oejŏ imgŭm) than with the central goal of organized labor's annual offensive, the family livelihood wage.[41] An example of this gendered wage demand practice can be found in a wage negotiation at an electronics factory in 1978, documented by Robert Spencer. The union documents he obtained revealed that each union member on average had to "support 0.95 of a person from their wages," but the union demanded a 32.7 percent across-the-board raise from 44,100 wŏn (about $88) per month to meet the "need for the single worker living alone," set at 58,538 wŏn, or $117, per month.[42] Even after the Great Workers' Struggle of 1987 that empowered trade unions, when most democratized unions made strong demands for a family livelihood wage based on the average number of dependents, for female workers the majority of unions continued to present wage demands based on a single-person cost of living.[43]

In the developmental scheme of the Park Chung Hee regime, female and male workers were mobilized through gender-specific ways. The labor market was structured to mobilize young women into lower-paid jobs labeled "unskilled," while channeling men into better paid, heavy-industry jobs with ample incentives including promotion ladders and job security.[44] Such bifurcated mobilization paths by gender meant that most textile workers were young and unmarried and had at best two or three years of seniority, confirming the hegemonic view of women workers as those free of the burden of the breadwinner role.[45] Overall, the basic assumption on women's wages seems to have changed little since the time of the 1930–31 rubber strikes in Pyongyang. A statement made by a Pyongyang businessman at the time could resonate seamlessly in the 1960s labor scene in

South Korea: "Since a yŏgong has a man and she earns money on the side, it is no problem that her wage is low."[46]

The Death of "Miss Kim" and the Power of Small-Group Organizing

One way to gauge the social perception of yŏgong around 1960, before the beginning in earnest of rapid industrialization under Park Chung Hee, is through factory women characters in contemporary movies. Industrial worker characters, either male or female, rarely appeared in top-rated movies produced during the "golden age" of South Korean cinema, from the mid-1950s to the mid-1960s. This fact alone says much about a lack of social visibility and influence of industrial workers during the period. Many successful films of the era featured urban working-class or lower-middle-class families in plots centered on a sympathetic portrayal of struggling yet endearing father figures.[47] Factory jobs were sometimes hinted at as a desirable new prospect for the younger generation as in the case of the second daughter, Okhŭi, in *Coachman* (*Mabu*, 1961, directed by Kang Taejin), but the actual factory life of women workers was seldom visible in films.

An interesting exception is *Housemaid* (*Hanyŏ*, 1960), an acclaimed movie by director Kim Kiyŏng, which is today celebrated as one of the best films ever produced in Korea. *Housemaid* tackles the salient social desire for bourgeois family formation that gripped the upwardly mobile urban population in 1950s South Korea and reveals contemporary concerns and fears about changing class and gender relations. The bourgeois dream in the movie is represented by the ownership of a new Western-style two-story house and accompanying material goods like a piano and a television set. And, as in the colonial period, women characters are striving to get music lessons to accumulate the necessary cultural capital to claim modern bourgeois womanhood. *Housemaid*, as the title hints, highlights and warns against a potential underclass intrusion into this bourgeois dream by unfolding a horrifying plot of a lower-class young maid seducing the head of the household and blackmailing and attacking the whole family.

What is germane to our story is the portrayal of factory women characters in the movie. The husband teaches music to a group of yŏgong in a choir club at a textile company, which is depicted as an idealistic capitalist institution that offers many after-work cultural activities to its employees.[48] Women workers are presented as cheerful and proud working women. Initially these yŏgong characters show up in their work uniforms, but that brief scene soon shifts into a locker room scene in which women workers show off their stylish Western-style attire. Actual production work is not shown in the movie, and most of the factory scenes are set in two spaces, the choir club room with a piano that the male protagonist plays, and a neat and modern dormitory room shared by two women workers. A lead character among the yŏgong, "Miss Cho," played by top actress Ŏm Aengnan, develops a crush on the music teacher and opts to take private piano lessons from him. She then introduces a less sophisticated newbie yŏgong, implied to be one fresh from the countryside, to the music teacher to work as his housemaid, thereby starting, albeit unintentionally, the fateful process toward the ruination of his whole family.

Yŏgong "Miss Cho" is a beautiful, smart, and assertive character, completely devoid of any hint of victimization under exploitative factory labor. Only in one instance does the music teacher bring up her occupation by observing that Miss Cho's hands are "quite rough" because she "works with machines," to which she responds by asking, "Can I still learn to play the piano with these hands?" He answers by giving her some lotion to put on her hands. Miss Cho, despite her factory woman status, is not a person of poverty either; she can pay for piano lessons and offer a substantial sum of additional monthly pay to the yŏgong-turned-housemaid to entice her to work at the music teacher's house on her behalf. In comparison to the middle-class music teacher who desperately clings to his factory teaching job and gives private lessons to improve his family's livelihood, Miss Cho seems to be free of financial concerns and is driven by romantic urges more than anything else.

This positive portrayal of a yŏgong is hard to reconcile with the lower-class victim image of yŏgong that took root in the following decade. By the early 1970s the use of a derogatory term for factory women, *kongsuni* (literally "Suni"—a common lower-class girl's name—of the factory), spread widely in society, and the term "yŏgong" also acquired highly negative connotations. The yŏgong in *Housemaid* resonated more closely with the 1950s *kongjang kasinae* (factory girl) image of yŏgong we saw earlier, which conveyed a positive social appreciation of young women willing to shoulder the responsibility of family livelihood, than what the 1970s *kongsuni* moniker conveys. A major change in social perception of factory women seems to have occurred between the 1950s and the early 1970s.

An obvious factor behind the cheapening of yŏgong's worth was the explosive growth in the number of factory women that accompanied the massive-scale export drive of the Park Chung Hee government, which depended on utilizing cheap labor as the country's primary comparative advantage in the world market. Manufacturing sector employees made up only about 8 percent of the total employed population in 1963, but their share grew to 13.2 percent in 1970 and shot up to 22.8 percent by 1979. The number of women employed in manufacturing increased 232 percent from 179,000 in 1963 to 416,000 in 1970, and continued to grow during the decade to reach 1,219,000 in 1979.[49] Among 293,112 women manufacturing sector employees in 1970 working at factories with five or more workers, close to 54 percent, or 157,427 women, were hired in the industry category composed of textile, garment, and shoe industries.[50] To link women's cheap labor to domestic and foreign capital for export-oriented production, gigantic industrial complexes were established, including the Kuro Export Industrial Complex in Seoul, the first section of which opened in 1965, and the Masan Free Export Zone near Pusan, and the majority of the new generation of young female industrial workers toiled in these factory complexes, called *kongdan*.

The massive scale of female labor mobilization was part of an equally massive scale of rural-to-urban migration in this period. Between 1960 and 1975 about 6.86 million people migrated to cities from the countryside looking for better life and jobs, and between 1966 and 1970 annually about 600,000 were moving into cities.[51] Following rapid industrialization was an increasing urban-rural income gap in the 1960s and 1970s, which worried the government and led to the launching of a new rural revitalization campaign, called the New Village Movement (Saemaŭl undong), in the early 1970s to address the problem.[52] The situation of having acute food shortages in rural areas in the springtime, called the "barley hump" (*porit kogae*) because people starved until barley harvests were in, continued until as late as 1977, according to the testimony of O Wŏnch'ŏl, a key planner of Park Chung Hee's Heavy and Chemical Industrialization Plan of the 1970s.[53] Financially strapped rural families often sent their young daughters to cities to obtain factory or housemaid jobs and, in many cases, their remittances supported their male siblings' education. The hope was that an educated son would one day lift up the whole family's class position. In the 1970s the capital city of Seoul had some two hundred thousand live-in housemaids, many of whom suffered harsh treatment, extremely low pay, and frequent cases of sexual violence.[54] Migrant women in the 1960s and 1970s hoped to get out of housemaid work and land a factory job and competition for entering large factories was stiff.

In conjunction with massive urbanization and the influx of rural people into major cities, the increasing affluence of emerging middle-class families and the advent of a consumer society began to produce significant cultural and social changes in South Korean society. In the mid-1960s we see early debates on new concepts like the "middle class" (*chungsanch'ŭng*) and the "masses" (*taejung*) appearing in the media. While conservative gender values persisted, people's attitudes toward money making and consumption changed rapidly, shaped by the "growth-first" ideology and economic policies of the developmental state. As the Park regime's promise of economic development materialized for a sizable segment of upwardly mobile middle-class people, the sympathetic perceptions of lower-class people that the *kyun* (equality) ideology inspired in past decades faded fast, replaced by a new status hierarchy determined by material wealth.

This solidifying culture of class-based discrimination in turn provoked fierce resistance among manual workers seeking social recognition of their worth and dignity.

Reflecting this conservative turn toward excluding the lower-class population as losers in the developmental race, by the early 1970s the usage of pejorative terms (ŭnŏ) kongdori (factory boy named Tori) and kongsuni (factory girl named Suni) spread in mainstream society. These terms referred to young factory workers toiling in kongdan, export-oriented factory complexes.[55] Calling them "Tori" or "Suni" connoted both their lower-class status and their preadult stage.[56] Kongdori was a demeaning term that implied a denial of the adult head-of-the-household status for a male industrial worker, but the use of the term was much more limited compared to that of kongsuni, reflecting the higher status in the workplace hierarchy and in society of male workers compared to women workers. The pejorative term kongsuni was widely in use in the 1970s and 1980s, to whose unambiguously negative connotations female workers reacted in intensely emotional ways. Kongsuni was also a term deeply colored by a sexualized view of the factory woman, one who, in the words of labor historian Ruth Barraclough, "is easily approachable, unprotected by social laws of etiquette and strict rules of honorific address," and thus vulnerable and morally suspect. Barraclough points out that South Korean women "who refused the cover of patriarchal protection, or were too poor to benefit from it, were huntable creatures," and when they asserted their rights as workers, management frequently unleashed "violence that often turned sexual."[57]

As the kongsuni moniker prevailed in society, the term "yŏgong" also came to be degraded and equated to kongsuni. Because their peers were attending secondary schools while they sweated in factories, the social distance between "normal young women" and kongsuni or yŏgong was conspicuously matched to the gap in educational attainment. Formal education, or rather lack thereof, became a much-resented marker of factory girl status.[58] The Park government encouraged companies to offer after-work secondary education, which helped draw young girls with strong educational aspirations into factories. Night schools that provided a curriculum for high school equivalency tests attracted many female workers who struggled to juggle arduous factory labor and after-work study in the hope of one day entering college. Alternative night schools that politically conscious university students developed became a site through which many female worker activists experienced moments of awakening to class and political realities.[59]

Many women participants of the minju labor movement testified how the term kongsuni casually hurled at them hurt them deeply. Chŏng Hyangja, a silk-reeling worker and Catholic labor activist, recalled how much she resented the commonly used phrase "as a mere kongsuni" (kongsuni chuje e), thrown at her when she protested prevalent sexual harassment at work.[60] Women workers at Control Data, an electronics assembly factory producing computer memory chips, resisted the company's move into the Kuro Export Industrial Complex in 1974 because they, mostly high school graduates and better educated than most yŏgong, did not want to be seen as *kongsuni*.[61] Even as late as 1991, the term maintained enough power to hurt. A female shoe industry worker in Pusan, Kwŏn Migyŏng, committed suicide in protest of exploitative speedup practices and managers' use of abusive language, including *kongsuni*, as a labor control measure (see chapter 6). She left a suicide note on her arm explaining her decision to die in order to speak out. In the note she cried, "My name is Migyŏng, not *kongsuni*!"[62]

While the number of factory women increased dramatically and social perception of them deteriorated under the Park government's ambitious and intensive economic modernization drive, women industrial workers' struggle against exploitative treatment at work continued to break out. The media, however, remained largely silent on female workers' suffering and activism. The emerging hegemony of the growth-first ideology in society meant that a strong social consensus existed on the unavoidability of a significant degree of exploitation of industrial workers as a necessary condition for national success. The suffering of female workers especially was understood as a sacrifice, one not intolerable albeit pitiful, for national economic development. Although major labor disputes broke out in female-dominated industries like textile and electronics in the late 1960s, it was not until the public suicide by self-immolation in November 1970 of a male garment worker Chun Tae-il (1949–70) in downtown Seoul that elite society and the media turned their attention to the female labor question in a meaningful way. The sweatshop working conditions and inhumane level of exploitation of teenage female workers in numerous small garment factories in the Peace Market garment district in Seoul, about which Chun and his fellow activists had tried hard to tell the larger society for years, were finally exposed through his tragic death and social reaction to his story was swift.[63]

We can access aspects of Chun Tae-il's journey to become a committed labor activist through diary entries and drafts of fictional stories he left behind. These documents reveal an exceptionally intelligent and perceptive thinker who grasped fundamental problems in the human conditions under capitalism, a kind of organic intellectual who grew out of his non-elite background. Before Chun resorted to the final option of sacrificing his own life for suffering young female workers, he, together with male worker friends, tried various ideas to pressure factory owners to change their inhumane labor practices and abide by the nation's labor laws and to make the larger society pay attention to their grievances.[64] Included in Chun's ideas was a model company plan, a plan to establish a company that followed all the provisions of the Labor Standards Act and still made a profit. Chun's model company plan was meant to demonstrate to the whole society that it was possible to run successful companies while treating workers well. Chun's vision for a desirable capitalist system that accommodates workers' needs, a system he believed the Labor Standards Act upheld, resonates with the 1930s dream of building worker-owned production cooperatives among Pyongyang's rubber workers. Chun Tae-il of the Peace Market in 1970 and Kang Churyong's worker friends of the Peace Rubber factory in Pyongyang in 1931 harbored similar dreams of a human-faced modernization, although they lived under quite dissimilar historical circumstances.

The intensity and swiftness of responses to Chun's suicide protest among university students and progressive Christian intellectuals was one product of a tense political environment before the 1971 presidential election and at the dawn of the *Yusin* (revitalization) constitutional revision in 1972 that began full-blown authoritarian rule by Park Chung Hee. Chun Tae-il's death occurred at the precise moment when the relationship between the dissident movement and the Park government was changing rapidly and the emerging democracy movement of the time, which began to criticize the developmental economic policies of the increasingly authoritarian regime, was beginning the process of discovering and reconceptualizing working-class people as potential allies in an epic battle against the regime. Chun's self-immolation, as many prominent dissident intellectuals and worker activists have testified, marked a transformative moment in their lives and their thinking. The tragic incident itself and the outpouring of support from dissident intellectuals and student movement activists engendered heightened media attention on the case. Media coverage and ensuing investigative reports dramatically exposed consequences of the celebrated capitalist developmental strategy of the Park regime to the public through images of the extreme suffering of teenage female workers.

Although media interest in sweatshop working conditions subsided after the April 1971 election, in which Park Chung Hee narrowly beat opposition leader Kim Dae-Jung (Kim Taejung), activists in the democracy movement and worker activists helped keep Chun's memory alive. An authoritative biography of Chun Tae-il, *The Critical Biography of Chun Tae-il* (*Chŏn T'aeil p'yŏngjŏn*), written in the mid-1970s by student activist turned human rights lawyer Cho Yŏngnae and first published in 1983, circulated widely among activists and workers as a manuscript before publication and later as a banned book. It became a bible of social movement activists and inspired a generation of university students and industrial workers to commit themselves to the cause of labor under the severe authoritarian repression of the 1980s.[65]

I have written elsewhere about the memory politics surrounding Chun Tae-il's death and the subsequent exaltation of the Chun Tae-il spirit in the labor movement. I analyzed how Cho Yŏngnae's biography defined Chun's life and death in the political context of the opposition movement against Park Chung Hee's *Yusin* authoritarian rule and what aspects of workers' aspirations and agency were left invisible in his book as a result. Standing in part on the tremendous success of the biography in providing the moral justification and the imperative to act in resistance, the Chun Tae-il story became the foundational story of the minju labor movement. The biography's narrative continues to reverberate in today's South Korean society, and Chun's death is acknowledged widely in South Korea as the "single spark" that ignited a new militant and democratic labor movement and the worker-intellectual alliance that buttressed it.[66] The historical account of the Cheonggye (Chŏnggye) Garment Workers' Union captures this understanding in the title of its prologue: "Everything started from him" ("Modŭn kŏsŭn kŭ saram ŭrobutŏ sijak toeŏtta").[67]

The "beginning" of the new minju labor movement thus defined has had the effect of making the history of the growth of women worker activism in the 1960s before Chun's death much less appreciated than it should be in the memories and narratives in the labor movement and in the study of labor history. That is because the concept of the "1970s minju labor movement" presumes a blank canvas for post-Chŏnp'yŏng South Korean labor history and begins a proud new labor history with Chun's martyrdom, making the pre-1970 worker activism of both men and women basically irrelevant. Chun's martyrdom occurred on the periphery of South Korea's industrial development, not in an export-oriented factory complex, not at a heavy-industry shop, nor in an organized textile mill. The exploited female workers Chun wanted to protect through his death were teenage sweatshop workers located largely outside of the industrial relations system and labor law protection. They were in the periphery of South Korea's industrial development. Highlighting the peripheral sector as if what was going on there represented the status of the South Korean union movement as a whole helped erase the history of activism and accomplishments at unionized workshops up to that point. The origin narrative exalting martyr Chun Tae-il has also affected the ways in which stories of women worker–led labor struggle in the post-1970 period were told and recorded. Highlighted in the conventional narrative of the minju labor movement is the power of the "Chun Tae-il spirit" and the sacrificial deeds of intellectual activists who responded to Chun's call for help by forging a *nohak yŏndae* (worker-student/intellectual alliance). This line of labor history narrative does not do justice to the female worker activism that continued to develop in the 1960s and 1970s and was not wholly governed by Chun Tae-il's death and subsequent intellectual praxis in the labor movement, although the impact of both were indeed significant.

One way to glimpse the numerous erased stories of pre- and post-1970 activism among female workers is to contemplate a case involving a "Miss Kim" in the southwestern city of Kwangju. Her suicide protest in 1962, unlike that of Chun Tae-il, failed to garner the social attention she desired, yet it contributed to the rise of a grassroots movement among fellow women workers in the area. Not much is known about "Kim-*yang*" (Miss Kim), not even her first name. The only access to her story is through the official historical account of the JOC (Jeunesse Ouvrière Chrétienne, or Young Christian Workers) Korea, which briefly mentions how the suicide of a certain textile worker, "Miss Kim," was a catalyst for the early development of the JOC movement among women workers in Kwangju.[68]

Textile worker-members of the JOC Korea were the ones who endeavored to discover the meaning of Kim's suicide, and their action alerts us to the importance of understanding the early history of Christian labor activism in South Korea. Understanding the relationship between the JOC movement, a Catholic lay apostle movement among young workers, and women worker activism is also important because the JOC movement, together with night schools and Protestant organizations, including the Christian Academy and the urban industrial mission (UIM) institutions, played a very significant role as "the incubator for female labor activists" in the late 1960s and the 1970s in South Korea.[69]

The JOC movement was started by Joseph Cardijn of Belgium in the 1920s as a Catholic alternative to the then-powerful socialist trade union movement in Europe. It grew into a well-organized international movement with millions of members in dozens of countries by 1957 when South Korean Catholics adopted it.[70] The JOC Korea (Han'guk Kat'ollik Nodong Chŏngnyŏnhoe) was officially launched with a "fighter" (*t'usa*) declaration ritual of nine female nurses held at a Mass on November 16, 1958, at the Myŏngdong Cathedral of Seoul, which was witnessed by Cardinal Cardijn himself and the vice president of the International JOC. The first *t'usa* declaration of male members followed in April 1960. Following the organization of the Seoul JOC Association in October 1960, many JOC organizations emerged in the country in subsequent years, including one in Kwangju in November 1961, a little less than a year before Miss Kim's death.[71]

The term *t'usa* was often used in the Protestant nationalist movement in the colonial period, and the media in that era applied it only in rare cases to women activists. Women workers who joined the JOC movement were at first a little taken aback by this unfamiliar military-style term, as JOC activist Pak Sunhŭi later recalled.[72] But soon women workers eagerly embraced the term and the meaning associated with it, the devoted apostle "who marches in the front line" following God's will, in Pak's understanding. The calling of each JOC member to become a *t'usa*, a position that lent respect and recognition, seems to have had a strong appeal to women workers who joined the JOC. Cardijn's JOC movement put inordinate emphasis on the principle of autonomous development by workers themselves, believing in the capacity of young workers to evangelize themselves by helping people around them in everyday life following Jesus Christ's footsteps. A central training method of the JOC was a practice called a "Review of Everyday Life" (*saenghwal pansŏng*), in which workers were to follow a three-step process of "see, judge, act." JOC Korea organized workers into small teams ranging from four to ten members each, led by a *t'usa* leader.[73] On the team, workers shared their experiences in life and at work while engaging in a variety of activities, and members often developed tight-knit "communities" (*kongdongch'e*) in which they enjoyed a long-lasting, sibling-like relationships, according to their testimonies.[74] It was a movement method geared toward ensuring the growth and empowerment of each worker member, which was quite different from the vanguard-led organizing tactics of the 1930s communist red union movement. JOC-trained worker-activists self-identified problems around them ("see"), made judgments on the nature of the problem among themselves ("judge"), and committed themselves to a course of action they decided on for the resolution of the problem ("act"). In Cardijn's words, "this kind of change in the everyday life of individual members of the JOC is greater than any generic revolution."[75] The belief was that each member's personal growth would bring about changes in their environs, and it would eventually lead to meaningful social changes. "Consciousness-raising" (*ŭisikhwa*) in JOC understanding meant "seeing the world in Jesus's eyes."[76]

The small group organizing that tapped into workers' shared experiences of hardship and unjust treatment in everyday life bred strong solidarity and devotion among worker members. It became the distinctive and very successful method of nurturing worker consciousness and solidarity in 1970s minju unions.[77] The first instance of a minju union that applied the small group method was the Cheonggye Garment Workers' Union, created in the wake of Chun Tae-il's death. In the initial phase of the union, the role of a JOC female *t'usa*, Chŏng Insuk, was crucial in building a critical mass for the union. Close to 90 percent of workers in the Peace Market were female, but the union leadership was monopolized by men. In such a situation the role of the Women's Department (Punyŏbu) was deemed crucial, but two women workers who stepped into the role quit one after another, having found that reaching out to female workers scattered in close to six hundred small workshops in the garment district was extremely taxing.[78] On the worker side, it was not easy to approach the union either. Yi Sukhŭi, a garment worker, recalled how she had to give up the idea of joining the union when she gathered up the courage and visited the union office during lunchtime, because the presence of the roomful of male union officials was intimidating.[79] After hearing a moving speech by Chun Tae-il's mother, Yi Sosŏn, at a church, Chŏng Insuk visited the union, together with the female president of the JOC national association, Yun Sunnyŏ, who enticed Chŏng to consider the role of Women's Department chair in order to help the Cheonggye Garment Union prosper.[80] Once assuming that position in May 1971, Chŏng introduced the union to the small-group system of the JOC, and by the end of the year she was able to organize eight teams with 130 members.

By October 1972 the number of small-group teams in the Peace Market increased to fifteen, and members of these teams became the core force in the Cheonggye Garment Union's movement.[81] The transformative impact of small-group activities on worker members is attested in many participant testimonies.[82] Chŏng Insuk encouraged women workers, many of whom were playing the breadwinner role. "Listen," she said, "we are all heads of the household responsible for family livelihood. We need to have pride in ourselves. Aren't we, who provide for the family, awesome people indeed?" Yi Sukhŭi remembered how deeply the small-group experience moved and changed her: "I really liked the fact that people who labor in factories can become good friends and develop a relationship in which we console and encourage each other. I began to have pride, understanding that to live the life of a worker [nodongja] in this land is not a shameful thing."[83]

Another important aspect of the JOC movement for our story is its emphasis on gender equality, which also stemmed from the focus on self-development of activist subjectivity among workers. Pak Sunhŭi believed that the greatest merit of the JOC movement was the "equal status" given to men and women in the organization.[84] Following the international JOC movement rules, JOC Korea established a separate organization for female members, called the JOCF (Jeunesse Ouvrière Chrétienne Feminine, or Kat'ollik Nodong Yŏja Chŏngnyŏnhoe) in 1961, after which time JOC associations were represented by a duo of one male and one female president. The idea was that such an arrangement would allow women members to speak up more freely and help nurture women's leadership skills. *A 50-Year Record of the JOC Korea* celebrates that practice as a pioneering move in a conservative society aiming at "securing the dignity and human rights of women." Applying their usual method of "see, judge, act," JOC women workers "saw" the accusation of the larger society that women of the JOC were "unfeminine" and seriously considered the matter as a key problem. A 1967 statement by the female chair of the Seoul diocese JOC association, Chŏn Chisuk, hints at the "judgment" JOC women came to hold on this issue. Contrasting two memorable yet starkly opposite women characters created by Norwegian playwright Henrik Ibsen—Solveig in *Peer Gynt* and Nora in *A Doll's House*—Chŏn beseeched women to take the position of Nora, who criticized patriarchal men, instead of following Solveig, who embraced patriarchal arrangements as fate. In this way JOC women workers learned to confront issues that "puzzled" and "tormented" them, including gender issues, and they grew to become confident *t'usa* who spoke truth to power and reached out to their workmates and less fortunate souls around them, people like bus girls.[85]

In Kwangju, the capital city of South Chŏlla Province, the first JOC team was born in November 1961, organized by fifteen female workers of Chŏnnam Spinning and Weaving and Ilsin Spinning and Weaving.[86] In late 1962 JOC members "saw" the suicide of twenty-five-year-old textile worker "Kim" at Chŏnnam Spinning and Weaving as an investigable issue because it was a death related to her union activities.[87] They visited the union, talked to Kim's close friends, and gathered "sufficient" corroborating evidence. Kim, who had worked at the factory for about seven years, was active in union affairs despite continuing harassment by managers. She was trusted by her fellow workers. A manager, seizing on a mistake made by a worker under Kim's supervision, harshly censured and insulted Kim to the extent of slapping her on the face. Kim allegedly decided to sacrifice her life for "current colleagues and all other workers," consumed a large quantity of vinegar, and soon died at a hospital. Despite the evidence they had gathered, because of insurmountable pressure from the company the JOC members regrettably decided against pursuing the case further.

This investigative effort in 1962 by Kwangju's JOC members, although it failed in engendering a worker alliance to fight against the managerial injustice that brought the suicide protest of one worker, had the broad impact of activating the JOC movement in the region and solidifying the movement's orientation toward labor issues.[88] In the spring of 1963 JOC members in Chŏnju, the capital city of North Chŏlla Province, strove to establish a regional union of textile workers as an alternative to the existing FKTU-affiliated union at Chŏnbuk Silk Reeling, which was resented as ŏyong, meaning doing the bidding of the company. Workers at the factory, in alliance with those at nearby Samyang Wool and supported by the Catholic diocese of Chŏnju, fought for six months and succeeded in founding the alternative union in September 1963, despite various maneuvers by the company to thwart the move.[89] In March 1964, seventeen months after Miss Kim's death, workers at Chŏnnam Spinning and Weaving and Ilsin Spinning and Weaving rose up against the powerful textile business interest the two companies represented and demanded a raise.[90]

The unfulfilled wish of Kwangju's women JOC activists to generate a wider alliance and social interest in women textile workers' suffering in 1962 was finally realized through a major textile dispute on Kanghwa Island near Seoul between the island's twenty-one textile companies and their workers. Many of these textile workers became members of a newly established JOC on the island, and in 1967 they began to organize unions, beginning with the Simdo Textile union. A massive union-busting campaign by well-organized and powerful local business association and government authorities ensued.[91] This time the whole Catholic order, from Bishop (later Cardinal) Kim Suhwan to the local parish priest, was ready to be mobilized for the workers' cause, and social movement forces stood behind female union workers, reflecting the progress that had been made by that time in the democracy movement against the Park government's developmental politics. In the official history of JOC Korea this Kanghwa textile dispute of 1967–68 is narrated as the historic turning point in JOC history in Korea. That dispute confirmed the Catholic Church's commitment to act for social justice and brought about significant changes in the identity, the mode of existence, and the scope of operation of the JOC movement.[92]

Paralleling the JOC movement, Protestant orders also began their work among industrial workers in the late 1950s, beginning with the Presbyterian (Jesus) Church of Korea (Yesugyo Changnohoe, or Yejang) in 1957.[93] Originally conceived as "industrial evangelism" (*sanŏp chŏndo*) to expand their popular base, committees set up by churches reached out to the management of major companies in the country, and some companies and government agencies were eager to cooperate with them, understanding that Christian teachings could promote industrial peace and be useful in disciplining workers.[94] By the late 1960s South Korean Protestant churches were embracing a new approach called an "urban industrial mission." It was partly a response to the overall lukewarm responses the "industrial evangelism" approach had received from workers, but international developments including the Bangkok meeting of the Asian Christian Council in 1968 were also influential. The council resolved to uphold the approach of the "urban mission" (*tosi sŏn'gyo*) and "industrial mission" (*sanŏp sŏn'gyo*) and move away from the previous focus on evangelism and individual salvation.[95] Various Protestant churches established regional Tosi Sanŏp Sŏn'gyohoe (urban industrial mission, or UIM) and coordinating bodies in the 1970s, which worked in cooperation with JOC associations.[96] By around 1973, facing increasingly brutal labor suppression policies of the Park government, UIMs began to collide head-on with government authorities, and the Catholic Church also sharpened its criticism of the government on behalf of suffering JOC workers.[97]

Entering the 1970s a "small-group" method, influenced in large measure by Saul Alinsky's organizing technique and Paulo Freire's educational philosophy centering on "conscientization" (*ŭisikhwa*), became a distinctive trend in Christian social movements in South Korea in general, and the UIM movement was no exception. Freire's ideas began to be introduced in Korea in the early 1970s, and Alinsky's works circulated among Korean activists beginning in the late 1960s.[98] In small-group practices of the early minju labor movement in the 1970s and early 1980s, the influence of Freire and Alinsky was particularly strong.[99] Among industrial missions, the Yŏngdŭngp'o UIM in Seoul and the Incheon UIM in particular played significant roles in organizing and supporting key minju unions, including unions at Tongil Spinning and Weaving, Pando Trading, and Wŏnp'ung Wool.[100] UIM's turn to small-group consciousness-raising in the early 1970s also meant a transition from a strategy of targeting male workers to that of organizing women workers, a change of strategies that resulted in part from their lack of success in reaching out to male workers.[101]

Thus, by the late 1960s both the UIM and the JOC were deeply involved in labor disputes and union organizing, in Seoul and surrounding areas in particular. JOC activism accelerated in the 1970s and "workplace teams" spread rapidly. During that decade about 150 JOC teams were in operation, and in many minju labor unions JOC members served as officials. The robust development of the JOC movement in the Kwangju region, which in some measure stood on Miss Kim's sacrifice in 1962, provides a good example of this 1970s development. JOC activist and silk reeler Chŏng Hyangja gathered together nineteen workers at Chŏnnam Silk Reeling and organized a JOC team. At the time there were about five JOC teams operating in the factory.[102] Chŏng, who became the president of the union local in 1975, emerged as one of the key leaders of the JOC movement in the Kwangju and South Chŏlla region, and later served as the head of the South Chŏlla headquarters of the national textile union, a rare case of a female worker playing such a prominent role in that heavily male-dominated institution. JOC small groups continued to multiply "like octopus tentacles" and functioned in close alliance with the area's night schools and the Kwangju YWCA. By the end of the 1970s JOC teams were operating in nine textile mills and three other workplaces in the area pursuing unionization or democratization of existing company-friendly unions.[103]

In extant labor archives it is difficult to uncover traces of "Miss Kim," and unlike Chun Tae-il she did not leave powerful writings for posterity. The conditions of the two deaths were also quite different, which partly answers the question of why her sacrifice was forgotten while Chun's came to define the minju labor movement. The political and social conditions that allowed Chun's suicide protest to galvanize activists of the budding democracy movement and brought them to plunge into an epochal alliance with industrial workers were lacking in Miss Kim's case, and unlike Chun, who immolated himself in bustling downtown street of Seoul, Kim died in a hospital in Kwangju, far away from the nation's capital, which was, and is, the center of the political, social, and cultural universe in South Korea.[104]

Another salient difference between the two protests by suicide was that while Chun Tae-il, a male worker, sacrificed his life on behalf of young female garment workers, "Miss Kim" struggled among fellow female workers and died for them. Following in Chun's footsteps, male intellectual activists and workers formed the dominant force in the ensuing garment workers' movement, albeit with spirited participation of female unionists. Inspired by Miss Kim's death, women workers of the JOC in Kwangju developed an autonomous grassroots movement that joined the growth of female activism from multiple locations to produce a robust Christian labor movement and a generation of women labor leaders. If Chun Tae-il was "a single spark" that ignited the wildfire of the democratic labor movement, as the mainstream activist narrative has it, Miss Kim represented one of the many small sparks lit by anonymous women workers at the dawn of the minju labor movement. Labor history narratives, shaped by the gender politics of the labor and democracy movements, highlight a historic single spark at the expense of numerous little sparks that evidenced the collective self-transformation of women industrial workers.

How these women who became involved in the labor movement via small group activities came to develop their perspectives on gendered discriminatory practices at work and in the movement is the focus of the next section, which surveys the progress made toward gender equality by women unionists in the minju union movement of the 1970s and 1980s.

Raising the Flag of Women's Liberation

In November 1976 a group of young female factory workers who had met in a labor education program at the Christian Academy decided to launch an organization of their own, and after much discussion they chose a name they thought best captured their collective vision. The name, the Society of Worker Flagbearers for Women's Liberation (Yŏsŏng Haebang Nodongja Kisuhoe), startled staffers in charge of labor and women's education programs at the Academy, Sin Illyŏng and Han Myŏngsuk. In the appellation workers came up with, seemingly subversive terms—*haebang* (liberation), *nodongja* (instead of *kŭlloja*, or "dedicated laborers"), and *kisu* (flagbearers)—were juxtaposed. The head of the Academy, Rev. Kang Wŏnyong, who wanted to steer the Academy movement carefully within the limits of the law so as not to provide excuses for government repression, was flabbergasted on hearing the name. But Academy activists in the end upheld the principle of respecting workers' own decisions with the condition that in public they would use a shortened name, Kisuhoe, as a cautionary measure. That trick, however, did not work well as pestering from government authorities continued on the use of subversive terms.[105]

Most significant and unprecedented in the naming decision was the fact that workers integrated the cause of women's liberation into their pledge to a life of committed labor activists. The bylaws of the society clearly delineated its goal as "the achievement of women's liberation through the labor movement." The society aimed at building solidarity among women workers and increasing their participation in the trade union movement. Kisuhoe members engaged themselves in discussions on gender issues that affected their workplaces and brainstormed ways to achieve women's liberation through the labor movement.[106] Kisuhoe participants—Pak Sunhŭi of Wŏnp'ung Wool (Kisuhoe president); Control Data unionists Yi Yŏngsun (Kisuhoe vice president), Yu Oksun, and Han Myŏnghŭi; Chang Hyŏnja and Cho Kŭmbun of Pando Trading; Yi Ch'onggak of Tongil Spinning and Weaving; Ch'oe Sunyŏng and Pak T'aeyŏn of YH Trading; and Yi Sukhŭi of the Cheonggye Garment Workers' Union—all fulfilled their pledge to live as "flagbearers" of the minju union movement in the 1970s and 1980s. Later, members of this group, together with a younger generation of women who lost their jobs during the 1980s because of their union activities, established the Women Workers' Association (Yŏsŏng Nodongjahoe) in Seoul and other cities, beginning in March 1987, with the dual goals of achieving "women's liberation" and "labor liberation" (*nodong haebang*).[107]

It is surprising to witness this level of heightened gender consciousness among women factory workers during the late 1970s because in conventional understandings, the 1970s have been viewed as a period when the gender question had not yet been taken up seriously in the democracy movement in general and in the minju union movement in particular—this despite the minju union movement being in large part led by women workers. And the existing literature on the minju union movement does not give sufficient attention to the extent to which women workers in the movement actually confronted gender-based discriminatory practices at work. Hagen Koo, in his classic account of the minju union movement, *Korean Workers*, states that feminist issues "were not important" in the 1970s and the early 1980s, and "feminist issues had been mute in virtually all labor disputes until the mid-1980s," although he does note a minor exception at Control Data, "where women workers fought to obtain maternity leave and fairer promotion opportunities."[108] Labor scholar Yu Kyŏngsun, who has written extensively about women workers' experiences in the 1970s minju union movement, also assesses that the movement in general "did not pay much attention to gender issues," except for several key minju unions, including those at Wŏnp'ung Wool and Control Data.[109]

It is true that the Kisuhoe perhaps represented the most advanced level of gender and class consciousness reached by women unionists in the mid-1970s, and Kisuhoe itself was gone by 1979 in the aftermath of the government persecution of Christian Academy education programs. But the impact of gender-oriented discussions through Kisuhoe on women union activists was much more substantial than the conventional understanding has it. At some unions led by Kisuhoe members, including the Control Data union and the Wŏnp'ung Wool union, we find gender-specific issues emerging as key objectives in union struggle in the late 1970s and early 1980s, at the time an unprecedented phenomenon in Korean labor movement history. Koo's argument that "in the 1970s and until the second part of the 1980s, the *majority* of Korean women workers did not possess a proper interpretive framework or language to understand their experiences in terms of dominant gender relations" is valid, but it is important to recognize and appreciate the fact that a vocal *minority* of women workers who actively participated in the minju union movement were rapidly developing a critical gender consciousness in the second half of the 1970s and acting on it in their union struggles.[110] This section, after briefly surveying the effect of Christian Academy labor education and the characteristics of the 1970s minju labor movement led by female workers, explores union activities that tackled gender-specific grievances of women workers at female-dominated workplaces.

It is abundantly clear from oral testimonies and written memoirs of worker activists in the minju union movement that Christian Academy education, together with training offered by UIMs, JOCs, and labor night schools, exerted a powerful influence on women workers.[111] The Christian Academy was founded in 1965 by Rev. Kang Wŏnyong with a goal of reforming South Korean society through research, open conversations, and social education. The post–World War II German Academy movement provided funding and the basic model.[112] Korean Christian Academy leaders defined the central problem that South Korean society faced at the time as that of "dehumanization" caused by political, economic, and social "polarization" (*yanggŭkhwa*), and they reasoned that the best way to reverse the trend of polarization and achieve "humanization" (*in'ganhwa*) of the society would be nurturing leaders of "intermediary groups" (*chunggan chiptan*).[113] The Academy's "intermediary group" education was launched in 1974 targeting five sectors, including the "Industrial Society" sector, which provided training for labor leaders.[114] The goal of Academy education was to spark self-awakening among participants by creating a thoroughly democratic environment and utilizing a task-based workshop format. Emphasis was placed on nurturing emotional bonding among participants through shared creative activities that peppered the four-night, five-day period of education, including singing, dancing, short plays, meditation, moments of silence, five-minute speech practice, and writing exercises in which each person composed his/her own epitaph and a letter to him/herself.

Many worker activists recall their experiences at the Academy as life-changing. Yi Chŏnghŭi, president of the Rocket Electrical union, the first female union local president in national metal union history, testified that Academy "conscientization" education awakened her to social problems, beginning with minor issues related to working conditions, and that she soon reached a realization that "we women" were treated unjustly vis-à-vis men. Academy-educated workers spearheaded building alliances with other unions across sectors and regions and also with social movement organizations and applied the "Academy method" they had learned to their own union activities, sometimes turning their dormitories into education camps.[115] Some graduates received another round of education after an interval of six or more months, and after the second-round program, staff members followed up with graduates with programs more tailored to individual needs. They sent workers relevant study materials and made calls to their shops to provide consultation and on-site education, which sometimes included closed-session seminars on gender issues and "social science" (a term meaning leftist) materials.[116] After successfully training more than six hundred worker leaders, the labor ("Industrial Society") education program was moving toward creating a labor college. But just as the impact of the Academy education became noticeable in the labor and farmers' movements, the Park regime decided to crush the Academy education program altogether in March 1979. Using a fabricated charge of anticommunist law violation, the Park government arrested six staff members, including Sin and Han, and subjected many trainees to harsh interrogation. The Christian Academy incident was a typical case in which the *Yusin* regime used the law and inhumane methods of interrogation that involved severe forms of torture of a physical, psychological, and sexual nature. The goal was to frame part of the democracy movement as treasonous operations connected to North Korean spy rings and also to create divisions in the movement.[117]

Foregrounding Kisuhoe women worker activists and their union struggle to end gender discrimination, albeit only a small part of the much larger and complex history of the 1970s minju union movement, brings into focus aspects of women worker activism in the minju union movement that have not been well known or appreciated in the existing literature.[118] Their actions can be best understood by examining how workers used the term "minju" and why they differentiated their minju unions from the rest of the unions under the FKTU umbrella. The term *minju nojo* (democratic unions) was a new coinage that emerged in the authoritarian political context of the 1970s, at a time when government authorities were putting maximum pressure on activist unions to conform to acceptable behavior. Already in the late 1960s the resistance of women factory workers was increasing rapidly, and disputes at foreign-invested firms in export sectors, exemplified by major disputes that engulfed Oak Electronics and Signetics Korea, worried policy planners eager to entice foreign investment.[119]

Labor activism had been rapidly gaining steam from around 1968 among both female and male workers in various sectors, including textile, mining, shipbuilding, and dockworkers, constituting a potential threat to Park Chung Hee's developmental plans.[120] Protests by unorganized workers, illustrated by Chun Tae-il's shocking self-immolation in 1970 and the occupation and arson of the Korean Air building in Seoul by four hundred Hanjin technicians in 1971, made an already tense economic and political situation even more volatile. In response the government swiftly slapped new legal restrictions on union actions. In January 1970 a law with a long name, the Provisional Exceptional Law Concerning Labor Unions and the Settlement of Labor Disputes in Foreign-Invested Firms, which restricted union organizing and labor disputes at multinational corporations, was promulgated. In December 1971 came the declaration of a national emergency and the promulgation of the Special Law Regarding National Security, which severely restricted collective bargaining and suspended collective action. In the fall of 1972 Park Chung Hee declared martial law, put tanks and troops in the streets, disbanded the National Assembly, and pushed through a new, revised constitution—the *Yusin* (revitalization) constitution—that gave him nearly limitless executive powers.

Under *Yusin* authoritarian rule, unions from the FKTU headquarters down to the local level were forced to do the bidding of the government and management, focusing on the task of mobilizing the rank and file in a "patriotic" endeavor to raise productivity. Unlike the wartime Japanese labor mobilization scheme of Sanpō, the FKTU trade union system itself escaped abolition, but FKTU unions were essentially charged with the role the "patriotic units" played at workplaces in the late colonial period. From the mid-1970s on, the Factory New Village Movement (Kongjang Saemaŭl Undong), an expansion into factories of the rural New Village Movement, began to be implemented through unions in an attempt to squeeze out more unpaid, supposedly voluntary, labor from workers.[121] By then the leadership of almost all national industrial unions had succumbed to this political pressure and adopted the pro-government, pro-company stance activists called *ŏyong*. A handful of courageous unions that refused to be *ŏyong* began to call themselves the *minju nojo* (democratic unions), distinguishable by their autonomous stance vis-à-vis management and upper-level unions and by their commitment to internal democracy and to workers' democratic rights.[122]

Representative unions in the minju union category included the Cheonggye Garment Workers' Union, organized soon after Chun Tae-il's death in November 1970, textile unions at Tongil Spinning and Weaving, Wŏnp'ung Wool (Han'guk Wool until 1974), and Pando Trading (initially a wigmaker but transformed into a garment manufacturer), and unions at YH Trading (wigmaking), Control Data (electronics), and Samsung (Samsŏng) Pharmaceutical. All these unions emerged at heavily female-dominated manufacturing firms between 1970 and 1975. Thereafter, the democratic leadership groups of these unions (except for the Samsung Pharmaceutical union, which continued to function as a minju union until the mid-1980s) were eliminated one by one under relentless union-busting campaigns coordinated between management and government authorities between 1978 and 1982.[123]

Instead of describing the numerous struggles these democratic unionists went through, which Yi Okchi, Hagen Koo, and others have documented in moving detail,[124] below I opt to summarize several key shared characteristics of women workers' "democratic" labor activism in this period. First, as discussed earlier, most minju unions had leaders and active rank-and-file members who had received education and training from Christian organizations like the UIM, the JOC, and the Christian Academy and from night schools. The learning, or the "knowledge of liberation," women workers obtained through study sessions and small-group activities at these institutions was of critical importance in producing a generation of active women unionists. By the late 1970s the leadership capacity of many women workers reached what might be called "a self-sufficient level," and the bulk of worker education came to be done by women union leaders themselves through the proliferation of educational programs each union established.[125] Growing solidarity among minju unions and the widening networking opportunities facilitated by minju unions' close linkage to the democracy movement also raised the level of political consciousness among many women unionists.[126] Minju unions' success in sustaining their arduous struggle depended on strong support from the rank and file, nurtured through the full-throttled deployment of union education programs and an array of engaging union programs, including small group activities, credit and consumer cooperatives, and social and cultural events.

Second, minju unions grew in constant struggle against concerted union-busting campaigns by management and government authorities. An unfathomable degree of violence, including sexual violence and torture, fills the incident reports produced by minju unions, and in many cases the upper-level industrial unions looked the other way or colluded with management. The repressive situation strengthened the ties between unionists and outside supporters, mostly Christian and student activists, to which government authorities and management responded by the late 1970s with a campaign of relentless red-baiting targeting, in particular, the UIM. Supported by the mainstream media and government agencies, management at minju union shops unleashed propaganda campaigns against the red *paehu*, or behind-the-scenes masterminds who were taking advantage of supposedly ignorant and gullible women workers for their own agenda. On many occasions family members who were misinformed that their daughters or sisters "had become red" rushed to the factory to pull the young women home. In a divided country with the very stringent National Security Law governing everyday life, the red-baiting tactic was a particularly challenging obstacle that often resulted in an internal division of the affected union. Unionists dismissed as subversives were then blacklisted to prevent them from finding jobs elsewhere. Still, in some rare cases unionists were able to fight back by reaching out to family members themselves. For example, Control Data unionists countered management's red-baiting campaign by organizing their family members, friends, and partners into action. In some cases they made protest calls to management or visited sit-in sites in a show of support.[127] Some mothers of union members even joined sit-ins, risking police arrest.

Another equally powerful union-busting tactic was utilizing economic pressure to create divisions among workers, especially along gender lines. In dealing with minju unions, some companies chose to delay hiring and resorted to disguised subcontracting practices to deplete the union of membership numbers.[128] Some companies used factory closure as a threat or opted to actually shut down the factory, blaming the union for causing company's financial trouble.[129] Whether the real reason for closure was business failure or improved wages and working conditions due to union activism, economic pressure tended to provoke anti-union actions among those male employees who had mostly adopted a bystander attitude toward union affairs.[130] Management often appealed to male pride, and many men were unwilling to support female union leadership because "working under the sway of women's skirts" was demeaning for them.[131] More fundamental was the structural position male workers occupied in the sex-segregated hierarchical workplace order of South Korea's manufacturing firms, which assigned better paid, secure, and allegedly more skilled jobs to men. Fear of losing a secure breadwinner job, combined with conservative gender norms they harbored, easily turned many male workers against the union. A conspicuous division by gender in union activism thus constitutes a third characteristic of the minju union movement. The union movement had been men's turf until women workers barged into their world in the early 1970s. Even in the Cheonggye Garment Workers' Union, which was the pioneer in the minju union movement, key leadership positions were virtually monopolized by men despite sporadic attempts by women unionists to elect a female president who could better represent the membership, more than 80 percent of which was female.[132]

The first female union local president did not come on the scene until May 1972, when Chu Kilja was elected to that position at Tongil. Her election constituted a major turning point in Korean union history, an event that cracked the gendered power structure of the labor movement. At the time women constituted 83.2 percent of the national textile union membership, and at Tongil 1,214 of 1,383 production workers were women. Electing a female president there was viewed by many as a coup d'état against the union establishment. Historian Kim Muyong interprets the meaning of the rise of a minju union at Tongil, which Chu Kilja's election jump-started, as in part a "cultural struggle" in which women workers expressed their values and desires rooted in their gender identity. He notes that women workers expressed "boundless hope and exhilaration" that "a woman could become a union local president and conduct something like politics by administering a union."[133]

In the key minju unions listed above, women eventually came to dominate the leadership positions, although some unions such as the Wŏnp'ung Wool union and the Cheonggye Garment Workers' Union also produced legendary male union leaders. Many women workers were keenly aware of their hierarchy-demolishing act of seizing the helm of the union movement, and management was quick to utilize the gender divide to drive a wedge into union solidarity. The developmental mobilization of the Park regime fostered the gender division in society, and male workers in the 1970s, assigned advantageous positions in the labor hierarchy, had much to lose in labor disputes compared to women workers.[134] Oftentimes in the 1970s and early 1980s male employees were mobilized by management in the name of "save-the-company corps" (*kusadae*) to violently disrupt women's meetings or sit-in demonstrations.

Sexual harassment and sexual violence as a tool of labor control was rampant in many labor disputes involving minju unions, and the police were not innocent in this regard. As women's studies scholar An Chŏngnam convincingly shows in her analysis of labor practices in Pusan's rubber industry in the 1980s, sexual violence was frequently deployed as a major means of labor control in female-dominated industries. An argues that in numerous cases managers of South Korean manufacturing firms applied, or threatened to apply, sexual as well as physical violence, often in combination, with two main goals: first, in order to secure the labor of a particular female worker by binding her to the shop through forced sexual relationship, and second, to create divisions among unionists and weaken union solidarity. Sexual attacks amplified insidious "fear of rape" among women workers, and threats to spread rumors about allegedly indecent sexual conduct of workers if they continued their union activism were deployed against both female and male unionists with powerful effect.[135] Labor struggle for women workers in the minju labor movement had thus become a highly sexualized affair, and women unionists became conscious of their vulnerability to this ongoing attack on their female body and their reputation as properly feminine and chaste women. Sometimes women unionists reacted to violence forced on them in extraordinary ways. For example, in a well-known yet difficult-to-understand case of so-called nude protest in July 1976, which sociologist Hagen Koo described as "an extremely surprising and dramatic form of resistance, probably unique in world labor history," Tongil's female unionists spontaneously took off their clothes. They did so after the clothes of some women were ripped off by the police while being dragged away from a sit-in. The decision to undress, which was simultaneously and instantly made by several hundred women sit-in strikers without any discussion, was later explained by participants as an emotional outburst of an intense feeling of solidarity for their colleagues wronged by the police and suffering the shame of nudity. It was also a desperate, albeit futile, effort to stop the police, all men, from approaching them.[136] The police did not hesitate long, however, before moving in and breaking up the sit-in. Seventy-two women were arrested while two hundred other women strikers, all half naked, fought to block the arrest. In the act these Tongil women strikers created a memorable moment in Korean labor history, simultaneously appropriating and subverting the conventional norms of proper femininity.

Male workers on occasion became party to the exercise of sexual violence on their women colleagues. In a particularly bizarre case a male anti-union employee of Control Data exposed himself and urinated in front of women workers engaged in a sit-in.[137] Even though the female leadership of minju unions never framed their struggle as one between male and female workers, in the sharply gendered and sexualized terrain of the minju union struggle of the 1970s and 1980s, it was difficult to effect the kind of cross-gender solidarity at the factory level seen in the 1930s among Pyongyang's male and female rubber workers.

Minju union activism for women workers also meant a growing awareness of gender-based discrimination as a problem and a new subjectivity as union activist/woman worker. In the process of building and sustaining a democratic union, women increasingly questioned gender as well as class hierarchies they had once viewed as natural. Most *minjung* practitioners and ideologues in this period did not consider gender-based exploitation and oppression as a primary problem, but women workers in the minju union movement showed a much higher level of gender consciousness than is recognized in conventional academic and popular understandings. The emergence of a women-specific agenda in union struggle by the late 1970s constitutes the fourth and last characteristic I wish to highlight here. The most advanced fight to tackle age-old gender discrimination practices occurred at Control Data, whose union leadership included Kisuhoe vice president Yi Yŏngsun and Kisuhoe members Yu Oksun and Han Myŏnghŭi.

Control Data Korea, a memory parts assembly firm for high-end industrial computers, was established in 1967 in Seoul by a US company that had branch companies in thirty-three countries by 1977.[138] The number of employees, only forty in 1969, grew to over a thousand by 1974, and 100 percent of union membership was composed of women because no man was hired in production jobs in a strictly sex-segregated setting. From early on the Control Data union, founded in 1973 as a local under the national metal union, tackled women workers' grievances in two areas as well as gaining significant raises for them. The union was able to clarify women's right to claim a monthly menstruation leave, albeit unpaid, in the collective contract so that women could use it without having to get checked by a nurse and also curry favor with supervisors.[139] It also obtained an equal annual bonus payment for women production workers to the level paid to male white-collar employees. After the first union president was removed by a rank-and-file vote of no confidence and Christian Academy–educated Yi Yŏngsun became the president in May 1977, a militant and systematic struggle for gender equality began in earnest.

The first fight for gender equality under Yi's leadership was prompted by a struggle that broke out on the company's commuter bus in late 1977 between female and male employees. When the company moved into the Kuro Industrial Complex in 1974, as mentioned earlier, the union demanded and obtained the company's commitment to commuter bus service, running twenty-six buses by 1977. Over time a customary practice developed on the bus, initially out of women's goodwill in consideration of the possible difficulty men as a minority might experience in the midst of a bus full of women. The custom was to leave the first two rows of seats for male employees even though that meant some women had to endure the cross-town commute standing. Men soon came to consider it their masculine privilege. One day a female worker, Kim Aehŭi, feeling sick, sat down in the supposedly male space, and a male employee insulted her.[140] The union demanded punishment of the male employee from the company and an apology from him, and it installed a handwritten wall poster (*taejabo*) denouncing verbal violence against women. Unfortunately, about seventy or so male employees, most of them in supervisorial ranks, decided to unite against the women, which escalated the "commuter bus struggle" into a kind of a gender battle. When the company sided with male employees on the matter, the union successfully flexed its muscle through an undeclared work slowdown of some 50 percent, which was possible because of the strong unity that existed among the women unionists. The man in question received a light, mostly symbolic, punishment of just one month's suspension, but the effect of the union victory in the language struggle was socially and culturally significant and transformative. Male employees began to refrain from their customary practice of talking down to women using *panmal* (language used by a higher-status person to a lower-status person) to avoid trouble.

The union then confronted more serious discriminatory practices in the shop step by step, beginning with the project of reversing employment regulations that forced women to quit at marriage, a widely shared employment practice in South Korean companies until recent decades. It was also a critical issue for union survival because the company froze hiring and let the workforce shrink by normal attrition, a large part of which was women resigning at marriage. The number of employees steadily declined from thirteen hundred in 1976 to about six hundred in 1979. Through a determined and persistent "continue-working-after-marriage" campaign, the union was able to reverse the practice and even obtained six days of marriage leave and a money gift for women workers at marriage, perks that only male employees had enjoyed in the past. Helped by intensive union education sessions on gender and labor issues, women workers began to change their own conservative attitudes toward employment after marriage and after pregnancy, and some brave souls volunteered to endure managers' harassment to make sure the new custom of lifelong employment for women could take root. By the time the factory closed in 1982, married women constituted 15 percent of the workforce, 30 percent of whom were pregnant, and the union was planning to set up a factory day care and fight for a sufficient nursing time.[141] Unionists also forced the company to abolish a ludicrously discriminatory practice of paying white-collar employees 50,000 wŏn at the birth of a son and 20,000 wŏn if it was a baby girl, while equivalent payment to production workers was 20,000 wŏn regardless of the baby's sex. The company had to agree to pay a uniform amount of 50,000 wŏn at any childbirth. Control Data's women production workers also broke the ceiling for women's promotion to the line head (*panjang*) position, and in 1977, for the first time in the company's history, three women in the rank of production worker reached the managerial position of supervisor (*kamdok*).[142]

Robust education and social programs run by the union, a democratic decision-making culture, and a track record of success strengthened women workers' commitment to the union (99.9 percent joined the union in an open-shop system), and collectively women unionists displayed an extraordinary degree of creativity and acumen in organizing their fights. Under the Special Law Regarding National Security, which made collective action illegal, the union used well-organized, prolonged work slowdowns, which on the surface seemed like a spontaneous occurrence without union involvement and thus difficult for the company to prove and respond to. When preparing for wage negotiation the union collected detailed information on company finances to improve their negotiation power and conducted market surveys themselves. Much information came from white-collar employees of the company, who were not union members but willing to help, and to acquire critical information on company finances the union used ingenious tricks. At one point, unionists, disguised as white-collar employees, obtained key data on the company's export records from the national trade association, and on another occasion a union official sneaked into the office of the company's production department chief and secured data on productivity increases. To break the customary practice of not paying family allowances to women workers with the excuse that they were unmarried, the union conducted a survey of union households, which revealed that a union member on average supported 2.6 family members.[143] In the end the company chose to close the Korea factory, blaming the militancy of the union as the reason, which had the effect of turning male employees against the union. Men then vented their anger by disrupting women unionists' anti–factory closure struggle.[144]

A similar pursuit of gender equality issues and a women-specific agenda was prominent at Wŏnp'ung Wool, where Kisuhoe president Pak Sunhŭi was a key official, and at Samsung Pharmaceutical, whose union was almost all female and "concentrated on issues women were facing."[145] The Wŏnp'ung union successfully pushed up women workers' wages from the lowest level in the textile industry in 1972 to the highest level by 1979 and alleviated the gender gap in wages. It also challenged the practice of resignation at marriage for women workers and rooted out rampant sexual harassment at work. The Samsung Pharmaceutical union took up women-specific issues such as menstruation leave, resignation at marriage, maternity leave, and nursing time, and challenged the entrenched male culture of sexual harassment and sexual violence against female production workers.[146] Rebellion against gender discrimination at work was also noticeable in the banking sector. A college-educated women's department chair of a banking union, having had a "life-changing" experience through the Christian Academy program for women unionists, worked together with women's department chairs of other banking unions to abolish the practices of resignation at marriage for women and of gender-based discrimination in wages and promotion opportunities.[147] In all these workplaces, significant cultural changes were occurring during the days of the minju union movement as unions singled out women's issues as serious and legitimate grievances. They put up a good fight against practices of sexual harassment at work and challenged male supervisors' pervasive use of *panmal* and other rude language regarding female production workers.[148]

Fighting to preserve the minju union, therefore, was for women unionists more than a pursuit of their class interest, as historian Kim Muyong has elucidated. Women worker subjectivity was being transformed through the flurry of democratic meetings, education programs, group activities, demonstrations, sit-ins, and experiences of state and company violence. Through union activism women workers were changing workplace culture and everyday life around them. Many former worker activists recall how they got to acquire a sense of pride in being a female worker (*nodongja*) through union involvement and how they were able to overcome the painful sense of inferiority that the much-hated term *kongsuni* had cast over them. Han Myŏnghŭi, a former Control Data union official, recalled how, after participating in an intense union struggle under Yi Yŏngsun's leadership, the union movement came across to her as an "awesome" and "exciting" (*sinbaram*) affair and how confident she became as if "there was nothing that could scare me."[149] She said she used to hide her *kongsuni* status and her allegedly "unfeminine" manual labor by acquiring trappings of bourgeois femininity like luxurious clothes and cosmetics, and she lied to family and friends saying she was a white-collar worker. But a year or so of union experience transformed her into an eager propagandist of labor's cause to strangers, including taxi drivers, as well as to her family and friends. In a symbolic and revolutionary move, she proudly wrote down "kongsuni" as her occupation on the ferry passenger declaration form when she traveled to Hongdo Island with worker friends.[150]

Although restricted to a few female-dominated large manufacturing factories, it is important to note that thousands of young female workers experienced exhilarating and effective union offensives against entrenched practices and cultures of gender discrimination. Considering the breadth and depth of their activism against gendered power relations at work, the paucity of attention to this aspect of the minju union movement is striking. Traces of Kisuhoe history and the gender revolution Kisuhoe members helped propagate in their shops remain scattered in oral history testimonies of former activists and in union records. Up against the weight of both activist and academic labor literature, which tends to portray women workers as victims of abuse and as good troopers who fought hard in the larger democracy movement, helped and guided by students and intellectuals, the women worker activists of the 1970s and early 1980s we met in this chapter have been speaking up and registering their dissent to mainstream interpretations of their past struggle.

Buoyed by the breadth of cross-firm networking and educational activities among minju union activists during this time, to which Christian Academy labor education contributed much, a growing awareness of gender-based discrimination on the shop floor and of a need for unions to address women's specific grievances was spreading among unionists beyond areas of minju union strength in Seoul and the surrounding Kyŏnggi Province.[151] For example, the Chŏnnam Silk Reeling union in Kwangju, led by union president and JOC *t'usa* Chŏng Hyangja, brought Academy labor educator Sin Illyŏng and several female unionists down from Seoul, including Kisuhoe members Yi Ch'ŏnggak, Ch'oe Sunyŏng, and Pak Sunhŭi, as part of the union's prolific education sessions, a fact that shows the reach of Academy education. Chŏng recalls that her union was preparing to directly tackle the issue of sexual violence and harassment on the shop floor, but the Kwangju Massacre of May 1980 and the ensuing repression unleashed on social movements made normal union affairs impossible.[152]

The final chapter of this book looks into the profound political impact of the shock caused by the massacre in Kwangju and turns attention to the growing body of memory work in the twenty-first century that seeks to capture the experiences of the female-dominated minju union movement of the 1970s and early 1980s. Then it assesses the continuing challenges South Korea's women strikers are facing today despite the remarkable achievements of the last hundred years.

6

FEMALE STRIKERS IN RECENT DECADES AND THE POLITICS OF MEMORY

The extraordinary struggle of women factory workers that had "coursed through the 1970s, raising sparks (*pulssi*),"[1] ended rather abruptly by 1982, but in a few years South Korean workers created another extraordinary moment in Korean history in the form of the Great Workers' Struggle of July–September 1987, which empowered organized labor to a level unimaginable to even ardent labor activists. The swift turnaround in labor's fortune generated a strong need in the labor movement and among concerned scholars to make sense of, and allocate credit for, workers' great success. What happened in this process of review and assessment of the past practices of labor activism demonstrates pervasive and deeply entrenched gendered assumptions and biases in the labor movement and the democracy movement at large. Looking back at the many years since 1987 during which women unionists suffered from undue criticisms about their shortcomings and failures despite the enormous contribution they had made in the minju (democratic) union movement of the 1970s and early 1980s, veteran female labor activist Yi Chŏlsun bitterly asks, "What if [we] had not been there [fighting] at that time? Would the 1987 Great Struggle occur? Could the democratization of this land have proceeded this far?"[2] The "sword of denouncement" (*pinan ŭi k'al*) wielded by intellectual activists against female unionists cut deep, while at the same time the effects of the neoliberal turn effectively dismantled the foundation of factory women's militant struggle.[3] Still, in the beginning of the twenty-first century we witness women workers, this time mostly in the position at the bottom of the labor market hierarchy as irregularly employed workers, rising up again spreading new "sparks" to defend workers' rapidly diminishing rights. This chapter follows this important yet not well-known history of South Korean women workers' fight in recent decades, focusing in particular on gender and memory politics manifested in it.

The story begins in the early 1980s when the minju union movement crumbled under repression. By then thousands of union activists had been dismissed and blacklisted, following a determined and well-coordinated joint assault on minju union activism by management and the military dictatorship of Chun Doo-Hwan (1981–88). After the assassination of Park Chung Hee in October 1979, Chun consolidated his grip on power in stages, the final step of which accompanied the bloody military suppression of peaceful demonstrations and the ensuing citizens' uprising in the southwestern city of Kwangju in May 1980. Thus opened a new, dynamic, and turbulent decade that fundamentally reshaped the course of South Korean history.

The unfathomable brutality of the country's military attacking and killing civilians in broad daylight in Kwangju changed the terrain of South Korea's democracy movement drastically. A bitter realization of how ineffective the student- and intellectual-centered pro-democracy movement of the 1970s was in the face of such naked power drove elite activists over the 1980s into a fundamental rethinking of the premises of the dissident movement. The fact that students and intellectual democracy activists were the ones who fled the besieged city of Kwangju first, while working-class citizens fought to the end, tormented the former group with a profound feeling of guilt. Historian Namhee Lee's book *The Making of Minjung* provides the best English-language analysis of this 1980s transformation in South Korea's dissident movement, in which she observes that Kwangju "became the cross to bear for 1980s activists" as "Chŏn T'aeil's death was the cross for 1970s activists."[4]

Under the heavy impact of the shock of the Kwangju Democracy Movement, in which several hundred mostly young people perished resisting the military crackdown, and following a long process of self-reflection into the reasons for the "defeat" of the 1970s minju union movement, activists proceeded to build a new kind of union movement. The emergent revitalized movement prioritized cross-firm solidarity and promoted struggle of a more political nature. It emphasized a more systematic and large-scale alliance between workers and students/intellectuals. Informed by a so-called scientific, meaning socialist, knowledge, intellectual activists of the new labor movement aimed at a radical transformation of politics and society. Many veteran unionists of the 1970s minju union movement, dissenting from this radical line of thinking, continued to argue for strengthening trade unions through efforts at union democratization and struggles for livable wages and working conditions. The worker-student alliance (*nohak yŏndae*), already a feature of the 1970s movement but confined then to small numbers of people and isolated instances, developed into a systematic and collective endeavor during the 1980s. Believing that awakening and organizing the working-class "masses" was the only way to defeat the military regime, many student groups began to prepare and send student activists to factories, most of them located in the capital region surrounding Seoul. No dependable statistics exist, but informed observers have estimated the number of university students who gave up their middle-class career paths and chose to become factory worker/organizers, called *hakch'ul*, in the range of one thousand to several thousand by 1985.[5]

A major accomplishment of this line of worker-student-alliance–based organizing was a solidarity strike in June 1985 in Seoul's Kuro Industrial Complex, where at least nineteen *hakch'ul* organizers had been in operation. In the six-day solidarity strike mostly female unionists from five textile and electronics companies struck together, and another five unions in the area publicly expressed their support through collective actions of their own. Some 2,500 workers participated in this first solidarity strike in South Korea since the Korean War.[6] The strike, however, ended in defeat. All the minju unions in the Kuro area, newly created or democratized in the previous two years, collapsed, and more than 1,300 unionists were dismissed. The outcome generated a bitter controversy regarding strategies. Still, the capacity of workers to execute a solidarity strike in the heart of Seoul's export industrial zone impressed many. The Kuro solidarity strike represented an important node in the gradual rise of worker militancy in the mid-1980s in various sectors, including male-dominated heavy-industry firms. The little sparks women workers had generated and nurtured since the 1970s, without much help from their male colleagues, began to grow and spread in all directions. This surging labor activism across sectors and regions eventually converged in an explosive manifestation of labor militancy, the Great Workers' Struggle, in the summer of 1987.

The 1987 Great Workers' Struggle greatly empowered organized labor. Following the June Struggle of that year, which extracted important political compromises from the ruling elite, including a direct presidential election, a strike wave of an unprecedented scale and intensity burst out in July and continued unabated into September. Between July and September that year 3,341 labor disputes occurred (averaging over forty-four disputes a day); in August an average of eighty-three disputes started each day, in comparison to fewer than three hundred disputes occurring annually in the previous two years when labor struggle was on the rise.[7] An estimated 1.22 million workers, about 37 percent of a total of 3.33 million workers employed at shops that hired ten or more workers, participated in these labor disputes, more than 94 percent of which took the form of illegal work stoppages and sit-in strikes.[8] A whopping 1,296 new unions were created in 1987 representing 336,507 workers, and numerous existing unions purged their pro-company leadership.[9]

As a result of this colossal upheaval of industrial workers, the extreme power imbalance between labor and capital narrowed to a significant degree. For the first time since the promulgation of the labor laws in 1953, the power of newly organized or democratized unions, especially those in male-dominated heavy industries and the transportation and infrastructure sectors, pushed the state and businesses to reformulate their labor control tactics and strategies. An alternative labor confederation of democratic unions that competed with the now more democratic FKTU became a reality in November 1995 through the successful launching of the Korean Confederation of Trade Unions (KCTU; Chŏn'guk Minju Nodong Chohap Ch'ŏngyŏnmaeng), and experimentations with labor parties also began.[10] Although unions soon faced a formidable counterattack by the state-business alliance that began in earnest in 1989, post-1987 industrial relations moved into a new era.

A major difference between pre- and post-1987 minju union movements was a conspicuous shift in movement leadership from women export-industry workers to heavy- and chemical-industry male workers, those at *chaebŏl* (huge family-owned and managed business conglomerates) companies in particular. But women workers were active participants in the 1987 struggle as well as in the post-1987 union movement. For example, the labor dispute at Pusan's Kukche Trading, in which thousands of mostly female shoe workers fought against violent suppression coordinated by the goons of the "save-the-company corps" and the police from July 28 to August 12, 1987, was one of the early struggles, together with the sit-in by 2,500 KSEC shipyard workers, that influenced the fast expansion of labor struggle in Pusan and across the country in the summer of 1987.[11] But the visibility and influence of women-dominated unions relative to male-dominated unions rapidly declined.

How did this rather abrupt marginalization of women workers happen in the minju union movement? The first section of this chapter addresses this question by looking into the experiences of women shoe workers in Pusan in the 1990s. The complex politics of the demotion of women unionists in the labor movement, a process that corresponded to their marginalization in the narratives and memories of the minju labor movement, is the subject of the second section. As women strikers of the 1970s were being forgotten and the everyday figure of *kongsuni* or female "industrial warriors" faded in social memory, women workers in the 1990s and the first decades of the twenty-first century were being channeled, under South Korea's increasingly neoliberal labor market transformation, into "irregular" or nonstandard (*pijŏnggyujik*) categories of employment.

The term *pijŏnggyujik* includes various forms of unstable employment including temporary, fixed-term, specially employed, subcontracted, on-call, and dispatched status. These "irregular" workers, especially women, are at the forefront of a new militant and innovative labor activism in today's South Korea. The last section explores this emerging new activism among *pijŏnggyujik* women workers in the last two decades. It attempts to understand the ways the gender question has become a major problem in today's South Korean labor movement by looking at the case of labor activist Kim Jin-Sook. Significantly, Kim's actions have provoked new memories of Kang Churyong, Pyongyang's rubber worker whose story began this book. Examining the ways in which those in South Korean society today frame these two legendary women labor activists offers us a window on the gender dynamics at work in today's South Korean labor and progressive movements.

The Disappearance of Factory Women: Capital Flight in the Shoe Industry

In the previous chapter we encountered a young female shoe worker who declared, "My name is Migyŏng, not *kongsuni*," just before she committed suicide in protest of conditions in her factory.[12] At the time she took her own life, Kwŏn Migyŏng (1969–91) was a twenty-two-year-old union activist and a senior machinist at Taebong, a large shoemaking company in Pusan. The company, facing industry-wide recession, squeezed workers to their limits of endurance with demands of ever-increasing speedup and unpaid extra labor in the name of a "Work-Thirty-More-Minutes" campaign, which was a version of a nationwide "Enterprise Ten-Percent-More Campaign," initiated in November 1991 by several national business associations, including the Korea Chamber of Commerce and Industry, the Federation of Korean Industries, and the Korea International Trade Association.[13] At Taebong in late November 1991, a new product line was set up for Adidas leather sneakers, and every hour managers checked the time each worker took to produce a pair of shoes. Slower performers like Kwŏn were severely scolded and forced to put in extra hours of work. A big wall poster with a slogan of "Let's Die Together, If We Fail to Reach the Production Target" was hung prominently in the shop to add psychological pressure on workers. Kwŏn and several other women workers had to forgo dinner one day because their supervisor kept them on the floor, all the while insulting them with abusive language. Suffering pangs of hunger, they tried to eat bread and tangerines while working, but they were subjected to insults from a supervisor who yelled at them, "How could you, those who are not even capable of meeting the production quota, take time to shove food into your traps [*agari*]?" Kwŏn endured the abuse in tears, according to her fellow workers, murmuring, "Is this not hell?"

According to fellow shoe workers' assessment, Kwŏn Migyŏng left "as much writing as martyr Chun Tae-il," mostly in the form of daily diary entries, excerpts of which were later included in *A Sourcebook of Rubber Worker Struggle*. Kwŏn's writings reveal a worker activist who felt a deep compassion for the younger, teenage female workers around her, whom she lovingly called "girls" (*sonyŏdŭl*), in a fashion that reminds us of Chun Tae-il's compassion for teenage apprentice (*sida*) girls in the garment industry.[14] Not being able to do much to help the "girls" whom she saw as "so pitiful" ("nŏmuna ant'akkapko aechŏropta") seems to have distressed her greatly. She wrote in the diary, "What can I do for those girls?" Then, on the fateful day of December 6, 1991, after witnessing a nineteen-year-old "girl" in her line bursting into agonizing sobs following her supervisor's vicious reproaches—a scene during which Kwŏn found herself unable to speak out against in protest—Kwŏn threw herself off the third-floor veranda of the company building. She left a "last diary entry" on her left arm: "My beloved siblings!" she wrote. "Please do not bury me in the icy land of repression but bury me in your bosoms. Only then I believe we could become a complete whole [*wanjŏnhan hana*]. I wanted to live like a human being. Do not repress us anymore. My name is Migyŏng, not *kongsuni*."

The string of events and circumstances leading up to her fatal decision remind us of the 1962 suicide of "Miss Kim," the Chŏnnam Spinning and Weaving worker whose action helped energize JOC activism among fellow women workers. Kwŏn's friends in 1991 were more prepared than Kim's colleagues in 1962 to commemorate and find meaning in her suicide protest. Kwŏn's death resonated widely among Pusan's rubber shoe workers, who, as we will see, were suffering from essentially the same harrowing conditions of speedup and workplace violence as Kwŏn had faced. Kwŏn's funeral was conducted as a "funeral of [all] Pusan workers," and her death began momentum for the founding of the Council of Rubber Workers in April 1992. Later, in 1995, at the time of its dissolution to become part of the KCTU, the council put together the previously cited document collection, *A Sourcebook of Rubber Worker Struggle*, in order to leave a record of their struggle, in which Kwŏn Migyŏng's actions and writings figure prominently.

The impact of Kwŏn's death occurred in the context of turmoil in Pusan's rubber shoe industry in the post-1987 years. Exploring what happened in the rubber shoe sector allows us to assess the turbulent history of South Korea's neoliberal reforms that soon followed the empowerment of organized labor after 1987. Of course, neoliberalism has been a worldwide phenomenon, which significantly weakened job security and union strength in many parts of the world. In South Korea the Asian financial crisis of 1997–98 provided proponents of neoliberal arrangements a propitious moment for instituting rapid and intense structural changes.[15]

Pusan, one of the three centers of shoe production in colonial Korea together with Pyongyang and Seoul, experienced a rapid rise in the shoe industry during the 1970s and 1980s and an even more rapid fall in the early 1990s. The total production of 70 million pairs of shoes in 1970, 21.1 percent of them for export, increased to 298 million pairs in 1980 (68.1 percent exported), and to 573 million pairs in 1988 (78.7 percent exported).[16] By 1993, only five years after the industry's peak year of 1988, production declined back to the 1970 level with 77 million pairs, and the ratio of export to total production slid to 62.3 percent.[17] Almost all shoe production was arranged in the OEM (original equipment manufacturing) method, in which South Korean firms assembled shoes for major shoe companies around the world, including Nike, Reebok, Adidas, and LA Gear. In 1990, for example, 97.95 percent of shoe production in South Korea was through the OEM method. During its heyday shoe exports grew to become the third-largest export sector in South Korea after electronics and textiles, and South Korea became the number-two shoe exporter in the world, after Italy. South Korean firms, regrettably, neglected investment aimed at designing their own brands and upgrading their technological capacity while enjoying the export boom that relied on the cheap and disciplined labor of women workers.

Pusan became the center of this surge in shoe production with the shoe industry accounting for about 30 percent of the city's economy.[18] According to South Korean Shoe Industry Association data, as of November 1991 Pusan and its surrounding areas housed 190 (65.1 percent) of 292 shoemaking firms and 95,000 (82.8 percent) of the 115,000 shoe workers. In the peak year of 1988 the shoe industry employed 155,000 workers, which means that the industry by 1991 had already lost forty thousand jobs in just three years. At the end of 1993, only 31,395 employees, including 27,944 production workers (6,404 men and 21,540 women), remained, a precipitous decline of more than 70 percent from the level in early 1988, when the industry boasted 164,000 workers. US shoe import statistics show where the multinational corporation buyers were moving to in these years. In 1988 South Korea accounted for 68.8 percent of US imports in the "leather sneakers" category, but by 1992 (January to August only) South Korea's share had fallen to 29.7 percent and trailed China (29.8 percent), with Indonesia (20.7 percent) not far behind. Some of these goods from Indonesia, in particular, were being produced by South Korean companies that had moved there seeking cheaper labor.

This sudden capital flight and gutting of a local economy was not just occurring in Pusan's shoe industry, of course. By the 1990s the era of export-driven industrialization, based on low-wage women's labor in manufacturing industries, was over. Women rubber shoe workers' ordeal in Pusan was repeated in many export sectors as affected companies downsized, resorted to subcontracting arrangements, moved orders to new factories abroad, engineered speedups for remaining workers, delayed wage payments, or abruptly closed shop, often without paying wages and severance pay. In the words of Pusan rubber workers on a hunger strike in June 1992, the "industrial warriors" (*sanŏp yŏkkun*) of yesterday suddenly found themselves in the status of "industrial garbage" (*sanŏp ssŭregi*) by the early 1990s.[19]

The devastation wrought by this abrupt and massive capital flight was aggravated by the worrisome trend of overinvestment and cutthroat competition that had plagued the industry in previous years, as more and more capitalists entered the shoe business, whose labor-intensive production process required relatively small capital investment while profit margins were high. To cope with the sudden collapse of the export shoe industry, the South Korean government came out with a three-year "shoe-industry rationalization" plan (1992–94), which prioritized a reduction in production capacity by shedding outdated equipment and slashing production costs through a wage freeze, mechanization, and layoffs to regain market competitiveness.[20] Encouraged by government support and blessed by the media, shoe companies mounted "save-the-company" campaigns, which the media praised as an innovative new model of labor-management relations.

Shoe shops in Pusan had been known for their "low wages, long hours, and forced-labor-like labor control," a labor control regime that was to a great extent a carryover from the labor control methods of the colonial era. And once the "save-the-company campaign," which was essentially a mix of speedup and union-busting measures, began, already notorious working conditions in Pusan's rubber shoe industry deteriorated even further.[21] Workers were routinely required to start work five or ten minutes earlier and end twenty or thirty minutes later than the regular schedule, and they were often forced to endure unpaid "extended" labor when the production target, set unreasonably high, was not met. Some companies gained cooperation from their unions and pressured workers to return bonuses or a portion of their hourly pay, or to work extended hours on Saturdays. Sometimes the biweekly Saturday as holiday, guaranteed by contract, was given up altogether. Worker performance was constantly checked and allegedly "lazy workers" were punished, as we saw in Kwŏn Migyŏng's case, and workers' bodily movement in and out of the factory, including late arrival, early departure, briefly going out of the factory, or absences, was strictly controlled.[22] Rubber companies also hired foreign laborers in "apprentice" positions at about 15 to 30 percent of the average wage of regular employees, and some larger firms began to open new shops abroad.[23]

Pusan rubber capitalists' attempt to compensate for declining profit rates caused by changing production strategies of multinational corporations primarily by further squeezing workers provoked desperate protests, and protest in turn was, according to striking rubber workers' statements, met by "beastlike" violence "that defies imagination" committed by the company-mobilized "save-the-company corps" (*kusadae*), which in many cases included not just male employees but also hired thugs.[24] Cases of "beastlike" violence committed as a labor control measure by management and documented by rubber workers are astoundingly cruel even in the context of the already low standards of repression-prone South Korea's labor control practices. On many occasions worker activists, both men and women, were forcefully taken to isolated locations on company premises, held against their will for hours or even days, mercilessly beaten up, sometimes for hours on end, until they agreed to sign a resignation letter or a false confession that accused a targeted union official with immoral acts, often of a sexual nature. Threats of or actual conduct of sexual violence were prevalent.[25] Often a top demand of striking workers in the late 1980s and early 1990s in Pusan's rubber industry was to end the violence of the "save-the-company corps" as well as the cessation of the "save-the-company" campaign. One of the most effective strategies of rubber companies during this time was to manipulate and nurture divisions among workers and claim that the violence they committed on worker activists was a result of internal conflicts among workers. Threats or rumors of factory closure or downsizing often generated the desired divisions among workers. Cases of actual factory closures and delinquency in wage payment were increasingly common.

This was the context in which Kwŏn Migyŏng committed suicide and fellow workers rallied to her cause in December 1991. But public opinion in Pusan, according to workers' understanding, was lukewarm at best toward rubber shoe workers in the early 1990s.[26] Instead of an uproar against blatant abuses of power by Pusan's big capitalists, society in general showed great sympathy toward the struggling shoe businesses caught in a massive economic downturn. The concern for Pusan's economy "in its final throes" trumped any concerns over workers' economic well-being or human rights, in the Council of Rubber Workers' assessment.[27] In the end rubber workers in Pusan were unable to turn the tide of public opinion against the so-called "rationalization" campaigns and lost their jobs.

The 1990s labor-management relations we see in the rubber shoe industry in Pusan, when compared side by side with those of the 1930s in the same industry in Pyongyang, show certain noticeable differences in terms of society's and the media's attitudes toward striking women rubber workers. The nationalist mooring of Pyongyang's bourgeoisie, to which rubber capitalists and journalists were tethered to a substantial degree, was no longer discernable in 1990s Pusan. Pusan's rubber capitalists in the 1990s showed no compunction in exploiting women workers to a maximum degree, and unleashed violence on them with impunity in order to crush their spirit of resistance. Rubber shoe companies were ready to move production abroad, depriving the lower-class population of Pusan of their livelihoods. The predicament of Pyongyang's rubber businessmen—they had to justify wage cuts to society and at the same time maintain their legitimacy as Christian nationalists committed to building the economic foundation of the nation—does not seem to have bothered either the management class of Pusan's rubber industry or the opinion makers in the media. The violence-ridden labor repression scenes painstakingly documented by workers themselves in *A Sourcebook of Rubber Worker Struggle* show that in terms of their stance toward labor, especially in the ways they treated women factory workers, by the early 1990s Korean capitalists in certain labor-intensive sectors had regressed far from earlier capitalist visions and practices in the 1930s.

Following similar processes in many industries and regions factory women largely disappeared from factory complexes in South Korea in the 1990s and the early twenty-first century.[28] The Kuro Industrial Complex in Seoul that had 44,856 workers in 1987 shed 18,000 women workers to shrink to a workforce of 27,027 six years later, and the size of the workforce in the Masan free export zone decreased during the same period from 28,022 to 10,799.[29] And this massive expunging of the export-industry yŏgong in the 1990s failed to generate alarm or an outcry either in society at large or in the now male-dominated organized labor movement.

The next section explores how women workers' struggle in the minju union movement of the 1970s and 1980s has been evaluated in the democracy movement and how some former women activists have been speaking up to problematize the regime of forgetting imposed on the cherished memories of their lives.

Remembering Women Workers of the Minju Union Movement

In a foreword to a collection of the life stories of eight former women activists of the 1970s minju union movement with the title *Rose Vines over Barbed Wire* (*Kasi chŏlmang wi ŭi nŏngk'ul changmi*), Yi Chŏlsun, the head of the

Council of Korean Women Workers' Associations (Han'guk Yŏsŏng Nodongjahoe Hyŏbŭihoe; now the Korean Women Workers' Association or the KWWA) and a respected leader of the JOC movement, raised the important questions mentioned at the beginning of this chapter.[30] Referring to not just those eight women represented in the book but to all former female minju union activists, Yi asked those poignant questions regarding women's critical yet underappreciated contributions to the labor and democracy movement and grieved over the fact that stories of "so many women workers" who had fought in the movement were "now remembered by no one," even though their stories constituted a "history that should not be buried."[31]

This concern about social forgetting was the reason her organization sponsored the publication of *Rose Vines over Barbed Wire* in 2004, as well as the massive two-volume account *The History of the Korean Women Workers' Movement* (*Han'guk yŏsŏng nodongja undongsa*), three years earlier.[32] Yi's statement represents widely shared sentiments among the veterans of the 1970s minju union movement. Chŏng Hyangja, whose activism at Chŏnnam Silk Reeling was recounted in chapter 5, articulated these women workers' grievance regarding the social disremembering of their contributions in another collection of worker testimonies, titled *A Hidden History of Korean Women* (*Sumgyŏjin Han'guk yŏsŏng ŭi yŏksa*). "The work of building worker organizations on the shop floor," Chŏng stated, "nurturing them, and making them unite, that work women workers of the 1970s pulled off brilliantly. People of today do not know that history and do not bother to learn about it, even though it is apparent that today's labor movement was born from this history of women workers."[33]

One of the factors that shaped the parsimonious recognition of women workers' contributions to the dual success of the June 1987 Struggle for democratization and the July–September Great Workers' Struggle of 1987 was the disappearance of the women-led minju union movement itself, largely resulting from the post-1987 structural changes in the economy as well as in the labor politics we have discussed. But more forces were at play in the consolidation of a generally negative assessment of the 1970s minju union movement over the course of the 1980s and 1990s, an evaluation fixated on the alleged shortcomings or "failures" of the movement. The first of these forces was the immense shock wave the massacre in Kwangju in 1980 generated and the ways in which the dissident movement changed in a comprehensive way in its wake. In the 1980s the goal of the dissident movement shifted from a loose consensus on the values of liberal democracy to socialist visions of a revolutionary transformation, termed *pyŏnhyŏk*, and in the new movement culture, *hyŏnjang t'usin* (literally, plunging oneself into where the action happens, meaning entering factories) became a rite of passage for student activists. Unlike previous episodes of *hyŏnjang t'usin* that occurred in small numbers beginning in the late 1950s, the 1980s students turned worker activists, or *hakch'ul* in movement jargon, conducted the act of "plunging" as a collective affair, which was carefully prepared and managed by underground activist circles.³⁴

The early- to mid-1980s labor movement developed in the context of large-scale practices of worker-student alliance and was squarely built on a negation of the 1970s minju union movement. The latter was condemned as a model not to follow in the evolving minju union discourse of the 1980s. The focus of the criticism was that women workers had failed to overcome their immature orientation toward "economic unionism," meaning prioritizing union building and shop-floor activism instead of fighting for explicitly political goals. Their alleged lack of solidarity work was also stressed as a major flaw that allowed the defeat of the 1970s enterprise-centered minju unions, as each of them was demolished individually. This unwarranted "sword of denouncement" was wielded by *hakch'ul* organizers and so-called advanced workers (*sŏnjin nodongja*) against veteran women activists of the earlier minju union movement. Many testimonies of women worker activists contain expressions of this sense of injustice done to them. Pak Sunhŭi protested the injustice indignantly, saying, "They say the 1970s labor movement neglected solidarity struggle, but solidarity struggle in the 1970s was more vigorous than ever. We just did not use the term 'solidarity' then. Do you know how much our members were beaten up because of their involvement in the struggle of other workplaces? We frequented police stations as if they were our houses." She declared that she and her fellow women workers "made sure to attend every event, every gathering, summoning all the might we had. That is 'solidarity.'"³⁵

The discourse that denounced the 1970s minju union movement and belittled women's struggle unfortunately proved to have staying power throughout the 1980s. It even developed deeper roots in the post-1987 era and merged into the consolidating "myth" of the men-led minju union movement, whose invented nature was dissected by political scientist Kim Wŏn in his scathing criticism of post-1987 minju union movement discourses. Kim argues that large-enterprise male unionists who seized the helm of the movement following the 1987 Great Workers' Struggle needed a new narrative to buttress their position as the dominant force in the labor movement. Chun Tae-il, a male hero, was hoisted as the "symbol of all Korean workers," and a new discourse endorsing male workers' militancy, class consciousness, and capacity for solidarity as much stronger than those of women was built on that foundation. In the new historical narrative of the labor movement, the ascendance of male workers was portrayed as a desirable progression into an upgraded, "scientifically" informed, and militant struggle by men who overcame the weaknesses of the past. In that mythmaking process it is not surprising that women workers and their struggle were marginalized. Kim Wŏn summarizes three essential claims the dominant post-1987 union discourse makes on the 1970s movement as follows: first, the women-led union movement with all its limitations posed an obstacle to the sound development of the Korean labor movement; second, what caused women unionists' tendency to concentrate on economic struggle and union-centered activism and imposed limitations in their activism was the temporary nature of women workers' employment; and third, the 1970s minju union movement led by women was essentially a movement that simply reacted to material poverty, lacking the essential foundation in an "ideology or philosophy."[36] In Kim Wŏn's assessment published in 2006, most of the materials and studies that had been published on the 1970s minju union movement more or less subscribed to this viewpoint, except for works by a handful of scholars who applied feminist perspectives, including sociologist Yi Okchi and anthropologist Kim Hyŏnmi.[37]

In this way the history of the 1970s women worker struggle was rewritten from the perspective of now-dominant union men, and the alleged "limitations" in women worker activism of the 1970s became commonsensical knowledge in the labor movement and in the labor studies literature. The idea of progress from a female-led to a male-led movement resonated effortlessly with male-centered habits of mind among progressive intellectuals in and around the labor movement in South Korea, making it very difficult for women activists to publicly raise questions about the "sword of denouncement," no matter how strongly they felt about the injustice done to them. Examining this process of history writing, or mythmaking, I came to understand my own experience in the post-1987 years in South Korea. I began to understand why such an acute, yet hard-to-articulate, feeling of unfairness gripped me witnessing this changing of the guard in the minju union movement and the accompanying criticism of what women workers had done. That strong sense of injustice has stayed with me over the past decades and driven me to persist in studying Korean labor history focusing on gender politics. A similar feeling of "history not being written right" seems to have been what motivated former women worker activists to agree to numerous oral history interviews during the past two decades.

Entering the twenty-first century, proliferating oral history projects have offered women activists a chance to speak up, and publications of their testimonies and autobiographical accounts have sharply increased. A salient example is a massive project of the Labor History Institute (Nodongsa Yŏn'guso) of Sungkonghoe (Sŏnggonghoe) University in Seoul, to which hundreds of women added their voices in the early 2000s.[38] The Korea Democracy Foundation has also accumulated testimonies of hundreds of activists, including women worker activists.[39] A historical account of the Korean labor movement centered on women workers' struggle came into being with the 2001 publication of *The History of the Korean Women Workers' Movement*. This two-volume series, sponsored by the Council of Korean Women Workers' Associations and written by Yi Okchi and Kang Insun, represents a multiyear effort by women scholars and activists to revitalize the fading memory of female worker activism.[40] Attentive to the effect of intellectual intervention in shaping memories of women worker activism, labor scholar Yu Kyŏngsun and others have experimented with "Workers Writing Their Own History" (*Nodongja chagi yŏksa ssŭgi*) programs, in which workers themselves write autobiographical essays supported by a small group of like-minded workers who share and discuss their writings among themselves.[41] This growing body of new materials reveals ample evidence of fissures and conflicts in the minju union movement that have been glossed over in the dominant narrative, and through their testimonies and writings we can glimpse women workers' emotions and desires and enhance our understanding of the culture and spirit of their union activism. Helped by these new sources, a new body of critical scholarship that unpacks the dominant discourse and conventional assumptions on the 1970s minju union movement has emerged in recent years.[42]

The newly emerging body of memories, however, mainly captures those of a small segment of the tens of thousands of women worker participants in the 1970s union movement. As Yi Okchi writes, we do not know the names of thousands, or even tens of thousands, of women factory workers in South Korea who "collectively created and experienced exhilarating days of democratic union activism in the 1970s, as well as dark days of defeat and unjust violence."[43] The life experiences and union experiences of the absolute majority of 1970s women workers are not accessible to us, and so is the complexity of and contradictions in their experiences. Many of those who volunteered to testify emphasized how joyous, happy, and high-spirited they felt in the thick of the movement and how their union involvement, although it may have ended in dismissal, a long period of unemployment via blacklisting, and/or jail time, helped them to live a meaningful and happy life afterward. Many of them grew to become conscientious citizens through the union movement and became involved in local grassroots movements of various kinds after leaving the factory.[44] It is important to be mindful of the fact that foregrounding these uplifting human stories produces an effect of pushing out the not-so-happy stories of former yŏgong. But at the same time, it is also meaningful to illuminate the hidden histories of women worker activism as we do here, helping women speak more freely, liberated from the weight of the dominant male-centered account of South Korean labor history.

While memories of factory women as "industrial warriors" and as *kongsuni* faded in society in the post-1987 decades, outside the realm of the labor movement no new hegemonic memory of 1970s yŏgong replaced them. In today's South Korean society contrasting memories and images of yŏgong circulate through various forms of cultural products, but without garnering much public attention nor generating much tension. One of the best films that confronts memories of 1970s yŏgong in ways that attempt to move beyond typical activist portrayals of victimized-yet-brave women unionists struggling for democracy and justice is *Factory Complex* (*Wiro kongdan*, 2015) by acclaimed director Im Hŭngsun. In that documentary film, images of yŏgong and narratives of their life and struggle come across ambivalently. Images of yŏgong in the film are poignant, even mysterious, provoking a sense of discomfort and bewilderment in viewers. The yŏgong in *Factory Complex* are a kind of ghostlike figures that haunt the audience and lead it to confront the shady side of the developmental past in which yŏgong labor was used and abused. Contrasting sharply with *Factory Complex*'s nuanced and thought-provoking portrayal of yŏgong, overtly celebratory memories and discourses about yŏgong's sacrifice for the nation also exist. This is a view that perhaps a multitude of former yŏgong quietly share. The most vocal propagator of this celebratory narrative is economic planner O Won-chol (O Wŏnch'ŏl), one of the brains behind Park Chung Hee's Heavy and Chemical Industrialization (HCI) drive in the 1970s. O, in straightforward fashion and without evoking a sense of irony, speaks of how the Park government calculated the usefulness of the yŏgong, whose "shelf life as labor," according to him, "only amounted to some 5 years," and how it skillfully mobilized them as a crucial resource in economic development.[45] He praises how much paternalistic care Park Chung Hee and his government showered on yŏgong in the form of company-sponsored after-work schooling and other welfare measures, and how in the end the "blood and sweat" of yŏgong, "pure-hearted patriots" who "should be viewed as [rising] to the defense of the homeland," saved the country under the guidance of Park, the great leader. As Kim Wŏn aptly decodes all this, the logic of the story is that the nation's patriarch Park and his loyal yŏgong "daughters" rescued the country from poverty.[46]

This fluid and murky terrain of memory work on yŏgong in the twenty-first century means that while yŏgong are forgotten as a social force to be reckoned with, the yŏgong of a bygone era remain potent as a signifier for South Korea's developmental past, either as embodiment of its tribulations or as heroines of its eventual triumph in economic success. What is conspicuously missing, however, in today's various yŏgong discourses is a seemingly obvious question: Where did all those yŏgong go, and what are they doing now? Yŏgong who were in their late teens and early twenties in the mid-1970s and who continued to labor as wage workers were middle-aged and older women in their late forties, fifties, and sixties in the first decades of the twenty-first century. In the context of vanishing factory jobs for women and the neoliberal restructuring of South Korea, which accelerated following the financial crisis of 1997, it is very likely that most of them had fallen into the category of "irregular" workers at the start of the twenty-first century.

More important than histories of personal transition from yŏgong to irregular worker status, which we see from time to time in women worker testimonies, is the structural linkage between 1970s yŏgong and today's female irregular workers, a linkage that has not been noticed or discussed much in today's discourses about 1970s yŏgong. Just like yŏgong in the developmental period, women irregular workers today, together with foreign migrant workers, find themselves in the structural position of a lowest-paid, disposable workforce, susceptible to social neglect and discrimination yet vital to continuing business success and economic growth. Instead of factory complex *kongsuni*, today, as we have seen, the new name for discriminated manual laborers is *pijŏnggyujik*, workers in irregular or nonstandard employment, the majority of whom are women.

Activists of the Korean Women Workers' Association (KWWA) comprehended this linkage from early on. Yi Chŏlsun, the head of the association, observed that 73 percent of women workers, most of them in their forties or older, were employed as irregular workers at the time of her testimony in the early 2000s, and they were "no other than those female workers who, twenty, thirty years ago, operated machines or assembled electronics parts at a factory."[47] Since the early 1990s the KWWA, in alliance with the Labor Committee of the Korean Women's Association United (Han'guk Yŏsŏng Tanch'e Yŏnhap; KWAU), has called attention to the problem of labor market polarization and exploitation of irregular workers and has run campaigns for unorganized workers at the periphery of the labor movement, including domestic workers, care workers, and unemployed workers.[48] The KWAU was instrumental in the August 1999 launch of the Korean Women's Trade Union (Chŏn'guk Yŏsŏng Nodong Chohap), a union of women workers mostly working at hard-to-organize small shops and in contingent employment. For the past two decades the KWTU has pursued a women-friendly and flexible form of union activism, addressing the needs of irregular women workers both in their workplaces and in their communities and developing small group–centered methods of nurturing a sense of community and leadership skills among members.[49] The founding declaration of the KWTU, which chose not to be affiliated with either the KCTU or the FKTU, clarified its connection to past women worker struggles: "The Korean Women's Trade Union inherits the struggle of our senior colleagues [*sŏnbaedŭl*] who developed the 1970s minju union movement as pioneers and the struggle of women workers who helped shape the flow of the 1980s trade union movement."[50]

The act of recognizing this connection is not an innocuous gesture but politically potent claim making. Women's studies scholar Jiwoon Yu-Lee, in her ethnographic study of the female janitorial workers' union struggle in Seoul in the 2010s, discerns a particular kind of memory politics at work—what she calls the "politics of forgetting"—in the minju union movement, which began the task of organizing contingent workers in the early 2000s.[51] Progressive intellectuals and KCTU-affiliated labor activists, according to Yu-Lee, have come to define the *pijŏnggyujik* or precarious labor as a "new" form of labor exploitation in South Korea's neoliberal era, and produced an "abstract homogeneous figure," the *pijŏnggyujik* worker, on which activists base their organizing strategy. This "newness narrative" has had an effect of erasing "heterogeneous histories" of female workers, separating them from the history of 1970s yŏgong. Although most of the janitorial workers Yu-Lee interviewed during her field research had long and varied employment histories, including stints at factories, and one particular interviewee happened to be a veteran union organizer who had devoted close to thirty years of her life to union work, their union, the Seoul-Kyŏnggi Local of the KCTU-affiliated Korean Public Service and Transport Workers' Union, has been indifferent to their personal histories. The KCTU-led *pijŏnggyujik* movement, Yu-Lee argues, summoned these female janitors only to speak about their "present hardship" as "new" subjects, as contingent workers with no history, although for many women interviewees experiences of various forms of contingent work had long been part of their lives and thus not really new. This form of erasure or forgetting, she argues, perplexes and alienates women union members and "forecloses a radical critique of the process of social reproduction of feminized labor."[52]

I agree that in discussing the figure of the *pijŏnggyujik* worker as a new subject of the labor movement, scholars and activists have fixed their gaze on the "newness" of the recent phenomenon of a rapid growth in the use of nonstandard, contingent labor as a consequence of neoliberal restructuring and have not paid sufficient attention to past histories of labor market segmentation and gender division of labor in South Korea. And I believe that not seeing gender as a key category of analysis in defining the phenomenon of irregularization has important consequences for the gender politics of the union movement today. In order to understand these consequences, we need, first of all, to look into the claim of newness more closely. Various forms of contingent labor have been used as an essential component of capitalist strategy in Korea throughout the twentieth century; using contingent labor is simply not a new practice that began with neoliberal restructuring of recent decades. This is true especially for the majority of women workers. For them contingent employment has been the norm. Even for those women fortunate enough to have a formal employment contract, like factory workers or bank employees, the customary practice was to terminate their employment in a few years or at marriage. The struggle to have lifetime employment beyond marriage and childbirth by a few female-dominated minju unions represented women workers' effort to break loose from an entrenched gender-segregated and tiered labor market system that in effect dictated temporary employment for women.

Historically, contingent employment was also common among male workers as well, although it is important to note that the passage from contingent to regular status was wide open for men during the developmental era.[53] Use of a temporary workforce to meet the fluctuations in business conditions was a long-standing and widely practiced strategy at heavy-industry sites like the Korea Shipbuilding and Engineering Corporation. It was only in the 1980s when acute shortages in the male skilled labor force that followed the South Korean economy's rapid expansion into heavy-industry sectors motivated companies to eliminate the temporary worker system so as not to lose skilled male workers to rival firms.[54] Large companies' efforts to retain skilled male production workers through internal labor market arrangements that boosted job security began in earnest after the 1987 empowerment of labor, which in turn segmented the labor market further and increased the gap between unionized *chaebŏl* company workers and less fortunate workers at small- and medium-sized firms.[55] From the perspective of large-firm male workers, so-called core insiders in the South Korean labor movement in the post-1987 period, what really changed with neoliberal restructuring, which accelerated following the Asian financial crisis of 1997–98, was the fact that large firms began to turn premier production jobs at unionized heavy-industry shops into contingent work, a process facilitated by adoption of various labor-saving and de-skilling measures since the late 1980s, including automation and the module production method. The employment security and middle class–level earning power male core workers had achieved through militant struggles in the 1980s and 1990s was slipping away, and with it their capacity to provide for the family as breadwinner heads of the household.

In sum, the focus of the *pijŏnggyujik* talk and *pijŏnggyujik* organizing strategies was male workers' ordeal, especially the demise of the male breadwinner model in the economic life of South Korea. For women workers, many of whom had already lost semi-secure large-company factory jobs in the 1990s, as in the case of Pusan's shoe workers, becoming contingent workers and facing insecurity in employment did not represent as novel an experience as it was for men. For men, especially for unionized *chaebŏl* company workers, the specter of losing their breadwinner jobs and falling down into a "feminized" position of *pijŏnggyujik* workers, whose job standards and employment patterns resemble those that had traditionally been associated with women's work, represented an existential crisis.[56] It is notable that what finally propelled the KCTU to take on the irregular worker problem was an explosion of male irregular workers' struggle that began around 2000.[57] Once the central motivation in KCTU's organizing drive targeting *pijŏnggyujik* workers was to safeguard male breadwinning jobs, it is not surprising that women's heterogeneous employment histories or past histories of gendered labor market segregation failed to attract the attention of male union leadership.

At most KCTU unions in the post-1987 period, the leadership has been dominated by men even where the absolute majority of members are women. For the male leadership of these unions, female workers are supposedly neophyte unionists under their tutelage. But if a more historically grounded appreciation of yŏgong activism develops, one that observes women's struggle through its decades-long dynamic history, it may expose the constructed nature of the minju union discourse that legitimizes male leadership and disrupt the current gendered power structure of the labor movement.

For, in point of fact, the decade of the 1970s represents a shameful time for male unionists because men largely remained quiescent during that decade while women workers shouldered the burden of the minju union struggle despite harsh repression. Although the post-1987 minju union discourse succeeded in taming the 1970s history of yŏgong struggle by entrenching the idea of women's limitations, no unionist can deny the fact that women workers in the 1970s and 1980s built a robust and politically significant union movement against all odds and proved their militancy, persistence, and leadership skills in the process. Even more disconcerting for the current male union leadership of the KCTU is the fact that women workers, now increasingly in the position of contingent workers in service industries, have again proved that, like their sisters in the 1970s, they are able to wage militant, persistent, democratic, and creative struggles against neoliberal arrangements.

By not seeing or ignoring the connection between today's women worker activists and 1970s yŏgong activists, the KCTU-led union movement is missing a precious opportunity to bolster women contingent workers' struggle and the fortunes of contingent workers, both male and female. Today, the conditions of precarious labor have expanded across the gender divide and across the long-standing divisions among industries and firm sizes. These new developments are thus engendering new conditions for a broad-based solidarity struggle among a large swath of workers against capitalist excesses. The spirit of solidarity and militancy women workers have consistently shown in their century-long labor struggle, if embraced by organized labor, may help reverse the trend of the declining power of labor in South Korea we witness today. This is why the history of the 1970s women-led union movement is important and has remained a contentious site of memory war in recent decades among scholars, activists, and the women who participated in those momentous struggles.

The Kim Jin-Sook Conundrum

A good way to access the complex and shifting terrain of gender politics in South Korea's labor movement today and gauge the potential of women worker activism to lift up the now socially isolated labor movement is through the life and struggle of an extraordinary female labor leader, Kim Jin-Sook (Kim Chinsuk). I first met Kim in 2004 as part of my research on the union movement at the KSEC shipyard in Pusan. A female welder at that male-dominated workplace, Kim was the unlikely spearhead of the union democratization movement at the KSEC in the mid-1980s. Dismissed by the company in 1986 because of her union activism, Kim Jin-Sook has steadfastly fought for the KSEC (from 1989, Hanjin Heavy Industries) shipbuilding union and the KCTU union federation for the past three and a half decades. Interviewing her and observing her speaking to fellow unionists in union education sessions, I was deeply impressed by her passion and sincerity, on the one hand, and her powerful storytelling skills, on the other. The more I got to know her through her writings, speeches, and actions, as well as occasional personal encounters over the following decades, the greater my interest in and respect for her life of activism became. I felt a growing urge to understand her presence in and influence on the landscape of South Korea's male-dominated union movement.

Kim Jin-Sook, who worked as a yŏgong during the 1970s, grew into a labor leader following a path somewhat different from the routes traveled by the women unionists of the 1970s and 1980s. In a 2009 article I explored the ways in which a small number of women, including Kim Jin-Sook, became integrated into the heavy-industry workforce in the 1980s and discussed how Kim not only survived the tough masculine environment of the shipyard as a young female welder but also emerged as a trusted union leader.[58]

The rapid expansion of the manufacturing sector and heavy industries in particular under the HCI drive by the Park Chung Hee government, launched in 1973, created conditions of acute labor shortage by the late 1970s. The economic boom of the mid-1980s, which was aided by the so-called three lows of exchange rates, oil prices, and interest rates, exacerbated the situation.[59] The incredibly rapid expansion of the shipbuilding industry in the 1970s under the HCI plan created a need to reconfigure the existing pattern of sexual division of labor at shipyards, and the KSEC and other giant shipbuilding companies founded by Hyundai and other *chaebŏl* groups began in the late 1970s to experiment with new programs of training and deploying women workers for traditionally male jobs like welding and metal cutting. To justify the hiring of women in men's work, KSEC executives argued that mechanization—electrical welding and gas-torch cutting—had rendered these jobs "safe and easy" and thus suitable for female labor at a semiskilled level.[60] Kim was hired in July 1981 together with a few dozen other women trainees when the KSEC briefly reopened its recruitment program for women. Unlike the rest of this female cohort, who were, as the company intended, middle-aged married women (*ajumma*) who came to work to supplement their family heads' income, Kim was a twenty-one-year-old unmarried woman (*chŏnyŏ*, literally meaning a "virgin"). She would acquire fame at the yard as an unprecedented case of a "*chŏnyŏ* welder."

Kim Jin-Sook's career path before she reached the KSEC yard follows a typical pattern of employment history for women in 1970s South Korea who belonged to what sociologist Yokota Nobuko calls the "urban lower class." The majority of these people migrated from the countryside, dwelled in urban slum areas, and moved in and out of formal- and informal-sector jobs. Kim Jin-Sook recalled how she had resented her family's poverty-stricken financial situation, which eventually forced her to quit schooling at the middle school level. After leaving home on Kanghwa Island near Seoul as a teenager and fleeing to Pusan, a place chosen because it was the farthest point from home, Kim started as a sweatshop worker printing gold and silver patterns on *hanbok* (Korean-style clothing). Disturbed by the routine sexual harassment a fellow female worker was enduring at the shop, Kim soon fled from that job and became an apprentice (*sida*) worker at a large garment factory owned by the Daewoo *chaebŏl*, which at the time employed eighteen thousand very young female workers. To escape the harsh conditions of factory life of which she became unbearably "fearful," she left the factory and tried without success to eke out a living as a soy milk and newspaper delivery person and an ice-cream peddler.[61] Then after working at a faux leather handbag factory for eleven months, Kim became a "bus girl." The horrendous working conditions of that job included standing half naked in front of male and female inspectors who checked the young women's bodies after each shift for potential theft of bus fees. Like many *yŏgong* of the 1970s, Kim's ardent dream was to go to college by saving enough money through hard work. But like many *yŏgong* of the period, she ended up supporting her younger brother's college education instead of pursuing her own dream.

An advertisement seeking female trainees for welding and cutting jobs she saw in the local newspaper, the *Pusan ilbo*, changed her life, opening a door for her to join the rank of elite workforce at the nation's premier heavy-industry shop. Contrary to the company's characterization of electrical welding as safe and easy work suitable for women, Kim found it extremely difficult and dangerous. She routinely had to carry forty kilograms of welding equipment on one shoulder and a toolbox on the other and maneuver through piles of steel plates and other objects, often climbing up the side of a hundred-meter-high ship on a vertical ladder. By sheer willpower and characteristic perseverance she was able to gain acceptance and respect as "a darn good worker" among fellow male workers on the shop floor, who at first did not believe that a young woman could last longer than a few days and were not happy about female intrusion into their world. Eventually older male workers at the yard, whom Kim calls *ajŏssi*, a term of endearment toward older men, took her under their wings and she settled into the shop floor community of male solidarity, a community that became the support base of her labor activism.

In early 1986, together with two young male workers she took on the dangerous task of challenging the existing pro-company union. Starting as a model worker, desperately clinging to her once-in-a-lifetime chance of being part of the elite core-worker stratum, Kim Jin-Sook's transformation into an activist came slowly over several years. She enrolled in 1984 in the Ŏksaep'ul ("reed") Night School, offered by a YMCA branch in Pusan, without knowing that it was a labor night school, not the equivalency-test-preparation night school she expected. At first, she was put off by the school's focus on labor-related issues instead of the English or mathematics classes she wanted to attend, thinking that the teachers smacked of being "commies." But she continued to attend the school because the Wednesday night sessions offered a precious reprieve from the "beastlike life" of a shipyard welder pressured to work extremely long hours in very dangerous and dirty conditions. The night school was also the only place she was called politely as "Jin-Sook-*ssi*" (Ms. Jin-Sook).[62] One evening a teacher at the night school handed her a copy of *The Critical Biography of Chun Tae-il*, a book she eventually read out of boredom one rainy day. (It was customary for shipyards to suspend outdoor welding work during downpours.) The book shook her to the core. "I felt as if a big mountain took a position in my heart," she described of her encounter with Chun Tae-il's story, and "many pieces of rocks tumbled down from that mountain and pounded on my conscience."[63] The reading changed her worldview, and she wept out of an acute sense of shame about her past behavior, including an attitude of looking down on fellow manual workers as lowly people beneath her, she later recalled. As she became increasingly enthusiastic about worker rights, *ajŏssi* workers allowed her to preach to them about the labor laws she learned at night school, joking as she approached, "Oh, here comes the Labor Standards Act!"

It was *ajŏssi* workers' nudging that made Kim decide in early 1986 to run for that year's election for union representatives at her shop, together with two of her like-minded male colleagues, Yi Chŏngsik and Pak Yŏngje. Those elections had become a pro forma affair arranged behind the scenes by the existing union leadership. Alarmed at the prospect of an open-ended election, management and union officials tried hard to isolate the three challengers and make them give up on their plan. On the election day Kim Jin-Sook snuck into a room on top of a crane that her coworkers used as their lunchroom and delivered a memorable speech, denouncing the corrupt behavior of union officials and the unjust ways the company treated production workers. She pointed at the company-provided lunches before her and asked whether it was any better than dog food. Hundreds of workers in the room erupted in roaring applause when Kim finished her speech, and when managers and security personnel tried to drag her out of the room, workers rose up to defend her. She and the two fellow activists handsomely defeated the foremen candidates sponsored by the union and the company in their shop's election, and workers from other shops followed suit and demanded democratic elections in their units. A union democratization movement at the KSEC (Hanjin) yard was born.

Kim, together with Yi and Pak, now acting as union representatives, used internal documents they obtained to reveal corruption in the union and fought to take back and distribute some of the union-embezzled money to workers. The company's harassment was severe, and Kim Jin-Sook in particular became a target of an intense red-baiting campaign coordinated by the company. Management also tried to provoke masculine anxiety among male workers by pointing to her sex, but without much success. In Pusan she was taken twice to the torture chamber of the dreaded Counter-Communist Detached Unit (Taegong Punsil) of the national police. This was the same institution that, eight months after Kim's interrogation, murdered a Seoul National University student, Pak Chongchŏl, during waterboarding in its Namyŏngdong office in Seoul, igniting a nationwide protest that led to the June 1987 Struggle. Kim Jin-Sook recalled that she had been kidnapped, carried to the chamber, beaten up, and hung by her ankles until blood trickled out of her eyes. In the end the torturers let her go, unable to find any connections between her and those activists in a North Korean spy ring they were fabricating, labeling her instead as "home-grown communist."[64]

The company then fired the trio of KSEC activists in July 1986. Undaunted, Kim, together with her male colleagues, continued to protest at the gate of the yard demanding reinstatement despite daily harassment and beatings by company security guards. She ended up spending all her savings to pay for the printing of flyers, which were then distributed across the shipyard and in worker neighborhoods. What she wanted most was to talk to fellow workers to let them know that she was not a "commie" and that what the company was doing to her was unjust. Composing flyers and putting them at the door of worker households was "the only thing I could do at the time" to communicate with *ajŏssi* workers, she recalled, activities that helped her survive the ordeal.⁶⁵

Support for Kim and the union democratization movement she led grew stronger despite the repression. The KSEC workers' union democratization struggle flared up in the midst of the nationwide June Struggle of 1987, and the KSEC strike that started on July 25 provided important momentum for the expansion of the strike wave into the nationwide explosion of the 1987 Great Workers' Struggle. By the 1990s Kim Jin-Sook was already on the way to becoming a legend at the yard and in the metal workers' movement. And the democratized Hanjin Heavy Industries union gained the reputation of being one of the most militant and powerful unions of the post-1987 era.

In her recollections, including her testimony in an acclaimed documentary about the Hanjin Heavy Industries union struggle titled *Island of Shadows* (*Kŭrimjadŭl ŭi sŏm*, 2014, directed by Kim Chŏnggŭn), what is most pronounced is her love of fellow workers, especially *ajŏssi* workers, and her longing for the olden days when she got to work side by side with them at the yard. The strong commitment Kim Jin-Sook has shown over the years to the union movement of metal workers is legendary. It reached epic proportions as she risked her life conducting hunger strikes and in 2011 mounted an unprecedented 309-day high-altitude sit-in on top of a crane at the yard. Her militancy and commitment can only be understood by pondering the long distance she had traveled as a female worker to finally land a secure (male) job and build an enduring community around it. Fighting to defend that community seems to have become her purpose in life. At important junctures, her bold and risky actions on behalf of the shipyard union helped the union extract significant concessions from the stubborn owner of the yard, the Hanjin *chaebŏl*. But while benefiting from her courage and the waves of broad-based support and solidarity in the larger society her daring actions have generated, male unionists have yet to resolve the vexing question her gender poses to their male-centered world.

That is because Kim Jin-Sook was and is an activist exceeding the gendered frame of the post-1987 minju union movement. Her unique status as the only female labor leader of worker background with national name recognition in the heavily male-dominated metal workers' movement has posed a conceptual challenge for all South Korean unionists.⁶⁶ A convenient way out of the predicament of accommodating a female factory worker as a respected leader representing male metal workers has been to highlight her exceptional personal qualities and bracket her femaleness. An amusing and rather extreme example of the kind of stories that functioned to elevate Kim, a gender-neutral worker hero, above and beyond other ordinary women workers was a rumor, which Kim heard from a young male worker, about her ability to use *chukchipŏp* (a magic method of contracting space), popular in martial art stories and folktales, which she allegedly utilized to stealthily and simultaneously distribute newsletters and flyers to many locations at the huge shipyard.

Kim Jin-Sook herself largely avoided the gender question until recently. Applying a feminist perspective, women's studies scholars Kim Hyŏn'gyŏng and Kim Chuhŭi problematize Kim Jin-Sook's self-representation as one that pivoted around her identification as a "brother" figure to male shipbuilding workers, a stance that bracketed her "female" identity while highlighting her "worker" identity. In order to express her sense of solidarity toward fellow workers and be heard in a politically meaningful way in the male-centered union movement, Kim and Kim explain, Kim Jin-Sook chose to appropriate masculine qualities and speak from the position of a masculine subject, especially that of "male breadwinner workers."[67] Kim and Kim argue that even though her bitter experiences of prevalent sexism and sexual harassment at work surfaced ever so often "in a delicately suppressed way" in her writings and testimonies, Kim Jin-Sook's representational strategy before the 2010s had an overall effect of sustaining the male-centered and degenderized labor movement discourse.[68] Her presence in the metal workers' struggle did not jump-start a serious discussion of gendered power relations in the movement nor help women unionists break out of their secondary status as family members or at best helpers of male political subjects.

Kim Jin-Sook was never allowed a chance at reinstatement at the shipyard, despite her ardent wish to go back to her previous welding job and notwithstanding her many contributions to the struggle to obtain the reinstatement of her male colleagues, including Yi and Pak, who were rehired in 2006, twenty years after dismissal. Although it is true that management's adamant refusal to deal with Kim has been the main reason for her thirty-some-year unsuccessful fight for reinstatement (which ended with a spirited solidarity campaign in 2020–21 as she reached the age for mandatory retirement), there have also been hints of a high level of uneasiness and tension her leadership role has generated in the union, including the criticism mounted by union leadership against her 2010 hunger strike and her 2011 crane sit-in.[69] As a dismissed worker, Kim has long served in an honorary position as an adviser (*Chido wiwŏn*) to the Pusan regional headquarters of the KCTU. But her authority and influence seem to have been rooted in her solidarity-building actions and speeches, more so than in her official role in the KCTU organization. Her speeches and writings have shown an unusual power to resonate widely and deeply among workers and also among citizens in the larger society. Over the past three decades Kim Jin-Sook has delivered many powerful and memorable speeches at labor events, at funerals of fellow unionists, in education sessions, and during her hunger strike and sit-in struggles. Her 2007 book, titled *Salt Flower Tree* (*Sogŭm kkot namu*), which is a collection of her writings and speeches, has become a best seller in progressive circles.[70] Kim's capacity to connect with people via storytelling and to convey, through selfless actions, the sincerity or authenticity (*chinjŏngsŏng*) of her heart, a key value in South Korean social movements and politics, was what has sustained her relevance and influence in the labor movement and allowed her to reach out to a broader audience. These qualities remind us of the case of rubber worker Kang Churyong, whose oratory skills and audacious high-altitude sit-in stirred up Pyongyang society and reached a national audience in 1931.

Kim Jin-Sook's identification with a KCTU union movement dominated by large-firm male workers began to show signs of important changes beginning in the early 2000s. She began to raise her voice to criticize organized labor's lack of a spirit of solidarity toward irregular workers and other less fortunate citizens in society.[71] A major turning point in her thinking, which helped her embrace a much broader scope of solidarity and develop a keen interest in feminism, came through her experience during her historic 309-day high-altitude sit-in, or "sky protest," in 2011. That protest started in the middle of the night of January 6, 2011, when Kim climbed up to the top of Crane no. 85 at the Yŏngdo shipyard of Hanjin Heavy Industries in Pusan to block the company's move to lay off four hundred regular workers. There she endured unfathomable hardship in the confined space of the crane driver's room, 115 feet above ground, until November 10, 2011 (see figure 3).

Hanjin Heavy Industries, following a typical strategy of large companies in the aftermath of the 1987 Great Workers' Struggle, steadily pursued the downsizing of its labor force in order to cope with rising labor costs and to roll back union power on the shop floor. The company also opened a gigantic state-of-the-art shipyard at the Subic Bay Freeport Zone in the Philippines in 2007, which was operating with 21,000 dispatched workers from nineteen subcontracting firms and only a handful of regularly employed Korean workers as of 2011.[72] At that time Hanjin's Subic yard was the world's fourth-largest shipyard. It utilized cheap irregular labor and succeeded in holding union organizing drives at bay, despite continuing challenges by worker organizations, including the Samahan ng Manggagawa Sa Hanjin Shipyard (the labor association at Hanjin Shipyard).[73]

FIGURE 3. Kim Jin-Sook on Crane no. 85, Yŏngdo, Pusan, August 17, 2011. Courtesy of photographer Jang Youngsik (Chang Yŏngsik). Kim is making the shape of a heart with her arms. On her left is the crane driver's room that served as her living quarters for 309 days.

Hanjin shipyard's labor conflict in Pusan was understood by both capital and labor as a pattern-setting battle, and management at Hanjin, partly buoyed by the success of the Subic yard, was determined to weaken its militant union at home at any cost. During the 1990s the number of regular employees engaged in production work shrank rapidly, and by 2002 the proportion of irregular production workers at the yard reached close to 70 percent.[74] On June 11, 2003, in the midst of a prolonged strike against a major management offensive, including a massive layoff of 650 workers, the union local president, Kim Chuik, took dramatic action. He climbed up Crane no. 85 at the yard, and after 129 days of a lonely high-altitude sit-in, "hanging onto the crane like a torn-apart flag," in Kim Jin-Sook's later words, he hanged himself on October 17. Kim Chuik's fatal decision was prompted by the gradual weakening of solidarity among unionists as a result of the company's novel strategy of claiming an exorbitant sum of damage compensation against the union and unionists, which then led to the continuing threat of "provisional attachment" not only on union dues but also on individual union officials' wages and houses. The practice of "damage compensation and provisional attachment" (*sonbae kaamnyu*) has become the most effective, as well as the most inhumane, management strategy aimed at weakening union power in contemporary South Korea. It has driven a number of unionists to suicide since the early 2000s.[75]

When Kim Jin-Sook climbed up the same Crane no. 85 at 3:00 a.m. on January 6, 2011, she knew full well that she might not be able to come down alive, she later recalled.[76] It was a bitterly cold winter night, and in the −13°C (9°F) weather her hands stuck to the metal rungs of the crane's ladder as she climbed. She filled her backpack to the brim with metal bolts to use for self-defense, repressing a desire to pack additional hiking socks (she dreaded the possibility of painful frostbite, which she had often suffered as a welder working outdoors during the winter months). Months into her high-altitude sit-in, on June 27, an attack by sixteen hundred policemen and company-hired security personnel evicted her union supporters below the crane, isolating Kim, and a special police counterinsurgency unit seized nearby Crane no. 84, built on the same track, and repeatedly tried, mostly at night, to get close enough to her crane to subdue her. Kim later recalled how hard it was living on the crane, not being able to sleep more than ten minutes at a time worrying about imminent police attack. With a characteristic sense of humor, she later reminisced about her exploits. Running out of bolts to throw, she resorted to her excrement as a weapon, a strategy that had, she later told an audience at Seoul National University, a great effect as the men were much more fearful of feces than metal bolts. "The reason the human species is the lord of all creatures is because of its capacity to auto-produce weapons," she declared.

Kim Jin-Sook recalled that she had battled each day against an urge to put an end to her ordeal. She said she clung to a wish to sustain her sit-in for 129 days, as her close friend and colleague Kim Chuik had done. By May, people on the ground had become frantic in fear of her desperation turning into an unthinkable decision. They feared she might follow in the footsteps of a long line of labor martyrs in South Korea and at the Hanjin yard, including Kim Chuik. The only communication channel between Kim and her supporters was her phone and her tweets, which she started in late February by learning to use a smartphone sent up to her by her close friend Hwang Yira (Hwang Ira), a union official of the Pusan headquarters of the KCTU. Hwang was a female irregular worker dismissed from her salesclerk job at the Pusan subway due to automation. Hwang had met Kim in 2006 when Kim came to support the struggle of subway workers for reinstatement.[77] The two soon became close friends and comrades, cherishing a shared experience of having been fired at age twenty-six. Hwang brought meals to Kim Jin-Sook every day during Kim's 309-day sit-in, even when the crane area was occupied by security guards. On those days she had to brave a gauntlet of harassment by hundreds of male guards to reach the crane.[78] The June 27 attack evicted all the unionists from underneath the crane, except for Hwang, who hid in a nearby container. But that night a group of Hanjin unionists, including Pak

Yŏngje, who started the union democratization movement with Kim in 1986, went up to the middle of the crane (see figure 4) to protect Kim from attacks from below. Three of them—Pak Sŏngho, Pak Yŏngje, and Chŏng Honghyŏng, all union activists who had worked with Kim for a long time—stayed put in the middle of the crane, exposed to the elements, for 137 days until the day Kim came down.

Following the June 27 attack, the company cut water and electricity to the crane. Kim's communication through tweets was aided by a solar battery that somehow passed thorough checks by security guards below the crane, who even stirred food with sticks to check for contraband or strategic items before allowing it to go up to her via ropes. Over time her daily tweets began to reverberate beyond the usual labor movement circles to reach a much larger audience.

What seems to have saved her life at some of the most critical moments of the sit-in was the miraculous arrival at the yard of the so-called Hope Bus caravans. These were voluntarily organized by people of all walks of life who were moved by Kim's Twitter pleas. The first Hope Bus caravan of about 750 people arrived in Pusan on the 157th day of Kim's sit-in and reached the crane at 1:00 a.m. on June 12 after fighting their way through the night against seven hundred company-hired security guards. A second caravan on July 9 numbered some ten thousand people traveling in 185 vehicles. Three more caravans were organized that summer and fall, at the end of July, in late August, and in early October.[79]

Hope Bus activists turned the Yŏngdo shipyard and Crane no. 85 into a festive zone for the celebration of labor and other progressive causes. The creative cultural energies of diverse groups of participants, mostly young people, poured out in the streets of Pusan. They sang, danced, and staged cultural performances, all in the midst of heavy and often violent police repression against participants.[80] It was a remarkable and unprecedented solidarity event in Korean labor history, which Kim called "a movement very new and mysterious," something she had never encountered in the labor movement.[81] A wide range of social movement groups and individuals from across the country showed up in person to express their support of her sit-in. The third Hope Bus, for example, included caravans of migrant workers, human rights activists, teenagers, people with disabilities, indie band musicians, and queer activists, and more than fifteen hundred people who came from all across the country walked three kilometers in monsoon rains to reach the shipyard after enduring water cannon attacks and spraying of toxic chemicals by the police. In a speech, conveyed by phone, to the caravanners gathered at a city park after failing to reach the yard, Kim demanded that before telling her to come down the mayor of Pusan and the government address the needs of "irregular and dismissed workers, people with disabilities, sexual minorities,

FIGURE 4. Hope Bus supporters and Kim Jin-Sook wave at each other, Yŏngdo, Pusan, October 10, 2011. Courtesy of photographer Jang Youngsik. This photo was taken just after the fifth Hope Bus caravan left the crane. Another sit-in by Kim's male union colleagues designed to protect her is visible in the middle of the crane.

women, and students who cannot afford tuition." In her later assessment she said, "The biggest power of the Hope Bus is to help us realize the fact that people can ride the same bus while each person is raising a different flag."[82]

Under the enormous pressure Kim's long-term high-altitude sit-in generated both domestically and internationally, the company finally caved and canceled its layoff plan. Kim Jin-Sook came down from the crane safely on November 10 to the enthusiastic cheers of the crowd below.[83]

The Hope Bus movement, Kim later recalled, not only reinforced her desire to live and persevere but also opened a new horizon for her, allowing her to see the possibility of a solidarity much bigger in scope than traditional organized labor, one that involved many more groups than just unionists. The Hope Bus movement occurred simultaneously as female janitors at Hongik University in Seoul were rousing social attention by generating solidarity actions from university students and new social activist groups like the "Nallary [punk-like] Outside Forces" (*Nallary oebu seryŏk*, coined in mockery of the accusation of "outside forces," or *paehu*, manipulating gullible workers), a cultural action group organized around actress Kim Yŏjin. Kim Yŏjin's Nallary group played key roles in both the Hongik University women janitors' strike and the Hope Bus movement. Performances and continuing cultural production by Hope Bus participants rattled hegemonic masculine cultural politics by generating sophisticated visual and media products with Kim Jin-Sook, a woman, at the center of the struggle and of a new solidarity network. The Hope Bus movement for Kim was often symbolized by a big bold flower painted in pink, and the color pink dominated Hope Bus cultural events and products.

Even before the 309-day sit-in, Kim Jin-Sook was becoming increasingly vocal in criticizing the masculine culture of the union movement, and she often spoke out critically against organized labor's neglect of the irregular worker issue.[84] Following her encounter with Hope Bus activists, Kim Jin-Sook's voice of criticism against KCTU practices that turned away from the interests of irregular workers became increasingly sharper, and she began to speak about gender issues in more forceful fashion.

What Kim said in an invited talk at Seoul National University's Women's Studies Interdisciplinary Program in September 2017 shows how far she has traveled in her thinking on these two intertwined challenges, the need for solidarity between irregular and regular workers, on the one hand, and the gender question in the South Korean union movement, on the other. In her talk Kim recalled her experiences of being subjected to rampant sexual harassment and vulgar sexual talk at work, which she only recently was able to conceptualize as expressions of *yŏhyŏm*, a newly coined word that contracts *yŏsŏng hyŏmo* (literally, "hatred of women"). Answering a student question, she explained how she was conflicted at the time not knowing how to respond because those explicit dirty jokes came from *ajŏssi* workers who were otherwise good-hearted, older men who helped her and trusted her. She told the students that everybody should "talk about the matter constantly" to change the minds of other people and thereby change the world. She explained that that was why she had been trying to say something about gender issues every day, however "clumsy" it might be, using her Twitter platform, and it was a practice of "self-reflection" on her past in which she might have, unknowingly, said hurtful things to others.

Kim Jin-Sook opened that Seoul National University lecture with a statement: "I was a female worker and am living as a female worker." And after describing the exploitation and sexual violence she witnessed as a factory worker in some detail, she asked, "What would have become of these [female] workers?" Answering the question herself, she continued, "All have become irregular workers. At subway stations, those janitorial workers hired by dispatched firms, workers who clean college campuses are all those workers who in the past toiled like that." She ended her talk with a clear prescription for the future direction of the union movement. One of the limitations of the current union movement, that is, its domination by heavy-industry male regular workers, mostly forty years or older, she declared, could be overcome by a movement that is led by irregular workers.

Irregular workers in South Korea have shown a phenomenal level of militancy and tenacity in recent decades, although their uphill battle against the management of private and public companies has registered only limited success in reversing or delaying the swift process of irregularization that has come to engulf the whole South Korean economy. Layoffs and disguised factory closures have provoked tenacious struggles by affected regular workers.[85] And among irregular workers we see equally fierce and long-term struggles, often lasting thousands of days and involving the dangerous tactics of high-altitude sit-ins and hunger strikes. Most of the long-term irregular worker struggles that have recently triggered social attention and broad-based solidarity action have been led by women workers. In addition to the female janitors' spirited struggles analyzed by Jennifer Chun and Jiwoon Yu-Lee, well-known recent irregular worker struggles include the high-speed train KTX female attendants' twelve-year (2006–18) struggle, the 2,822-day (2007–15) fight by private tutor unionists of the JEI Corporation (Chaenŭng Kyoyuk) to have their "worker" status recognized, and the 510-day E-Land/Homeplus supermarket workers' struggle (2007–8)—the subject of a well-received feature film, *Cart* (*K'at'ŭ*, 2014, directed by Pu Chiyŏng) and a Webtoon turned TV drama, *Awl* (*Songgot*, 2015).[86] These were all struggles by irregular women workers in the service sector. In the manufacturing sector women unionists at Kiryung Electronics, a producer of satellite radio and navigation and GPS equipment, continued a gripping struggle for more than ten years, from 2005 to 2015. Kiryung's women unionists conducted hunger strikes, which at one point lasted a mind-boggling ninety-four days. These workers also launched several high-altitude sit-ins in 2008 and 2010, feats that preceded Kim Jin-Sook's crane sit-in at the Hanjin shipyard and represented the first cases of female high-altitude sit-ins since Kang Churyong's in 1931.[87]

The proportion of irregular employment in total employment has grown among both men and women in recent decades. But in the context of the profoundly gender-segregated labor market system of South Korea, women workers were the ones who faced the brunt of the new management strategy of eliminating regular employment that burdened employers with protective regulations, mandatory insurance coverages, and unionization. During the Asian financial crisis of 1997–98, female workers were the first group receiving pink slips (allegedly as non-breadwinners), and male unionists, in their desperate attempt to safeguard male jobs, showed no qualms about agreeing to management's plan of sacrificing female union members' jobs by turning them into irregular jobs. A notorious early example was the case of the Hyundai Motors union, which in one of the early strikes protesting irregularization in 1998 agreed to sacrifice 144 elderly female cafeteria workers to save male jobs, even though most of these female workers were providers for their families, and they earnestly supported the strike by preparing hot meals for male strikers.[88] The union then agreed to a 16.9 percent ceiling for irregular worker hiring in return for a promise of no layoffs for regular workers in 2000. In effect that decision authorized the company to use irregular workers at will, and the proportion of irregular employees at Hyundai Motors spiked up to 30 percent in the ensuing decade.[89]

Statistics on these developments vary, depending on whose definition of "irregular employment" one follows. A key issue is whether to include workers employed regularly in temporary or day laborer positions. Another is how to categorize the "specially hired" workers caught in the gray area between small proprietorship and wage labor. Also, workers dispatched by subcontracting firms to work side by side with regular workers at large firms are counted as regular workers of those subcontracting firms, despite the fact that they are in effect dispatched irregular workers enduring second-class laborer status with no job security nor benefits of union representation. After a careful analysis of data sets, sociologist Yokota Nobuko takes the statistics put out by the Korean Contingent Worker Center (KCWC) as the most reasonable, according to which 56.9 percent of male workers held regular jobs while a whopping 64.4 percent of women workers were employed as irregular workers in 2008, showing the heavily gendered dynamics of South Korea's irregularization process.[90] By 2013,

8.3 million irregular workers—3.84 million men and 4.49 million women—constituted 45.7 percent of all workers in South Korea. That means that 57.2 percent of female workers and 37 percent of male workers were hired in *pijŏnggyujik* worker categories, the biggest of which were temporary workers working full time (31.3 percent) or part time (16 percent).[91]

Meanwhile, since the 1990s women's employment in general, especially that of married women, has rapidly increased in South Korea. Most of these women were making a transition from the unpaid family labor of small urban businesses to irregular wage work.[92] The bulk of irregular workers as of 2008, in Yokota's analysis, were temporary or day workers of urban small businesses, many of which had fewer than five employees and thus remained outside of legal protection, including many articles of the Labor Standards Act. The majority of these workers were women.[93] Overall the gender pay gap remains very large in South Korea, although it is slowly improving. While women workers made on average 63.1 percent of male workers' average wage in 1998, government statistics announced on July 1, 2019, show that women workers now make a little over two-thirds—69.8 percent—of what men make.[94] The pay gap is immense between female irregular workers and male regular workers. In 2013 the average wage of female irregular workers was 40.7 percent of the average wage of male regular workers. Meanwhile, male irregular workers made 53.3 percent of the male regular worker wage.[95]

As a two-tier labor market system composed of a small, exclusive labor market for male "core insiders" and a large, lower-tier market for irregular and small business workers became consolidated in the new century, it has become increasingly difficult to move from the second-tier to the first-tier labor market.[96] And, as we have seen, for women workers the situation has been much worse than it is for men. The neglect of the organized labor movement, including the KCTU, of this emerging group of second-class or urban lower-class workers is revealed in union organization rates. Union density in 2013 was an abysmal 1.4 percent for female irregular workers and 2.8 percent for male irregular workers. Meanwhile, 23 percent of male regular workers and 17.3 percent of female regular workers enjoyed union representation.[97] This is the context in which irregular workers, especially women irregular workers, have mounted their desperate and persistent struggles to block, reverse, or delay the process of irregularization and gain union protection.

Gender has thus been a key organizing principle in this labor market transformation in the new century in South Korea. Because that transformation has moved in the direction of the feminization of labor, and because women workers have formed the core of resistance against the new kind of exploitative labor control regime, it is not an overstatement to say that without tackling the gender discrimination and pervasive sexism in the labor movement as well as labor market polarization, it will be impossible to revive the declining fortunes of the union movement. In facing this reality, the power of memory and history looms large.

Women in the Sky, the title of this book, encompasses Korean women factory workers' struggle over a full century from the 1920s to the 2010s, and Kang Churyong and Kim Jin-Sook, both of whom created historic "woman-in-the-sky" moments, stand at the beginning and end of the book's narrative. The choice of these two "women in the sky" to open and close the book was propelled by a very recent development that links Kang and Kim in South Korea. Kang Churyong had remained forgotten in South Korea for a long time, although since the 1970s a few labor history accounts have included a few lines on her rooftop sit-in during the 1931 P'yŏngwŏn rubber strike.[98] But popular interest in the Kang Churyong story is primarily a very recent phenomenon stimulated by the prevalence, beginning in the 1990s, of high-altitude sit-ins as a tactic in the Korean labor movement. "Sky protest" became a major weapon in the arsenal of the minju labor movement following the epoch-making sit-in in 1990 by male workers on top of a gigantic Goliath crane at the Hyundai shipyard in Ulsan.[99] But it was Kim Jin-Sook's crane sit-in in 2011, the longest high-altitude sit-in up to that point in history, that stirred up a durable interest in Kang Churyong.[100] Her bold action recalled the iconic image of Kang Churyong on the Ŭlmiltae Pavilion in Pyongyang in 1931. In fact, it was while watching Kim's suffering on Crane no. 85 that the idea occurred to me of beginning and ending the book I wanted to write on the history of Korean female workers' struggles with Kang Churyong and Kim Jin-Sook. As Kim's sit-in became widely publicized, especially after the phenomenal appearances of the Hope Buses, many nonscholarly accounts by bloggers and news reporters linking Kang Churyong's Ŭlmiltae sit-in and Kim Jin-Sook's crane-top sit-in began to appear. Even a full-length novel depicting Kang Churyong's life, titled *Woman-in-the-Sky Kang Churyong*, was published in 2018.[101] A narrative connecting the two female worker heroes, albeit without much analysis, has now become commonplace.[102]

A new direction of memory making on Kang Churyong became visible in 2018 with the Liberation Day speech by President Moon Jae-in on August 15, 2018, discussed in the introduction to this book. Perhaps the most powerful celebration of Kang's memory so far, Moon's speech elevated Kang Churyong to the level of "women independence fighters" that the nation is obligated to discover and commemorate. By calling Kang Churyong a woman independence fighter, President Moon's speech integrates Kang Churyong's story seamlessly into the hegemonic nationalist narrative celebrating the resistance of the whole nation, except for a few evil collaborationists, against Japanese colonial rule. And by inventing a visual image of her shouting the slogan of "women's liberation and workers' liberation" on the roof of the Ŭlmiltae Pavilion, Moon's narrative in effect defined Kang Churyong as a pioneering feminist worker activist.

In this way Kim Jin-Sook's 309-day crane sit-in helped add another potentially powerful layer of historical memory of yŏgong struggle. While being used as a canvas on which to project today's desires and politics, however, the politics of this memory work has been left largely unexamined. What are we asking and answering by juxtaposing Kang Churyong on the Ŭlmiltae in Pyongyang in 1931 and Kim Jin-Sook atop a crane in Pusan in 2011, eighty years later? What aspects of their experiences are these popular narratives highlighting and obscuring? Emergent memories of "women in the sky" Kang Churyong and Kim Jin-Sook largely remain ambiguous and unsettled, just like memories and assessments of a century-long struggle by yŏgong, factory women, continue to constitute a site of memory war among both activists and scholars. In this book I have endeavored to situate Kang, Kim, and numerous other yŏgong activists, including the 1950s Chobang textile unionists, the 1970s and 1980s minju union activists, and the 1990s rubber shoe industry women strikers, in the broader historical context of place and time. A fuller understanding of the voices and actions of factory women requires a century-long look at the depth of female industrial workers' insurgency and the complex and changing historical situations in which they operated. Such historical examination can equip us with a capacity to visualize a web of connections, old and new, between Kang and Kim, and between these "women in the sky" and thousands of other women labor activists over the years.

As the chapters of the book reveal, not only Kang and Kim but many other factory women of the past century demonstrated similar qualities and characteristics as autonomous, audacious, and capable activists who built and prospered in the communities of working women they nurtured. They protested and sometimes overcame deep-rooted gender domination in the labor movement and in society at large while providing crucial momentum for democratic changes time and time again. Only a small minority among them, beginning in the 1970s, raised "women's liberation" as their goal, but many women strikers we have met in this book showed a clear awareness of their gendered position as "female" workers or yŏgong and cherished the principle of autonomy in their activism. They believed in the power of solidarity among women and impressed those willing to listen with their storytelling ability.

This final chapter opened with a fundamental question raised by Yi Chŏlsun, a "big sister" figure among veterans of the minju union movement: "What if [we] had not been there?" This question, having informed this whole book, can serve as its closing question to readers. It is my hope that after following the century-long journey of inspiring yŏgong characters presented here, readers will find it impossible to imagine Korea's twin success in development and democracy without acknowledging the role of these yŏgong fighters demanding justice and respect for workers while appealing to society's conscience and to the democratic promises of the republic. My wish in writing this book is to shine new light on Korea's modern history through the lens of yŏgong and their many contributions to major historical developments. I hope readers will find this new angle convincing. And I hope they will engage in the ongoing struggle to define the contents of "democracy" in today's South Korea and in the larger world, always mindful of the importance of the politics of gender as well as the politics of class.

Notes

INTRODUCTION

1. *Dong-A ilbo*, May 30 and 31, 1931.

2. Muhojŏngin (O Kiyŏng), "Ŭlmiltae sang ŭi ch'egongnyŏ," 40; Kim Ch'angsul, "Ŭlmiltae sang ŭi t'usa," 51.

3. The labor history literature on colonial-period Korean women workers primarily deals with working and living conditions in certain sectors, the textile and rubber industries in particular, and examines their labor activism. Often the goal is to gauge the level of class consciousness or nationalist commitment women workers attained. More recent works have made attempts to assess women worker subjectivities through their work life and activism. Examples include Janice Kim, *To Live to Work*; Yoo, *Politics of Gender in Colonial Korea*. But works that directly engage the question of how the larger society and women themselves viewed female industrial workers are rare. Works on postcolonial South Korean labor history that discuss women workers and gender issues include Barraclough, *Factory Girl Literature*; Kim Chun, "1970-yŏndae yŏsŏng nodongja" and "1950-yŏndae ch'ŏlto nojo"; Kim Kyŏngil, "1970-yŏndae minju nojo undong" and "1950-yŏndae Han'guk ŭi nodong undong"; Seung-Kyung Kim, *Class Struggle*; Koo, *Korean Workers*; Moon, *Militarized Modernity*; Nam, *Building Ships*, "Shipyard Women," and "Reading Chun Tae-il."

4. Nam, "Shipyard Women."

5. This phrase is taken from a question raised by veteran female labor activist Yi Ch'ŏlsun in her foreword to Pak Minna, *Kasi ch'ŏlmang*. This question is discussed further in chapter 6.

1. A "WOMAN-IN-THE-SKY"

1. *Dong-A ilbo*, May 30 and 31, 1931. The original Ŭlmiltae was built as the Pukchangdae (northern military station) in the sixth century, when the kingdom of Koguryŏ (37 BCE–668 CE) constructed the inner fortress of the larger Pyongyang fortress. The current building was constructed in 1714. Academy of Korean Studies, *Han'guk minjok munhwa taebaekkwa sajŏn* [Encyclopedia of Korean Culture], accessed May 3, 2016, http://encykorea.aks.ac.kr/.

2. Nationalist leader Cho Mansik, who served as president of the Northwest Sports Association (Kwansŏ Ch'eyukhoe) from 1931 to 1937, created a program in February 1932 for Pyongyang citizens. They gathered at 7:00 every morning at the Western Shrine (Sŏmyo) plaza, performed a fifteen-minute calisthenics routine, and then fast-walked to Ŭlmiltae. He himself developed a habit of an early morning walk, in which he passed by the scenic Pubyŏk Pavilion on the Taedong River and reached the Ŭlmiltae on the Moran Peak. Chang Kyusik, *Minjung kwa hamkke han Chosŏn ŭi Kandi*, 148.

3. *Dong-A ilbo*, May 30 and 31, 1931; *Chosun ilbo*, May 30, 1931; *Maeil sinbo*, May 30, 1931; *Dong-A ilbo*, May 31, 1931.

4. As of 1931, *Dong-A ilbo* had the largest circulation (33,035) in Korea. *Chosun ilbo*, representing the left wing of the bourgeois nationalist movement, followed *Dong-A ilbo* with 26,883 copies. The colonial government–owned *Maeil sinbo* had the third largest circulation with 22,258, and *Chungang ilbo* was fourth with 19,130. *Chungang ilbo*

was previously *Chungoe ilbo* and from March 1933, *Chosŏn chungang ilbo*. Kim Sujin, *Sinyŏsŏng, kŭndae ŭi kwaing*, 493-94.

5. The journal *Tonggwang* (May 1926-January 1933) was the organ of the Suyang Tonguhoe, which stood at the center of the bourgeois nationalist movement in Korea. Kang's interview in the journal thus helped push Kang Churyong into the national limelight, albeit briefly.

6. Muhojŏngin, "Ŭlmiltae sang ŭi ch'egongnyŏ," 40.

7. See *Dong-A ilbo*, August 17, 1932; *Chungang ilbo*, December 30, 1931. Contemporary documents often used *nyŏ* for *yŏ* (female), the latter being today's South Korean orthography when the character comes at the beginning of the word. In this book, I render both as *yŏ* in order to avoid confusion.

8. He also used the term *ch'egongnyŏ* for Kang and called women strikers "our brave sisters" (*uri ŭi yonggamhan chamaedŭl*) in his short piece admiring Kang's feat in *Tonggwang*. Kim Ch'angsul, "Ŭlmiltae sang ŭi t'usa," 51.

9. *Dong-A ilbo*, June 10, 1931.

10. As communists were being weeded out by state repression and new directives from the Comintern, which highlighted the need to struggle against "reformists" to strengthen a mass base for the task of establishing a communist party, gained adherence in Korea, a segment of communists in the Sin'ganhoe moved in the direction of dissolving the organization rather than handing over the control of the movement to the nonsocialist nationalists. On the history of the Sin'ganhoe, see Yi Kyunyŏng, *Sin'ganhoe yŏn'gu*; Kim Kyŏngil, *Han'guk kŭndae nodongsa*, 170, 264n9; Ch'oe Kyujin, *Chosŏn kongsandang chaegŏn undong*, 283-84. Kŭnuhoe's dissolution followed the same path.

11. For example, the page of the June 11, 1931, issue of *Dong-A ilbo* that reported on the P'yŏngwŏn rubber strike and the arrest of Kang and another leader, Ch'oe Yongdŏk, by the Pyongyang police also reported the re-jailing into Seoul's notorious Sŏdaemun Prison of Hŏ Chŏngsuk, a famous socialist woman activist and Kŭnuhoe leader. Hŏ had been temporarily released due to childbirth after receiving a one-year prison sentence for allegedly being the mastermind behind a major anticolonial rally by Seoul's female students. On the Seoul female student demonstration incident (otherwise known as the Kŭnuhoe incident), see chapter 2.

12. Colonial statistics show that in 1930 only 5.1 percent of girls and 26.7 percent of boys entered elementary school in the countryside, while in the cities 30.2 percent of girls and 60.4 percent of boys did. According to a secret report prepared by the colonial government in May 1944, even after an extensive governmental effort to increase the educational level of Koreans, about 89 percent of Korean women in the colony did not have any formal education, and the rates of secondary and higher education among women remained extremely low, 0.3 percent and 0.02 percent, respectively. Kim Sujin, *Sinyŏsŏng, kŭndae ŭi kwaing*, 66-67, 73 (table 1-4).

13. *Chungang ilbo*, December 30, 1931.

14. Muhojŏngin's interview article in *Tonggwang* repeats this point in the *Dong-A ilbo* report as well as the "Woman-in-the-Sky" moniker, a fact not surprising because Muhojŏngin was the pen name used by O Kiyŏng, the *Dong-A ilbo* reporter based in Pyongyang. Historian Chŏng Yonguk revealed the identity of Muhojŏngin as O Kiyŏng in his recent contribution to *Han'gyŏre sinmun*. Chŏng Yonguk, "Ch'egongnyŏ Kang Churyong twi en." O's background is discussed in more detail in chapter 3.

15. On Tanabe Kiyoshi (1903-33) and the Fuji Gas Cotton Spinning strike of 1930, see Hashimoto, "Entotsu otoko Tanabe Kiyoshi shōron." As noted, after Tanabe's feat, multiple similar incidents occurred in Japan. These activists also acquired the "chimney man" moniker.

16. See *Dong-A ilbo*, November 24, 1930, February 5 and May 15, 1931; *Chungang ilbo*, April 30, 1932. For example, the May 15, 1931, *Dong-A ilbo* article reported a worker

"chimney man" at Japan Dyeing and Spinning Company in Tokyo. He lasted 306 hours on a chimney and forced the company to reverse a harsh layoff order.

17. For example, in 1931 the number of *Osaka asahi shinbun* copies delivered to Korea was 41,187 (2,757 to Koreans and 38,430 to Japanese residents). In the early 1930s thousands of Koreans in Korea subscribed to Japanese "general culture" journals, including *Kaizō* and *Chuo koron*, and the total number of subscriptions for Japanese magazines by residents in Korea was 120,919 in 1929. Kim Sujin, *Sinyŏsŏng, kŭndae ŭi kwaing*, 112, 494–95. Leftist writer Yi Pukmyŏng, who was celebrated as a worker turned labor novelist, published a short story, titled "Yŏndol-nam" (Chimney Man), in the February 1937 issue of the leftist magazine *Pip'an* (Criticism). The imagery of the tall chimney (*yŏndol* or *kulttuk*) in the colonial period was often used to conjure up the formidable force of industrialization and class struggle, similar to the imagery of shipyard cranes and worker sit-ins on top of them since the 1990s in South Korea. In recent years the more than two decades of desperate worker sit-ins in South Korea on top of tall structures such as factory chimneys and various towers created a new term, *kulttuk-in* (chimney people), and spawned a Facebook newspaper, *Kulttuk ilbo* (Chimney Daily; https://www.facebook.com.gultukilbo).

18. *Chosŏn chungang ilbo*, October 31, 1933.

19. *Dong-A ilbo*, May 20, 1931.

20. P'yŏngwŏn Rubber was established in September 1930, much later than other rubber shoe companies in the city. For a list of twelve Pyongyang rubber companies founded in the 1920s, see Chu Ikchong, "Singminjigi Chosŏn esŏ ŭi komu kongŏp," 96. The official exchange value of Korean wŏn, issued by the colonial government, was set to be equal to the Japanese yen, and 1, 5, 10, and 100 wŏn bills were circulated in the Korea colony and parts of China under Japanese control. See Bank of Korea (Han'guk Ŭnhaeng), *Ilche sidae mit haebang ihu Han'guk ŭi hwap'ye*, 3, 8–19. Exchange rates between the Japanese yen and the US dollar remained a little over two yen to a dollar between 1928 and 1931 (for example, 2.15 yen to a dollar in 1928 and 2.02 yen in 1930) and jumped to 3.56 yen to a dollar in 1932. Lawrence H. Officer, "Exchange Rates between the United States Dollar and Forty-one Currencies," http://www.measuringworth.com/exchangeglobal/.

21. Muhojŏngin, "Ŭlmiltae sang ŭi ch'egongnyŏ," 40, 42; *Dong-A ilbo*, May 31, 1931.

22. *Dong-A ilbo*, June 3, 1931. This seventy-six hours is longer than the duration of her arrest (8:40 a.m. on May 29 to 11:30 p.m. on May 31) reported by the newspaper, which was about sixty-three hours. The reporter probably calculated Kang's fasting time from her last meal in the evening of May 28.

23. The Pyongyang Labor Alliance passed a resolution to actively support the strikes, and some workers started sympathy work slowdowns. *Dong-A ilbo*, June 1, 1931; *Chosun ilbo*, May 20, 1931.

24. *Dong-A ilbo*, June 4 and 5, 1931.

25. *Dong-A ilbo*, June 5, 1931; *Chōsen shinbun*, June 7, 1931. *Chōsen shinbun* articles on labor issues are available in Yŏngjin, *Ilcheha Chosŏn kwan'gye sinmun*, vols. 1–6. This is a collection of newspaper clippings on mostly labor and tenancy issues from thirty-five local and national newspapers that circulated in colonial Korea, including Japanese-language newspapers. *Chōsen shinbun*, based in Seoul, was the Japanese language national newspaper with the largest circulation. Chi Sugŏl, "Singminji sidae sinmun charyo," 278.

26. *Dong-A ilbo*, June 4 and 6, 1931.

27. *Dong-A ilbo*, June 3 and 10, 1931.

28. On the arrest of Kang and Ch'oe and their hunger strike, see *Dong-A ilbo*, June 11 and 13, 1931; *Chōsen shinbun*, June 17, 1931.

29. *Dong-A ilbo*, June 15, 1931.

30. Sŏn'gyo-ri, located south of the Taedong River in the southwestern part of the city, was a newly developed site for factories during the 1920s, following the urban

development plan negotiated between the colonial government and local capitalists. O Miil, *Kŭndae Han'guk ŭi chabon'gadŭl*, 413, 415.

31. *Dong-A ilbo*, June 5, 1931.

32. Muhojŏngin, "Ŭlmiltae sang ŭi ch'egongnyŏ," 40.

33. Kim and Ch'oe were recognized as worker leaders at P'yŏngwŏn Rubber. We know that at the meeting of Pyongyang rubber workers held on May 23, which more than a hundred female workers attended, Kim Ch'wisŏn presided as the chair and Ch'oe Yongdŏk represented the P'yŏngwŏn rubber workers on the newly elected steering committee. *Chosun ilbo*, May 28, 1931.

34. In the chemical sector nationally, the rubber industry's portion in terms of the number of employees reached 67.2 percent in 1925, decreased to 55.7 percent in 1930, and fell further to 45.5 percent in 1935. Meanwhile, the portion of the fertilizer industry in the sector increased from 5.7 percent in 1925, to 21.1 percent in 1930, and 45.1 percent in 1935 as large-scale investment by Japanese heavy and chemical industry companies increased in Korea over the 1930s, including the Chōsen Chisso, Nihon Chisso's branch company built in Hŭngnam. See Yi Chŏngok, "Ilcheha kongŏp nodong," 171–72. The ratio of women workers in the rubber industry remained around 67–68 percent from the mid-1920s to the mid-1930s, but it was much lower in the fertilizer industry, increasing from 6.8 percent in 1925 to 16.6 percent in 1930 and to 24.2 percent in 1935. Ibid., 173.

35. Yi Chŏngok, "Ilcheha kongŏp nodong," 190–91.

36. The discussion of the conditions of Pyongyang rubber industry in this section is based on O Miil, "P'yŏngyang chiyŏk Chosŏnin chabon'gadŭl," 133–37; O Miil, "1910–1920-yŏndae kongŏp palchŏn tan'gye," 214–17; Song Chiyŏng, "1930-yŏn P'yŏngyang komu kongjang p'aŏp," 237.

37. Chu Ikchong, "Singminjigi Chosŏn esŏ ŭi komu kongŏp," 101–2.

38. Yi Ch'ungnyŏl, *Kŭrim ŭro ingnŭn Han'guk kŭndae*, 125–26; Kim Kyŏngil, *Han'guk kŭndae nodongsa*, 110. The first rubber shoe company in Korea was Taeryuk Rubber Company, established in Seoul in 1919. See Pak Sŭngdon, "Han'guk komu kongŏp 50-yŏn sosa 1." The first in Pyongyang was Tonga Rubber, established in 1921. See ibid.; O Miil, "1910–1920-yŏndae kongŏp palchŏn tan'gye"; and Chu Ikchong, "Singminjigi Chosŏn esŏ ŭi komu kongŏp" for the early history of the industry.

39. Chu Ikchong, "Singminjigi Chosŏn esŏ ŭi komu kongŏp," 87; Academy of Korean Studies, *Han'guk minjok munhwa taebaekkwa sajŏn* [Encyclopedia of Korean Culture], accessed November 19, 2018, http://encykorea.aks.ac.kr/.

40. The consumption of *komusin* increased from 600,000 pairs in 1921 to 22 million pairs in 1930, and 37 million in 1937. The self-sufficiency rate of *komusin* reached 75 percent in 1931 and almost 100 percent by 1937. Chu Ikchong, "Singminjigi Chosŏn esŏ ŭi komu kongŏp," 85–87.

41. O Miil, "P'yŏngyang chiyŏk Chosŏnin chabon'gadŭl," 113–16.

42. Ibid, 109. In 1936 a contributor to *Dong-A ilbo* celebrated the economic achievements of Korean businesses in Pyongyang, especially the fact that Koreans were dominating the rubber and knitwear industries, calling Pyongyang "the Manchester of Korea." *Dong-A ilbo*, June 3, 1936.

43. Chang Kyusik, *Ilcheha Han'guk Kidokkyo minjokchuŭi*, 259.

44. See O Miil, "1910–1920-yŏndae P'yŏngyang Chosŏnin chabon'ga" and *Han'guk kŭndae chabon'ga*.

45. The split between the bourgeois ("cultural nationalist") movement and the "socialist" movement and the fierce struggle between them in colonial Korea are analyzed in Michael E. Robinson, *Cultural Nationalism in Colonial Korea*. On the ideology and economic programs of the cultural nationalist group, see O Miil, *Han'guk kŭndae chabon'ga*, chap. 6 and 9.

46. Chu Yosŏp, "10-yŏn man e pon P'yŏngyang," *Pyŏlgŏn'gon* 5, no. 8 (1930): 47, cited in Chang Kyusik, *Ilcheha Han'guk Kidokkyo minjokchuŭi*, 266. Chu's father was a Presbyterian minister, and Chu Yohan, who wore many hats as poet, reporter, businessman, and politician, was his elder brother.

47. *Dong-A ilbo*, December 28, 1931. The account reviews what happened in Pyongyang that year under the title of "The Features of the Pyongyang Society in 1931," and it also mentions, in an indirect and cautious way, "the sudden incident of last July that made Pyongyang notorious in one more way," a reference to the anti-Chinese race riots of July 5–6, 1931. The riot exploded when news accounts of the Wanbaoshan incident (July 3, 1931) in Manchuria that exaggerated Korean victimization at the hands of Chinese farmers circulated in Korea. While Incheon, Seoul, and many other cities also witnessed looting, lynching, and killing of Chinese merchants and workers (more than four hundred incidents in all), casualty numbers in Pyongyang exceeded other places by a large margin. While the death toll was around ten in other areas, in Pyongyang at least ninety-four Chinese were killed, more than three hundred were wounded, and 289 Chinese houses were destroyed. Chu Ikchong, "Singminjigi P'yŏngyang meriyasŭ chabon," 120; Chŏn Ponggwan, "P'yŏngyang Chunggugin paech'ŏk p'oktong sakŏn." In the aftermath of the massacre, more than twelve hundred people were arrested by the police in Pyongyang, according to a heavily censored article in *Tonggwang*, titled "P'yŏngyang p'oktong sakŏn hoego" [Reminiscing about the Pyongyang Riot]. It was penned by *Dong-A ilbo* reporter O Kiyŏng, who laments the "misuse of nationalist consciousness" in that tragic night in downtown Pyongyang by hundreds of people in angry mobs that did not flinch from killing even children and women. On the racial riots in Seoul and other cities, see Chŏn Ponggwan, "P'yŏngyang Chunggugin paech'ŏk p'oktong sakŏn"; Jung, "Migrant Labor and Massacres"; Chŏng Pyŏnguk, *Singminji puron yŏlchŏn*. The fierceness of the racial violence in Pyongyang reflected the high degree of competition Korean workers and businesses experienced in the region resulting from the heavy presence of Chinese migrant laborers and merchants. North and South P'yŏngan Provinces were close to the border and received the brunt of Chinese migration. This 1931 pogrom resulted in a drastic reduction of Chinese merchant power in Pyongyang and helped Korean businesses, knitwear companies in particular, that had been suffering from robust Chinese production based in Sinŭiju on the Yalu River border and strong Chinese merchant networks in the region. The rubber industry was less affected by these events. See Chu Ikchong, "Singminjigi P'yŏngyang meriyasŭ chabon," 119–23.

48. Kim Kyŏngil, *Ilcheha nodong undongsa*, chap. 7; O Miil, *Han'guk kŭndae chabon'ga*, chap. 6.

49. After the Russian Revolution of 1917, "socialist" ideas gained traction among Korean anticolonial fighters as in other parts of Asia, and the "socialist" wing soon emerged as a force in the independence movement challenging the leadership of the bourgeois nationalist camp. Anarchist and Marxist-Leninist groups waged fierce and often violent battles among themselves over the course of the 1920s, a process dubbed the Ana-Bol Struggle by contemporaries, from which the Bolsheviks emerged as the winner by the late 1920s. The early history of the colonial labor movement reflects these political developments in the larger nationalist movement.

50. Kim Kyŏngil, *Ilcheha nodong undongsa*, 379–80.

51. Song Chiyŏng, "1930-yŏn P'yŏngyang komu kongjang p'aŏp," 239–40.

52. Kim Kyŏngil, *Han'guk kŭndae nodongsa*, 97. From the late 1930s, however, youth labor began to replace adult female labor in rubber industry as the industry was reorganized to produce military goods. Yi Chŏngok, "Ilcheha kongŏp nodong," 193.

53. Yi Chŏngok, "Ilcheha kongŏp nodong," 212.

54. Ibid., 201–3.

55. On rubber industry associations, see Kim Kyŏngil, *Han'guk kŭndae nodongsa*, 85.

56. Kim Kyŏngil, *Han'guk nodong undongsa* 2, 46, table 2-3; Yi Chŏngok, "Ilcheha kongŏp nodong," 175, table 4-21. This gender ratio was stable between 1928 and 1940, around 31.7 to 34 percent.

57. The largest group (15,373 women) worked in the textile sector, comprising 80.9 percent of the sector total of 19,011 workers. The food industry sector had the second largest concentration of women workers, with 6,362 women (23.5 percent of the sector workforce total of 27,055), followed by the chemical industry sector, which employed 5,173 women (35.1 percent of the sector total of 14,720). Kim Kyŏngil, *Han'guk nodong undongsa* 2, 46, table 2-3. According to *Chōsen Sōtokufu tōkei nenpō* (Statistical Yearbook of the Government-General in Korea) statistics, which collected data from companies hiring five or more workers on a regular basis, the ratio of women in the total industrial workforce (manual workers, categorized as *chikkong*) remained stable around 33 percent throughout the 1930s, while the total number of industrial workers grew from 83,900 in 1930 to 135,797 in 1935, and to 230,688 in 1940. Yi Chŏngok, "Ilcheha kongŏp nodong," 175. By 1940, 73,202 women worked in factories, a 259 percent jump from the 1930 level. Kim Kyŏngil, *Han'guk nodong undongsa* 2, 46.

58. By 1935 the fertilizer industry caught up with the rubber industry and emerged as the leading employer for women in the chemical sector by 1940, although the ratio of women workers in the fertilizer industry was much lower (16.6 percent in 1930, 24.2 percent in 1935, and 20.9 percent in 1940) than in the rubber industry (67.9 percent in 1930, 68.6 percent in 1935, and 59.3 percent in 1940). Yi Chŏngok, "Ilcheha kongŏp nodong," 171-73.

59. Kim Kyŏngil, *Han'guk kŭndae nodongsa*, 92, table 2-5.

60. Sŏ Hyŏngsil calculates the percentage of married women workers in the chemical sector in 1930 as 80.7 percent, using the *Chōsen Sōtokufu* statistics published in 1935. Sŏ Hyŏngsil, "Singminji sidae yŏsŏng nodong undong," 36. Kim Tongwŏn, the president of P'yŏngan Rubber, noted in 1935 that more than twenty thousand people, roughly two-tenths of the total population of Pyongyang, depended on the rubber shoe and knitwear industries. O Miil, "P'yŏngyang chiyŏk Chosŏnin chabon'gadŭl," 136. In 1930 the colonial government statistics show the total number of gainfully employed persons (*yuŏpcha*) in Pyongyang as 41,989 (Sŏ Hyŏngsil, "Singminji sidae yŏsŏng nodong undong," 43), while the population of the city as of 1930 was 140,703, which included 116,899 Koreans, 20,073 Japanese, and 3,534 Chinese (Korean Statistical Information Service, "In'gu ch'ongjosa, in'gu pumun, ch'ongjosa in'gu (1930-yŏn)" [Population Census, Population Sector, Population by Census (1930)], available at kosis.kr). The population of Korea as a whole in 1930 was a little over 21 million (21,058,305), which included 527,016 Japanese and 91,783 Chinese.

61. Korean reckoning of age ("se") counts the year of birth as one, and adds one each following year, regardless of the date of birth. Also, in the colonial period the lunar calendar was widely used for everyday life, including birthday celebrations. It is not easy, therefore, to pinpoint her birth year from the recording of her age in extant documents. In our best estimate Kang appears to have been born in 1901 and was thus thirty-one years old in the Korean way of counting age in 1931. News media reported her age as thirty at the time of the 1931 P'yŏngwŏn strike (*Dong-A ilbo*, May 30 and 31, 1931), but listed her age as thirty-two at her death in 1932 (*Dong-A ilbo*, August 17, 1932). Information on Kang's life story is taken from Muhojŏngin, "Ŭlmiltae sang ŭi ch'egongnyŏ," 40-41.

62. The *Dong-A ilbo* report on her death (August 17, 1932) mentions that Kang, age 32, was survived by her mother (age 65), father (age 61), older brother (age 33), and younger brother (age 15).

63. Kim Kyŏngil, *Han'guk kŭndae nodongsa*, 107.
64. Kim Kyŏngil, *Han'guk nodong undongsa 2*, 102. Kim summarizes the history of colonial-era rubber strikes (102–13); see also FKTU, *Han'guk nodong chohap undongsa*, 50–52, 56, 195–201, 205–6.
65. With the help of an umbrella labor organization, the Nodong Yŏnmaenghoe (Labor Alliance), women workers were able to establish the Kyŏngsŏng (Seoul) Rubber Female Employees' Association (Kyŏngsŏng Komu Yŏjikkong Chohap). Kim Kyŏngil, *Han'guk nodong undongsa 2*, 110–13.
66. *Dong-A ilbo*, July 8 and 9, 1923; Kim Kyŏngil, *Han'guk nodong undongsa 2*, 111–15.
67. According to a list of strikes in major cities compiled from contemporary news media by Kim Kyŏngil, between the 1923 Seoul rubber strike and the 1930 Pyongyang rubber strike at least fifteen cases of rubber strikes occurred in Seoul, Pyongyang, and Pusan, often involving more than one factory. After the August 1930 strike in Pyongyang, at least thirty-eight more strikes occurred in these three cities before the end of the colonial period. Kim Kyŏngil, *Ilcheha nodong undongsa*, 530–67, and *Han'guk kŭndae nodongsa*, 92, 116–17, 134–35.
68. The year 1933 represented another peak in rubber disputes with three strikes in Seoul, four strikes in Pusan (including a massive solidarity strike by 626 workers of six rubber companies in October and November 1933 that lasted about twenty-five days), and ten strikes in Pyongyang. The number of rubber strikes declined thereafter, registering only one small-scale strike in 1934, five strikes in 1935, two in 1938, and two in 1939, after which reports on strike activity ceased to exist. See Kim Kyŏngil, *Han'guk kŭndae nodongsa*, 111, 116–17, 134–35.
69. On the 1930 Pyongyang rubber strike, see Kim Kyŏngil, *Han'guk nodong undongsa 2*, 327–33; Kim Kyŏngil, *Han'guk kŭndae nodongsa*, 114–29; FKTU, *Han'guk nodong chohap undongsa*, 195–201; Song Chiyŏng, "1930-yŏn P'yŏngyang komu kongjang p'aŏp," 235–53; Kim Chungyŏl, "P'yŏngyang komu kongjang p'aŏp."
70. From the mid-1920s until 1931, rubber prices went down, leading to higher profitability and heated investment in the sector, but between 1931 and 1936 the price of rubber shot up 400 percent, while companies were unable to increase prices more than 25 percent because of severe competition. Chu Ikchong, "Singminjigi Chosŏn komu kongŏp," 102. By 1933 the production capacity of 60 million pairs far exceeded actual output of 20 million pairs. Faced with dwindling profit margins, Korean rubber companies tried to open new markets in Manchuria, diversify product lineup, and collectively regulate production and sales, but without much success. Ibid., 101–4, 107–11.
71. Ibid., 105. According to 1935 industry statistics, wages accounted for 12 percent of the total production cost, while the cost of rubber material constituted 38 percent. Yi Chŏngok, "Ilcheha kongŏp nodong," 192.
72. Chu Ikchong, "Singminjigi Chosŏn komu kongŏp," 105–7. Economic historian Chu Ikchong provides a detailed description of the components of production costs in the rubber industry (101–11).
73. *Dong-A ilbo*, September 5, 1930; O Kiyŏng, "P'yŏngyang komu chaengŭi chinsang," no. 4.
74. O Kiyŏng, "P'yŏngyang komu chaengŭi chinsang," nos. 4 and 7; O Kiyŏng, "P'yŏngyang komu kongjang chaengŭi chŏnjŏk"; *Maeil sinbo*, August 25, 1930; *Chungoe ilbo*, August 25 and 27, 1930.
75. On the Wŏnsan general strike of 1929 to 1930, see Kim Kyŏngil, *Han'guk kŭndae nodongsa*, chap. 7. Kim Kyŏngil, *Han'guk nodong undongsa 2*, 210n120 lists key literature on the strike, which is vast. According to Kim, the labor movement in Pyongyang got out of the doldrums in 1930, with a major stimulant for the rejuvenation of

the movement coming from the Wŏnsan general strike. Kim Kyŏngil, *Han'guk kŭndae nodongsa*, 145.

76. Kim Kyŏngil observes that this strike represented a war the colonial government waged "against the working class" and "a strategic move" by the colonial authority "on the eve of imperialist wars" to subjugate the labor movement in the colony. Organized labor in Wŏnsan was not prepared for this "decisive battle" (*iltae kyŏlchŏn*). Kim Kyŏngil, *Han'guk nodong undongsa 2*, 223–24.

77. Kim Kyŏngil, *Han'guk kŭndae nodongsa*, 160.

78. Kim Kyŏngil, *Ilcheha nodong undongsa*, 549–52. Kim Kyŏngil points out the "subjective conditions" of Pyongyang's industrial workers around 1930 that led to intensive strike activities in Pyongyang, including the concentration of workers in certain industrial areas of the city, the long history and vitality of the city's labor and social organizations that ran educational programs for workers, and the experiences of participating in strikes, all of which helped workers attain "common class consciousness." Kim Kyŏngil, *Han'guk nodong undongsa 2*, 328.

79. Yi Horyong, *Han'guk ŭi anak'ijŭm: Sasang p'yŏn*, 97–98. Historian Dongyoun Hwang argues that the association, which was not yet an anarchist organization, demonstrates "the popularity of anarchist ideas in colonial Korea, especially that of the mutual aid idea of Peter Kropotkin." Hwang, *Anarchism in Korea*, 96–97. According to historian Yi Horyong, anarchist thought began to filter into Korea through Japan and China beginning in the 1880s. Anarchism's appeal to "the self-consciously internationalist radical Left" was felt strongly across the globe in the last two decades of the nineteenth century. Anderson, *Age of Globalization*, 2. In addition, key figures in the international anarchist movement were interacting with Japanese thinkers and activists by then. Konishi, *Anarchist Modernity*. A major attraction anarchism had for Korean intellectuals was that its ideas, especially the notion of "mutual aid" and solidarity as the engine of human progress championed by Kropotkin, provided a much-needed solution to the dilemma they faced: how to justify Korean survival as a nation against the power of the hegemonic imperialist discourse of "civilization and enlightenment" undergirded by social Darwinism. The anarcho-communism of Kropotkin became mainstream in the Korean anarchist movement from the 1910s until the emergence of anarcho-syndicalism as a force at the end of the 1920s. Yi Horyong, *Han'guk ŭi anak'ijŭm: Sasang p'yŏn*, 92–93, 107; Yi Horyong, *Han'guk ŭi anak'ijŭm: Undong p'yŏn*, 22–32.

80. Kim Kyŏngil, *Han'guk nodong undongsa 2*, 165–74. According to Kim, it was an "unfortunate" development for nonsocialist nationalists because "by turning a blind eye to the life of workers who were the majority of the population in a colonial context, and by ignoring their resistance, nationalism as an ideology failed in securing its legitimacy at the popular level." In this book I follow the contemporary usage in general and use "communist" to refer to those who were members of the Communist Party or the Marxist-Leninists who worked in the international communist movement and accepted guidance from the Comintern. The first socialist parties emerged among Koreans overseas in the late 1910s, and the first Korean Communist Party in Korea proper was secretly formed in April 1925. Yi Chunsik, *Chosŏn kongsandang sŏngnip kwa hwaltong*.

81. Kim Kyŏngil, *Han'guk nodong undongsa 2*, 174.

82. Ibid., 177; Yi Horyong, *Han'guk ŭi anak'ijŭm: Undong p'yŏn*, 144–50, 160–62. Both Kim Kyŏngil and Yi Horyong focus on the appearance of "work's bureaus" or "industrial cooperatives," which were often formed during or in the aftermath of a strike with the purpose of securing strike funding or supporting the livelihood of fired workers. They see these entities as distinctive experimentations based on tenets of anarcho-syndicalism. Kim Kyŏngil, *Han'guk nodong undongsa 2*, 178; Yi Horyong, *Han'guk ŭi anak'ijŭm: Undong p'yŏn*, 157. On the role of anarchists in the labor movement in Korea,

see Kim Kyŏngil, *Han'guk nodong undongsa 2*, 176–81; Kim Kyŏngil, *Ilcheha nodong undongsa*, 413–26; Yi Horyong, *Han'guk ŭi anak'ijŭm: Undong p'yŏn*, 143–70.

83. *Chungoe ilbo*, August 11, 1930; *Dong-A ilbo*, September 10, 1930. In the case of Kyŏngsŏng Spinning and Weaving (Kyŏngbang), studied by Eckert, dividends to shareholders remained high at 8 percent during this period while the company cut wages by 20 percent using the Depression as an excuse. Kyŏngbang executive Yi Kanghyŏn claimed that the company "had no choice but to reduce wages to some extent, even though it was not [the company's] original intention [to do so]," and *Dong-A ilbo* repeated the company's stance. Eckert notes that during the time of a general strike of knitwear workers in Pyongyang in 1925, in which one thousand workers participated, *Dong-A ilbo* came to the defense of Korean capitalists in its editorial (April 14, 1925), arguing that to buttress the Korean industry suffering from stiff competition from Chinese and Japanese makers, "the workers movement in it will have to be content with a less than satisfactory standard." Eckert, *Offspring of Empire*, 209–11.

84. See Kim Kyŏngil, *Han'guk kŭndae nodongsa*, 98, table 2–6, which is based on *Chōsen Sōtokufu* statistics. In 1932, when rubber strikes against wage cuts were coming to an end, adult female workers' average daily wage was 0.70 wŏn, and it continued to decrease to 0.62 by 1936. According to surveys of women's wages in Seoul in the early 1930s, monthly wage income for factory women in silk reeling, rice milling, and the tobacco industry came out at 20–30 wŏn, 10–30 wŏn, and 6–25 wŏn, respectively. Housemaids' income averaged 7.6 wŏn a month. The top wage-earning professionals were nurses (33–70 wŏn), followed by primary schoolteachers (35–60 wŏn) and reporters (25–60 wŏn). In the middle were preschool caretakers, office workers, telephone switchboard operators, department salespersons, and bus girls. Kim Sujin, *Sinyŏsŏng, kŭndae ŭi kwaing*, 90, table 1–12. Adult women workers at Chōsen Spinning and Weaving (Chōbō) in Pusan in 1930 earned on average 0.60 wŏn a day, while the numbers for women workers in the textile industry and in manufacturing were 0.41 and 0.46, respectively. Pak Chaehwa, "1930-yŏn Chosŏn Pangjik p'aŏp," 13.

85. Song Chiyŏng, "1930-yŏn P'yŏngyang komu kongjang p'aŏp," 239–40.

86. Ibid., 240.

87. Kim Kyŏngil, *Han'guk kŭndae nodongsa*, 104–5. In addition to the withdrawal of the plan to cut wages workers also called for severance pay, holiday and nighttime extra pay, and yearend bonuses. Song Chiyŏng, "1930-yŏn P'yŏngyang komu kongjang p'aŏp," 243.

88. Song Chiyŏng, "1930-yŏn P'yŏngyang komu kongjang p'aŏp," 239.

89. "Life was ridiculously unfair," he continued, since workers who could barely afford "millet gruel" had to see their already meager wages being slashed further. Ibid., 240. On abject working conditions, long working hours, and the sexual harassment and violence that many women factory workers faced daily at the time, see Yi Chŏngok, "Ilcheha kongŏp nodong," chap. 5; Kim Kyŏngil, *Ilcheha nodong undongsa*, 58–80; Yi Songhŭi, "Ilcheha Pusan chiyŏk yŏsŏng nodongjadŭl"; Janice Kim, *To Live to Work*.

90. *Dong-A ilbo*, September 9 and 10, 1930; *Chosun ilbo*, May 25, 1931; Kim Kyŏngil, *Han'guk kŭndae nodongsa*, 100; *Dong-A ilbo*, November 9, 1933.

91. Eckert, *Offspring of Empire*, 214.

92. *Chungoe ilbo*, August 11, 1930.

93. Chang Kyusik, *Ilcheha Han'guk Kidokkyo minjokchuŭi*, 266–68.

94. Among them were Ch'oe Ch'anghwan of Chŏngch'ang Rubber and Kim Tongwŏn and Yi Yŏngha of P'yŏngan Rubber. On the Sinminhoe incident, see Chang Kyusik, *Ilcheha Han'guk Kidokkyo minjokchuŭi*, 104–7; Yun Kyŏngno, *105-in sakŏn kwa Sinminhoe yŏn'gu*; O Miil, "1910–1920-yŏndae P'yŏngyang Chosŏnin chabon'ga," 273–76.

95. Chang Kyusik, *Ilcheha Han'guk Kidokkyo minjokchuŭi*, 105.
96. O Miil, "1910-1920-yŏndae P'yŏngyang Chosŏnin chabon'ga," 280–82. The names and backgrounds of Pyongyang businessmen who led the March First Movement are listed on p. 281 and include Yi Tŏkhwan, Yun Wŏnsam, Yun Sŏngun, Sŏ Kip'ung, and Kim Tongwŏn.
97. Chang Kyusik, *Ilcheha Han'guk Kidokkyo minjokchuŭi*, 268; *Chosun ilbo*, August 12, 1930; Yi Chŏkhyo, "Ch'ongdongwŏn," 214.
98. Chang Kyusik, *Ilcheha Han'guk Kidokkyo minjokchuŭi*, and "1920-yŏndae kaejoron," 111–34.
99. "New people" were also defined as *sa*, as in the name "Hŭngsadan" (Young Korean Academy). *Sa*, a Confucian concept of "gentlemen" qualified to serve the king as government officials, became reimagined as the citizen subject of modern and Christian nation-building.
100. Chang Kyusik, *Ilcheha Han'guk Kidokkyo minjokchuŭi*, 139. The Hŭngŏp Kurakpu was the domestic counterpart of the Tongjihoe (Comrade Society) led by Syngman Rhee from the United States, and the Suyang Tonguhoe was linked to An Ch'angho's Hŭngsadan (Young Korean Academy), whose base was also in the United States. Chang sees the differences in orientation between the two groups as stemming partly from the differences in their social backgrounds. Northwestern Christians were of non-elite (*p'yŏngmin*) background while many in the Hŭngŏp Kurakpu group, or the Kiho (Seoul and Kyŏnggi and Ch'ungch'ŏng Provinces) Christians, boasted their elite pedigree. In addition, as mentioned earlier in this chapter, special characteristics of the northwest region helped create a particular kind of culture and dynamism within the bourgeois entrepreneurial class, what Chang Kyusik calls the "autonomous middle class" (*charipchŏk chungsangch'ŭng*), as the northwestern Protestant movement was strongly rooted in the ranks of small- to medium-sized merchants and industrialists, small landlords, and owner-cultivator farmers of the region, unlike its counterpart based in Seoul. Chang Kyusik, *Ilcheha Han'guk Kidokkyo minjokchuŭi*, 35–41, and "'Chosŏn ŭi Kandi' Kodang Cho Mansik," 87.
101. Seoul-based Suyang Tongmaenghoe was launched in February 1922 by mostly intellectuals, including the famous novelist Yi Kwangsu, and Pyongyang-based Tongu Kurakpu was established in January 1923 by mostly entrepreneur activists led by Kim Tongwŏn. Suyang Tonguhoe was created when, following the wishes of An Ch'angho, the two groups merged in October 1925. Suyang Tongmaenghoe was reorganized into the Seoul headquarters and Tongu Kurakpu into its Pyongyang chapter. Direct negotiations between Yi Kwangsu and Kim Tongwŏn in 1923 and again in 1925 made the merger possible. See Yi Hyŏnju, "Ilcheha (Suyang) Tonguhoe," 187–89. The membership numbers fluctuated around one hundred, and as of February 1933 there were 148 members. Chang Kyusik, *Ilcheha Han'guk Kidokkyo minjokchuŭi*, 141–43. On Suyang Tonguhoe and Hŭngŏp Kurakpu, see ibid.; Yi Hyŏnju, "Ilcheha (Suyang) Tonguhoe"; and Kim Sangt'ae, "1920-1930-yŏndae Tonguhoe-Hŭngŏp Kurakpu."
102. Yi Kihun, *Ch'ŏngnyŏn a*, 130–31.
103. Chang Kyusik, *Ilcheha Han'guk Kidokkyo minjokchuŭi*, 167–72.
104. Ibid., 171. This tendency was also in resonance with An Ch'angho's group's new reformist formulation, *taegongjuŭi* (ideology of great public-mindedness), which emerged in the late 1920s as a way to legitimize cooperation between Christian and socialist fighters for independence. Thus, efforts at reformulating Christian evangelism and social practices within Korea paralleled developments among overseas Korean nationalists, mostly based in China, which resulted in the formation of a strong consensus on a platform based on the principles of democracy, republicanism, and equality (*kyŭndŭng*) by the late 1930s to the early 1940s. Later, the urgent need to combine forces against the

Japanese imperialist expansion on the continent and in preparation for eventual Japanese defeat and Korean liberation propelled these serious united-front endeavors among Korean fighters. The merging of these two strains of reformist ideas, one domestic and one from the Korean nationalist movement in China, in the postcolonial space of southern Korea under US control merits additional study.

105. Kim Hyŏngsik served as the head of the branch from March 1921 to May 1924, and Kim Sŏngŏp succeeded him, serving as branch head until December 1927 and again from June 1928 to February 1938. Chu Yohan stepped into the role from December 1927 to June 1928. All these three men and reporters O Kiyŏng and Yi Chehak were members of Suyang Tonguhoe. Chang Kyusik, *Ilcheha Han'guk Kidokkyo minjokchuŭi*, 280. Many of these Suyang Tonguhoe/Hŭngsadan leaders later found influential positions in the United States Army Military Government in Korea (USAMGIK) following the Japanese surrender in 1945, and their Christian reformist views had a significant impact on the early nation-building process in South Korea (see chapter 4). An important example is Yi Taewi, a key leader of the reformist wing of Suyang Tonguhoe. He was recruited as the head of the Labor Bureau by USAMGIK, influencing the direction and institutionalization of the industrial relations system in South Korea.

106. On the Kŭnuhoe movement, see Nam Hwasook, "1920-yŏndae yŏsŏng undong" and "Kŭnuhoe undong."

107. The development of the united-front movement provoked diverse responses from nationalists. In nationalist circles, the "left-wing" forces, centered on the Old Faction of Ch'ŏndogyo and the Chosun Ilbo group, supported the united-front movement along with socialists and opposed the "self-government" (*chach'i*) argument entertained by the Dong-A Ilbo group and the New Faction of Ch'ŏndogyo. The latter, the self-government advocates, formed the "right wing" of the nationalist movement. The Suyang Tonguhoe was regarded as one of the bases of the self-government movement, and its leader, Yi Kwangsu, was a major ideologue in the self-government discussion. Yi Hyŏnju, "Ilcheha (Suyang) Tonguhoe," 186, 194–96.

108. The alienation of the Suyang Tonguhoe from the Sin'ganhoe movement prompted Chu Yohan (Pyongyang) and Cho Pyŏngok (Seoul) to launch a reform movement from within. An Ch'angho's direct involvement in the dispute in late 1927 eventually led to the deletion of the word *suyang* from the organization's name by November 1929 and the retirement of Yi Kwangsu, the leader of its conservative and collaborationist wing who had been suffering from illness, from the leadership role. Chang Kyusik, *Ilcheha Han'guk Kidokkyo minjokchuŭi*, 148–49.

109. The Suyang Tonguhoe reformists set out to expand their organizational base by capturing the national association of Presbyterian Young People's Society of Christian Endeavor, the largest Christian youth organization in the country. Yi Taewi worked as its president or secretary from its beginning in 1928 to 1937, when he was arrested in the Suyang Tonguhoe incident. These reformists also organized the Kidok Sinuhoe as a united-front organization of reformist Christians and created a rural bureau of the Presbyterian General Assembly. Cho Mansik's Kidokkyo Nongch'on Yŏn'guhoe coordinated their work with the rural bureau. Chang Kyusik, *Ilcheha Han'guk Kidokkyo minjokchuŭi*, 148–53.

110. Yi Hyŏnju, "Ilcheha (Suyang) Tonguhoe," 205. The Christian reform movement of the late 1920s and early 1930s evolved in a complicated way, but what is important to our discussion is that by the early 1930s the majority of Korean Christian leaders were leaning in the direction of collaboration with the colonial power, choosing the protection of their "class" interests over their "nationalist" mission. Meanwhile, the reformist wing trying to engage social issues, including the thorny labor question, remained small in number.

111. These projects include the launching of the Pyongyang Chamber of Commerce and Industry (P'yŏngyang Sanggong Hyŏphoe) in December 1928, which aimed at protecting ethnic Korean businesses against the Japanese-dominated Pyongyang Chamber of Commerce.

112. On Kim Tongwŏn, see Chu Ikchong, "P'yŏngyang Chosŏnin kiŏpka," 148, 157–63; O Miil, "1910–1920-yŏndae P'yŏngyang Chosŏnin chabon'ga," 276, 281, 292; O Miil, "1910–1920-yŏndae kongŏp palchŏn tan'gye," 207. The companies Kim owned included a wooden goods (*mongmul*) factory, established in 1910; P'yŏngan Rubber, established in 1924; and the P'yŏngan Knitwear, established in 1929.

113. The most influential among Christian leaders in the region was An Ch'angho (1878–1938), and Cho Mansik was regarded as An's representative in the Christian nationalist community in the northwest, although Cho maintained a certain level of independence from An's line. Cho Mansik was very close to and worked together with Suyang Tonguhoe members, and people viewed him as a "Tonguhoe person," but he did not join the organization out of concern over factionalism. Chang Kyusik, *Minjung kwa hamkke han Chosŏn ŭi Kandi*, 169, 199.

114. The Pyongyang Society for the Promotion of Chosŏn Native Goods, established in June 1922, represented the most robust part of the Christian self-strengthening movement of the 1920s. Demonstrating the vitality of the nationalist movement of the northwest, it operated independently from the national Society for the Promotion of Chosŏn Native Goods, which was established half a year later in Seoul, in January 1923.

115. Chang Kyusik, *Minjung kwa hamkke han Chosŏn ŭi Kandi*, 169, 199. On Cho Mansik, see Chang Kyusik's works, including ibid., 236; *Ilcheha Han'guk Kidokkyo minjokchuŭi*, 140–43, 209–11; "'Chosŏn ŭi Kandi' Kodang Cho Mansik," 92; "1920-yŏndae kaejoron," 134.

116. Over the 1930s Cho Mansik's followers, led by Pae Minsu and Yu Chaegi, vigorously pursued rural campaigns through the Kidokkyo Nongch'on Yŏn'guhoe (Christian Rural Research Association, established in 1929), and Chang Kyusik sees the association as the first case of Christian socialism taking root in colonial Korea in both theory and practice. The Christian Rural Research Association was already discussing land reform ideas in the 1930s, and Cho was positive about the idea, unlike other right-wing leaders. After the Soviet takeover of northern Korea, Cho tried hard to mediate a land reform policy between the communists and the conservatives as the head of the P'yŏngnam People's Political Committee. Chang Kyusik, *Minjung kwa hamkke han Chosŏn ŭi Kandi*, 235–36.

117. His views appeared in a series of *Dong-A ilbo* articles, titled "The Real Story of the Pyongyang Rubber Dispute" (P'yŏngyang komu chaengŭi chinsang), which reviewed the 1930 Pyongyang rubber strike after the fact. (*Dong-A ilbo* was suspended by the colonial government from April to early September 1930 and was unable to cover the 1930 rubber strike.) It is reasonable to assume that this *Dong-A ilbo* series, published in the name of one "Special Correspondent O" of the Pyongyang branch, was written by reporter O Kiyŏng, who served as the special correspondent at the time. An article published in his name the following month in *Pyŏlgŏn'gon* (O Kiyŏng, "P'yŏngyang komu kongjang chaengŭi chŏnjŏk") is a condensed version of the "Real Story."

118. O Kiyŏng, "P'yŏngyang komu chaengŭi chinsang," no. 6, *Dong-A ilbo*, September 10, 1930.

119. Even though Kim Tongwŏn and other business leaders boycotted the Sin'ganhoe, in the Pyongyang chapter Christian and business elements still constituted the dominant force, and some officials in the local Sin'ganhoe chapter were rubber factory owners. Song Chiyŏng, "1930-yŏn P'yŏngyang komu kongjang p'aŏp," 238.

120. Yi Hyŏnju, "Ilcheha (Suyang) Tonguhoe," 205; O Miil, *Han'guk kŭndae chabon'ga*, 311.

121. Kim Kyŏngil, *Han'guk nodong undongsa 2*, 170.

122. North Korean scholarly literature on the strike concurs with this evaluation and cites the "reformist" nationalist elite as a major reason for the defeat. Kim Kyŏngil, *Ilche ha nodong undongsa*, 264. Although several Sin'gan and Kŭnu chapters passed resolutions siding with workers or developed pro-labor platforms, including calls for a minimum wage law, an eight-hour workday, protection of women and youth workers and union rights, and a ban on ethnic discrimination at work sites, actual intervention in local labor disputes by Sin'gan and Kŭnu chapters was not frequent overall.

123. The Kŭnuhoe Pyongyang chapter was, like other chapters in the country, created by an earnest collaboration between socialist and nonsocialist Christian women activists on January 30, 1928. Nam Hwasook, "1920-yŏndae yŏsong undong," 91, 96.

124. The Pyongyang Kŭnu chapter, together with the Unggi chapter in North Hamgyŏng Province, was able to acquire a headquarters building, a feat even the Kŭnu national headquarters was unable to pull off. Ibid., 101. On the Kŭnuhoe Pyongyang chapter, see ibid., 96; Pak Yongok, *Han'guk yŏsŏng hangil undongsa*, 55–56, 392–99. Nationalists at the Kŭnu Pyongyang chapter continued its operation after the Sin'ganhoe Pyongyang chapter closed down at the end of 1930.

125. These included night schools, and even a plan to set up an underwear factory to create jobs for unemployed women. Nam Hwasook, "1920-yŏndae yŏsong undong," 96.

126. *Dong-A ilbo*, June 13, 1931, and March 25, 1933 (figure 2); *Kyŏngsŏng ilbo*, July 25, 1931.

127. Early news reports recorded her surname as "Kang," but I take "Cho" as the correct surname based on official legal records contained in Kim Kyŏngil, *Ilcheha sahoe undongsa charyojip*, vol. 6, sections 9 through 11.

2. FACTORY WOMEN IN THE SOCIALIST IMAGINATION

1. Many newspaper articles in the early 1930s, collected in Yŏngjin, *Ilcheha Chosŏn kwan'gye sinmun*, vols. 1–2, relayed police concerns with "behind-the-scenes" agitators and underground organizations, using language like "the hand of labor activists" (*nodong undongja ŭi son*) or "the hand behind the black curtain" (*hŭkmak ŭi son*) that was conspiring to provoke labor disputes.

2. The information on the activities of Chŏng Talhŏn and his group, unless otherwise noted, comes from the following three documents produced by the Pyongyang District Court, which are reproduced in Kim Kyŏngil, *Ilcheha sahoe undongsa charyojip*, vol. 6: "Chŏng Talhŏn oe 7-in ŭi yesim ch'ŏnggusŏ" (July 1931); "Chŏn Chosŏn chŏksaek nodong chohap chojik kyehoek ŭi yesim chonggyŏl kyŏlchŏngsŏ songbu ŭi kŏn" (April 10, 1933); "Chŏng Talhŏn oe 7-in ŭi p'an'gyŏlmun" (May 8, 1934).

3. On the "June 10 *Manse* movement," see Chang Sŏkhong, *6.10 manse undong*. More than a thousand people were arrested in the police roundup linked to this movement. Among them was Kwŏn Osŏl (1897–1930), the Communist Party leader who recruited Chŏng Talhŏn into the party and was in charge of the preparation committee for the June 10 movement on the communist side. He was brutally tortured and perished in prison.

4. The university, called the "Moscow Communist University" (Mosŭk'ŭba kongdae) in Korea, was established by the Comintern in 1921 to train Asians as well as Russians of the Far East and lasted until 1938. In addition to Chŏng Talhŏn, illustrious Korean graduates included Cho Pongam and O Sŏngryun, and female communists Hŏ

Chŏngsuk, Chu Sejuk, Kim Myŏngsi, Kim Choi, and Pak Chŏngae. Ho Chi Minh and Deng Xiaoping are among the best-known graduates of the school.

5. On the communist campaigns to build a "Bolshevik" party through revolutionary or "red" labor and farmers' movements in the late 1920s and the 1930s, see O Miil, "1920-yŏndae mal—1930-yŏndae Pusan-Kyŏngnam," 95–188; Kim Kyŏngil, *Han'guk kŭndae nodongsa*, chap. 8–11; Ch'oe Kyujin, "1930-yŏndae ch'o Chosŏn 'Polsyebik'i tang'" and *Chosŏn kongsandang chaegŏn undong*. From the late 1920s the Comintern and the Profintern began to pay close attention to the Korea question and issued a series of directives to Korean communist activists, the most important of which were the "December Thesis" of 1928 by the Comintern, the "September Thesis" of 1930 by the Profintern, and the "October Letter" of 1931 by the Secretariat of the T'aero. Comintern policies toward Korea were based on the understanding crystalized at the Sixth World Congress in 1928, which maintained that the world's capitalist system had entered the third and last stage of a system-wide revolutionary crisis. Comintern communists believed it was thus time to reveal the true nature of "reformist" forces and organize a coordinated revolt of the revolutionary masses. Ch'oe Kyujin, *Chosŏn kongsandang chaegŏn undong*, 18–35. History had entered "an era of revolutions and wars," and in such conditions it was urgent that revolutionaries establish a "Bolshevik" party founded on the power of industrial workers and farmers and resolved to overcome all obstacles and work toward *the* revolution, imagined to be within reach. On the effect of the directives from the Comintern, Profintern, and the T'aero Secretariat, see Ch'oe Kyujin, "1930-yŏndae ch'o Chosŏn 'Polsyebik'i tang'" and *Chosŏn kongsandang chaegŏn undong*.

6. The last, and fourth, Korean Communist Party was destroyed in 1928 by the Japanese colonial government.

7. By 1942 Chōsen Chisso accounted for a whopping 36 percent of the total Japanese manufacturing investment in its colony of Korea and 27 percent of the total manufacturing capital in Korea. Kwak Kŏnhong, "1930-yŏndae ch'oban Chosŏn Chilso Piryo," 46.

8. On Chŏng Talhŏn group's organizing activities in the Hamhŭng-Hŭngnam area, see Isogaya, *Uri ch'ŏngch'un ŭi Chosŏn*; Ch'oe Kyujin, "'K'ommyunisŭt'ŭ kŭrup' kwa T'aep'yŏngyang Nodong Chohap," 148–50; Kim Kyŏngil, *Han'guk nodong undongsa 2*, 272–73.

9. Around that time communist activists, including the legendary female labor organizer Pak Chinhong, were also infiltrating rubber factories in Seoul. Leafletting efforts of various groups in support of labor strikes in Seoul, Pyongyang, and Pusan in the 1930s are detailed in Kim Kyŏngil, *Han'guk kŭndae nodongsa*, 155–59.

10. Kim Kyŏngil, *Ilcheha sahoe undongsa charyojip*, 6:229.

11. Ibid., 6:232–33.

12. A red union organization called Hŭngnam Leftists (Hŭngnam Chwaik, established in 1932), operating under T'aero's guidance, constructed a list of must-read texts for reading clubs it organized among workers. These were mostly T'aero-issued pamphlets and newsletters. Ch'oe Kyujin, "'K'ommyunisŭt'ŭ kŭrup' kwa T'aep'yŏngyang Nodong Chohap," 158. We can also get a glimpse of the kind of text materials workers were exposed to in the labor and social movements of the time in contemporary leftist novels. For example, Song Yŏng's *O Suhyang* (1931) mentions some leftist literature circulating among women activists, including Hosoi Wakizō's *Jōkō aishi* (The Pitiful History of Female Factory Workers), *Women and Socialism* (Puinnon) by August Bebel, *Techniques of Capitalism* (*Chabonjuŭi ŭi kigyo*), and *How to Fight* (*Ŏttŏkke ssaulkka*). Also mentioned were Korean journals *Musanja* (Proletariat) and *Chosŏn chi kwang* (Light of Chosŏn). Song Yŏng, *O Suhyang*, 120, 141.

13. Kim Kyŏngil, *Ilcheha sahoe undongsa charyojip*, 6:222.

14. *Dong-A ilbo*, June 13, 1931.
15. *Dong-A ilbo*, March 25, 1933.
16. After Chŏng Talhŏn's arrest, another T'aero organizer, Yi Chuha, tried to help striking workers at P'yŏngwŏn Rubber, mainly through disseminating flyers, and he continued his activities during the Sech'ang Rubber strike in July.
17. For examples of Japanese participation in "thought crimes," see articles in Yŏngjin, *Ilcheha Chosŏn kwan'gye sinmun*, 2:81, 188, 200, 208, 212, 222, 224, 236, 247, 253. Sonobe Hiroyuki's study of Japanese participation in Korean social movements during the 1930s, which introduces eighteen prosecuted incidents involving Japanese nationals between 1930 and 1934, provides the names of five Japanese workers who joined the red union movement in Hŭngnam (at Chōsen Chisso), as well as in Pusan and Seoul. Sonobe, "Zaicho Nihonjin no sanka shita kyosanshugi undo," 213–39. The most famous case of a Japanese worker fighting together with his Korean comrades is that of Isogaya Sueji, whose 1984 memoir *Korea, My Youth* (translated into Korean in 1988) provides a rare firsthand account of T'aero organizing activities in the Hŭngnam-Hamhŭng area in the 1930s. Isogaya came to Korea as a soldier and stayed as an employee of Chōsen Chisso. He was arrested in the second of the four T'aero incidents and returned to Japan in 1947. Isogaya, *Uri ch'ŏngch'un ŭi Chosŏn*, 80–83, 103–13.
18. Japanese activists dropped out of the movement increasingly from the late 1930s by choosing the option of *tenko* (thought conversion), although there were exceptions like Isogaya Sueji, who spent ten years in a prison in Korea. Kim Kyŏngil, *Han'guk kŭndae nodongsa*, 497; Isogaya, *Uri ch'ŏngch'un ŭi Chosŏn*.
19. The modern girl "emerged quite literally around the world in the first half of the twentieth century" and served as a marker of modernity in specific ways at each locale. Weinbaum, *Modern Girl around the World*, 1–8.
20. Kim Kyŏngil argues that in Japan the term "new woman" was applied to the members of an early feminist group, the Seito (Bluestockings), in the 1910s, and the *moga* (modern girls) gained currency in the following decade as a visible group of young wage-earning women, armed with a consumerist penchant for Western modern products and lifestyles and a bold desire to pursue romantic love. In Korea, however, the two terms began to circulate one after another during the 1920s, when the economic basis for such modern living had yet to be developed for women. The Korean version of "new women" thus became tangled up with knowledge about the "modern girl phenomenon" in Japan. As a result, Kim argues, the Korean "new women" suffered inordinate criticism from social reformers and the media. Kim Kyŏngil, *Yŏsŏng ŭi kŭndae, kŭndae ŭi yŏsŏng*, 28–33.
21. Literary scholar Sunyoung Park explains that in Japan, "the word *moga* generally connoted an independent urban professional woman who wore Western fashions and spent money lavishly on herself," while in Korea the figure of a *moga* "lacked of referents in real life," and in the late 1920s and early 1930s Korean context the term tended to function as an alias for "a deplorably consumerist New Woman." Sunyoung Park, *Proletarian Wave*, 207. Job opportunities for educated women increased somewhat and "modern girl" existence became possible by the 1930s in Korea, but the historical context had changed dramatically by then. The historic turn from a pro-Western orientation that defined the Taisho Democracy period in Japan toward a critique of the "modern"/the West over the 1930s—a hegemonic cultural current that reverberated in Japan's colonies as well—condemned the figure of the Korean "modern girl" (*modŏn kkŏl* in Korean pronunciation) practically at its birth. "Modern girl" became a marker of irresponsible Western decadence and extravagance. Kim Sujin, *Sinyŏsŏng, kŭndae ŭi kwang*, 450–71.
22. Editors of the "Modern Girl around the World" project state, "The Modern Girl was an object of nationalist scrutiny and thus provoked a full range of nationalist desires.

In all national contexts in which she appeared she was a contested figure and image, either an object of celebration or of attempted control." Weinbaum, *Modern Girl around the World*, 15. Kim Sujin in *Sinyŏsŏng, kŭndae ŭi kwaing* discerns and analyzes three separate yet overlapping categories of Korean "new women" that evolved out of the nationalist rendering of the woman question during the 1920s and 1930s: the "new woman," the "modern girl," and the "good wife" (*yangch'ŏ*). The "new woman" was envisioned as the modern subject who, under male intellectuals' guidance, would embrace the noble goal of enlightening and transforming the female population, the so-called "old-style women" (*kuyŏsŏng*) who had not yet reached modern womanhood. The "modern girl" figure, which in Korea was largely a media construct lacking real presence, was deployed as the bad subject of Westernizing modernization. Lastly, the "good wife" type of new woman was hoisted as the desirable subject of modernization. Armed with modern scientific knowledge, she properly manages the household and educates her children while embracing her gender role as the dedicated supporter of her husband. The "good wife" ideal was vigorously promoted by colonial authorities as the Korea colony became an indispensable part of the Japanese Empire's war machine in the 1930s and 1940s.

23. There is a growing literature, mostly in cultural studies, literature studies, and gender studies, that focuses on the figures of the "new women" and the "modern girls" and the cultural milieu surrounding their emergence. A body of literature also exists on women's activism in anticolonial movement history and colonial labor history. But the two largely remain separate. A few scholars, including Jennifer Jung-Kim, Sŏ Chiyŏng, and Theodore Jun Yoo, have attempted to include women workers in the scope of their inquiry into colonial gender relations, but there is still much work to be done to have a more comprehensive picture of evolving gender politics of the period. See Jung-Kim, "Gender and Modernity in Colonial Korea"; Sŏ Chiyŏng, *Kyŏngsŏng ŭi modŏn kŏl*; Yoo, *Politics of Gender in Colonial Korea*.

24. Yun Chŏngnan, "Singminji sidae chesa kongjang yŏgongdŭl," 39–41.

25. T'ae Hyesuk and Im Okhŭi, *Han'guk ŭi singminji kŭndae wa yŏsŏng konggan*, 325. "Girls" appeared globally during the 1920s and 1930s "as a modern social and representational category and as a style of self-expression." The term "denoted young women with the wherewithal and desire to define themselves in excess of conventional female roles and as transgressive of national, imperial, and racial boundaries." Weinbaum, *Modern Girl around the World*, 9. Literary scholar Yi Sanggyŏng notes that the English loan word "girl" (*kkŏl*) connoted frivolous behavior of young women, including that of thoughtlessly following whatever was trendy, and that was why major socialist women activists like Hŏ Chŏngsuk and Chŏng Chongmyŏng, who were a bit older than typical "Marx girls" and acknowledged for their expertise in Marxist theories, were not called "Marx girls." Instead, Hŏ and Chŏng each earned the dubious sobriquet of "Korea's Kollontai," after the famous Soviet diplomat and feminist revolutionary Alexandra Kollontai, for their pursuit of free ("red") love as well as socialist feminism. Yi Sanggyŏng, *Im Sundŭk*, 27.

26. Chŏng Ch'ilsŏng, "Amnal ŭl parabonŭn puin nodongja," 70. On Chŏng Ch'ilsŏng's life and activism, see Pak Sunsŏp, "1920–30-yŏndae Chŏng Ch'ilsŏng ŭi sahoejuŭi undong."

27. *Ch'ŏngnyŏn Chosŏn*, July 31, 1928, cited in Sŏ Chiyŏng, *Kyŏngsŏng ŭi modŏn kŏl*, 232.

28. Sunyoung Park says that the "radicalization of socialist feminist discourse in the mid-1920s" in Korea followed the trend in socialist thought in East Asia, in which Marxism was replacing "anarchism, which tended to be more liberal and individualist." Park, *Proletarian Wave*, 202.

29. In 1925 Korean female students in Tokyo, including Chŏng Ch'ilsŏng, Yi Hyŏn'gyŏng, and Hwang Sindŏk, organized the Samwŏrhoe (the March Society), which

gained support from Yamakawa Kikue. Ibid., 203; Pak Yongok, *Han'guk yŏsŏng hangil undongsa*, 270. Chŏng Ch'ilsŏng published the journal *Rosa Luxemburg* in Tokyo that introduced Yamakawa Kikue's work in Korean translation. Pak Sunsŏp, "1920-30-yŏndae Chŏng Ch'ilsŏng ŭi sahoejuŭi undong," 252. Members of the Samwŏrhoe, as they returned to Korea the following year, played an important role in moving the women's movement toward accepting the idea of forming a united-front organization among women, in coordination with the movement to establish the Sin'ganhoe.

30. Park, *Proletarian Wave*, 201–9. The liberal feminists in Korea, in addition to their inability to deal with the labor question in a rapidly industrializing society, had their hands tied because the colonial situation made a women's suffrage movement or demands for legal reforms impractical. These colonial conditions partly explain why there were no sustained debates in Korea on core issues of the women's movement such as suffrage rights or factory regulations for motherhood protection, which contrasts sharply with a long history of lively debates on a whole gamut of women's issues among female and male intellectuals in Japan.

31. In her essays published in *Sidae ilbo* ("On the Women's Liberation Movement," May 16, 1924) and *Dong-A ilbo* ("Fundamental in the Liberation of Women Is Economic Independence," November 3, 1924), Hŏ Chŏngsuk pointed out class differences among women and prioritized the need to develop a "proletarian women's movement" over a "bourgeois women's movement." She emphasized a need to "take as the object of struggle not men but 'the mode of life,'" that is, the capitalist class system. Yi Hyŏn'gyŏng was a major theorist behind the Kŭnuhoe movement. Yi published her most substantial and comprehensive theoretical work on socialist feminism in 1927 in four installments in the journal *Hyŏndae p'yŏngnon* (Contemporary Critiques), and its content, like most essays penned by socialist feminists in the period, very closely reflected two classics on the subject: *The Origin of the Family, Private Property and the State* by Friedrich Engels and *Women and Socialism* by August Bebel. Bebel's book had been translated into Korean in 1925 and became very influential among socialist women. Nam Hwasook, "1920-yŏndae yŏsŏng undong," 19–20.

32. Discussion of the Kŭnuhoe movement is based on my 1989 master's thesis, "1920-yŏndae yŏsŏng undong," unless otherwise noted.

33. By the time of its dissolution in 1931, which took place in steps along with the controversial dissolution of the Sin'ganhoe from within, Kŭnuhoe's total membership number swelled to several thousand strong, as the who's who among women in local society flocked to Kŭnu chapters, including women active in Christian, Ch'ŏndogyo, and Buddhist organizations.

34. It ends with three slogans: "Women are already not a weaker party," "The day women liberate themselves the world will be liberated," and "Sisters of Korea, unite!" Kŭnuhoe, "Kŭnuhoe sŏnŏn" [The Declaration of the Kŭnuhoe], *Kŭnu* (May 1929): 3–4.

35. Hŏ Chŏngsuk, "Kŭnuhoe undong ŭi yŏksajŏk chiwi wa tangmyŏn immu" [The historical status and current task of the Kŭnuhoe movement], *Kŭnu* (May 1929): 5–13; Nam Hwasook, "1920-yŏndae yŏsŏng undong," 50–52. The Comintern, at its third convention in 1921, opposed the idea of organizing women separately into women-only organizations and instead encouraged the establishment of a "women's bureau" (*puinbu*). As a consequence, in Japan a major debate on the legitimacy of the Kanto Women's Alliance (Kwandong Puin Tongmaeng) broke out in 1927. But in Korea I have not located any objections to the decision to create the Kŭnuhoe as a sister organization of the Sin'ganhoe. This was the case even after Pae Sŏngnyong made known the Comintern policy on organizing women in an article published in *Sidae ilbo*, titled "The Trend in the International Women's Movement," on January 3, 1926. Pae Sŏngnyong was the one who translated *Women and Socialism* by Bebel. Pae was a socialist theorist who wrote many

articles on women's issues. His position on the location and direction of the Kŭnu movement, expressed in his article in the inaugural issue of *Kŭnu*, titled "The Current State of the Korean Women's Movement," is very similar to that of Hŏ Chŏngsuk and other national leaders of the Kŭnuhoe. He himself seems to have been a key ideologue and supporter of the Kŭnuhoe movement. Nam Hwasook, "1920-yŏndae yŏsŏng undong," 45, 49–50.

36. Kŭnuhoe, "Kangnyŏng" [The Objectives], *Kŭnu* (May 1929): 2. These objectives were revised at the 1929 national convention of the Kŭnuhoe in the direction of revealing the organization's progressive character more fully. The revised objectives were: "We promote solid unity and conscious training [among women] in order to accomplish the historical mission of the women of Chosŏn" and "We strive to protect political, economic, social, and all [*chŏnchŏk*] interests of Korean women." The 1929 convention also modified the action programs (*haengdong kangnyŏng*) of the Kŭnuhoe. Nam Hwasook, "1920-yŏndae yŏsŏng undong," 105–11.

37. Park, *Proletarian Wave*, 205; Chŏng Ch'ilsŏng, "Ŭisikchŏk kaksŏng ŭrobut'ŏ: Musan puin saenghwal esŏ" [From an awakening of consciousness: In proletarian women's lives], *Kŭnu* (May 1929): 35–37. In the essay Chŏng calls factory women "kongjang puin" (women of the factory), a more respectful term than yŏgong, and also alerts readers to the wretched life conditions suffered by rural women, sex workers, and housemaids. Kŭnuhoe, aspiring to be a democratic institution, did not elect a president; instead, the head of the Central Steering Committee represented the organization. Chŏng Chongmyŏng was elected to that position at the first Central Steering Committee meeting in July 1928, and a year later, Chŏng Ch'ilsŏng took over that role by winning, by a large margin, over Chŏng Chongmyŏng and Pyongyang's Cho Sinsŏng in an election held at the July 1929 national convention of chapter representatives. Nam Hwasook, "Kŭnuhoe undong," 159.

38. The Kŭnuhoe incorporated certain gender-specific demands of women workers in its action programs, which included paid maternity leave before and after birth, the banning of dangerous work and nighttime work for women and youth workers, the abolition of wage discrimination against women, and the prohibition of sex trafficking. Nam Hwasook, "1920-yŏndae yŏsŏng undong," 105–11, contains a discussion of the nature of the revised Kŭnuhoe action programs adopted at its 1929 national convention.

39. *Chosun ilbo*, March 31, 1929; *Dong-A ilbo*, January 18, 1931; *Chosun ilbo*, October 27, 1929; *Dong-A ilbo*, May 6, 1931; Nam Hwasook, "1920-yŏndae yŏsŏng undong," 100; *Chosŏn sinmun*, April 16, 1930; "Kŭnuhoe hoehwang illam" [An overview of the Kŭnuhoe membership], *Kŭnu* (May 1929), 82–93.

40. According to membership data published in the inaugural issue of *Kŭnu* cited above, of 2,103 members (in twenty-five chapters) whose occupation was categorized, only 131 (6.2 percent) were laborers and 34 (1.6 percent) were farmers while the majority (1,256) were housewives. Worker members were reported by seven chapters: Kunsan (50 members out of a total chapter membership of 70), Pyongyang (30/452), Nanam (18/58), Tokyo (15/105), Pusan (9/127), Tamyang (5/38), Sinŭiju (3/40), and Seoul (1/224). In contrast, Sin'ganhoe's membership of 39,410 as of 1931 included 6,041 laborers and 21,514 farmers. Colonial police data put Kŭnuhoe membership as of June 1930 at 3,749 in fifty-eight chapters. "Kŭnuhoe hoehwang illam," *Kŭnu* (May 1929): 82–93; Pak Yongok, *Han'guk yŏsŏng hangil undongsa*, 347, 372. The journal *Irŏt'a*, published in July 1931, reported the Kŭnuhoe membership number as approximately six thousand, and novelist Ch'oe Chŏnghŭi left a record of a specific membership number of 6,542 for the year 1931. Nam Hwasook, "Kŭnuhoe undong," 161.

41. Kim Yunjŏng, "1930-yŏndae ch'o Pŏm T'aep'yŏngyang Nodong Chohap kyeyŏl"; Ch'oe Kyujin, *Chosŏn kongsandang chaegŏn undong* and "'K'ommyunisŭt'ŭ kŭrup' kwa T'aep'yŏngyang Nodong Chohap."

42. They are preserved in the National Archive on Society and Politics of Russia in Moscow and were made available as photocopies in 1998. See Pak and Yi, *T'aep'yŏngyang rodongja*, 2 vols.

43. Ch'ae Rin, "P'yŏngyang komu chikkong kongdong p'aŏp"; Paektusan, "P'yŏngyang P'yŏngwŏn komu chikkong p'aŏp."

44. When referring to women workers in their everyday roles, the term "female factory operatives" (yŏgong or yŏjikkong) was used, and a variety of terms all meaning "working women" were used when referring to them as an abstract entity. Terms used included *nodong yŏja, noryŏk yŏja, nodong puin, puin nodongja,* and *yŏja nodongja.* All meant "working" (*nodong* or *noryŏk*) women but used different signifiers for "women" (*yŏja* or *puin*). According to a linguistic-statistical study of competing signifiers used for women by historian Yi Chŏngsŏn, during the period of active social movements (1920-33), *yŏja* tended to refer to an object of education or a nationalist subject, and *yŏsŏng* and *puin* were often associated with a socialist subject. From the late 1920s to the early 1930s, the time when criticism of "new women" was soaring, *yŏja* lost its activist color as sexual connotations of the term became stronger. In the early 1930s the signifier preferred by communists was *puin*, but as the socialist movement went underground by the mid-1930s, the term *puin* began to lose its association with activism. Together with *yŏsŏng, puin* was coopted by the colonial authorities during the final years of colonial rule as women were turned into loyal subjects of mobilization. Yi Chŏngsŏn, "Kŭndae Han'guk ŭi 'yŏsŏng' chuch'e," 93-94, 121-22.

45. Paektusan, "P'yŏngyang P'yŏngwŏn komu chikkong p'aŏp," 232-37.

46. Ibid., 236.

47. Ch'oe Kyujin, "'K'ommyunisŭt'ŭ kŭrup' kwa T'aep'yŏngyang Nodong Chohap," 120.

48. Analyzing a particular political culture among Indian jute workers focusing on the nature of authority that elite leaders of the labor movement held over industrial workers, historian Dipesh Chakrabarty points to the pronounced tendency among workers to make "a spectacle of [their] sufferings, and thus obtaining the compassion and assistance of the rich," which "was, and still is, a familiar sight in societies marked by precapitalist cultures." Chakrabarty, *Rethinking Working-Class History*, 142-43. Workers in colonial Korea and South Korea also utilized the tactic of a public display of suffering on occasions when strong empathy and support coming from the public were deemed essential for the positive outcome in disputes. I thank Ruth Barraclough for alerting me to this potentially useful comparison point. Historical contexts, however, differed much between India and Korea. When the jute workers of India that Chakrabarty studied exhibited a strong desire to display their sufferings in great detail, their pleas were directed toward elite authority figures who would then intervene on behalf of the workers in disputes. But when colonial Korean workers chose to expose their sufferings caused by the allegedly starvation-level wages, the target audience was often the larger society, not some individual elite labor leaders who exerted authority over workers within a still strongly precapitalist social nexus. Often the spectacle of women workers' suffering in colonial Korea was deployed by the media and intellectual knowledge producers in order to accentuate the helplessness of yŏgong, expecting the humanist sentiment of pity as response from readers, rather than being staged by workers themselves. (See chapter 3.)

49. In his study of the communist struggle to build a new Korean Communist Party in the 1930s, historian Ch'oe Kyujin highlights four major streams of the party reconstruction movement, which involved numerous groups of committed activists in many parts of the Korean Peninsula. The earliest party reconstruction movement (1929-32) involved at least four separate groups of activists, including the Seoul Shanghai faction, the ML (Marxist-Leninist) faction, the Leninist group, and the communist group. The second (1933-36), third (1936-38), and fourth (1939-41) movements were led by the Yi

Chaeyu group, the Wŏnsan group, and the Kyŏngsŏng (Seoul) K'om (communist) group, respectively. Ch'oe Kyujin, *Chosŏn kongsandang chaegŏn undong*. Ch'oe includes some names of arrested female activists, as does Kim Kyŏngil, *Han'guk kŭndae nodongsa*, chap. 8 to 11.

50. Kim Kyŏngil, *Yi Chaeyu*; An Chaesŏng, *Kyŏngsŏng t'ŭroik'a*; Yi Sanggyŏng, *Im Sundŭk*, 79–82.

51. On the involvement of the Kŭnuhoe in the student movement, see Nam Hwasook, "Kŭnuhoe undong," 168–69.

52. Kim Kyŏngil, *Han'guk kŭndae nodongsa*, 454–67. A list of schools where RS organizations were discovered is given on 465.

53. Yun Yŏdŏk, *Han'guk ch'ogi nodong undong yŏn'gu* [A study of the early labor movement in Korea], 201, cited in Kim Kyŏngil, *Han'guk nodong undongsa 2*, 269. A scholar who examined the ages of worker activists who were arrested in relation to T'aero red union cases found that fifty-three (78 percent) out of sixty-eight workers whose ages at the time of the arrest were known were younger than twenty-five years of age. Kim Kyŏngil, *Han'guk nodong undongsa 2*, 268. During a five-year period from 1928 to March 1933, one prison in Hamhŭng alone housed 1,101 "thought criminals," and more than 73 percent of them (809) were twenty-five years old or younger, and another 20 percent (219) were between ages twenty-six and thirty. Ch'oe Kyujin, "'K'ommyunisŭt'ŭ kŭrup' kwa T'aep'yŏngyang Nodong Chohap," 149.

54. An article in *Chosŏn chungang ilbo*, August 24, 1936, reported on Yi Sun'gŭm and Yi Kyŏngsŏn as "audacious intellectual women who bravely operated among factory workers" and commented that they were like "two red dots in the vast green forest," meaning only two women among the more than five hundred arrestees in the Korean Communist Party reconstruction alliance incident. Yi Sanggyŏng, *Im Sundŭk*, 66, 77–78.

55. Yi was arrested in the Kyŏngsŏng RS Association incident in 1931 together with her school friend Pak Chinhong, and, like Pak, she later joined the Yi Chaeyu group. She had a high reputation among labor organizers in the Seoul area as a militant and effective organizer. Kang Man'gil and Sŏng Taegyŏng, *Han'guk sahoejuŭi undong inmyŏng sajŏn*, 373; Kim Kyŏngil, *Yi Chaeyu*, 82.

56. O Miil, "Pak Chinhong," 289.

57. Kim Kyŏngil, *Han'guk kŭndae nodongsa*, 155–59. Arrested in December 1931 and tortured and incarcerated for twenty-three months, Pak Chinhong was released in November 1933, but by August 1934 she joined the Yi Chaeyu group, which was also attempting to organize school RS cells and red unions in the Seoul area. Pak Chinhong was arrested six times and indicted three times. O Miil, "Pak Chinhong," 288–90; Ch'oe Kyujin, *Chosŏn kongsandang chaegŏn undong*, 146. Pak worked as a *rep'o* (messenger) and an *ajit'ŭ k'ip'ŏ* (housekeeper) for Yi Chaeyu until her arrest in January 1935. After her release in May 1937, Pak tried to connect with Yi Kwansul, her former teacher at Tongdŏk and her friend Yi Sun'gŭm's brother. But she was arrested again only two months after her release. Freed in September thanks to insufficient evidence, she continued her work as a *rep'o* and also as a labor organizer. Pak was again arrested at the end of 1937 in relation to the "Kyŏngsŏng Preparatory Group for the Reconstruction of the Korean Communist Party" incident. She was sentenced to a one-year prison term and served until July 1939. Then she joined the Kyŏngsŏng *K'om* (communist) group movement led by Pak Hönyŏng, which led to another round of incarceration from the end of 1941 to October 1944. Soon after her release she made a daring and dangerous move, fleeing to Yenan, China, with Kim T'aejun, a famous literary scholar, and reaching her destination in April 1945. After liberation Kim T'aejun became an official of the South Korean Workers' Party and was later executed by the South. Pak disappeared from public view after the September 1948 Supreme People's Assembly in the north, where she served as an elected

representative. She was likely a victim of political purges of southern communists by Kim Il-sung (Kim Ilsŏng).

58. Hŏ was a member of the Yi Chaeyu group, which also had Yu Sunhŭi, Yi Chonghŭi, and Pak Chinhong as members. Yi Chaeyu group's activities are detailed in O Miil, "Pak Chinhong"; Kim Kyŏngil, *Yi Chaeyu*.

59. Kang Man'gil and Sŏng Taegyŏng, *Han'guk sahoejuŭi undong inmyŏng sajŏn*, 536; Ch'oe Kyujin, *Chosŏn kongsandang chaegŏn undong*, 153–54, 167.

60. Hwang Dongyoun describes the harsh prison conditions that Korean anarchists faced in the colony as follows: "If arrested and tried, it is said, no anarchist would be able to walk on his or her own two legs or even remain alive after having spent time in prison, due to brutal and repeated torture, malnutrition, and an unspeakable environment." Hwang, *Anarchism in Korea*, 89.

61. The group, according to the prosecutor's office, attempted to make factories in Pusan and Taegu "red" and also tried to reach out to rural areas in the region. The age of the indicted thirty-nine activists ranged from eighteen to twenty-seven, and Pak, a nineteen-year-old yŏgong, was one of the youngest members. *Pusan ilbo* (a Japanese-language regional paper), March 17, 1935, contained in Seoul National University, *Sŏuldae kugwan sinmun palch'we charyo*.

62. Ch'oe Kyujin, *Chosŏn kongsandang chaegŏn undong*, 154, 163–65; Kim Kyŏngil, *Yi Chaeyu*, 78–83. A pamphlet written by Yi Chaeyu and titled "Central Slogans among Industrial Worker Masses in the Years 1933 to 1934" presents sixteen slogans to use among workers, including a seven-hour workday (forty-hour work week) and a promotion of national industrial unions. Several gender-specific issues are also listed, including calls to "Oppose all feudal dormitory-style impingement on workers!"; "Achieve a system of equal pay for equal work!"; and "Absolutely oppose the year-long [*nyŏn'gi*] contract and purchase of women and children!" Kim Kyŏngil, *Yi Chaeyu*, 75–76.

63. The contemporary media sensationalized this controversial communist practice of assigning an *ajit'ŭ k'ip'ŏ* (agitation point, or "agit," keeper) or "housekeeper" role to a young female activist when a high-ranking male activist went into hiding. Going through a precarious underground life while disguising themselves as a couple, sometimes sexual relations developed between the man and the woman, and when revealed that relationship was profitably utilized in anticommunist propaganda. The case involving three communists in a love triangle—aforementioned school friends Pak Chinhong and Yi Sun'gŭm, and the legendary male activist Yi Chaeyu—gained notoriety when Pak, who worked as a housekeeper for Yi Chaeyu, gave birth to a son by Yi in prison. Her friend Yi Sun'gŭm, who became the next housekeeper for Yi Chaeyu, had by then become romantically involved with Yi. This housekeeper question, which touches on intimate personal relationships and changing cultures and norms of gender and sex among radical activists in colonial Korea, has not been examined much in the Korean history field. An exception is historian Chang Yŏngŭn's study of female socialists' views of love and revolution vis-à-vis those of men, centered on the case of Pak Chinhong. Chang Yŏngŭn, "Ajit'ŭ k'ip'ŏ wa hausŭ k'ip'ŏ."

64. Alexandra Kollontai's *Red Love* (or *Love of Worker Bees*) was translated into Korean in 1928, only one year after its English and Japanese translations came out, and the book brought socialism to the attention of a wide audience. Barraclough, "Red Love and Betrayal," 91. The pursuit of "red love" by some famous socialist women, including Hŏ Chŏngsuk and Chŏng Chongmyŏng ("Korea's Kollontai"), came at great personal cost, and personal "scandals," either real or fabricated, tended to define the public perception of socialist women thinkers, rather than the intellectual merit of their ideas. On "red love" and negative public perception of socialist women, see ibid.

65. The extremely conservative culture of the day in terms of proper gender roles and behaviors was revealed in the ultimately unsuccessful project of three socialist women

(Hŏ Chŏngsuk, Chu Sejuk, and Kim Choi) in August 1925 when they staged a collective haircutting to express their modern self-consciousness. As portrayed in Cho Sŏnhŭi's two-volume historical novel, *Se yŏja* (Three Women), which follows the lives of the trio, the public reception was cold, and the women soon had to renege on their vow to keep a "modern" bobbed hairstyle.

66. Literary scholar An Sŭnghyŏn compiled ninety-eight "labor novels" by forty writers, mostly short stories of the colonial period, in a three-volume collection, titled *Ilche kangjŏmgi nodong sosŏlsŏn*. For analyses of women worker characters in colonial period labor novels, see Park, *Proletarian Wave*; Yoo, *Politics of Gender in Colonial Korea*, chap. 3 and 4.

67. Author Yi Chŏkhyo was in the notorious Sŏdaemun Prison in Seoul when the short story was published in the August 1931 issue of *Pip'an*. An Sŭnghyŏn, *Ilche kangjŏmgi nodong sosŏlsŏn*, 2:213.

68. Perry, *Recasting Red Culture in Proletarian Japan*, 106.

69. An Sŭnghyŏn, *Ilche kangjŏmgi nodong sosŏlsŏn*, 2:213-37.

70. This short novel, originally serialized in *Chosun ilbo* (March 1-26, 1931), is included in ibid., 2:111-51.

71. Ibid., 2:150. Song Yŏng used the same "mad lioness" metaphor in another short story, "Representatives of a Stonemason's Union" ("Sŏkkong chohap taep'yo," 1927). The protagonist is Ku Oksun, a distressed young wife and rubber factory worker in Pyongyang, whose husband Ch'angho's decision to attend a meeting in Seoul as a representative of his union of stonemasons leads to violent clashes between his employer and Oksun. Oksun is described as "a woman of the west [northwestern region] with dashing spirit and adventurousness." The cruel employer hits Ch'angho's old father and Oksun becomes "enraged and rushes like a lioness" toward the cruel boss yelling and pushing him away. An Sŭnghyŏn, *Ilche kangjŏmgi nodong sosŏlsŏn*, 1:118.

72. It was published in the July 1931 issue of *Pip'an* and reproduced in ibid., 2:252-58.

73. *The Human Predicament*, serialized in *Dong-A ilbo* in 1934, is today in South Korea regarded as "one of the most accomplished products of colonial-period literature." Park, *Proletarian Wave*, 221.

74. Park, *Proletarian Wave*, 222-28, offers an excellent analysis of characters in *The Human Predicament*. Another well-developed yŏgong character is the aforementioned O Suhyang in Song Yŏng's novel of the same name. Sŏ Chiyŏng, *Kyŏngsŏng ŭi modŏn kŏl*, 231-32. The role of the title character of Ri Kiyŏng's playscript *Wŏlhŭi* (1929), who is a café waitress who transforms herself into a class-conscious trade unionist at a textile factory, is also revealing.

75. Park, *Proletarian Wave*, 200. Park assesses Kang Kyŏngae's other masterpiece, *Salt* (*Sogom*, 1934), as a work that "provides a clearly feminist counterpoint to the idealized image of a self-sacrificial mother-savior," if "read against the contemporary patriarchal glorification of women's domestic virtues." Park, *Proletarian Wave*, 200, 212-21.

76. Ibid., 200, 222-28.

77. Yi Sanggyŏng, "Kang Kyŏngae munhak," 343.

78. Sŏ Chŏngja, *In'gan munje (oe)*, 525.

79. Muhojŏngin, "Ŭlmiltae sang ŭi ch'egongnyŏ," 40.

80. The phrase "knowledge of liberation" is borrowed from Kim Kyŏngil, "Ch'ulse ŭi chisik, haebang ŭi chisik."

3. COPING WITH WOMEN STRIKERS

1. Kim Kyŏngil, *Han'guk nodong undongsa 2*, 46, table 2-3. Kim's table is based on data sets from Chōsen Sōtokufu, *Chōsen Sōtokufu tōkei nenpō* [Statistical Yearbook of the

Government-General of Korea]. Only factories that employed five or more workers on a regular basis and were not government-owned were included in the statistics. In 1930 a total of 83,900 industrial workers met the criteria (55,612 men and 28,288 women), and chemical workers numbered 14,720 (9,547 men and 5,173 women) among them. The total number of industrial workers shot up to 337,269 (250,956 men and 86,313 women) by 1943, an increase of 302 percent overall and 205 percent for women. By then there were 54,690 chemical workers (42,879 men and 11,811 women).

2. National Institute of Korean History (Kuksa P'yŏnch'an Wiwŏnhoe), Korean History Database, db.history.go.kr. *Chosun ilbo*, another major Korean-language newspaper, is unfortunately not part of this database service.

3. Contemporary orthography had the terms as *nyŏjikkong* and *nyŏgong*, but, as explained in chapter 1, I render them as *yŏjikkong* and *yŏgong* in this book, following today's South Korean orthography.

4. A keyword search of colonial-period publications using *(n)yŏjikkong* and *(n)yŏgong* yields a total of 1,458 entries, 669 of which—124 articles containing the word *(n)yŏjikkong* and 545 containing *(n)yŏgong*—come from the five-year period between 1929 and 1933. Of these 669 entries the most represented are *Dong-A ilbo* articles (52 cases for *yŏjikkong* and 180 cases for *yŏgong*). If we eliminate overlapping entries and irrelevant articles, the net number of entries containing the two terms would become somewhat smaller. National Institute of Korean History, Korean History Database, db.history.go.kr, searched April 22, 2016. In addition to major Korean-language newspapers and magazines, the database also contains, in digitized format, an extensive colonial-period newspaper scrap collection held at Seoul National University Library, which adds articles from Japanese-language newspapers to our sample. The Seoul National University collection covers mainly Japanese-language papers, but some Korean-language papers are included also. The collection, which covers the period between 1928 and 1940 in 459 volumes (a total of 106,700 articles), is divided into seven categories; the first category, titled "Korea-related matters" (249 volumes), contains newspaper articles on labor and tenancy disputes. Seoul National University, *Sŏuldae kugwan sinmun palch'we charyo*.

5. Kim Pongu, *Chibangbyŏl kisa moŭm*, vol. 4, P'yŏngan Namdo [South P'yŏngan Province].

6. Sŏ Chiyŏng, *Kyŏngsŏng ŭi modŏn kŏl*, 222–23. In the 1920s sensitive writers did not miss aspects of factory employment and urban life that had the potential to empower young women migrants from rural areas. And in some media accounts we can encounter images of factory girls enjoying modern city life during their leisure time, listening to Western music and reading magazines. Ibid., 221–36.

7. Muhojŏngin, "Ŭlmiltae sang ŭi ch'egongnyŏ," 41.

8. Sŏ Hyŏngsil, "Singminji sidae yŏsŏng nodong undong," 67–68.

9. O Kiyŏng, "P'yŏngyang komu chaengŭi chinsang," no. 4, *Dong-A ilbo*, September 7, 1930.

10. In 1930, for example, about nineteen thousand workers participated in 160 strikes in colonial Korea, and Pyongyang saw fourteen strikes, including four large-scale rubber strikes involving a total of 2,800 workers. Kim Kyŏngil, *Ilcheha nodong undongsa*, 308, table 6–1, and 311, table 6–3; Kim Kyŏngil, *Han'guk kŭndae nodongsa*, 116, table 2–11. In the same year in Japan the number of women strikers exceeded that of male strikers in some industries, and the Tōyō Muslin strike of 1930, "one of the most violent of strikes" waged by thousands of workers over sixty days, became "famous as a 'women's strike.'" Historian Vera Mackie concludes that although the number of organized women workers remained small, "such strikes were significant in facilitating new ways of seeing working women: as workers and as comrades." Mackie, *Creating Socialist Women in Japan*, 124–26.

11. For examples, see *Dong-A ilbo*, July 31, 1931, and November 11, 1932; *Chungoe ilbo*, August 21, 1930, and June 1, 1931.

12. The earliest cases include a Hamhŭng Silk Reeling strike in December 1928 in Hamhŭng, a Chobang strike in January 1930 in Pusan, a Chosŏn Silk strike in January 1931 in Seoul, and a Sech'ang Rubber strike in July 1931 in Pyongyang. *Dong-A ilbo*, December 25, 1928; January 11, 15, and 20, 1930; January 6 and July 31, 1931. A search of *Dong-A ilbo* (1920–40) with keywords *tanghwang* and *ch'anghwang mangjo* using the News Library service offered by South Korean web portal Naver (https://newslibrary.naver.com, searched January 12, 2019) yielded 1,789 usages of the word *tanghwang* and 123 usages of the phrase *ch'anghwang mangjo*. Only a small subset of those entries dealt with labor conflict, and almost always the labor disputes these terms were applied to involved women workers. Although the first labor dispute case associated with the expression was a strike of transportation workers at Samnŭng Steel in Kyŏmip'o, Hwanghae Province, in December 1927 (*Dong-A ilbo*, December 11, 1927), I have not found any other cases in which the expression was used in relation to heavy-industry male worker strikes.

13. Kim Ch'angsul, "Ŭlmiltae sang ŭi t'usa," 51.

14. For example, *Chōsen shinbun*, a Japanese-language newspaper, reported that the police tried to feed her but she "adamantly continued her hunger strike." "Worried about her life," the article goes on, the police released her right after midnight on June 1 (*Dong-A ilbo* on June 3, 1931, reported the release time as 11:30 p.m. on May 31). "Seventy-eight Hours of Hunger Strike, a *Han Sŭt'o-nyŏ* [a woman on a hunger strike] Released," *Chōsen shinbun*, June 2, 1931.

15. From 1926 to 1931 the proportion of the "people in poverty" (*pinmin*) in the total population of Korea jumped from 11.3 percent to 26.7 percent (5,415,324 of 20,262,958 people), that is, more than a quarter of the population. The category of *pinmin* in colonial statistical data included the *semin* (those who barely maintained a subsistence-level livelihood), the *kungmin* (the very poor who required emergency measures by the state), and the *kŏrin* (beggars). Among these subcategories the fastest growing in this period was the *kungmin*. As of 1933, 17.4 percent of the Korean residents of five major cities—Seoul, Incheon, Taegu, Pusan, and Pyongyang—belonged to the *pinmin* category. Yi Sangŭi, *Ilcheha Chosŏn ŭi nodong chŏngch'aek*, 36–37.

16. The age range of arrested *yŏgong* from the P'yŏngwŏn Rubber strike and Pusan's Marufuto (Hwandae) Rubber strike, both of which occurred in the spring of 1931, was between twenty-nine and thirty-nine years of age. *Dong-A ilbo*, June 5, 1931; *Pusan ilbo*, March 13, 1931, cited in Kim Kyŏngil, *Han'guk kŭndae nodongsa*, 149.

17. O Miil, "1910–1920-yŏndae P'yŏngyang Chosŏnin chabon'ga" and *Han'guk kŭndae chabon'ga*.

18. It is also noteworthy that the main reporter and interviewer who so ardently flagged this *yŏgong* question for the consideration of the nation was O Kiyŏng (Muhojŏngin), who also penned many pieces of reportage for magazines exposing various social problems, including labor-related issues. At the time of the rubber strikes of 1930 and 1931, O Kiyŏng was serving as a *Dong-A ilbo* special correspondent for the company's Pyongyang branch office (he served in that function from March 1928 to March 1936), and Kim Sŏngŏp was the branch head (Kim headed the Pyongyang branch office from June 1924 to December 1927, and again from June 1928 to February 1938). Both were central figures in the northwestern Christian nationalist movement and also members of the reformist wing of the (Suyang) Tonguhoe. Chang Kyusik, *Ilcheha Han'guk Kidokkyo minjokchuŭi*, 141, 260, 272. What he was unable to publish in the pages of *Dong-A ilbo* O Kiyŏng published in magazines like *Tonggwang* or *Pyŏlgŏn'gon*. Critical pieces he authored for the two magazines include "An Overview of Social Organizations in Pyongyang" (*Pyŏlgŏn'gon*,

September 1930), "The Battle Site of the Pyongyang Rubber Dispute" (*Pyŏlgŏn'gon*, October 1930), and "Reminiscing about the Pyongyang Riot" (*Tonggwang*, September 1931), in addition to a key material in our discussion, that is, his interview of Kang Churyong (*Tonggwang*, July 1931).

19. Kang was called *yŏt'usa* in a *Dong-A ilbo* article (May 31, 1931), a *Chungang ilbo* article (December 30, 1931), and in Muhojŏngin's piece and Poet Kim Ch'angsul's short essay in *Tonggwang* (July 1931). Kim Ch'angsul called Kang Churyong *yŏt'usa* as well as *ch'egongnyŏ* in his essay. It is interesting that he calls Kang's colleagues "brave sisters" ("yonggamhan chamaedŭl") rather than applying the term *yŏt'usa* to them. Kim Ch'angsul, "Ŭlmiltae sang ŭi t'usa," 51.

20. A search in the Korean History Database of the National Institute of Korean History with keyword *yŏt'usa* (and *nyŏt'usa*) yields just eighteen cases from the entire colonial period (searched April 27, 2016), of which nine entries refer to non-Korean women abroad. Among the nine remaining cases, two entries were about women activists of the Korean independence movement in China, and four involved well-known female social movement activists who operated in Korea, including Kŭnuhoe leader Hŏ Chŏngsuk and "Woman General" Kim Myŏngsi. Kim was trained at the Communist University of the Toilers of the East in Moscow and was arrested while working to build red unions in Incheon in 1932. Later she fought in the Communist Eighth Army and in the Korean Righteous Army (Chosŏn Ŭiyonggun) in China, earning the nickname *yŏjanggun* ("woman general"). An Chaesŏng, *Irŏbŏrin Han'guk hyŏndaesa*, 323.

21. It was Japanese language newspapers that gave the *yŏt'usa* title to the other two yŏgong. One was a yŏgong arrested in 1933 as a member of the red union at Chōsen Nitrogen Fertilizer in Hamhŭng (*Chōsen shinbun*, December 14, 1933), and the other yŏgong, Pak Sunhŭi, was arrested in 1934 in relation to a red union case in Pusan (*Pusan ilbo*, March 17, 1935). In the Korean-language newspapers the next time the term *yŏt'usa* appears after Kang Churyong's case was in the postliberation period on March 3, 1946, in a piece reminiscing about the March First Movement.

22. *Dong-A ilbo*, June 15, 1931.

23. A search in the Korean History Database with keyword *yŏjangbu* yields thirty-four entries from the colonial period (searched April 27, 2016). Those who were called *yŏjangbu* included socialist women activists Chŏng Chongmyŏng and Hŏ Chŏngsuk, and Christian nationalist activist Kim Maria.

24. *Dong-A ilbo*, June 10, 1932.

25. A keyword search using *yŏsa* (and *nyŏsa*) in the Korean History Database (searched April 27, 2016) yields thousands of entries from the colonial period.

26. *Dong-A ilbo*, June 8 and 13, 1931; *Chungoe ilbo*, June 2, 1931.

27. Sŏ Hyŏngsil, "Singminji sidae yŏsŏng nodong undong," 56, 67–75. Sŏ concludes that women workers in the colonial period overall subscribed to the patriarchal gender notions prevailing in society and thus mostly remained obedient and passive. But she also argues that given certain opportunities, women workers, especially married women, could overcome their passive characteristics and mount fierce resistance through strikes.

28. Kim T'aesu, *Kkot kach'i p'iŏ maehokk'e hara*, 41.

29. Chang Kyusik, *Ilcheha Han'guk Kidokkyo minjokchuŭi*, 238. Chu Yohan, An Ch'angho's disciple and a leader of the reform movement within the (Suyang) Tonguhoe, also emphasized the importance of the task of nurturing *t'usa* in an article in the July 1927 issue of *Tonggwang*. Ibid., 204, 236. This association of the term *t'usa* with the northwestern Christian movement partly explains why three of the four articles attaching the term to Kang Churyong appeared in *Dong-A ilbo* and *Tonggwang*.

30. *Dong-A ilbo*, July 31, 1931.

31. *Dong-A ilbo*, August 23 and September 10, 1931.
32. Yi Chŏngok, "Ilcheha kongŏp nodong," 215–20.
33. Sŏ Hyŏngsil, "Singminji sidae yŏsŏng nodong undong," 67.
34. Mackie, *Creating Socialist Women in Japan*, 108.
35. Muhojŏngin, "Ŭlmiltae sang ŭi ch'egongnyŏ," 41.
36. The relationship between Kang's literary works and her experience in Manchuria is explored in Yi Sanggyŏng, *Han'guk kŭndae yŏsŏng munhaksaron*, chap. 8, and "Kang Kyŏngae munhak"; Kim Hyŏnsaeng, "Kang Kyŏngae ŭi 'Kando' ch'ehŏm"; Kwon, *Intimate Empire*, chap. 9.
37. *Chungoe ilbo*, August 21–25, 1930; O Kiyŏng, "P'yŏngyang komu chaengŭi chinsang," no. 3, *Dong-A ilbo*, September 6, 1930. These women workers were all arrested, but the police soon released them following mediation by the Sin'ganhoe Pyongyang chapter.
38. When communist activist Kim Myŏngsi was sent to Incheon from Shanghai in March 1932 by the T'aero and began organizing female workers at spinning and matchmaking factories, she used copies of communist journals, including T'aero's newspaper, the *Pan Pacific Trade Union*, as key educational texts for women workers. An Chaesŏng, *Kyŏngsŏng t'ŭroik'a*, 322. This seems to have been a typical practice in the red union movement.
39. Muhojŏngin, "Ŭlmiltae sang ŭi ch'egongnyŏ," 40.
40. Yi Chaeyu, the legendary communist organizer who died in prison from brutal torture in 1944 at age forty, summed up this attitude in his final court statement in 1938: "We communists are determined to discard our lives for the movement, and [only] such a person can be called a genuine communist." Ch'oe Kyusik, *Chosŏn kongsandang chaegŏn undong*, 126–27. We again see this level of intenseness among unionists and student movement activists in late twentieth-century South Korea. On politics surrounding labor and student martyrs (*yŏlsa*) in South Korea, see Nam, "Reading Chun Tae-il"; Cheon, "Untimely Death and Martyrdom"; Sun-Chul Kim, "Construction of Martyrdom."
41. Pak Chaehwa, "1930-yŏn Chosŏn Pangjik p'aŏp," 36. Historian Yun Chŏngnan examines working conditions and labor disputes in the silk-reeling industry in the 1920s and early 1930s and argues that as "modern women" these women workers were developing a "modern self-consciousness" and "a new women's culture" over the period, although from the late 1930s until the time of the liberation in 1945, the potential of female workers had to lay dormant because of harsh wartime control measures. Yun Chŏngnam, "Singminji sidae chesa kongjang yŏgongdŭl," 38, 71–73.
42. Other demands included "meals worthy of human beings," a ten-hour workday, "clean" work clothes, and a demand that supervisors not be allowed to "severely abuse workers." In their earlier strike in January 1930, five hundred Yamajū workers demanded a raise and an improvement in working conditions. That strike ended in a compromise. Pak Chaehwa, "1930-yŏn Chosŏn Pangjik p'aŏp," 55; *Chosun ilbo*, April 27, 1930.
43. Sŏ Hyŏngsil, "Singminji sidae yŏsŏng nodong undong," 98; Pak Chaehwa, "1930-yŏn Chosŏn Pangjik p'aŏp," 36.
44. *Dong-A ilbo*, June 13, 1931, June 10 and August 17, 1932. Kang Churyong's temporary release on June 7, 1932, was reported as due to serious illness, including a breakdown of nerves and digestive problems.
45. *Chungang ilbo*, December 30, 1931.
46. *Dong-A ilbo*, August 13 and 17, 1932.
47. *Dong-A ilbo*, August 17, 1932.
48. Nationalists continued to address the question of labor-capital cooperation throughout the 1930s. In the late 1930s Korean nationalist thinkers like Yi Hun'gu, Yi Sunt'ak, and Yi Chongman presented their own theories of labor-capital cooperation as

a solution to the labor question. And the colonial government also began emphasizing the concept of "labor-capital cooperation" as part of the ideology of wartime labor and economic control and development. Yi Sangŭi, *Ilcheha Chosŏn ŭi nodong chŏngch'aek*, 87.

49. Policy discussions on the matter within the colonial government ended by 1936 when the final evaluation was made that deemed the legislation "premature." Ibid., 86, 94–107.

50. Ibid., 87–89. The voices in the bourgeois nationalist movement that called for attention to distribution issues between classes remained in the small minority, however, as most nationalists saw a "distribution struggle" being "premature" in the current Korean economic situation. O Miil, *Han'guk kŭndae chabon'ga*, 522–25.

51. Albert L. Park, *Building a Heaven on Earth*; Yi Kihun, *Ch'ŏngnyŏn a*, 143–48.

52. Chang Kyusik, *Ilcheha Han'guk Kidokkyo minjokchuŭi*, 342–75; Chang Kyusik, "1920-yŏndae kaejoron," 124; Park, *Building a Heaven on Earth*, chap. 5. The Danish cooperative system was a key component of a national movement to stabilize the Danish state and society that began in the eighteenth century. The movement had three major components: land reform, the folk-school movement initiated by Frederik Severin Grundtvig, and the cooperative movement. By the 1920s the Danish model became popular globally. In Korea, beginning in 1920, "the discourse on Denmark exploded." Park argues that the Danish system was attractive to Korean Christian reformers because Denmark was "the only country to install a comprehensive cooperative system that enabled it to become the most respected modern agrarian nation-state in the world" and also because if the colonial situation did not allow land reform, the Danish system "could become a viable alternative for agrarian reform in place of comprehensive land reforms." Park, *Building a Heaven on Earth*, 20, 154–55, 161, 164.

53. O Miil, *Han'guk kŭndae chabon'ga*, chap. 9.

54. Ch'oe Kyujin, *Chosŏn kongsandang chaegŏn undong*, 211. A survey by the Dong-A Ilbo company found ninety-three cooperatives in the country in the spring of 1932. O Miil, *Han'guk kŭndae chabon'ga*, 498.

55. Ch'oe Kyujin, *Chosŏn kongsandang chaegŏn undong*, 510.

56. It was named the Kwansŏ Hyŏptong Chohap Kyŏngnisa (Northwest Cooperatives Administration). Chang Kyusik, *Ilcheha Han'guk Kidokkyo minjokchuŭi*, 276.

57. Chang Kyusik, "1920-yŏndae kaejoron," 131.

58. *Osaka Mainichi Shinbun*, Korean edition, September 7, 1930; *Pusan ilbo*, October 15, 1930; Yŏngjin, *Ilcheha Chosŏn kwan'gye sinmun*, 1:456, 464.

59. Yi Horyong, *Han'guk ŭi anak'ijŭm: Undong p'yŏn*, 144–63; Kim Kyŏngil, *Han'guk nodong undongsa 2*, 177.

60. Yi Horyong, *Han'guk ŭi anak'ijŭm: Undong p'yŏn*, 11, 19–50, 471. The Korean anarchist movement was composed of domestic anarchists, exiles in China, and exiles in Japan, and, according to Yi Horyong, it developed three strategies of struggle for social revolution in the colonial period. The first was an emphasis on direct action through terrorist methods, and the second was a movement to build revolutionary bases or ideal communities (*isangch'on*), which was mainly the strategy of Korean anarchists operating in China. The third was the anarcho-syndicalist strategy of prioritizing economic direct action and everyday struggle. Yi Horyong, *Han'guk ŭi anak'ijŭm: Sasang p'yŏn*, 266–93.

61. Yi Horyong, *Han'guk ŭi anak'ijŭm: Sasang p'yŏn*, 93.

62. Yi Horyong argues that as a consequence, an internal split developed in 1929 between the mainstream anarchists who continued to uphold anarcho-communism (or "pure anarchism") and those with anarcho-syndicalist tendencies. It followed a similar split that had occurred among Japanese anarchists the previous year. According to Yi, this rise of anarcho-syndicalism in Korea was stimulated by the return of anarcho-syndicalists

from Japan, including Yi Honggŭn and Ch'oe Kangyong. Ibid., 236–37; Yi Horyong, *Han'guk ŭi anak'ijŭm: Undong p'yŏn*, 157–58. Refuting Yi's argument that emphasizes the 1929 split and the resulting deterioration of the movement, a recent book by historian Dongyoun Hwang on Korean anarchist history downplays the division and persuasively shows that Korean anarchists developed diverse practices and methods addressing local conditions and demands. Hwang, *Anarchism in Korea*, 116, 211–12.

63. Yi Horyong, *Han'guk ŭi anak'ijŭm: Undong p'yŏn*, 157–80.

64. They were also influential in the Pyongyang chapter of the General Alliance of Korean Workers (Chosŏn Nodong Ch'ongyŏnmaeng), organized labor's national peak association. Ibid., 147–49, 159–62.

65. The Sin'ganhoe movement stimulated anticommunist struggle by anarchists greatly, especially in the northern cities of Pyongyang and Wŏnsan, where anarchism had a strong base. Ibid., 472.

66. The plan to convene the All Korea Anarchist Social Movement Activists Convention (Chŏn Chosŏn Hŭksaek Sahoe Undongja Taehoe) ultimately failed because of repression by the colonial state. Ibid., 125–28, 150–54.

67. Ibid., 158–63; Yi Horyong, *Han'guk ŭi anak'ijŭm: Sasang p'yŏn*, 243.

68. Yi Horyong, *Han'guk ŭi anak'ijŭm: Undong p'yŏn*, 157–60.

69. Ibid., 160–62. According to contemporary news reports, Pyongyang workers who installed and ran "work bureaus" or "industrial cooperatives" included Western suit makers (*Dong-A ilbo*, November 29, 1926), gold- and silversmith workers (*Dong-A ilbo*, December 11, 1928), Western shoemakers (*Chungoe ilbo*, March 27, 1930; *Chosun Ilbo*, December 2, 1930), carpenters (*Chosun Ilbo*, January 14 and 16, 1931), and knitwear factory workers (*Dong-A ilbo*, December 20, 1927).

70. Its official name was the Rubber Industry Bureau (Komu Kongŏppu) of the Pyongyang Mutual Aid Production Cooperative (P'yŏngyang Kongje Saengsan Chohap). Information on Mutual Aid Rubber comes from Ch'ae Rin, "Sin ch'akch'wi pangbŏp," 177–79; Yi Horyong, *Han'guk ŭi anak'ijŭm: Undong p'yŏn*, 160–62; *Dong-A ilbo*, September 18, October 8, October 12–13, October 16, October 19, November 6–7, December 1, and December 18, 1930; *Chungoe ilbo*, September 5, 12, and 18, 1930; *Chosun ilbo*, September 7 and 18, October 29, and November 6, 1930; *Maeil sinbo*, September 8 and November 1, 1930.

71. Yi Horyong, *Han'guk ŭi anak'ijŭm: Undong p'yŏn*, 162; *Dong-A ilbo*, October 8 and 19, November 6, and December 1, 1930; August 23 and September 10, 1931.

72. *Dong-A ilbo*, July 11, 1931.

73. *Dong-A ilbo*, October 7 and 13, 1931; *Chungang ilbo*, December 16, 1931. In his two short stories, "Factory Newsletter" ("Kongjang sinmun," published in *Chosun ilbo* in July 1931) and "Worker Friends Association" ("Konguhoe," published in *Chosŏn chi kwang*, January–February 1932), novelist Kim Namch'ŏn named the rubber factory that was the site of labor organizing "Peace Rubber." Both stories are contained in An Sŭnghyŏn, *Ilche kangjŏmgi Han'guk nodong sosŏlsŏn*, vol. 2. "Factory Newsletter" portrays a meeting between a male union member and an underground labor organizer as if the author got a cue from the revelation of the Chŏng Talhŏn group's infiltration into the P'yŏngwŏn Rubber strike, which happened in the month prior to the story's publication.

74. Kim Kyŏngil, *Han'guk nodong undongsa 2*, 180; *Dong-A ilbo*, January 7, 1932, editorial.

75. *Chungang ilbo*, December 16, 1931; Yi Horyong, *Han'guk ŭi anak'ijŭm: Undong p'yŏn*, 162.

76. Yi Horyong, *Han'guk ŭi anak'ijŭm: Undong p'yŏn*, 169–71, 179. According to Yi, anarcho-communist organizations mounted strong criticism of the anarcho-syndicalists in the Northwest Black Friends Society. In the anarcho-communists' view, the latter were "compromising reformists" who, instead of empowering workers to join the struggle

to overthrow capitalism, succumbed to workers' desires to pursue their own economic interests, a position that essentially constituted a compromise with capitalists. Ibid., 170–71; Yi Horyong, *Han'guk ŭi anak'ijŭm: Sasang p'yŏn*, 243–45.

77. Yi Horyong, *Han'guk ŭi anak'ijŭm: Undong p'yŏn*, 292–93, 472–73.

78. Ch'ae Rin, "Sin ch'akch'wi pangbŏp."

79. Ch'oe Kyujin, *Chosŏn kongsandang chaegŏn undong*, chap. 4, analyzes the reception of the popular-front strategy among Korean communists. The Profintern opposed reformist cooperatives because they would spread the fantasy that a solution could be found in "socialization" through cooperatives "peacefully and gradually" within the framework of capitalism. But the Profintern reserved a more positive stance toward consumer cooperatives because such cooperatives, like trade unions, could function as important "contact points with the proletarian masses." Based on this understanding and also in order to gain necessary legal cover for their movement, some red farmers' and workers' unions actively promoted the consumer cooperative movement in the early 1930s, as in the case of the Chŏngp'yŏng Farmers' Union. The Wŏnsan Group communists in the late 1930s also vigorously promoted industrial workers' consumer cooperatives as a training ground and a material base for struggle, calling it a "military supply depot for workers." Ch'oe Kyujin, *Chosŏn kongsandang chaegŏn undong*, 212–15.

80. *Dong-A ilbo*, July 11 and October 7, 1931. The preparatory committee was headed by Kim Tongsŏk, and members included Kim Yongsŏn, Pak Pongch'ung, Kim Imgwan, and five others in addition to P'yŏngwŏn yŏgong Ch'oe Yongdŏk. *Dong-A ilbo*, July 11, 1931.

81. *Dong-A ilbo*, December 7, 1932.

82. Ibid.

83. Kim Kyŏngil, *Ilcheha nodong undongsa*, 426; *Chosun Ilbo*, October 16, 1930, cited in Yi Horyong, *Han'guk ŭi anak'ijŭm: Undong p'yŏn*, 179.

84. *Akahata* 122, February 28, 1933, cited in Hashimoto, "Entotsu otoko Tanabe Kiyoshi shōron."

85. *Chosŏn Chungang ilbo*, March 25 and October 31, 1933; *Dong-A ilbo*, March 25, 1933; *Dong-A ilbo*, April 21 and May 1, 1934.

86. We know of the existence of this material because a censorship record for it exists as part of the Kyŏngsŏng Regional Court Prosecutors Office material (in Japanese), which is accessible through the Korean History Database. The magazine is listed as *Chagongdŭng* (*Kodomora* in Japanese), vol. 1, no. 1, and the result of the prepublication censorship review is recorded as "not permitted." Literary scholar Yi Sanggyŏng speculates that the Korean title must have been *Aidŭl*, meaning "children." According to Yi, available historical records show that *Aidŭl* was published by Pak Wansik in Ŭiju, North P'yŏngan Province. Pak Wansik published another magazine, *Chosŏn sonyŏn* (Young-age Koreans), for several years in Ŭiju; it suffered continuously under heavy censorship and eventually folded. It seems that *Aidŭl* was Pak's next venture after the closing of *Chosŏn sonyŏn*, but *Aidŭl* also met with harsh censorship and folded. Neither magazine is extant. Pak, who worked at the Ŭiju branch of the Chosun Ilbo company, was arrested and served a prison term in relation to the second KAPF (Korea Artista Proleta Federatio) incident of 1934. Personal communication, Yi Sanggyŏng, e-mail message to author, July 7, 2016.

87. Song Chiyŏng, "1930-yŏn P'yŏngyang komu kongjang p'aŏp," 251.

88. Kim Yŏnggŭn, "Rodong kyegŭp ŭi ttal Kang Churyong nyŏsŏng."

4. FACTORY WOMEN IN THE POSTWAR SETTLEMENT

1. An Chongu, "Chobang chaengŭi 1," 120. The wall poster incident is based on An's recollection in "Chobang chaengŭi 1 and 2," unless otherwise noted.

2. Song Chongnae et al., *Han'guk nodong undongsa 4*, 333.

3. Nam, *Building Ships*, chap. 2.
4. Nakao, "1950–52-yŏn Chosŏn Pangjik chaengŭi," 63.
5. Ibid., 4.
6. Pak Chaehwa, "1930-yŏn Chosŏn Pangjik p'aŏp," 55.
7. *Dong-A ilbo*, January 17, 1930. An eight-hour workday was a common demand of unions under the influence of communist groups.
8. Pak Chaehwa, "1930-yŏn Chosŏn Pangjik p'aŏp," 17.
9. Ibid., 23, 33–34, 37, 45–46; Yi Songhŭi, "Ilcheha Pusan chiyŏk yŏsŏng nodongjadŭl," 378.
10. For example, in October 1930, in relation to a strike plan, Chobang yŏgong Yi Chŏngsim and her partner were arrested, and their mimeograph machine was confiscated. *Dong-A ilbo*, October 7, 1930. In May 1931 four Chobang yŏgong were arrested, including Kim Kyejŏng, who was a student turned labor activist. Kim was freed but the other three yŏgong (Che Yŏngsun, Cho Pokkŭm, and Chŏng Kŭmja) were indicted. *Dong-A ilbo*, May 30, 1931. In 1933 ten Chobang yŏgong were arrested in May and another in September. *Dong-A ilbo*, May 7 and September 24, 1933.
11. *Pusan ilbo*, March 17, 1935.
12. Yi Songhŭi, "Ilcheha Pusan chiyŏk yŏsŏng nodongjadŭl," 385.
13. Pak Chaehwa, "1930-yŏn Chosŏn Pangjik p'aŏp," 22–25. Discussion of the strike process is based on this MA thesis, unless otherwise noted.
14. Ibid., 49. Historian Yi Songhŭi notes that this Chobang dispute "clearly revealed the capacity and autonomous subjectivity of working women of Pusan." Yi Songhŭi, "Ilcheha Pusan chiyŏk yŏsŏng nodongjadŭl," 386.
15. *Chungoe ilbo*, January 21, 1930.
16. For example, *Dong-A ilbo*, January 17, 1930, editorial.
17. *Dong-A ilbo*, September 8, 1933, editorial. In a statement, women strikers in the 1930 Chobang strike claimed that in spite of public perception of them as "stupid and ignorant know-nothings and weak beings," they "startled the company executives" with "the strong power of solidarity" and "will continue to fight without bending a bit." *Dong-A ilbo*, January 19, 1930, cited in Pak Chaehwa, "1930-yŏn Chosŏn Pangjik p'aŏp," 36. During the same strike a yŏgong explained workers' grievances and said, "Until our demands are accepted, we will never return to work, and we won't eat." *Dong-A ilbo*, January 13, 1930.
18. Workers also expressed their frustration and indignation through work slowdowns, absenteeism, fleeing in cases of conscripted labor, graffiti, and rumors. Yi Sangŭi, *Ilcheha Chosŏn ŭi nodong chŏngch'aek*, 363–65.
19. On the complex history of the wartime Sanpō movement and its legacies in Japan, see Notar, "Japan's Wartime Labor Policy"; Gordon, *Evolution of Labor Relations in Japan*, chap. 7 and 8; Saguchi, "Historical Significance of the Industrial Patriotic Association," 266–74.
20. Saguchi, "Historical Significance of the Industrial Patriotic Association," 271.
21. Critiquing existing literature that assumes the existence of the Sanpō in colonial Korea, such as George E. Ogle's *South Korea: Dissent within the Economic Miracle* and Soon-Won Park's "Colonial Industrial Growth and the Emergence of the Korean Working Class," sociologist Sin Wŏnch'ŏl clarifies the limited nature of the new labor policy experiments in Korea, including the lack of Sangyō Hōkoku (Sanpō) associations. Historians Yi Sangŭi and Kwak Kŏnhong provide detailed analysis of the Japanese colonial government's wartime labor policies in Korea. Overall, Sin Wŏnch'ŏl and Yi Sangŭi argue, the colonial context of Korea made the form and effect of the experiment in Korea quite different from counterparts in Japan. The "colonial fascist-type wartime mobilization system" constructed in Korea was a "much more brutal" version of the Japanese system,

and in that context the "effect of the statist ideology was very limited," Sin concludes. Sin Wŏnch'ŏl, "Chŏnsi nomu tongwŏn," 171–72, 180, 185; Kwak Kŏnhong, *Ilche ŭi nodong chŏngch'aek kwa Chosŏn nodongja*; Yi Sangŭi, *Ilcheha Chosŏn ŭi nodong chŏngch'aek*, 366–68, 380–81.

22. Contemporary estimates were that to supply and equip a million soldiers on the front, twelve to thirteen million workers were needed in production. The twenty-million-strong and fast-growing Korean population accounted for close to a quarter (23.4 percent in 1935) of the total population in the Japanese Empire, making it the most appropriate pool of human resources to mobilize from the imperial government's perspective. It is estimated that between 7 and 7.8 million Koreans were forcefully mobilized through various methods between 1939 and 1945, which accounted for one-third of the total population in Korea. About 280,000 Koreans were conscripted as military service workers between 1939 and 1945. Yi Sangŭi, *Ilcheha Chosŏn ŭi nodong chŏngch'aek*, 159, 161, 320–21.

23. In February 1944 "current-employee conscription" went into effect, turning 260,145 workers in key factories and mines into conscripted laborers unable to leave their jobs. By November 1944, workers at seventy-two factories and seventy-one mines were conscripted. Yi Sangŭi, *Ilcheha Chosŏn ŭi nodong chŏngch'aek*, 252–53. In August 1944 the general conscription of labor started, mobilizing men ages sixteen to forty to work in factories, construction sites, and mines in Korea and abroad for two years.

24. Important works on the industrial relations of the late colonial period include Kwak, *Ilche ŭi nodong chŏngch'aek kwa Chosŏn nodongja*; Yi Sangŭi, *Ilcheha Chosŏn ŭi nodong chŏngch'aek*; Janice Kim, *To Live to Work*. Kim's study examines textile workers in this period but does not discuss processes and effects of the Sanpō mobilization on women workers.

25. An T'aejŏng, *Chosŏn Nodong Chohap Chŏn'guk P'yŏngŭihoe*, 117. Chŏnp'yŏng's meteoric rise and precipitous fall, the fate of the worker-led self-management movement, and the nature of the Taehan Noch'ong are discussed in Nam, *Building Ships*, chap. 1. Statistics on Chŏnp'yŏng membership vary, and historian An T'aejŏng provides the most detailed discussions of available data. In April 1946 the North Korean Labor Federation (Puk Chosŏn Nodong Ch'ongdongmaeng) seceded from the Chŏnp'yŏng, and the southern Chŏnp'yŏng's membership strength seems to have hovered around 300,000 until early 1948, when the harsh repression began to decimate the movement. When Chŏnp'yŏng was founded in November 1945, its membership number of more than 217,000 represented about 10 percent of the total number of industrial workers in the northern and the southern zones, which was approximately 2.12 million. An T'aejŏng, *Chosŏn Nodong Chohap Chŏn'guk P'yŏngŭihoe*, 111–12, 117–21, 460.

26. Labor statistics on Chŏnp'yŏng-related strikes between August 1945 and February 1948 put the number of strikes at 3,251, in which a total of 762,913 workers participated. Of these 10,732 workers were arrested, 18,599 workers were fired, and 25 workers were killed. FKTU, *Han'guk Noch'ong 50-yŏnsa*, 286.

27. Nam, *Building Ships*, chap. 1. Japan also saw a very similar movement among workers in the same period.

28. FKTU, *Han'guk Noch'ong 50-yŏnsa*, 258. We can imagine the scale of the eruption from 1944 statistics that show that 195 (92 percent) of the 212 large companies with more than one million yen in capital stock were Japanese-owned. Nam, *Building Ships*, 27.

29. In 1947, out of 134 labor disputes, thirty-two cases involving 4,818 workers occurred in the textile industry. The second-highest number was recorded by the machine tools industry with thirty-one disputes in 1946 (4,403 workers) and another thirty-one disputes in 1947 (4,131 workers). Pak Yŏnggi and Kim Chŏnghan interpret

these numbers as a result of the left-wing dominance of these industries. Pak Yŏnggi and Kim Chŏnghan, *Han'guk nodong undongsa 3*, 504–5.

30. An Chaesŏng, *Chosŏn Nodong Chohap Chŏn'guk P'yŏngŭihoe*, 90.

31. Nakao, "1950–52-yŏn Chosŏn Pangjik chaengŭi," 22; FKTU, *Han'guk nodong chohap undongsa*, 337.

32. Pak Yŏnggi and Kim Chŏnghan, *Han'guk nodong undongsa 3*, 604–5.

33. An Chaesŏng, *Chosŏn Nodong Chohap Chŏn'guk P'yŏngŭihoe*, 59–60.

34. The original name of the Taehan Noch'ong was the Taehan Tongnip Ch'oksŏng Nodong Ch'ongyŏnmaeng; at its August 1948 convention of representatives, the name was changed to Taehan Nodong Ch'ongyŏnmaeng (Taehan Noch'ong in short). In this book I refer to both as the Taehan Noch'ong.

35. An Chongu, "Chobang chaengŭi 1 and 2." An was a veteran of an anti-Chŏnp'yŏng campaign at Mokto Shipbuilding and Ironworks, where he had "struggled against the 'commies' under the Chŏnp'yŏng, wiped them out, and was elected union president." An Chongu, "Chobang chaengŭi 1," 115. Chosŏn Heavy Industries, the biggest company in Mokto (Yŏngdo), was also going through the same kind of conflict. Nam, *Building Ships*, chap. 1. Song Wŏndo, who had been sent to Pusan as the Taehan Noch'ong organizer after the February 1947 general strike and organized a dockworkers' union as the first right-wing union in Pusan, became a staunch ally in An's anti-Chŏnp'yŏng struggles. The head of the South Kyŏngsang Province Unit of the notorious youth organization, the Northwest Youth Corps, was another key ally of An's. Nakao, "1950–52-yŏn Chosŏn Pangjik chaengŭi," 23; An Chongu, "Chobang chaengŭi 1," 115. An and Song founded the Pusan Regional Federation and the South Kyŏngsang Province Federation in 1948 and 1949, respectively. They were the major architects of the Taehan Noch'ong victory in Pusan. Nakao, "1950–52-yŏn Chosŏn Pangjik chaengŭi," 23.

36. An Chongu, "Chobang chaengŭi 1," 115–16; Nam, *Building Ships*, 33–35; Nakao, "1950–52-yŏn Chosŏn Pangjik chaengŭi," 24.

37. Recollection of Song Wŏndo, the head of the Pusan Regional Federation, cited in Nakao, "1950–52-yŏn Chosŏn Pangjik chaengŭi," 23. Statistics vary but the trend of rapid reversal of fortunes between the two national labor organizations was clear. By 1948, according to the statistics of the Labor Bureau (Nodongguk) of the Ministry of Social Affairs, Chŏnp'yŏng unions disappeared and the Taehan Noch'ong grew to an organization of 683 unions and 127,618 members. FKTU, *Han'guk Noch'ong 50-yŏnsa*, 303. As a result of this process, the Taehan Noch'ong–affiliated Chobang union, like other Taehan Noch'ong unions of the period, ended up with many members who had been transferred from the Northwest Youth Corps, as well as the National Youth Corps (Chokch'ŏng) of Yi Pŏmsŏk. An Chongu, "Chobang chaengŭi 1," 115; Nakao, "1950–52-yŏn Chosŏn Pangjik chaengŭi," 34.

38. Nam, *Building Ships*, 63.

39. Nakao, "1950–52-yŏn Chosŏn Pangjik chaengŭi," 22.

40. Pak Yŏnggi and Kim Chŏnghan, *Han'guk nodong undongsa 3*, 195; Nakao, "1950–52-yŏn Chosŏn Pangjik chaengŭi," 12; Kim Nakchung, *Han'guk nodong undongsa*, 145; Sŏ Munsŏk, "1960-yŏndae taep'yojŏk kwisok kiŏpch'e," 339.

41. An Chongu, "Chobang chaengŭi 1," 117. Kim Chit'ae had been a well-established businessman in Pusan and the inaugural and second chair of the Pusan Chamber of Commerce from 1946 to 1952. He was elected to the National Assembly in the May 1950 election. He became the manager of another major vested property in Pusan, Chosŏn Silk (formerly Asahi Silk), in 1946 and, based on that connection, purchased the company in March 1951. Kim served as a board member at Chobang beginning in March 1948. Nakao, "1950–52-yŏn Chosŏn Pangjik chaengŭi," 14.

42. Song Chongnae et al., *Han'guk nodong undongsa 4*, 339.

43. Ibid., 338-39; Nam, *Building Ships*, 50. In 1951 the net annual profit of the company reached 8.5 billion wŏn.

44. Such a union, even if it were to be unsuccessful in purchasing the company, could still claim the right to buy 30 percent of the company shares. Nakao, "1950–52-yŏn Chosŏn Pangjik chaengŭi," 29. Nam, *Building Ships*, 41–50, contains a discussion of Chŏn Chinhan's life and work.

45. Nakao, "1950–52-yŏn Chosŏn Pangjik chaengŭi," 30.

46. The ideological terrain of the period is detailed in Nam, *Building Ships*, chap. 2.

47. Important recent studies on the nature of the Constitution of South Korea include Pak Ch'ansŭng, *Taehan Min'guk ŭn minju konghwaguk ida*, and Kim Yukhun, *Minju konghwaguk Taehan Min'guk ŭi t'ansaeng*.

48. Im Songja, *Taehan Min'guk nodong undong*, 68–69; Yi Chŏngŭn, "1950-yŏndae nodong chibae damnon," 153. According to Yi, in the 1950s workers were routinely called "warriors" as in "transportation warriors" (*susong chŏnsa*) or "transit warriors" (*kyot'ong chŏnsa*).

49. Key works on Chokch'ŏng and the influence of the Chokch'ŏng group include Fujii, *P'asijŭm kwa che-3-segyejuŭi*, and Im Chongmyŏng, "Chosŏn Minjok Ch'ŏngnyŏndan kwa Mi kunjŏng."

50. Yi worked closely with Syngman Rhee until the mid-1950s when Rhee finally severed his ties to him under strong US pressure. Fujii, *P'asijŭm kwa che-3-segyejuŭi*, 395–456. The third manager who arrived at Chobang in May 1947 was Chŏng Myŏngsŏk, who was the head of the Industrial Bureau in the Commerce and Industry Department of the US occupation government. An Chongu recalls that when he came to Chobang in late 1947 to break the Chŏnp'yŏng union at the factory, he found that Chŏng had already brought in Chokch'ŏng people as his defense force against the union. An Chongu, "Chobang chaengŭi 1," 115.

51. Yi Chŏngŭn, "1950-yŏndae nodong chibae damnon," 159. On *ilminjuŭi*, see Sŏ Chungsŏk, "Yi Sŭngman chŏngkwŏn ch'ogi ŭi ilminjuŭi"; Fujii, *P'asijŭm kwa che-3-segyejuŭi*, 225–70.

52. Chang Kyusik, "Mi kunjŏng ha Hŭngsadan kyeyŏl chisigin." As of 1924 about half of the students who studied in the United States were from North and South P'yŏngan Provinces, and 90 percent of them were Christians. Yi Sangŭi, "Ilcheha Miguk yuhaksaeng," 418–19. A large portion of the high-ranking Korean officials in the USAMGIK were Christians from the northwest, especially those of the Hŭngsadan group, thanks to their education in the United States, English proficiency, and close connections to US missionaries on whose advice and expertise the USAMGIK relied. For example, out of thirteen department heads of the South Korea Interim Government, established in 1947 by the USAMGIK, five (Cho Pyŏngok of the Police Affairs Department, Yi Taewi of the Labor Department, O Ch'ŏnsŏk of the Education Department, O Chŏngsu of the Commercial Affairs Department, and Yi Yongsŏl of the Public Health and Welfare Department) belonged to the Hŭngsadan group. Of 141 long-term Hŭngsadan members residing in Korea as of November 1947, at least forty-three worked in the US occupation government or military. Kim Tongwŏn, the Pyongyang nationalist businessman and rubber factory owner we met in chapters 1 and 2, was one of them and served as an administrative adviser (*haengjŏng komun*) to the US Army military governor. Ibid., 248, 250–58.

53. Chang Kyusik, *Ilcheha Han'guk Kidokkyo minjokchuŭi*, 167–85; Chang Kyusik, "Mi kunjŏng ha Hŭngsadan kyeyŏl chisigin"; Yi Sangŭi, "Ilcheha Miguk yuhaksaeng." Yi Sangŭi introduces differing views on the issues of economic development and the labor question among nationalist intellectuals who studied in the United States during the colonial period and played important roles after liberation in the USAMGIK and

in the South Korean government and politics. He differentiates the "economic liberalism" group whose focus was on the production side of the economy and the "economic democracy" group whose focus was on the distribution side and analyzes labor-capital cooperation discourses of the thinkers in the latter group, which included, in addition to Yi Taewi, Chang Tŏksu, Han Sŭngin, Cho Pyŏngok, Yi Hun'gu, and Kim Hun.

54. Chang Kyusik, "Mi kunjŏng ha Hŭngsadan kyeyŏl chisigin," 261, 264–75. O Kiyŏng also advocated nationalization of vested companies, arguing that those companies should become the basis of an autonomous national economy. In this period O Kiyŏng worked as the operations bureau chief at a major vested company, Kyŏngsŏng Electric.

55. Sin Chubaek, "'Minju konghwaje' ron kwa pi chabonjuŭi," 122–24. This discussion on the evolving nationalist consensus on *kyun* and noncapitalist development draws largely from Sin's article.

56. Song Chongnae et al., *Han'guk nodong undongsa 4*, 125.

57. Chŏn, who was a champion of the cooperative movement in the 1920s, dubbed his ideology "cooperatism" (*hyŏptongjuŭi*), and together with many anarchist thinkers he transitioned into a "democratic socialism" in the late 1950s.

58. Nakao, "1950–52-yŏn Chosŏn Pangjik chaengŭi," 25–26.

59. Nam, *Building Ships*, chap. 5 and 7.

60. Yi Chŏngŭn, "1950-yŏndae nodong chibae damnon," 160.

61. Despite its historic importance Chobang workers' struggle has not garnered much scholarly attention. Official histories produced by the FKTU (*Han'guk nodong chohap undongsa*; *Han'guk Noch'ong 50-yŏnsa*) and chronological labor history accounts (Kim Nakchung, *Han'guk nodong undongsa*; Song Chongnae et al., *Han'guk nodong undongsa 4*) give weight to the dispute and its political repercussions, but so far only one scholar—labor historian Nakao Michiko—has produced a monograph on the dispute (in the form of an MA thesis), plus a short article summarizing her findings. Nakao, "1950–52-yŏn Chosŏn Pangjik chaengŭi" and "1950-yŏndae Han'guk nodong undong ŭi pun'gichŏm."

62. Article 18 on workers' profit sharing was not removed until a 1962 revision under Park Chung Hee.

63. An Chongu, "Chobang chaengŭi 1," 116. The sale of the companies recovered from the Japanese resumed in November 1950 when UN forces pushed back the invading North Korean army beyond the Thirty-Eighth Parallel after MacArthur's Incheon landing, and the sale of Chobang was scheduled for March 1951. Nam, *Building Ships*, 264n65.

64. Nakao, "1950–52-yŏn Chosŏn Pangjik chaengŭi," 37.

65. In the end the trial was transferred to a civil court in May, and six were found guilty in August. Kim Chit'ae and Chang Chaebong were both sentenced to a ten-month prison term with a year and a half of probation, and Chŏng Hojong received a two-year prison term with four years of probation. Nakao, "1950–52-yŏn Chosŏn Pangjik chaengŭi," 38; Pae Sŏngman, "'Chobang sakŏn,'" 182–86.

66. An Chongu, "Chobang chaengŭi 1," 118–19; Pae Sŏngman, "'Chobang sakŏn,'" 202–3.

67. Pegged on the nationwide wholesale price index of 1947 as 100, that of 1950, when the war began, registered 348. From there the number shot up to 2,194.1 in 1951, when the country was engulfed in war, a 530.5 percent increase, and the next year it went up to 4750.8, a 116.5 percent increase. Song Chongnae et al., *Han'guk nodong undongsa 4*, 71, table 2–5. In 1951 the number of unemployed reached around 1.1 million according to government statistics, out of a total population of about 20 million people. Ibid., 82.

68. Nakao, "1950–52-yŏn Chosŏn Pangjik chaengŭi," 30.

69. Kang did not have any significant experience in industrial management, although he had held a manager position at a department store. His private ties to Rhee have not been verified, but Syngman Rhee documents—*Unam Yi Sŭngman munsŏ* [Documents of Unam Syngman Rhee] (Seoul: Chungang Ilbosa, 1998)—show Kang as a recipient of substantial funds from Rhee in 1947 and 1948. Cited in Pae Sŏngman, "Haebang hu Chosŏn Pangjik," 91–92. According to Kim Chit'ae's recollection, he and company president Chŏng were persecuted through the so-called Nangmyŏn incident because he refused to provide political funds to Rhee. Kim Chit'ae, *Munhangna chŏgori nŭn*, 263, 295–300. Kim Chit'ae would have assumed the presidency of Chobang if the Chobang manager-employee coalition had succeeded in purchasing the company. Nakao, "1950–52-yŏn Chosŏn Pangjik chaengŭi," 14; Pae Sŏngman, "'Chobang sakŏn,'" 182–83.

70. The Liberal Party (Chayudang) was supposed to be the party of "working masses." Nam, *Building Ships*, 39, 255. The party would have as its foundation five social movement federations, representing industrial workers (Taehan Noch'ong), farmers (Taehan Nongch'ong), women (Taehan Puinhoe), youth (Taehan Ch'ŏngnyŏndan), and the general citizenry (Kungminhoe).

71. Ibid., 51. It is statistically difficult to determine exactly how large a proportion the vested assets accounted for in terms of total assets in the country, but no one denies its overwhelming weight in the mining and manufacturing industries. As of September 1947, according to Bank of Korea statistics there were 1,551 vested factories, which had 50,770 employees, in southern Korea. In comparison, 3,959 nonvested factories employed 77,922 workers. Pak Yŏnggi and Kim Chŏnghan, *Han'guk nodong undongsa 3*, 184–88. The Ministry of Commerce and Industry was swamped with disputes over managerial rights at many of these vested firms under its control. Nam, *Building Ships*, 265n71.

72. Nakao, "1950-yŏndae Han'guk nodong undong ŭi pun'gichŏm," 152; Pae Sŏngman, "'Chobang sakŏn,'" 183–84; Nakao, "1950–52-yŏn Chosŏn Pangjik chaengŭi," 33.

73. An Chongu, "Chobang chaengŭi 1," 119.

74. Kim Nakchung, *Han'guk nodong undongsa*, 146.

75. Nam, *Building Ships*, 51.

76. An Chongu, "Chobang chaengŭi 1," 123; *Dong-A ilbo*, May 20, 1952; Kim Nakchung, *Han'guk nodong undongsa*, 147–48.

77. An Chongu, "Chobang chaengŭi 2," 158.

78. *Dong-A ilbo*, February 9, 1952.

79. An Chongu, "Chobang chaengŭi 2," 159; Kim Nakchung, *Han'guk nodong undongsa*, 148–49.

80. Kim Nakchung, *Han'guk nodong undongsa*, 150.

81. An Chongu, "Chobang chaengŭi 2," 163.

82. Yi Oesŏn was the niece of Yi Sangok, the Chobang sub-local's vice president. Ibid. That must have been why An Chongu remembered and stated Yi's name in particular among key yŏgong leaders.

83. Song Chongnae et al., *Han'guk nodong undongsa 4*, 337.

84. Kim Nakchung, *Han'guk nodong undongsa*, 152. Soon after Chŏn's call for a strike, Rhee made a terse announcement against the strike plan, which read in part: "It seems that some people still are discussing the Chosŏn Spinning and Weaving company matter, but any amount of debate on this issue would do no good. The policy of the government is to separate the industry and the political party movement." Rhee went on to clarify his intention not to let Chobang, "an especially big company" in Korea, "fall into the hands of a political party" and declared his decision to eliminate the troublemakers and entrust the company to "those who simply promote production development." Ibid., 151.

85. An Chongu, "Chobang chaengŭi 2," 164.

86. Sŏ Munsŏk, "1960-yŏndae taep'yojŏk kwisok kiŏpch'e," 343; An Chongu, "Chobang chaengŭi 2," 164.

87. FKTU, Han'guk nodong chohap undongsa, 366. Rhee maintained his honorary position at the Taehan Noch'ong as well as other mass organizations as the "supreme leader" (ch'ongjae).

88. Sŏ Munsŏk, "1960-yŏndae taep'yojŏk kwisok kiŏpch'e," 343–44.

89. Kim Sŭng introduces twenty primary source documents on the 1951–52 dispute and the 1958 dispute at Chobang. The collection also includes materials of the Committee to Recover Rights Deprived in the Chobang Dispute, organized by Pak Chŏngt'ae and Yi Sangok in August 1960 after the April Revolution of 1960. Kim Sŭng, "Charyo sogae."

90. Sŏ Munsŏk, "1960-yŏndae taep'yojŏk kwisok kiŏpch'e," 343, 344.

91. Nakao, "1950–52-yŏn Chosŏn Pangjik chaengŭi," 63; Song Chongnae et al., Han'guk nodong undongsa 4, 297–323. Kang Ilmae installed a "Headquarters for Mobilizing People's Wishes" at Chobang, and after the Chobang dispute ended he mobilized Chobang workers to join often violent right-wing street demonstrations in Pusan against the National Assembly and in support of Rhee. Ibid., 319–20, 333.

92. I argued this point expanding on insights of labor historian and activist Kim Nakchung (Han'guk nodong undongsa) and labor law scholar Sin Illyŏng (Nodongpŏp kwa nodong undong) in Nam, Building Ships, 48–53.

93. Economist and labor scholar Song Chongnae credits the Chobang dispute of 1951–52 with the birth of what he calls "shop-floor [hyŏnjang] unionism" in South Korea. He highly evaluates the level of consciousness among Chobang's rank-and-file workers, although he does not note the fact that most of them were yŏgong. Song Chongnae et al., Han'guk nodong undongsa 4, 347.

94. An Chongu, "Chobang chaengŭi 2," 157.

95. The Chŏn'guk nodongja sinmun (National Workers' Daily), a Chŏnp'yŏng organ, was a major conduit of propaganda. Its circulation reached sixty thousand copies by May 1946. An Chaesŏng, Chosŏn Nodong Chohap Chŏn'guk P'yŏngŭihoe, 465.

96. Kim Chun, "1950-yŏndae ch'ŏlto nojo," 219–21, 229–30, italics added.

97. About half a year after the mass firing at Chobang, a local newspaper, Kukche sinbo (International News), while reporting on the conditions of life for dismissed Chobang workers, noted that "especially [dismissed] female workers [yŏjikkong] fell so low as to become women of the night." Kukche sinbo, September 9, 1952, cited in Pae Sŏngman, "'Chobang sakŏn,'" 187. It seems that the tragic outcome that befell some fired Chobang yŏgong was widely noticed in the larger society as well.

98. Song Chongnae et al., Han'guk nodong undongsa 4, 99. In 1955 the number of farmers (4.5 million, 67.9 percent of the economically active population) dwarfed the 310,000 industrial workers. Ibid., 80–81.

99. Ibid., 83.

100. Yi Hŭiyŏng, "1950-yŏndae yŏsŏng nodongja," 172–73.

101. Ibid., 187–88. "The stylish work uniform" women factory workers wore became an object of envy in this situation. A comparable textile factory, Seoul's Kyŏngsŏng Spinning and Weaving (Kyŏngbang), had an admission ratio of more than ten applicants to every one hired until the early 1960s. Ibid., 190–93. The relatively positive views of factory jobs for women in this period are reminiscent of the 1920s situation discussed earlier.

102. Ibid., 199–200.

103. An incident that shows the lingering influence of the Chŏnp'yŏng union experience and also the tense ideological situation of wartime Pusan occurred in September 1952, half a year after the end of the Chobang strike. The media broke a sensational news story about the roundup of a North Korean spy ring, a "corps of beautiful spies composed of female college students, yŏgong, and typists." Led by Pak Chŏngja (twenty-five years old),

a medical school graduate and "North Korea-trained spy," who worked as a typist at a US military base in Pusan, this group of thirteen activists allegedly operated in connection with partisan fighters in the region. Among the arrested were two white-collar female employees at Chobang (Yun Ch'ilsŏng and Yi Malsun) and two blue-collar Chobang yŏgong (Sŏk Okhŭi and Im Mija), in addition to a female doctor, female medical school students, and female civilian employees at US bases. *Kyŏnghyang sinmun*, September 5, 1952; *Dong-A ilbo*, September 15, 1952.

5. WOMEN WORKERS IN INDUSTRIALIZING KOREA

1. A major exception is a series of textile disputes and protests by dismissed women workers in Taegu, involving Taehan Spinning and Weaving (from 1956 to 1960) and Cheil Wool (June–August 1960). These textile disputes were closely connected to the rise of a reform movement within the Taehan Noch'ong and the eventual establishment in 1959 of the Chŏn'guk Nohyŏp, a rival organization to the Taehan Noch'ong. Taehan Spinning and Weaving in Taegu was formerly the Taegu factory of Chobang, which was sold to powerful Liberal Party politician Sŏl Kyŏngdong in 1955. Sŏl then fired 2,600 workers, provoking a persistent struggle by workers. On the Taehan Spinning and Weaving and Cheil Wool disputes, see Song Chongnae et al., *Han'guk nodong undongsa 4*, 380, 536; Kim Kyŏngil, "1950-yŏndae Han'guk ŭi nodong undong."

2. Even the lowest estimates show more than 100,000 war widows and some 59,000 orphans. Ham Inhŭi, "Han'guk chŏnjaeng, kajok kŭrigo yŏsŏng," 166–67. Women's historian Yi Imha includes in her estimates wives of those who were kidnapped and missing and of those who were killed in relation to the persecution of alleged "leftists," and she concludes that at least 300,000 "war widows" (*chŏnjaeng mimangin*) existed during the 1950s, which was around 30 percent of the total number of widows at the time. In Japan, as of May 1947, among a widow population of 1.88 million, 29.8 percent, or 560,000, were war widows. Yi Imha, *Yŏsŏng, chŏnjaeng ŭl nŏmŏ irŏsŏda*, 28–34.

3. Chŏng Pisŏk's novel *Chayu puin* was serialized in *Sŏul sinmun* (Seoul Daily) from January to August 1954, during which time the paper's circulation numbers increased exponentially. When published as a book, it became the first book that sold more than a hundred thousand copies in Korea. The movie was the number-one box office hit in 1956. A combined total of about 1.2 to 1.5 million readers and movie audiences consumed the story at the time, according to literary scholar Hŏ Yun. "Naengjŏn Asiajŏk chilsŏ," 92.

4. Ibid. The quoted passage is from the 1954 Chŏngŭmsa edition of the novel.

5. Kim Chun, "1950-yŏndae ch'ŏlto nojo."

6. Nam, *Building Ships*, chaps. 3–5.

7. The union archives of the National Railway Workers' Union and the KSEC Union are now available in digitized format as part of a vast digital collection of union documents, the *Korean Labor History Collection*. Sŏnggonghoe Taehakkyo Nodongsa Yŏn'guso (Labor History Institute, Sungkonghoe University), *Chŏn'guk Ch'ŏlto Nodong Chohap hwaltong* and *Taehan Chosŏn Kongsa Nodong Chohap hwaltong*.

8. Nam, *Building Ships*, chap. 5.

9. Ham Inhŭi, "Han'guk chŏnjaeng, kajok kŭrigo yŏsŏng," 182.

10. As of August 1962, among forty-two local unions of the national textile union, only one, which had 209 members, was protected by a collective contract, and the rest, which represented 99 percent of national textile union membership, worked without a contract. The situation contrasts sharply with contemporary unions in male-dominated and government-managed industries such as railway, electric power, communications, and the government-monopoly sector, which boasted 100 percent contract coverage. FKTU, *Han'guk Noch'ong saŏp pogo*, year 1962, 368.

11. Hwang Chŏngmi, "Kajok, kukka, sahoe chaesaengsan." Under the US occupation government, women-related tasks were assigned to a "Women's (*punyŏ*) Bureau," which concentrated on the issues of eliminating public prostitution and enlightening the female population to promote modern motherhood. Under the Rhee government, the Women's (*punyŏ*) Department under the Ministry of Society (later, the Ministry of Health and Society) focused on lifestyle reforms and job training for women, and it largely stayed away from labor-related issues.

12. Contemporary news articles clearly pointed out the fact that many women workers were breadwinners. For examples, see *Dong-A ilbo*, February 25, 1965; *Maeil kyŏngje*, September 17, 1969.

13. The communist labor agenda included nursing time and parturition leaves, and sometimes an idealistic and political demand of "equal pay for equal work" found its way onto lists of strike demands. Chŏnp'yŏng's action programs advocated, together with an eight-hour workday and a minimum-wage system, certain gender-specific goals, including equal pay for equal work, parturition leaves, and provision of childcare and nursing rooms for women. Presenting women's demands did not lead to active debates among activists and unionists in the colonial period or in the immediate postliberation years, either in the Chŏnp'yŏng or in the Taehan Noch'ong. This was unlike what happened in Japan, where union activists and socialist feminists like Yamakawa Kikue engaged themselves in substantial debates on how to define women's demands and what would be the proper organizational structures in which to house women workers in the labor movement. Mackie, *Creating Socialist Women in Japan*, 105–15.

14. Gordon, *Evolution of Labor Relations in Japan*, 262, 275–80, 338. Gordon defines the livelihood wage as a wage "which in theory would meet the basic material needs of a worker and his family by rising automatically with age, seniority and greater family responsibility." Ibid., 275.

15. Ibid., 295–97, 338.

16. Examples include Parr, *Gender of Breadwinners*; Kessler-Harris, *In Pursuit of Equity*; Frader, *Breadwinners and Citizens*; Self, *All in the Family*.

17. Land, "Family Wage"; Glickman, *Living Wage*; Kessler-Harris, *Woman's Wage*.

18. Saguchi, "Historical Significance of the Industrial Patriotic Association," 276. The September 1941 wage policy, which dictated the establishment of a standard wage, along with maximums and minimums, helped shape the idea of a fair wage, which "provided stability in income and did not produce large differentials between high and low." Ibid., 276–77. Saguchi argues that such wartime labor policies and Sanpō experimentations, although not very successful in generating enthusiastic worker responses, "powerfully constrained postwar labor-management interaction, wage systems, and employment systems" in Japan (261).

19. Hein, *Fueling Growth*, chap. 9.

20. Ibid., 100, 105; Gordon, *Evolution of Labor Relations in Japan*, 352–55. Gordon calls the Densan plan "the labor version of the aborted bureaucratic plans for a livelihood wage conceived in the Welfare Ministry during the war." The Densan livelihood wage formula established the base wage (98.8 percent) as the main source of income, which was composed of small "regional allowances" (6.8 percent) and a "livelihood guarantee" that was about two-thirds of the wage (63.2 percent). The "livelihood guarantee" portion was based wholly on the individual worker's age (44.3 percent) and family size ("family allowance," 18.9 percent). The remainder derived from "ability pay" (24.4 percent) and "seniority pay" (4.4 percent). Gordon, *Evolution of Labor Relations in Japan*, 353.

21. Gordon, *Evolution of Labor Relations in Japan*, 374–86.

22. Sin Wŏnch'ŏl, "Chŏnsi nomu tongwŏn," 171–72, 179–80, 184.

23. Lim Chai Sung, *Senji keizai to tetsudō un'ei*, 76–77, cited in Sin Wŏnch'ŏl, "Chŏnsi nomu tongwŏn," 184.

24. The Iwŏn Ch'ŏlsan mine encouraged workers' wives, using prize money, to participate in the no-absence movement, and plans were made to visit frequent absentees at home. A train station headmaster in Andong, North Kyŏngsang Province, a Japanese, took it upon himself to visit worker households and investigate the "thoughts and character (hobbies, tastes, entertainments)" of family members and also "relatives and friends" to promote "correct" economic and political behaviors. Lim Chai Sung, *Senji keizai to tetsudō un'ei*, 130–31; Sin Wŏnch'ŏl, "Chŏnsi nomu tongwŏn," 183–84. There is sporadic evidence of large-scale companies in Korea, in railway and mining sectors in particular, adopting the Sanpō movement in earnest, but we have little knowledge of how Sanpō was practiced in corporations in various other sectors in Korea, including Korean-run companies in this period.

25. As I argued in *Building Ships, Building a Nation*, key elements in trade union demands at heavy-industry sites in South Korea in the 1960s showed resonance with radical ideas Sanpō generated in the late colonial period. These included the idea of family living wages, wage distribution methods that prioritized reducing wage gaps among workers, and challenges to status discrimination against manual workers vis-à-vis white-collar employees. They also included the ways workers couched their demands employing the language of patriotism and stressing workers' role in building the nation's economy.

26. Hwang Ŭinam, "Han'guk ŭi imgŭm chŏngch'aek"; T'ak Hŭijun, *Han'guk ŭi imgŭm munje*; Sin Wŏnch'ŏl, "Kiŏp naebu nodong sijang."

27. T'ak Hŭijun, *Han'guk ŭi imgŭm munje*, 186–89; Sin Wŏnch'ŏl, "Kiŏp naebu nodong sijang," 154–74.

28. Hwang includes family allowances, together with a "livelihood" (*saenggye*) allowance, a separation allowance, and a housing allowance, in the category of "living wages." Hwang Ŭinam, "Han'guk ŭi imgŭm chŏngch'aek," 445–48.

29. Many unions in the postliberation period demanded living wages, and the Taehan Noch'ong and its successor, the Han'guk Noch'ong (FKTU), continued to list "securing the livelihood wage" as part of its agenda into the 1970s.

30. FKTU, *Han'guk Noch'ong 50-yŏnsa*, 445.

31. *Dong-A ilbo*, October 18 and December 30, 1963, and January 29, February 1, and February 10, 1964; *Kyŏnghyang sinmun*, February 1, February 10, and March 2, 1964; FKTU, *Han'guk Noch'ong 50-yŏnsa*, 369; Sŏnggonghoe Taehakkyo Nodongsa Yŏn'guso, *Chŏn'guk Ch'ŏlto Nodong Chohap hwaltong*, vol. 4, *Saenghwalgŭp hwakpo t'ujaeng kwan'gyech'ŏl* [A document collection regarding the struggle to secure a living wage] (1963); FKCU (Federation of Korean Chemical Workers' Union), *Hwahak nojo 20-yŏnsa*, 155. The Chŏn'guk Chŏnmae Nodong Chohap (currently the Korea Tobacco and Ginseng Workers' Union or KTGWU) has as members tobacco and ginseng workers of the government-owned Korean Monopoly Corporation (renamed in 1989 as the Korean Tobacco and Ginseng Corporation), which was privatized in 2002 as KT&G.

32. See KSEC union documents contained in volumes titled *1963 1964* and *1965–yŏndo imgŭm insang mit (pudang) nodong haengwi kwan'gyech'ŏl* [A document collection regarding the 1965 wage increases and (unfair) labor practices] held in the KSEC union archive.

33. Hwang Ŭinam, "Han'guk ŭi imgŭm chŏngch'aek," 280–81.

34. FKTU, *Han'guk Noch'ong saŏp pogo*, year 1963, 701–19. For example, in early 1963 Alice Cook, a Cornell University professor, and John Herring, a former Harvard University professor and then a labor reporter covering the White House, visited South Korea to introduce US practices of labor relations and labor administration. With Professor Cook's help the FKTU came to receive Cornell University's Industrial Research Institute publications regularly.

35. For example, the 1962 issue of *Han'guk Noch'ong saŏp pogo* shows that four Korean unionists were sent to the Asian Trade Union College (ATUC) seminar in Tokyo, and seven students were dispatched for training at ATUC, based in Calcutta, India. FKTU, both its headquarters and its individual industrial unions, actively conducted diplomacy with the ICFTU and its Asian Regional Organization. FKTU, *Han'guk Noch'ong saŏp pogo*, year 1962, 571–618.

36. On the FKTU union struggle against the law, see FKTU, *Han'guk Noch'ong 50-yŏnsa*, 458–61. The law was abandoned in February 1964.

37. *Maeil kyŏngje*, January 1, 1968.

38. Sŏnggonghoe Taehakkyo Nodongsa Yŏn'guso, *Chŏn'guk Ch'ŏlto Nodong Chohap hwaltong*, vol. 4.

39. FKTU, *Han'guk Noch'ong 50-yŏnsa*, 445–46. Professor Im Chongch'ŏl of Seoul National University and Ch'oe Kyuwŏn of the Korean Productivity Center conducted the commissioned research.

40. On the 1969 textile dispute launched by the Korean Textile Workers' Union, see ibid., 378–80. As of August 1962, the average monthly wage of white-collar and technical employees (*chigwŏn*) among FKTU union members was 6,713 wŏn, while workers in the "skilled workers" category made 4,712 wŏn and those in the "yŏgong" category made 3,308 wŏn. Meanwhile, the average monthly "real-life living expenses" (*silt'ae saenggyebi*) of worker households surveyed by the Bank of Korea was 11,000 wŏn. From its 1970 activity report the FKTU eliminated the "yŏgong" category and began to survey wages using the gender-neutral categories of white-collar employees, technical employees, skilled workers, unskilled workers, and temporary workers. Ibid., 443, 445.

41. In a roundtable in the midst of the 1969 textile wage dispute, the head of the national textile union, Yi Ch'unsŏn, explained that because more than 80 percent of textile workers were around twenty years of age and relatively less burdened by the obligation to support the family, the union was requesting 11,570 wŏn per month for textile workers when its calculation of the minimum cost of living for a five-person household came in at 19,772 wŏn. *Maeil kyŏngje*, September 17, 1969. The minimum wage law was promulgated on December 31, 1986, and implemented in stages beginning in 1988, starting with companies of ten or more employees in the mining, manufacturing, and construction industries. As of 1986, 27.3 percent of women workers were hired at companies that had fewer than ten workers and thus remained outside the purview of the law. The 1990 minimum wage of 5,520 wŏn per day (about 165,000 wŏn per month) was much lower than the FKTU-estimated monthly minimum cost of living for a single female worker, 331,054 wŏn. Han'guk Yŏsŏng Yŏn'guso, *Yŏsŏng nodongja wa imgŭm*, 101–2. An "equal pay for equal labor" article was finally added to the employment equality law in 1989, following an active campaign by women's movement organizations. Ibid., 106–12.

42. Spencer, *Yogong*, 67.

43. Han'guk Yŏsŏng Yŏn'guso, *Yŏsŏng nodongja wa imgŭm*, 117–19. The reasons given for this practice of pegging women's wage demands to a single-person cost of living were: (1) because women's wages were so low, it would be an unreasonable demand of a more than 100 percent raise if two persons' cost of living were used; (2) because of the capitalist ideology that women were not breadwinners; and (3) because of the nonexistence of industry-level bargaining that could push for a gender-neutral wage demand based on the average family size of all the workers in the industry. Because of the gender-segregated market situation and also the enterprise-centered union system in South Korea, unions at female-dominated work sites, unlike those at male-dominated shops, tended to produce cost of living estimates for single-worker households as the basis of their wage bargaining.

44. Seungsook Moon sees this gendered scheme of developmental politics as a core aspect of what she calls the "militarized modernity" of South Korea. Moon, *Militarized Modernity and Gendered Citizenship*.

45. An FKTU survey in 1970 found that more than two-thirds of surveyed women workers had fewer than three years of seniority, 78.9 percent were unmarried, and 73 percent were between eighteen and twenty-four years of age. *Maeil kyŏngje*, July 22, 1970. As of 1968, the FKTU had 120,000 women workers as members, and the country had an estimated 600,000 women industrial workers. *Dong-A ilbo*, July 25, 1968.

46. *Dong-A ilbo*, November 9, 1933.

47. Representative films include *Coachmen* (*Mabu*, 1961, directed by Kang Taejin), *Mr. Park* (*Pak sŏbang*, 1960, directed by Kang Taejin), *Romance Papa* (*Romaensŭ p'ap'a*, 1960, directed by Sin Sangok), and *Under the Sky of Seoul* (*Sŏul ŭi chibung mit*, 1961, directed by Yi Hyŏngp'yo). On the nature of father images in these films and the list of films produced in the 1950s and 1960s, see Yi Kilsŏng et al., *Kim Sŭngho*. An unusual case of a presentation of an entrepreneurial working-class young female figure is also found in this period in *Ttosuni* (1963, directed by Pak Sangho), a hit box office movie that featured a strong-willed, confident, modern female subject named Ttosuni, which hints at the still fluid terrain of gender politics in the early 1960s. Film scholar Pak Yuhŭi observes that characters like Ttosuni disappeared by the late 1960s. Pak Yuhŭi, "Ttosuni."

48. The 2010 remake of the film *Housemaid* completely changed the setting, and the housemaid figure is not from a factory but from a middle-class background. Also, the family she works for is portrayed as an extremely upper-class family.

49. The rate of increase for men in manufacturing was a little slower than that for women at 202 percent between 1963 and 1970, and 221 percent between 1970 and 1979. The total number of male employees in manufacturing was 422,000 in 1963, 852,000 in 1970, and 1,879,000 in 1979. The number of people fifteen years of age or older increased from 14.6 million to 23.8 million from 1963 to 1979. National Statistical Office (T'onggyech'ŏng), *Chinan 20-yŏn'gan koyong sajŏng ŭi pyŏnhwa*, 282, 291.

50. Women made up 70 percent of the workforce in that category. Yi Okchi, *Han'guk yŏsŏng nodongja undongsa 1*, 127, table 11. By 1980 the proportion of women manufacturing workers in the combined category of "textile, garment, and shoe industries" decreased somewhat to 50.7 percent, or 451,091 of 890,007 total women manufacturing employees, as women workers in the "electronics machinery" industry jumped up to 128,673 in 1980 from a low base of 14,767 in 1970.

51. Ch'ŏn Sŏngho, *Han'guk yahak undongsa*, 248. Rural-to-urban migration began to accelerate around 1967. Compared to the period between 1966 and 1970, during the period between 1955 and 1966 the number of people who moved from rural areas to cities annually was much smaller, averaging about 180,000. Ibid., 221.

52. This information is from Kim Yŏngmi's talk at the University of Washington, October 14, 2016, titled "Han'guk Saemaŭl undong ŭi saeroun ihae" [A new perspective on the New Village Movement in South Korea]. The Park government's concern over the severe rural-urban income gap at the time was related to its political concern over the declining rate of support for the government party in rural areas. The rural revitalization campaigns of Japan and Korea in the 1930s were policy measures addressing the problem of the rural-urban gap, and Park Chung Hee, working as an elementary schoolteacher in the 1930s, witnessed the campaign.

53. O, *Korea Story*, 432.

54. Ch'ŏn Sŏngho, *Han'guk yahak undongsa*, 254. Seoul's population grew from 5.43 million (1.1 million households) in 1970 to 8.36 million (1.84 million households) in 1980.

55. *Dong-A ilbo* and *Kyŏnghyang sinmun* articles confirm that *kongsuni* and *kongdori* used to have been "nicknames for industrial workers working at factory complexes geared toward export" (*such'ul kongdan*). *Dong-A ilbo*, August 27, 1980; *Kyŏnghyang sinmun*, October 6, 1989. A search of Naver's Newslibrary with keyword *kongsuni* shows forty-three articles between 1974 and 1996. There were eight articles from *Kyŏnghyang sinmun*, twenty-five from *Dong-A ilbo*, seven from *Han'gyŏre sinmun*, and three from *Maeil kyŏngje*. The first usage appears in *Dong-A ilbo*, February 11, 1974, in an article titled "Have Kongsuni Really Fallen? Erotic Provocative Reporting Covers Up Bigger Social Issues." A JOC leader and former chair of the Korean Women Workers' Association, Yi Ch'ŏlsun, recalled an interesting story behind that article. On reading the article written by reporter Yi Puyŏng, she became so angry that she went to see him and criticized him. Two weeks later reporter Yi wrote another article for the paper, titled "Women Workers in Darkness and Agony." He later served as a night-school teacher for workers. Yi Ch'ŏlsun's testimony in Pak Sujŏng, *Sumgyŏjin Han'guk yŏsŏng ŭi yŏksa*, 205. The Media Ethics Committee in March 1977 announced that it banned a hundred vulgar terms and thirty-eight slang terms (*ŭnŏ*), including *kongsuni* and *kongdori* among the banned slang terms. *Dong-A ilbo*, March 14, 1977.

56. Similarly, bus attendants were called *ch'asuni* (bus girls), and high school graduates who, on failing college admissions in their graduation year, chose to spend a year cramming for another round of college entrance examinations were dubbed *chaesigi, chaedori*, or *chaesugi*, where *chae* means "second time" (*sigi, dori*, and *sugi* refer to common characters used in male and female names). *Dong-A ilbo*, March 14, 1977. This method of making up pejorative slang names for those regarded as "losers" continues. A new slang term, *mundori* (*Tori* of humanities) appeared in 2019, which refers to university students who allegedly out of stupidity chose to major in humanities disciplines.

57. Barraclough, *Factory Girl Literature*, 72, 73. Barraclough observes that "the ways in which women laboring in factories and women laboring in brothels were defined—sometimes in opposition to each other, sometimes equated—reveals the instability of the image of a woman worker and the threat she posed to a society that found the prospect of her economic and sexual independence disturbing." She argues that this oppressive sexual politics nudged yŏgong activist writers of the 1970s and 1980s to adopt a defensive strategy of highlighting "factory girl virtue" in their autobiographical writings and skirting the issues of "ubiquitous sexual harassment or sexual assault" at workplaces. Ibid., 88.

58. In 1963, 277,149 (54.2 percent) out of 510,918 elementary school graduates were unable to move on to middle school, and the rate decreased to 50.2 percent in 1965, and to 38.2 percent in 1969. The rates were 16 to 20 percent higher for girls than for boys in the 1960s. Ch'ŏn Sŏngho, *Han'guk yahak undongsa*, 231–32.

59. The first "labor night school" (*nodong yahak*) opened at the Cheonggye Garment Workers' Union in May 1972, and many such schools began to appear in the 1970s, although the absolute majority of night schools in the 1970s, as well as in subsequent decades, were night schools that prepared workers for high school equivalency tests and were called "equivalency test night schools" (*kŏmjŏng kosi yahak*). In the early 1980s the city of Seoul had two to three hundred night schools of various kinds, and a survey conducted in 1980 by the Ewha Womans University's student newspaper estimated that about one-third of these night schools were "labor night schools." Ibid., 292, 343, 349.

60. O Miran and An Chin, *Minju changjŏng 100-yŏn*, 74–75. Chŏng was a JOC activist and a worker at Chŏnnam Silk Reeling.

61. Control Data by then had a union, organized in December 1973, but workers clung to the idea that they were "not *kongsuni*" and demanded and obtained commuter

busing service from the company. Getting to the factory in a fancy bus, they felt superior to all those *kongsuni* and *kongdori* who did not have such a privilege. Union education in the following years eventually helped them overcome their prejudices against less fortunate workers. Yu Oksun's testimony in Yu Kyŏngsun, *Na, yŏsŏng nodongja 1*, 250–52. Some companies tried to accommodate female workers' resentment toward the term by coining a neutral alternative like "skilled employees" (*kinŭngjik sawŏn*) or "production employees" (saengsanjik sawŏn). *Kyŏnghyang sinmun*, March 22, 1978; *Dong-A ilbo*, May 10, 1980.

62. *Han'gyŏre sinmun*, December 7, 1991.

63. For representative accounts in English of the significance of Chun Tae-il's suicide, see Koo, *Korean Workers*, 69–72, and Ogle, *South Korea*, 72–75, 113. The discussion of Chun's death and its impact on the labor movement in this section is drawn from Nam, "Reading Chun Tae-il."

64. Chun and fellow activists conducted surveys of working conditions and grievances among garment workers, visited the Office of Labor Affairs with survey results, persuaded news reporters to run their story (a major daily *Kyŏnghyang sinmun* showcased their story at the top of the society section on October 7, 1970), and organized demonstrations. What became Chun's immolation was originally planned as a symbolic funeral ritual in which a copy of the *Labor Standards Act* book would be burned.

65. The book came to be regarded as the primer for activist training in the democracy movement throughout the 1980s and 1990s. Over the 1980s the biography became the "classic of the era" and sold very well, despite the government's banning of the book. Already about 100,000 copies had been sold by the early 1990s, and more than 300,000 copies had been sold by the mid-2000s. Nam, "Reading Chun Tae-il," 193.

66. The literature presenting this viewpoint is large. For representative examples, see the preface of Cho Yŏngnae's biography of Chun Tae-il (Cho Yŏngnae, *Ŏnŭ ch'ŏngnyŏn nodongja ŭi sam kwa chugŭm*); Cumings, *Korea's Place in the Sun*, 375–76; Lee, *Making of Minjung*, 218–22, in addition to Koo, *Korean Workers*, and Ogle, *South Korea*.

67. An Chaesŏng, *Ch'ŏnggye, nae ch'ŏngch'un*, 33. Tan Pyŏngho, the respected labor activist and president of the Korean Confederation of Trade Unions (KCTU), which was established in 1995 as the democratic counterpart to the FKTU, begins his foreword to KCTU's 2001 publication of documents related to the minju union movement from 1970 to 2000 as follows: "The minju union movement that was rekindled in this land by the momentum-creating event of martyr Chun Tae-il's self-immolation has ceaselessly grown and developed against numerous hardships and adversities." He then argues that the progress in democratization in South Korea was "to a great extent helped by the minju labor movement." KCTU, *1970–2000 Minju nojo t'ujaeng*, 13.

68. JOC and KDF, *Han'guk Kat'ollik Nodong Ch'ŏngnyŏnhoe 50-yŏn*, 43–44.

69. O Miran and An Chin, *Minju changjŏng 100-yŏn*, 77–80, 84. For a brief history of the involvement in the labor movement by Christian organizations and night schools, see Lee, *Making of Minjung*, 222–33. My focus on JOC history here is to trace the case of Miss Kim and does not imply that JOC's contribution to women's activism was greater than that of the UIM, nor it is an endorsement of the view that overemphasizes the role of church organizations as "the critical factor that accounts for the Korean female workers' exceptional role" in the minju labor movement. Koo, *Korean Workers*, 94.

70. The history of the JOC movement in South Korea is taken from JOC and KDF, *Han'guk Kat'ollik Nodong Ch'ŏngnyŏnhoe 50-yŏn*, 11–40, unless otherwise noted. A Korean Catholic intellectual, Yi Haenam, who had a deep interest in labor issues, attended the World Lay Apostolate Conference in Rome in 1957 and procured JOC materials in multiple languages by visiting the JOC headquarters in Belgium. Early in the next year he penned a magazine article introducing the JOC movement and Pope Pius II's vision

emphasizing the importance of the labor question and the church's mission to tackle it for humanity's survival. Using the JOC documents Yi brought, nurses at Seoul National University Hospital began to study the JOC movement and applied the JOC method in their effort to improve working conditions at the hospital.

71. At first the JOC teams focused on providing social services to the underclass population under the motto of "Bible and bread," including medical service in slum areas, free meal service through restaurants named Barley Sprout, and hygiene and literacy lessons to youth who collected rags for a living (*nŏngmajui*). Soon the scope of their operations expanded to wage workers as well as rural youth, and "workplace teams" were organized in factories. In 1964 the Rural Youth Department was created within the JOC, which separated from the JOC in 1966 and later, in 1972, established the influential Catholic Farmers' Association (Kat'ollik Nongminhoe).

72. Song Kiyŏk, "Arŭmdaun t'ujŏng."

73. Two or three teams formed a "section," which was then supervised by a JOC association each diocese set up. According to Kim Wŏn's study, in the 1970s about five thousand *t'usa* and about thirty thousand JOC members or trainees existed. Twelve out of thirteen dioceses in South Korea established diocese JOC associations and oversaw at least 150 teams and eighty sections. Kim Wŏn, "1970-yŏndae Kat'ollik Nodong Ch'ŏngnyŏnhoe," 330.

74. O Miran and An Chin, *Minju changjŏng 100-yŏn*, 77–78. Membership was kept confidential, as in an underground organization.

75. JOC and KDF, *Han'guk Kat'ollik Nodong Ch'ŏngnyŏnhoe 50-yŏn*, 52.

76. Kim Wŏn, "1970-yŏndae Kat'ollik Nodong Ch'ŏngnyŏnhoe," 334.

77. For example, the Wŏnp'ung Wool union, one of the representative minju unions of the 1970s, had at least seventy small groups in operation, into which five hundred or more workers were organized. Hong Hyŏnyŏng, "Tosi Sanŏp Sŏn'gyohoe," 421.

78. Yi Okchi, *Han'guk yŏsŏng nodongja undongsa 1*, 320; An Chaesŏng, *Ch'ŏnggye, nae ch'ŏngch'un*, 129–30, 133. According to a Bureau of Labor Affairs survey in 1970, there were 570 workplaces in five markets in the Peace Market district. Together, they supplied 70 percent of domestic garment demand. The Cheonggye Union's 1975 survey found that about 80 percent of a total of 25,000 workers working in the market were women. Yu Kyŏngsun, "Ch'ŏnggye P'ibok Nodong Chohap," 104–5.

79. Yi Okchi, *Han'guk yŏsŏng nodongja undongsa 1*, 319.

80. JOC and KDF, *Han'guk Kat'ollik Nodong Ch'ŏngnyŏnhoe 50-yŏn*, 103–8; An Chaesŏng, *Ch'ŏnggye, nae ch'ŏngch'un*, 129. Chŏng later served as the "female president" of the JOC Korea.

81. Yu Kyŏngsun, "Ch'ŏnggye P'ibok Nodong Chohap," 128–33. These small-group teams or clubs created the Acacia Association, and many Acacia members served as union officials. Another club association, called the Tonghwa group, was created in 1977 and organized male worker teams, including the Tolmengi ("pebble") team. Tolmengi members played a key role until the forceful disbandment of the union in 1981. Ibid., 172. Sin Sunae, who supervised the Tonghwa group, testified that "male teams didn't work very well" as they tended to have infighting and some men were "not sincere" (*sŏngsil*). Yu Kyŏngsun, *Na, yŏsŏng nodongja 1*, 102–3.

82. For examples, see worker testimonies contained in Yu Kyŏngsun, *Na, yŏsŏng nodongja 1*, and in Sŏnggonghoe Taehakkyo Nodongsa Yŏn'guso, *Han'guk sanŏp nodongja*.

83. JOC and KDF, *Han'guk Kat'ollik Nodong Ch'ŏngnyŏnhoe 50-yŏn*, 106.

84. Song Kiyŏk, "Arŭmdaun t'ujŏng."

85. JOC and KDF, *Han'guk Kat'ollik Nodong Ch'ŏngnyŏnhoe 50-yŏn*, 37–52.

86. The first men's team was formed in January of the following year. Ibid., 123. Chŏnnam Pangjik began as Kanegafuchi Spinning (Chongyŏn Pangjŏk; Kanebō) in the

colonial period. Kanebō established one silk-reeling factory in Seoul in 1925 and another in Kwangju in 1930 before expanding into multiple industries establishing mining, metal, and trading firms in addition to various textile mills. Chŏnnam Spinning and Weaving in Kwangju was sold as a vested property in 1953 to Kim Yongju, who became the first chair of the powerful Spinning and Weaving Manufacturers' Association. The company was separated into two entities (Chŏnnam Pangjik and Ilsin Pangjik) in 1961. Yi Suae et al., *Chŏnnam yŏsŏng 100-yŏn*, 89.

87. The information on the case of "Miss Kim" and related events is from JOC and KDF, *Han'guk Kat'ollik Nodong Ch'ŏngnyŏnhoe 50-yŏn*, 43–45, and Kim Sŏksun, "Kat'ollik Nodong Ch'ŏngnyŏnhoe."

88. Kim, "Kat'ollik Nodong Ch'ŏngnyŏnhoe," 117–20, cited in Chŏng Hogi, *Minju changjŏng 100-yŏn*.

89. JOC and KDF, *Han'guk Kat'ollik Nodong Ch'ŏngnyŏnhoe 50-yŏn*, 44–45.

90. Chŏng Hogi, *Minju changjŏng 100-yŏn*, 61. In the following months several hundred workers were fired by the two companies.

91. Because Simdo Textile stood at the center of the conflict, this dispute is often called the Simdo Textile dispute in labor studies and Catholic accounts. Han Sanguk suggests "Kanghwa textile union incident" as a more appropriate term. Han Sanguk, "60-yŏndae Kanghwa chingmul nojo sakŏn," 129.

92. On the Kanghwa textile disputes of 1967–68, see ibid.; JOC and KDF, *Han'guk Kat'ollik Nodong Ch'ŏngnyŏnhoe 50-yŏn*, 61–69; Yi Okchi, *Han'guk yŏsŏng nodongja undongsa 1*, 116–19.

93. It was followed by the Methodist and the Anglican orders in 1961, the Presbyterian (Christ) Church of the Republic of Korea (Kidokkyo Changnohoe, or Kijang) in 1963, and the Salvation Army in 1965. Yi Okchi, *Han'guk yŏsŏng nodongja undongsa 1*, 111–16.

94. Hong Hyŏnyŏng, "Tosi Sanŏp Sŏn'gyohoe," 386–91.

95. On the history of South Korean UIMs and debates on their contributions to the labor movement, see Kim Chun, "Minju nojo undong kwa kyohoe"; Kwŏn Chin'gwan, "1970-yŏndae sanŏp sŏn'gyo hwaltong"; Hong Hyŏnyŏng, "Tosi Sanŏp Sŏn'gyohoe"; Kim Wŏn, "1970-yŏndae minju nojo wa kyohoe tanch'e." Kim Chun divides the history of the UIM movement in South Korea into three periods: (1) 1957 to 1963 (a period of industrial evangelism), (2) 1964 to 1970 or 1971 (a period of enlightenment-focused movement centered on educating laypeople and working through existing unions), and (3) 1971 or 1972 to 1979 (a period of consciousness-raising and organizing through small-group activities). Kim Chun, "Minju nojo undong kwa kyohoe," 128.

96. Hong Hyŏnyŏng, "Tosi Sanŏp Sŏn'gyohoe," 394–402. Christian institutions interested in spreading the Gospel to industrial workers, including the Christian UIM, the JOC, the Korea Student Christian Federation (KSCF), the Catholic Student Assembly, and the Christian Academy, in 1971 jointly established a coordinating body, the Christian Social Action Council (Christian Sahoe Haengdong Hyŏbuihoe), which provided training for labor organizers based on Freire's and Alinsky's methods. Ch'ŏn Sŏngho, *Han'guk yahak undongsa*, 305–6. The number of personnel involved in labor ministries was not very high, however. As of March 1978, Protestant "industrial mission" institutions had a total of forty-four full-time staff members, of which thirty-six worked in the capital area, and Protestant "urban mission" institutions employed fifteen staff members. Kim Chun, "Minju nojo undong kwa kyohoe," 127. Some key staffers, especially in the late 1970s, were non-Christian activists, and some, including Hwang Yŏnghwan, were of worker backgrounds. Kwŏn Chin'gwan's article "1970-yŏndae sanŏp sŏn'gyo hwaltong" discusses the backgrounds and activities of key staffers at the Yŏngdŭngp'o and Incheon UIMs.

97. Kim Chun, "Minju nojo undong kwa kyohoe"; Kim Wŏn, "1970-yŏndae minju nojo wa kyohoe tanch'e"; Kwŏn Chin'gwan, "1970-yŏndae sanŏp sŏn'gyo hwaltong."
98. Alinsky's books that circulated in South Korea included *From Citizen Apathy to Participation* (1957), *Citizen Participation and Community Organization in Planning and Urban Renewal* (1962), *Reveille for Radicals* (1969), and *Rules for Radicals* (1971). Kim Chun, "Minju nojo undong kwa kyohoe," 115–16, 118. Sin Illyŏng, who led labor education at the Christian Academy in the 1970s, recalled that Christian urban and rural mission work in the 1970s was heavily influenced by Alinsky's methods. Sin Illyŏng, *Na ŭi inyŏn iyagi*, 291. On Sin Illyŏng's life and activism, see Nam, "Shin In-ryung." Cho Wha Soon testified that at the Incheon UIM, Rev. Cho Sŭnghyŏk had talked about Alinsky "until she was sick of it" (*chillidorok*), while Rev. George Ogle was instead into the theology of Dietrich Bonhoeffer. Cho Wha Soon's testimony (CD no. 356) in Sŏnggonghoe Taehakkyo Nodongsa Yŏn'guso, *Han'guk sanŏp nodongja*. Freire was first introduced to a South Korean audience in the December 1971 issue of the magazine *Segye wa sŏn'gyo* (World and Mission) by Mun Tonghwan, who encountered Freire's work during his study at the Union Theological Seminary. The 1979 Korean translation of Freire's *Pedagogy of the Oppressed* made his philosophy popular and highly influential in the student and social movements and at alternative night schools. Hong Ŭnnang, "P'aullo P'ŭreiri kyoyuk sasang," 350–57.
99. Hong Ŭnnang, "P'aullo P'ŭreiri kyoyuk sasang," 370. After the mid-1980s, with the rise of interest in Marxist-Leninist literature, Freire's influence in consciousness-raising programs declined.
100. Tongil Pangjik began as Tongyang Pangjŏk (Tōyōbō) in the colonial period.
101. Minister Cho Chisong of the Incheon UIM stated that UIM leaders initially did not see women workers as prime targets of their organizing effort. According to him, it was only after the initial plan of forging cooperative relationships with management failed in the early 1960s and the effort to organize workers by educating male union officials also failed that they eventually turned their attention to women. Chŏng Misuk, "70-yŏndae yŏsŏng nodong undong," 127.
102. On Chŏng Hyangja's activism, see O Miran and An Chin, *Minju changjŏng 100-yŏn*, 75–78.
103. Yi Yunjŏng, "O-wŏl Kwangju hangjaeng ŭi Songbaekhoe undong," 86.
104. In Miss Kim's case, a union was already in existence, and she tried to work through the dysfunctional union system, while Chun Tae-il based his labor actions on unofficial organizations he and his male colleagues in the market had created in the absence of a union. How the existence/absence of a union affected the outcome of their deaths needs further study.
105. Sin Illyŏng, *Na ŭi inyŏn iyagi*, 126.
106. Chŏng Yŏnsun, "1970-yŏndae nodong kyoyuk," 44, 66–67, 87.
107. There were two other members, Kwŏn Sun'gap and Im Kŭmja, in Kisuhoe, whose identity needs more exploration. The list is from Sin Illyŏng, *Na ŭi inyŏn iyagi*, 126. Ch'oe Sunyŏng testifies that six women workers—herself, Pak Sunhŭi, Yi Yŏngsun, Chang Hyŏnja, Yi Ch'onggak, and Yi Kyŏngsim—held private seminar sessions with Sin Illyŏng, whose study topics included "capitalist economic history." Ch'oe Sunyŏng's testimony in Pak Sujŏng, *Sumgyŏjin Han'guk yŏsŏng ŭi yŏksa*, 99, 104. They were interrogated harshly when Sin was arrested in the Christian Academy incident. Five of these women unionists, except for Catholic labor organizer Yi Kyŏngsim, who was in charge of Incheon JOC, were Kisuhoe members, and from their relationship we can see that the nation's top women unionists across industries and firms were developing a strong bonding, facilitated by intellectual Sin's labor education. Kisuhoe did not develop its own action programs, and mostly functioned as a site of communication and solidarity among women

unionists through monthly meetings. The Christian Academy had a plan to develop Kisuhoe into a larger organization of women workers, which did not materialize because of the Christian Academy incident of March 1979. Yi Imha, "1970-yŏndae K'ŭrisŭch'yan Ak'ademi," 570.

108. Koo, *Korean Workers*, 96.

109. Yu Kyŏngsun, "Nodong chohap ŭi chidoryŏk kwa chendŏ chŏngch'i," 97. Yu asks why some minju unions actively worked to challenge and reverse gender discrimination at work sites while others did not, and she concludes that the degree to which minju unions pursued a women-specific agenda and challenged the discriminatory gender hierarchy at work and in the union movement depends on several factors, including the gender characteristics of a particular industry and workplace, whether the union was led by men, women, or jointly by men and women, and the longevity and stability of the union.

110. Koo, *Korean Workers*, 96, italics added.

111. The Christian Academy labor education program was respected as the best union activist education program at the time and a sought-after opportunity among union activists. Kwŏn Chin'gwan, "1970-yŏndae sanŏp sŏn'gyo hwaltong," 211; Chŏng Yŏnsun, "1970-yŏndae nodong kyoyuk," 81. Chŏng Yŏnsun provides some worker testimonies on the ways Academy education changed their lives (81–91).

112. On the history of the Christian Academy movement, see Chŏng Yŏnsun, "1970-yŏndae nodong kyoyuk"; Yi Imha, "1970-yŏndae K'ŭrisŭch'yan Ak'ademi."

113. "Intermediary groups" were defined as "voluntarily organized social pressure groups," which would perform "the function of reconciliation and integration." Chŏng Yŏnsun, "1970-yŏndae nodong kyoyuk," 22.

114. The five sectors were the Student Society, the Industrial Society, the Rural Society, the Women's Society, and the Religious Society. Christian Academy programs were regarded by contemporaries as the most advanced form of social education practiced by progressive Christians. In the planning stage many specialists from relevant disciplines including education, sociology, political science, and psychology were brought in, and, together with staff people, they worked on developing effective education methods. Practices they witnessed in the West, including the workshop method they learned from the Chicago Ecumenical Institute, were selectively adopted and mixed with indigenous culture forms and rituals such as meditation and the mask dance. The "intermediary group" education program at the Academy, which lasted five years from 1974 to 1979, provided opportunities to fine-tune the method, and the "Academy education method" spread over the 1970s and 1980s to influence the practices of the student, labor, and farmers' movements. Chŏng Yŏnsun, "1970-yŏndae nodong kyoyuk," 18, 49, 77.

115. O Miran and An Chin, *Minju changjŏng 100-yŏn*, 78, 80–81. For example, Pak T'aeyŏn of YH Trading transformed her factory dormitory into an Academy-like education scene, and the company countered by ramming through a dormitory reassignment plan, which then led to a heated confrontation and further solidified worker solidarity. Pak T'aeyŏn states that the Academy education and staffer Sin Illyŏng had "the biggest influence on her life as a labor activist." Pak Minna, *Kasi ch'ŏlmang*, 137.

116. O Miran and An Chin, *Minju changjŏng 100-yŏn*, 79. A total of 602 people in nineteen separate sessions went through the first-round program under Sin Illyŏng's watch between June 1974 and February 1979. Among them 103 activists joined the second-round program offered on five occasions. Two or three intellectuals were allowed to join in during each session, and, according to Sin, there was a long waiting list for the opportunity. In addition to regular labor education sessions, the "Women's Society" and the "Industrial Society" education staffers Han Myŏngsuk and Sin Illyŏng jointly conducted separate "women worker education" sessions from April 1977 to April 1978

on five occasions, in which key leaders from minju unions gathered to discuss labor and women's issues. Fifty or so graduates of the Industrial Society education program formed the Labor Case Study Research Group (Nodong Sarye Yŏn'guhoe) in May 1975 and continued a monthly forum in which several female labor activists, including Yu Chŏngsuk of the Cheonggye Garment Workers' Union, Han Sunim of the Pando Trading union, Pak Sunhŭi of the Wŏnp'ung Wool union, and Ch'oe Sunyŏng of the YH Trading union, had a chance to present their cases to the audience of intellectuals and male and female unionists. Yi Imha, "1970-yŏndae K'ŭrisŭch'yan Ak'ademi," 559, 565–68.

117. Between 1973 and 1979, the Park government arrested 1,931 activists using the anticommunist law, which accounted for 62.1 percent of the total number (3,108) of political arrestees in the period. Yi Imha, "1970-yŏndae K'ŭrisŭch'yan Ak'ademi," 586–607.

118. The literature on the minju union movement is fairly large; this book only features a small slice of its complex history. Interested readers can get a good overview of the history of the movement in English from sociologist Hagen Koo's *Korean Workers* and learn about the dynamics and representational politics of the worker-student alliance from historian Namhee Lee's *Making of Minjung*. In Korean, Yi Okchi's *Han'guk yŏsŏng nodongja undongsa* (The History of the Korean Women Workers' Movement) *1*, along with collections of oral history testimonies, offer detailed histories of representative minju union struggles of the 1970s and 1980s. Yi Okchi (143–311) details labor dispute cases, which were led by women or in which women participated, at more than seventy small and large companies, and she showcases seven representative minju unions at female-dominated garment, textile, wig, electronics, and pharmaceutical companies (317–424). Oral testimony collections include Pak Minna, *Kasi ch'ŏlmang*; Pak Sujŏng, *Sumgyŏjin Han'guk yŏsŏng ŭi yŏksa*; Yu Kyŏngsun, *Na, yŏsŏng nodongja 1*; Sŏ Chunsŏk, *Mising ŭn tolgo toragane*. Also helpful are Ogle, *South Korea*; Kim, *Class Struggle*; Soonok Chun, *They Are Not Machines*.

119. At Oak Electronics Corporation, a US-owned TV assembly company in Puch'ŏn, Kyŏnggi Province, unionization in July 1968 led to a dispute and a sudden factory closure in October. Although union militancy was not the main reason for the company's decision to close up shop, the Korean media criticized the union for the decision, and this incident alarmed the Park government greatly. Signetics Korea, located in Seoul, was also a US subsidiary company and produced transistors for export. The Signetics Korea union, established in 1966, continued to struggle against union-busting efforts by the company, and its disputes in 1968 and 1969, together with the Oak Electronics case, led to legislation banning union activities at foreign-owned firms. Yi Okchi, *Han'guk yŏsŏng nodongja undongsa 1*, 102–6.

120. Nam, *Building Ships*, 184–89.

121. Ibid., 190–92. To ensure worker loyalty to the company, companies and the Park government promoted the "company-as-family" ideology, which, unsupported by evidence of fatherly commitment to worker well-being in return for loyalty, did not seem to have much effect in generating the desired submissive attitudes among workers.

122. Yi Okchi, *Han'guk yŏsŏng nodongja undongsa 1*, 315. Sin Illyŏng claims that the term was first used in Christian Academy's labor education. Sin Illyŏng, *Na ŭi inyŏn iyagi*, 278.

123. Yi Okchi, *Han'guk yŏsŏng nodongja undongsa 1*, 316–17.

124. Ogle, *South Korea*; Yi Wŏnbo, *Han'guk nodong undongsa 5*; Yi Okchi, *Han'guk yŏsŏng nodongja undongsa 1*; Koo, *Korean Workers*.

125. Kwŏn Chin'gwan, "1970-yŏndae sanŏp sŏn'gyo hwaltong," 227–29. For example, the Tongil Pangjik union conducted forty-three instances of rank-and-file education per year. Yi Okchi, *Han'guk yŏsŏng nodongja undongsa 1*, 339. The Wŏnp'ung Wool union

aimed at training all 2,500 members to attain competency at the same level as union officials and required all union representatives and officials to conduct small-group activities. Testimony of Chŏng Sŏnsun, the last president of the Wŏnp'ung union, cited in Pak Minna, *Kasi ch'ŏlmang*, 206.

126. Kwŏn Chin'gwan, "1970-yŏndae sanŏp sŏn'gyo hwaltong," 228–29.

127. Yi Okchi, *Han'guk yŏsŏng nodongja undongsa 1*, 384.

128. The case of Pando Trading provides a good example. After unionization in 1974, the company shrank the size of the main factory, which decreased from about twelve hundred female production workers at the time of unionization to about seven hundred by the end of the decade, while the bulk of production work was siphoned off to subcontracting firms. Ibid., 349.

129. Wŏnp'ung Wool stopped hiring new workers after June 1980, diverted work orders to subcontracting firms, and threatened factory closure, which caused a serious internal division in the union by 1982. Ibid., 402–3. YH Trading shut down in August 1979, Pando Trading closed its unionized Pup'yŏng factory in March 1981, and Control Data pulled out of Korea in July 1982.

130. In a major clash between the union and the company in the fall of 1982, prompted by an all-out union-busting effort coordinated between government authorities and the company, the Department of Labor conducted a survey of Wŏnp'ung workers' political nature and categorized workers into four groups. Recommendations for the top two groups were arrest and immediate dismissal, and the third, "sympathetic," group was required to produce a letter pledging loyalty or voluntarily resign. The fourth, "bystander," group was allowed to get back to work. Among 636 female workers, 289 belonged to the top two groups, to which only 30 of 233 male workers belonged. The "bystander" group had 30 women and 203 men. The union, led by a male president, Pang Yongsŏk, a respected leader who later, in 2002, became the minister of labor, tried to increase women's presence in the leadership group in the 1970s, and in time the sex ratio in the steering committee came to correspond to that of the workforce at eight women to two men. Men's attitude in general in those days, women activists recall, was that women who could get married and leave the factory work should fight on the front lines while men, to whom the job was as important as life itself, would "help from behind." Yi Okchi, *Han'guk yŏsŏng nodongja undongsa 1*, 397, 411.

131. The quote is a description of male production worker attitudes at Samsung Pharmaceutical. At the time men composed about 10 percent of the production workforce as technicians or transport workers. Most of these men refused to join the union and sometimes opted to disrupt union struggle by serving as replacement workers. Ibid., 420.

132. The highest position allowed women at the Cheonggye Garment Workers' Union was that of vice president, which was essentially a ceremonial position, and women officials were usually assigned to the women's department or the welfare department. Women members tried to elect a female president in 1976 and again in 1978, motivated by a growing awareness among women that it was not natural that men, who were not well connected to the majority of largely female rank-and-file members on the shop floor, should always represent the union. Their efforts failed both times under the weight of the hegemonic gender discourse that naturalized male leadership, which was propagated by male intellectual influencers around the union and largely accepted by workers themselves. In two periods in the union's history, between 1981 and 1982 and between 1986 and 1987, women occupied the entire leadership in the absence of male leaders who were kept behind bars, but when men came back from their exile, women unionists were severely and unjustly criticized by them and had to turn over the leadership positions to men. Yu Kyŏngsun, "Nodong chohap ŭi chidoryŏk kwa chendŏ chŏngch'i," 424, 430–36, 440.

133. Kim Muyong, "1970-yŏndae Tongil Pangjik nodong undong," 211, 214. Kim argues that the minju union was thus a place in which women workers, as a marginalized group, expressed their consciousness, cultures, values, and utopian desires to leave work entirely as well as their class consciousness against capitalist labor relations (215).

134. On the gendered mobilization scheme of the Park government, see Moon, *Militarized Modernity and Gendered Citizenship*. On the economic conditions that ensured quiescence of male heavy-industry workers in the 1970s, see Nam, *Building Ships*, chap. 9.

135. An Chŏngnam, "Pusan chiyŏk yŏsŏng nodong undong," 31–38, esp. 34–36.

136. Koo, *Korean* Workers, 80–81; Ch'u Songnye testimony (CD no. 391), Tongil Pangjik group testimony (CD no. 420), and An Sunae testimony (CD no. 195) in Sŏnggonghoe Taehakkyo Nodongsa Yŏn'guso, *Han'guk sanŏp nodongja*.

137. Yu Oksun's testimony in Yu Kyŏngsun, *Na, yŏsŏng nodongja 1*, 268.

138. Information on Control Data and its union is based on Yi Okchi, *Han'guk yŏsŏng nodongja undongsa 1*, 373–89, and Han Myŏnghŭi's testimony (CD no. 382) in Sŏnggonghoe Taehakkyo Nodongsa Yŏn'guso, *Han'guk sanŏp nodongja*.

139. To make the privilege stick, according to Yu Oksun's testimony, the union combed through attendance records to locate members not using the leave privilege and persuaded them to use it. Yu Kyŏngsun, "Chendŏ kwan'gye esŏ pon 1970-yŏndae minju nojo," 138.

140. A particularly offensive wording for Kim was "how dare women [not toeing the line] act rudely like good-for-nothings" ("yŏjadŭl i ssagaji ŏpke"). Han Myŏnghŭi's testimony (CD no. 382) in Sŏnggonghoe Taehakkyo Nodongsa Yŏn'guso, *Han'guk sanŏp nodongja*.

141. When the company closed in 1982, the average age of women workers was 28.5 years, which was very high for female manufacturing workers, and their average length of service was also longer than usual at 7.5 years. Han Myŏnghŭi's testimony (CD no. 382) in Sŏnggonghoe Taehakkyo Nodongsa Yŏn'guso, *Han'guk sanŏp nodongja*.

142. Yu Kyŏngsun, "Chendŏ kwan'gye esŏ pon 1970-yŏndae minju nojo," 143.

143. Yu Oksun's testimony in Yu Kyŏngsun, *Na, yŏsŏng nodongja 1*, 259–60, 262–63.

144. Ibid., 269. In Han Myŏnghŭi's understanding, the government was eager to use the Control Data incident as an exemplary case to prove that UIM's agitation of workers would lead to the flight of multinational corporations from Korea. At the government's urging, KBS and MBC broadcasting stations produced three special programs against the Control Data union and the UIM. The company, on the other hand, wanted to negotiate with the union, according to Yu, so as not to harm its global corporate image by news of fierce labor disputes and also because the productivity of women workers at Control Data Korea was very high thanks to longer than usual levels of seniority and a shorter than usual work week of forty-two hours. In the end, in Yu's understanding, the South Korean government refused to allow reinstatement of dismissed activists and thereby set a precedent. Frustrated by the impasse, the company made the final decision to close the South Korean factory. Han Myŏnghŭi's testimony (CD no. 382) in Sŏnggonghoe Taehakkyo Nodongsa Yŏn'guso, *Han'guk sanŏp nodongja*.

145. Yi Okchi, *Han'guk yŏsŏng nodongja undongsa 1*, 420. Yu Kyŏngsun uses the Samsung Pharmaceutical union case to demolish women's studies scholar Yi Sukchin's argument that outside influence coming from the women's movement played an important role in raising women workers' gender consciousness in the minju union movement. Yu points out that the Samsung Pharmaceutical union was not connected to church or intellectual activists. Yu Kyŏngsun, "Chendŏ kwan'gye esŏ pon 1970-yŏndae minju nojo," 102–14.

146. Yi Okchi, *Han'guk yŏsŏng nodongja undongsa 1*, 395–97, 420–22.

147. Chŏng Yŏnsun, "1970-yŏndae nodong kyoyuk," 86–87.
148. Yi Okchi, Han'guk yŏsŏng nodongja undongsa 1, 348, 377, 396, 421.
149. Han Myŏnghŭi's testimony (CD no. 382) in Sŏnggonghoe Taehakkyo Nodongsa Yŏn'guso, Han'guk sanŏp nodongja.
150. Ibid. Cho Wha Soon of Incheon UIM recalled that she tried to "be humble and look shabby, wearing blue jeans and a T-shirt, but it was strange to the laborer's eye," and despite her good intentions to "appeal to them," they thought she "looked shabby and different." Cho, Let the Weak Be Strong, 125. In a more recent interview in 2003, Cho described another revealing episode on sartorial class culture. When a meeting with Ewha Womans University students was arranged, women workers of Incheon showed up wearing what they thought were respectable clothes, while students came wearing what they thought of as a properly working-class outfit. Cho resented the fact that university women looked so sophisticated and stylish in their simple clothing while workers in their clumsy effort to look nice ended up looking like country bumpkins. After a while, she happily reported, workers began to change their sartorial habits and it became hard to tell apart students and workers. Cho Wha Soon's testimony (CD no. 356) in Sŏnggonghoe Taehakkyo Nodongsa Yŏn'guso, Han'guk sanŏp nodongja.
151. Yu Kyŏngsun argues that among many recipients of Christian Academy education, only Wŏnp'ung and Control Data unions pursued a women-specific agenda, and thus the Academy education also cannot be said to have meaningful impact on the gender-conscious practices at Wŏnp'ung and Control Data. Yu Kyŏngsun, "Chendŏ kwan'gye esŏ pon 1970-yŏndae minju nojo," 102–14. But our discussion shows a far more expansive reach of the radical effect of Academy education beyond the two unions.
152. Chŏng Hyangja's testimony in Pak Sujŏng, Sumgyŏjin Han'guk yŏsŏng ŭi yŏksa, 253, 259, 261.

6. FEMALE STRIKERS IN RECENT DECADES AND THE POLITICS OF MEMORY

1. The quotation is from novelist Cho Chŏngnae's statement of recommendation (ch'uch'ŏnsa) featured in Pak Minna, Kasi ch'ŏlmang.
2. Yi Ch'ŏlsun, foreword to Pak Minna, Kasi ch'ŏlmang.
3. The phrase "sword of denouncement, not of critique" was used by author Pak Sujŏng to capture the indignation expressed by Pak Sunhŭi, a veteran female unionist and one of the key protagonists in this chapter. When released from prison in 1983 after a year of incarceration, Pak Sunhŭi found that her fellow workers had been "doubly trampled upon." They were being victimized by employers at work and at the same time mauled by students turned labor activists. She told the interviewer that even at the time of the interview in the early 2000s she was unable to "forgive the fact that those students turned activists made a habit of bombarding workers with denunciation" without taking into account the structural and social contexts of the time. Pak Sujŏng, Sumgyŏjin Han'guk yŏsŏng ŭi yŏksa, 170–71.
4. Lee, Making of Minjung, 218.
5. A conservative magazine, Sindonga (New East Asia), speculated in its June 1989 issue that many of the 1,363 college students who had been expelled from school between May 1980 and December 1983 because of their student activism joined the ranks of the hakch'ul. Cited in Yu Kyŏngsun, Arŭmdaun yŏndae, 41. Around 1985, media reports and statistical data produced by the Ministry of Labor and by a business association in Puch'ŏn, an industrial town near Seoul, suggested numbers ranging from 160 to 699. But Yu Kyŏngsun concludes that there probably existed many more hakch'ul organizers than what these numbers revealed. Ibid., 41–42. Ch'ŏn Sŏngho, who studied the night-school

movement, estimates that "several thousand" students entered factories in the capital region in the early 1980s. Ch'ŏn Sŏngho, *Han'guk yahak undongsa*, 447.

6. Yu Kyŏngsun provides a detailed account of the Kuro solidarity strike, including the list of *hakch'ul* activists involved in the strike and their organizational affiliations. Yu Kyŏngsun, *Arŭmdaun yŏndae*, 258.

7. Kim Wŏn et al., *Minju nojo, nohak yŏndae*, 11. This book summarizes and assesses major incidents and developments in the South Korean labor movement in the 1980s in an encyclopedia-like format. A total of 265 labor disputes occurred in 1985 and 276 in the following year, which represented a significant jump from an average annual occurrence of around a hundred labor disputes during the early 1980s. Yokota, *Kankoku no toshi kasō to rōdōsha*, 43.

8. Kim Wŏn et al., *Minju nojo, nohak yŏndae*, 11; Kang Insun, *Han'guk yŏsŏng nodongja undongsa 2*, 22.

9. Kang Insun, *Han'guk yŏsŏng nodongja undongsa 2*, 22. By 1989, 1.93 million workers were represented by 7,883 unions, a remarkable increase compared to the June 1987 statistics of 1.05 million members and 725 unions. Ibid., 360.

10. The process through which various democratic union associations, including the Chŏn'guk Nodong Chohap Hyŏbŭihoe (Chŏnnohyŏp or the National Congress of Trade Unions, formed in January 1990), merged into a new national center of democratic unions, the KCTU, in November 1995 is discussed in Koo, *Korean Workers*, 188–98.

11. Kang Insun, *Han'guk yŏsŏng nodongja undongsa 2*, 108–9. The Kukche shoe workers' struggle spread to many rubber shoe factories in Pusan, and in September women workers from six shoe factories, driven out of their shops by "save-the-company corps" violence, gathered at the Catholic Center in Pusan and began a solidarity sit-in struggle. Examples of acts of violence at these six companies—Hwasŏng, P'ungyŏng, Kukche Trading, Samhwa Rubber, Taeyang Rubber, and Puyŏng Chemical—are described in ibid., 125–30.

12. Information on Kwŏn Migyŏng's death is from ibid., 439–41, and Komu Nodongja Hyŏbŭihoe, *Komu nodongja t'ujaeng charyojip*, 466–79.

13. Taebong belonged to the Taeyang Rubber group, which had several branch factories in Pusan. Taeyang Rubber had about four thousand employees until 1990, and in 1993 Taebong was merged into Taeyang Rubber following Taeyang group's downsizing strategy, and by 1994 only thirteen hundred employees remained. Meanwhile, the company was expanding its operation in China. Komu Nodongja Hyŏbŭihoe, *Komu nodongja t'ujaeng charyojip*, 226. The "Enterprise-Ten-Percent-More Campaign," also known as the "Five-More Campaign," was presented as a way to overcome economic crisis, and as targets of the campaign, a 10 percent increase in resource savings, bank deposits, productivity, actual exports, and voluntary extra work was suggested. Kang Insun, *Han'guk yŏsŏng nodongja undongsa 2*, 440.

14. Komu Nodongja Hyŏbŭihoe, *Komu nodongja t'ujaeng charyojip*, 476–77. Kwŏn's suicide note and excerpts from her diary entries are on 476–79.

15. For an excellent analysis of the process of South Korean neoliberal transformation in the context of worldwide developments, see Chi Chuhyŏng, *Han'guk sinjayujuŭi ŭi kiwŏn*.

16. Industry data here and below are from Komu Nodongja Hyŏbŭihoe, *Komu nodongja t'ujaeng charyojip*, 11–16; Kang Insun, *Han'guk yŏsŏng nodongja undongsa 2*, 422–25.

17. The total export income in dollars hit a peak of $4.3 billion in 1990 and declined to $2.8 billion by 1993.

18. Komu Nodongja Hyŏbŭihoe, *Komu nodongja t'ujaeng charyojip*, 76.

19. Ibid., 57.

20. Ibid., 52.
21. Ibid., 471.
22. Various methods of speedup are documented in ibid., 71, 469–71. The most notorious method was PQM (product quality management), which Samhwa Rubber successfully deployed to obtain large productivity gains. It was soon copied by other shoe companies. Samhwa Rubber set up a test line, and thirty to forty managers and company officials surrounded workers on the line all day long measuring each move of the workers, including the time they consumed to go to the bathroom. The highest record of production thus achieved under enormous pressure was then applied to other lines. Workers had to refrain from bathroom visits, forgo lunch, and volunteer to work after hours to meet production goals. Two older women workers collapsed and died at Samhwa not long after the project began there in 1989. At Hwasŭng a seventeen-year-old male worker died while sleeping in the locker room after extended hours of work when a fire broke out. Workers called the program the "PQM that kills people" ("Saram chamnŭn PQM"). Ibid., 472.
23. Ibid., 71–72. Eleven companies in 1988 and nine companies in 1989 opened branches abroad, and as of October 1991, fourteen out of a total of twenty-five companies that expanded abroad chose Indonesia as their new production sites.
24. Ibid., 59, 443–44. According to Chu Kyŏngmi's study, about twenty to thirty *hakch'ul* female activists entered rubber shoe factories in Pusan before 1987. Chu Kyŏngmi, "80-yŏndae Pusan chiyŏk yŏsŏng undong," 162. Pak Sinmi, a *hakch'ul* activist who worked at Taeyang Rubber, recalled that from her alma mater, the University of Pusan, some two hundred students entered factories each year, but most of them dropped out within a year. Pak Sinmi's testimony in Pak Minna, *Kasi ch'ŏlmang*, 103.
25. Komu Nodongja Hyŏbŭihoe, *Komu nodongja t'ujaeng charyojip*, 90. Particularly heinous cases are documented on 128–29, 139–41, 374–76, 443, and 460–65. In an exceptionally vicious case of violence at Wŏnch'ang, a company of about eight hundred workers producing high-end shoes for Fila, a woman worker, Yang T'aeim, was held against her will by company men for more than twenty days and suffered a nightmarish ordeal in a makeshift torture chamber set up in a company elevator, in which management personnel allegedly beat her up, removed her clothes, caressed her breasts, threatened rape, applied iron pipes between her legs and pressed them against her bones mimicking a notorious premodern torture method, and tried to force unknown liquids down her throat. She finally gave in and signed the letter of resignation they produced. Ibid., 374–76. What was especially striking is the fact that Yang became a target of such an extreme degree of physical and sexual violence simply because the company had discovered that she had been involved in a sit-in struggle at Pusan's P'ungyŏng Rubber, which was one of the earliest strikes in the summer of 1987. The episode shows how fearful rubber companies became toward the possibility of labor activism in their factories under the post-1987 conditions of industrial relations.
26. Ibid., 74, 471.
27. Ibid., 471.
28. The size of the female manufacturing workforce in South Korea grew rapidly from 416,000 in 1970 to 1,155,000 in 1980, which represented 39.1 percent of all manufacturing workers, and continued to increase to 2,073,000 by 1990, constituting 42.2 percent of the total manufacturing workforce. As industrial restructuring proceeded, however, a precipitous drop in the number of female factory workers followed, shrinking from the peak of more than two million to 1,345,000 by 1998 (the number increased somewhat to 1,443,000 the following year), and the proportion of women in the total number of manufacturing employees also declined to 34.5 percent. Meanwhile, women workers in the service sector increased from 3,800,000 in 1990 to 5,758,000 in 1999, showing that

this was the sector that absorbed women workers discarded by manufacturing industries. Kang Insun, *Han'guk yŏsŏng nodongja undongsa 2*, 349.

29. Ibid., 348.

30. The Council of Korean Women Workers' Associations was established in 1992 as the coordinating body of women workers' associations that appeared in key industrial cities, including Seoul (1987), Incheon (1988), Puch'ŏn (1989), Kwangju (1990), and Pusan (1990). These associations were organized jointly by dismissed women workers and feminist activists. By 2004 the council grew to have thirteen chapters and five thousand members. Kang Insun, *Han'guk yŏsŏng nodongja undongsa 2*, 323–26, 476–77; Pak Minna, *Kasi ch'ŏlmang*, 301.

31. Yi Ch'ŏlsun's foreword to Pak Minna, *Kasi ch'ŏlmang*.

32. Yi Okchi, *Han'guk yŏsŏng nodongja undongsa 1*; Kang Insun, *Han'guk yŏsŏng nodongja undongsa 2*.

33. Pak Sujŏng, *Sumgyŏjin Han'guk yŏsŏng ŭi yŏksa*, 255.

34. Yu Kyŏngsun, *Arŭmdaun yŏndae*, 41–42, 47, 256; Yu Kyŏngsun, "Haksaeng undonggadŭl ŭi nodong undong chamyŏ," 80–83; O Hana, *Hakch'ul*.

35. Pak Sujŏng, *Sumgyŏjin Han'guk yŏsŏng ŭi yŏksa*, 157.

36. Kim Wŏn, *Yŏgong 1970*, 730–31.

37. Yi Okchi, *Han'guk yŏsŏng nodongja undongsa 1*; Kim Hyŏnmi, "Han'guk nodong undong ŭi tamnon punsŏk"; Kim Hyŏnmi, "Han'guk ŭi kŭndaesŏng kwa yŏsŏng ŭi nodongkwŏn."

38. Sŏnggonghoe Taehakkyo Nodongsa Yŏn'guso, *Han'guk sanŏp nodongja*.

39. Some of the testimonies are accessible through the KDF website at db.kdemocracy.or.kr.

40. In commemoration of its tenth anniversary, the Council of Korean Women Workers' Associations in 1997 published a worker-testimony collection, titled *Wildflowers! Flames! Your Name Is Women Nodongja* (*Tŭlkkot iyŏ! pulkkot iyŏ! kŭdae irŭm ŭn yŏsŏng nodongja*) and decided to publish a history of women workers' struggle. The result after four years of painstaking work came out as the two-volume *History of the Korean Women Workers' Movement* (*Han'guk yŏsŏng nodongja undongsa*).

41. Yu Kyŏngsun's *Na, yŏsŏng nodongja 1* and *Na, yŏsŏng nodongja 2* are the outcome of Yu's experiment with activists of the Kuro solidarity strike. Yu defines "Workers' Writing Their Own History" as a process in which a worker "experiences the history through her own experience and creates another kind of history." Yu Kyŏngsun, *Na, yŏsŏng nodongja 2*, 579. A recent example is Asahi Pijŏnggyujik Chihoe, *Tŭlkkot kongdan e p'ida*, a collection of writings by members of the local.

42. Representative works include Kim Wŏn, *Yŏgong 1970*; Kim Chun, "Minju nojo undong kwa kyohoe"; Kim Muyong, "1970-yŏndae Tongil Pangjik nodong undong"; Nam, "Narratives of Women Workers."

43. Yi Okchi, *Han'guk yŏsŏng nodongja undongsa 1*, 338.

44. For examples, see testimonies of Yi Ch'onggak, Ch'oe Sunyŏng, Pak Sunhŭi, and Chŏng Hyangja in Pak Sujŏng, *Sumgyŏjin Han'guk yŏsŏng ŭi yŏksa*; Yi Kyŏngok's testimony in Yu Kyŏngsun, *Na, yŏsŏng nodongja 2*; Hwang Sŏn'gŭm testimony (CD no. 412) in Sŏnggonghoe Taehakkyo Nodongsa Yŏn'guso, *Han'guk sanŏp nodongja*.

45. O, *Korea Story*, 436.

46. Ibid., 444–50; Kim Wŏn, *Yŏgong 1970*, 340.

47. Yi Ch'ŏlsun's testimony in Pak Sujŏng, *Sumgyŏjin Han'guk yŏsŏng ŭi yŏksa*, 229.

48. Kang Insun, *Han'guk yŏsŏng nodongja undongsa 2*, 472–77. The Labor Committee was established in 1988, and as of 1996 it was composed of the Seoul Women Workers' Association, the Incheon Women Workers' Association, the Council of Korean Women Workers' Associations, and the Korean WomenLink (Han'guk Yŏsŏng Minuhoe).

49. Kim Sangsuk, "Sinjayujuŭi sidae ŭi taeanjŏk nodong undong," details the history of the KWTU and its organizing strategy. In 1999 two other women's unions were organized in addition to the KWTU. The Seoul Women Workers' Trade Union (Sŏul Yŏsŏng Nodong Chohap) emerged sharply criticizing the patriarchal stance of both the KCTU and the FKTU, while the Federation of Women Workers' Trade Unions (Chŏn'guk Yŏsŏng Nodong Chohap Yŏnmaeng) prioritized the class question and soon joined the KCTU for the sake of the unity of organized labor. Kim Kyŏnghŭi, "Han'guk yŏsŏng nodong chohap undong," 140–44. In July 2019 the KWTU formed a coalition with two organizations representing irregular K–12 workers affiliated with the KCTU and jointly led a successful three-day general strike in which striking workers demanded that the Ministry of Education, the main employer, work on legislative measures to provide better employment security, better wages, and a path to regular employment for 150,000 irregular education workers, the majority of whom are women. *OhmyNews*, July 5, 2019; *Ch'amsesang*, July 5, 2019.

50. From KWTU's website at blog.daum.net/kwunion99. As of 2009 it had ten locals, seventy sub-locals, and more than six thousand members, of whom 99 percent were irregular workers. The largest group represented was of primary and middle school employees (4,500), and other groups included six hundred janitors, a hundred golf game assistants, three hundred workers in the category of "calculators of medical workers' wages," and five hundred workers who joined as individuals. In the early 2000s the union also organized employees of broadcasting stations and other enterprises. Yokota, "New Attempt at Organizing Irregular Workers," 82–88.

51. Yu-Lee, "Expressive Struggles," chap. 1.

52. Ibid., 56, 64.

53. Sociologist Yokota Nobuko argues that during the developmental era, from the late 1960s until the early 1980s, South Korea maintained a single labor market in which various groups of the "urban lower class" (*tosi hach'ŭng*) and production workers participated. Heavy-industry male workers of the 1970s were no exception. Most of the people in the urban lower class and most production workers shared a common social background as migrants from the countryside. According to Yokota's analysis based on a wide array of statistical and survey data, it was only after the 1987 Great Workers' Struggle that a two-tier labor market emerged and consolidated, as companies pursued a "new management strategy" to cope with rising labor costs and the presence of an empowered union on the shop floor. Internal labor market arrangements at large firms developed, protecting "core insider" workers in the post-1987 decade, and it became increasingly harder for "peripheral" workers in the lower tier of the labor market to move into core jobs, unlike the situation in the pre-1987 developmental era. Yokota, *Kankoku no toshi kasō to rōdōsha*.

54. Nam, *Building Ships*, 197–98.

55. Song, *Inequality in the Workplace*, 121; Yokota, *Kankoku no toshi kasō to rōdōsha*, chaps. 2 and 3.

56. Guy Standing observes a global trend of "feminization through flexible labor," a convergence toward "the type of employment and labor force participation patterns associated with women." After analyzing worldwide statistical data accumulated by the International Labor Organization, he concludes that in effect, "there has been a convergence of male and female patterns of labor force participation. While there has been an overall trend toward more flexible, informal forms of labor, women's situation has probably become *less* informal, while men's has become more so." Standing, "Global Feminization through Flexible Labor," 583, 600.

57. Jennifer Jihye Chun, "Legal Liminality," 544. Sociologist Cho Tonmun divides the history of the *pijŏnggyujik* struggle in South Korea into three periods: (1) a period

of emerging social interest in the *pijŏnggyujik* issue (1998–2002); (2) a period of KCTU mobilization of an offensive nature (2003–6); and (3) a period of mobilization of a defensive nature (2007 to the present). He points out central limitations of the KCTU movement in each period: a lack of interest (the first period), a lack of capacity (the second period), and an absence of strategy (the third period). Cho Tonmun, *Pijŏnggyujik chuch'e hyŏngsŏng*, 196.

58. Nam, "Shipyard Women."

59. According to economist Pae Mugi's study, by 1975 the condition of unlimited labor supply in South Korea provided by rural-to-urban migration was changing into that of a limited supply. As a result, beginning in the late 1970s unemployment rates declined, and real wages rose rapidly despite government policies repressing wages. Yokota, *Kankoku no toshi kasō to rōdōsha*, 38.

60. Nam, "Shipyard Women," 85–86. This article and Kim's recollections contained in Kim Jin-Sook, *Sogŭm kkot namu* and "Yŏsŏnghak hyŏptong kwajŏng t'ŭkkang" provide the material for Kim Jin-Sook's life story unless otherwise noted.

61. Kim Jin-Sook, *Sogŭm kkot namu*, 43–44.

62. Ibid., 46.

63. Ibid., 46–49.

64. Ibid., 19–20, 24–32. Kim recalled that the first time the interrogation room was "red," meaning everything in the room was red, and on her second visit, ten days later, she was taken to a "yellow" room. Later, when her male colleagues Yi Chŏngsik and Pak Yŏngje went missing, Kim found her way back to the building and demanded their release, believing that they had met the same fate. She was taken in again and beaten. Afterward her interrogators dumped her at the Yŏngdo police station, where to her surprise she found her two friends. This recollection was provided in the context of how much she appreciated and depended on the comradeship of Yi and Pak.

65. Ibid., 8.

66. Kang Insun concludes that the KCTU is a "sexist" and "male-centered" organization, which has a very limited capacity to plan and administer programs targeting women members. Kang Insun, *Han'guk yŏsŏng nodongja undongsa 2*, 366–67.

67. Kim Hyŏn'gyŏng and Kim Chuhŭi, "'(Yŏsŏng) nodongja' Kim Chinsuk," 1, 4, 15.

68. Ibid., 15, 19.

69. Kim Jin-Sook waged a twenty-four-day hunger strike from January 13 to February 5 in downtown Pusan, protesting a massive layoff by the Hanjin shipyard. On the twenty-third day, when her health had deteriorated to a dangerous degree, she sent an open letter to the Hanjin CEO, Cho Namho, titled "Dear Chairman Cho Namho, I . . . want to live." In the letter Kim Jin-Sook revealed that the union leadership refused to help print her flyers, which explained the reasons why she had started a hunger strike. They also ordered rank-and-file members not to provide her with gas to run a generator in her outdoor tent in the dead of winter. The letter was published in its entirety in a progressive online newspaper, *Minjung ŭi sori*, http://www.vop.co.kr/A00000281347.html, accessed February 5, 2010. During her 2011 sit-in, the union leadership led by Ch'ae Kilyong criticized Kim for starting a sit-in without union approval and tried to weaken the effect of Kim's action. Hŏ Sohŭi et al., *Chongi pae rŭl chŏmnŭn sigan*, 44–48. Ch'ae and a metal union official went up on the no. 17 crane at the yard on February 14, but their sit-in did not get much support from workers. Ch'ae unilaterally signed an agreement with management in June, allowing the company to mobilize hundreds of security guards who, together with more than a thousand military police, violently removed the strikers and occupied the area beneath Crane no. 85, isolating Kim Jin-Sook. Ch'ae was replaced by Ch'a Haedo, a supporter of Kim Jin-Sook's struggle, in the October election for union president. Ibid., 171.

70. Among a series of legendary public speeches Kim delivered at labor rallies, some are reprinted in Kim Jin-Sook, *Sogŭm kkot namu*, including "Pae Talho ch'umosa" (In commemoration of Pae Talho, January 25, 2003) and "Kim Chuik ch'umosa" (In commemoration of Kim Chuik, November 9, 2003).

71. For example, in a memorable speech in commemoration of Kim Chuik in 2003 she asked, "When the solidarity of capital is this strong, how much are we practicing solidarity?" Then she warned, "Irregular workers, people with disabilities, farmers, women, if we neglect them, we cannot beat capital." Kim Jin-Sook, *Sogŭm kkot namu*, 123. In her aforementioned open letter, "Dear Chairman Cho Namho, I . . . want to live," she sharply criticized the KCTU movement. After declaring that "during the last dozen or so years the labor movement has deteriorated," she presented her diagnosis as follows: "The labor movement that ignores irregular workers, street peddlers, farmers, and the urban poor who are fighting against slum redevelopment is destined to be isolated. The labor movement that does not practice solidarity is a dead one."

72. Kim Tohyŏng, "'Nodongja ŭi mudŏm' Hanjin Chung Subik Chosŏnso siwi kyŏkhwa" [Demonstrations escalate at "workers' grave," Hanjin Heavy Industries Subic shipyard], *Han'gyŏre sinmun*, June 30, 2011.

73. Al Jazeera English TV ran a twenty-five-minute documentary in 2011 on dangerous working conditions at the Hanjin Subic yard and the efforts of workers to organize a union. Al Jazeera English, *Philippines: Storm in Subic Bay*, December 16, 2011, https://www.youtube.com/watch?v=rz9XY65zMJ0. A Senate probe in the Philippines found that from 2006 to 2009, thirty-two workers died and five thousand were injured at the yard, which workers called "the graveyard." Progressive South Korean news media paid attention to the labor struggle at the Subic yard in 2011, prompted by Kim Jin-Sook's crane sit-in. Kim Tohyŏng, "'Nodongja ŭi mudŏm' Hanjin Chung Subik Chosŏnso"; Kim Ŭnji, "Hanjin Subik Chosŏnso edo hŭimang pŏsŭ issŏtta" [There also existed Hope Buses at the Hanjin Subic shipyard], *Sisain* 200, July 18, 2011. Once hailed as a success story that set a new model of industrial relations for South Korean businesses, the Hanjin Subic shipyard was near bankruptcy by early 2019 as net losses snowballed. The crisis at the Subic yard destabilized its mother company, Hanjin Heavy Industries and Construction, to the point that trading of its stocks was suspended for three months in early 2019. *Kukche sinmun*, February 25, 2019, editorial; *P'ainaensyŏl nyusŭ* (Financial News), May 21, 2019.

74. Kim Chuik Kwak Chaegyu Yŏlsa 1-jugi Ch'umo Saŏp Ch'ujin Wiwŏnhoe, *85-ho k'ŭrein*, 566.

75. In 2003, when union president Kim Chuik was trying to shore up support for the strike, union officials were overwhelmed and distraught by management's damage claims in the amount of 744 million wŏn (about $620,000). Four days before Kim's suicide, the company notified more than two hundred union members of its intention to go through with provisional attachment on their assets. Ibid., 254, 365–66, 566. In 2003 combined damage claims to unionists at fifty-one KCTU-affiliated shops reached 57.5 billion wŏn ($50 million), and by 2011 the amount grew to 158.27 billion wŏn ($148 million), which targeted twelve KCTU shops. As of 2016, a total of 152.3 billion wŏn ($136 million) in damage claims was threatening twenty KCTU shops in fifty-seven cases, and close to $96 million of it was imposed on ten metal unions in forty-seven different cases, including Hyundai, Kia, and Ssangyong Motors as well as Hanjin Heavy Industries. Yi Chongnae, "Damage Compensation Claims."

76. Kim Jin-Sook, "Yŏsŏnghak hyŏptong kwajŏng t'ŭkkang." In addition to this lecture, Kim Jin-Sook's recollection of her crane sit-in is from Hŏ Sohŭi et al., *Chongi pae rŭl chŏmnŭn sigan*, and from her two talks at the University of Washington on April 15 and 17, 2017. The talks were part of a series of events, including a workshop, organized by

Hwasook Nam and Jiwoon Yu-Lee and attended by Kim Jin-Sook, her colleague Hwang Yira, and the documentary director of *Island of Shadows*, Kim Chŏnggŭn. The workshop, "'Sky Protest' and 'Hope Bus': The South Korean Labor Movement Confronts Neoliberal Restructuring," was funded by the UW's Harry Bridges Center for Labor Studies and the Center for Korea Studies. During the visit Kim spoke at a book talk (April 15) and in Q&A sessions following showings of the documentary on campus (April 17) and at the hall of the International Longshore and Warehouse Workers' Union Local 19 in Seattle (April 27).

77. Kim Jin-Sook, *Sogŭm kkot namu*, 151–57.
78. *Han'gyŏre sinmun*, November 15, 2011.
79. The fourth Hope Bus met in downtown Seoul, not in Pusan, from August 27 to 28. On Hope Bus events, see Hŏ Sohŭi et al., *Chongi pae rŭl chŏmnŭn sigan*.
80. Subsequent Hope Bus gatherings occurred on July 9–10, July 30–31, August 27–28, and October 8–9. Ibid., 278–90. Hope Bus caravans were organized for major high-altitude sit-ins in subsequent years, including that of Hyundai Motors' irregular workers in Ulsan in July 2013 (they appeared on the 280th day of the sit-in) and that of Star Chemical worker Ch'a Kwangho's chimney sit-in in August 2014 on its eighty-ninth day. A caravan of ninety-seven Hope Buses showed up in March 2014 at the Okch'ŏn interchange of the Seoul-Pusan Express Highway in the middle of what became a 295-day sit-in by Yusŏng Corporation unionists. Angkko et al., *Sŏm kwa sŏm ŭl itta 2*, 136; Yi Kyŏngsŏk et al., *Sŏm kwa sŏm ŭl itta 1*, 224; *Han'gyŏre sinmun*, March 16, 2014.
81. Kim Jin-Sook's interview in *Han'gyŏre sinmun*, June 20, 2011.
82. Hŏ Sohŭi et al., *Chongi pae rŭl chŏmnŭn sigan*, 124; Kim Jin-Sook, "Hŭimang pŏsŭ ka oji anattamyŏn nan . . . irŭm morŭl kŭdaedŭl, komapsŭmnida" [If the Hope Buses hadn't come, I . . . you, whose names I don't know, thank you], *Han'gyŏre sinmun*, December 22, 2011.
83. The terms of agreement, in addition to Kim's decision to descend from the crane, included a promise to rehire all ninety-four remaining laid-off workers within a year and a modest lump-sum payment of up to 20 million wŏn (about $16,600 at the exchange rate of $1 to 1,200 wŏn) per dismissed worker to defray living costs. Hŏ Sohŭi et al., *Chongi pae rŭl chŏmnŭn sigan*, 157.
84. Among Kim's recent speeches and lectures to that effect are the aforementioned "Pae Talho ch'umosa" and "Kim Chuik ch'umosa" contained in Kim, *Sogŭm kkot namu*, and her Labor Day speech at Pusan Station on April 30, 2005. See also Kim Jin-Sook, "Pijŏnggyujik kwa hamkke pap mŏkki silt'ani . . ." [They don't want to eat meals together with irregular workers?], *OhmyNews*, January 13, 2005.
85. The best-known examples are disputes at Ssangyong Motors, guitar-making companies Cort and CorTec, and Star Chemical. Many of these long-lasting labor disputes finally wrapped up in 2018 and 2019 under the government of President Moon Jae-in. Moon won the May 2017 presidential election thanks in large part to a historic wave of candlelight demonstrations in the winter of 2016–17 and the ensuing impeachment of President Park Geun-hye (Pak Kŭnhye), the eldest daughter of Park Chung Hee. In September 2018 laid-off workers of Ssangyong Motors ended their ten-year-long struggle (2009–18) by winning the company's promise of reinstating all dismissed workers over a period of time. *Han'gyŏre sinmun*, June 24, 2019. During their long struggle, which received the brunt of labor repression under the conservative governments that preceded Moon, a total of thirty workers and family members perished by suicide, revealing the unusually high level of trauma the labor conflict inflicted on unionists and their family members. In April 2019 guitar workers of Cort Guitars and Cor-Tec Corporation ended their struggle that had lasted 4,464 days, or more than twelve years, from 2007 to

2019, on management's concession to rehire dismissed workers. *Yŏnhap nyusŭ* (Yonhap News), April 22, 2019. The Cort-CorTec struggle has been well known for its success in building a broad-based solidarity network of musicians and cultural activists, domestically and internationally. The Cort-CorTec Guitar Workers' Band, an amateur group that strikers put together, became popular at music venues and even recorded an album in 2018 that contains six songs written in commemoration of the tenth-year anniversary of their struggle. The title song is appropriately named "High Altitude" (*kogong*). The long-running dispute at Star Chemical (formerly Han'guk Synthetic Textile and later, Pine Tech) from 2013 to 2019 produced the longest high-altitude sit-ins in Korean and world history: first a 408-day sit-in on top of a forty-five-meter-high chimney in the Kumi Industrial Complex in 2014 and then a 426-day sit-in on a power plant chimney in Seoul in 2017. In April 2019 the company finally agreed to reinstate workers, ending the seven-year dispute. *Nyusŭ 1* (News 1), April 23, 2019; Yi Kyŏngsŏk et al., *Sŏm kwa sŏm ŭl itta 1*; Angkko et al., *Sŏm kwa sŏm ŭl itta 2*.

86. Jennifer Jihye Chun's book *Organizing at the Margins* and her article "Legal Liminality" introduce several cases of female irregular worker struggle, including janitorial workers, KTX attendants, E-Land/Homeplus cashiers, golf game assistants at the 88 Country Club, and cafeteria workers at Hyundai Motors. Yi Kyŏngsŏk et al., *Sŏm kwa sŏm ŭl itta 1* contains a chapter on the JEI case, and Angkko et al., *Sŏm kwa sŏm ŭl itta 2* features the Kiryung Electronics case. KTX female attendants achieved their dream of returning as regular workers in a July 2018 agreement, following a twelve-year, 4,526-day protest, and a year later, on July 1, 2019, Homeplus announced its plan to hire all 14,283 irregular employees as regular workers, which would make 99 percent of its workforce regular. *Nyusŭ 1*, July 21, 2018; *Dong-A ilbo*, July 1, 2019.

87. Angkko et al., *Sŏm kwa sŏm ŭl itta 2*, 163–99. The Kiryung union succeeded in uniting regular workers, who constituted a tiny minority of the production workforce, and irregular workers. Kiryung strikers participated in the Hope Bus campaign for Kim Jin-Sook in 2011 as a way to express their gratitude for all the support and solidarity they had received. Kim Soyŏn as union president led a sit-in struggle in 2000 demanding severance pay at Kabŭl Electronics, which was about to close the factory. Charged with National Security Law violations in relation to another labor organizing case, she was sentenced to a ten-month prison term with two years of probation in 2001. She then entered Kiryung Electronics as a contract worker, founded a union local in 2005, and served as the local president until 2011. In the 2012 national presidential election she ran for the nation's top office as a "workers' president" (in this election a female janitor and president of the KCTU union local at Ulsan Science College, Kim Sunja, also ran). Kim Soyŏn's testimony in Yu Kyŏngsun, *Na, yŏsŏng nodongja 2*, 182–287.

88. Kim Kyŏnghŭi, "Han'guk yŏsŏng nodong chohap undong," 137–38. In the end more than 170 female regular workers were laid off. Of them 95 percent were the main breadwinners for their families. The terms the Hyundai Motors union accepted included a layoff of 277 mostly female workers and a leave without pay for a year and a half for 1,261 workers, which sociologist Chi Chuhyŏng regards as "probably the best" option available for the union at the time. Chi Chuhyŏng, *Han'guk sinjayujuŭi ŭi kiwŏn*, 302–5.

89. Yokota, *Kankoku no toshi kasō to rōdōsha*, 167. On the self-interest–driven exclusionary practices of large-firm heavy-industry unions, see Cho Tonmun, *Pijŏnggyujik chuch'e hyŏngsŏng*, 110–51; Chang Kwiyŏn, "Taegiŏp nojo ŭi pijŏnggyu nodongja paeje." Chi Chuhyŏng argues that the outcome of the August 1998 Hyundai Motors strike marked a definite moment in the Kim Dae-Jung government's labor policy, moving away from that of "coordination" and to a "politics of control." The compromise of the union

symbolized organized labor's acceptance of the "principle of layoffs" and its defeat in the struggle over the critical issue of labor market flexibility. Chi Chuhyŏng, *Han'guk sinjayujuŭi ŭi kiwŏn*, 303–5.

90. Yokota, *Kankoku no toshi kasō to rōdōsha*, 174; Yokota, "New Attempt at Organizing Irregular Workers," 76.

91. Other categories included fixed-term employees (25.1 percent), on-call employees (9 percent), and subcontracted workers (7.8 percent). Yokota, "New Attempt at Organizing Irregular Workers," 76–77.

92. Yokota, *Kankoku no toshi kasō to rōdōsha*, 168.

93. Ibid., 177–86.

94. *Yŏnhap nyusŭ*, July 1, 2019.

95. Yokota, "New Attempt at Organizing Irregular Workers," 78.

96. Yokota, *Kankoku no toshi kasō to rōdōsha*, 195–97. Cho Tonmun cites a study that calculates the chance of an irregular worker with four years of seniority landing a regular job at a mere 9 percent. Cho Tonmun, *Pijŏnggyujik chuch'e hyŏngsŏng*, 34.

97. Yokota, "New Attempt at Organizing Irregular Workers," 81. Union density among regular workers increased somewhat from 15.3 percent in 2003 to 17.1 percent in 2018, while that of irregular workers as a whole stayed in the 3 percent range between 2009 (2.5 percent) and 2018 (3.1 percent). Korean Labor Institute (KLI), *2003–18 KLI pijŏnggyujik nodong t'onggye*, 62.

98. Feminist sociologist Yi Hyojae's 1983 article on colonial-period women workers offered the first account on Kang Churyong in some detail. Yi Hyojae, "Ilcheha ŭi yŏsŏng nodong munje."

99. An analysis of "sky protests" in South Korea from 1990 to 2013 is provided in Yoonkyung Lee, "Sky Protest."

100. Kim's record was replaced by a 408-day chimney sit-in from May 2014 to July 2015 by Ch'a Kwangho, a male irregular worker at Star Chemical.

101. Author Pak Sŏryŏn delves into the imagined inner world of Kang from her Manchurian days of marriage and independence struggle to the moment she climbed up on the roof of the Ŭlmiltae Pavilion. Loosely based on extant documentary evidence, this compelling historical fiction portrays Kang Churyong as an organic intellectual hero with a sharp feminist consciousness, one she developed herself, thus projecting a twenty-first-century feminist consciousness on Kang's story. Pak Sŏryŏn, *Ch'egongnyŏ Kang Churyong*.

102. Even a newly published English-language Korean labor history sourcebook edited by respected labor scholars Hagen Koo, Kim Kyŏngil, and Kim Chun establishes a causational link between the two sit-ins: "[Kang Churyong's] one-person demonstration atop the Eulmildae roof inspired the over-300 day aerial sit-in in 2011 by Kim Jin-Suk atop a crane in the Yeongdo (Busan) shipyard, protesting Hanjin Heavy Industries." Koo et al., *Modern Korean Labor: A Sourcebook*, 16–17. This statement, I believe, simplifies and distorts the historical record since there is no known evidence that establishes the fact that Kim Jin-Sook was inspired by Kang Churyong's Ŭlmiltae sit-in.

Bibliography

Colonial-Period Periodicals and Compilations

This section contains newspapers and magazines published in Korea during the colonial period (1910–45) and articles printed in them. It also includes postcolonial compilations of colonial-period news articles and/or court documents pertaining to social movements.

Ch'ae Rin. "P'yŏngyang komu chikkong kongdong p'aŏp ŭi kyohun" [A lesson from the Pyongyang rubber workers' solidarity strike]. *T'aep'yŏngyang rodongja* 1, nos. 11–12 (November–December 1930). In Pak and Yi, *T'aep'yŏngyang rodongja*, 1:401–7.
———. "Sin ch'akch'wi pangbŏp ŭi silhyŏn in P'yŏngyang Kongje Sanŏp Chohap e taehaya" [On Pyongyang's Mutual Aid Industrial Cooperative, which is a realization of a new method of exploitation]. *T'aep'yŏngyang rodongja* 2, nos. 4–5 (April–May 1931). In Pak and Yi, *T'aep'yŏngyang rodongja*, 2:176–80.
Chŏng Ch'ilsŏng. "Amnal ŭl parabonŭn puin nodongja" [Women workers who gaze at the future]. *Tonggwang* 29 (January 1932): 70.
Chosŏn chungang ilbo [Korea Central Daily] (Seoul, March 1933 to November 1937)
Chosun ilbo [Chosŏn ilbo; Korea Daily] (Seoul, March 1920 to August 1940; November 1945 to present)
Chungang ilbo [Central Daily] (Seoul, November 1931 to February 1933; continued as *Chosŏn chungang ilbo*)
Chungoe ilbo [Inside-Outside Daily] (Seoul, November 1926 to June 1931; continued as *Chungang ilbo*)
Dong-A ilbo [Tonga ilbo; East Asia Daily] (Seoul, April 1920 to August 1940; December 1945 to present)
Kim Ch'angsul. "Ŭlmiltae sang ŭi t'usa" [A fighter on the Ŭlmiltae]. *Tonggwang* 23 (July 1931): 51.
Kim Kyŏngil, ed. *Ilcheha sahoe undongsa charyojip* [A sourcebook for social movement history in the colonial period]. Vols. 1–10. Seoul: KSI, 2002.
Kim Pongu, ed. *Chibangbyŏl kisa moŭm: Ilcheha sahoe undongsa charyojip* [A collection of news articles by region: A sourcebook for social movement history in the colonial period]. Vol. 4, *P'yŏngan Namdo* [South P'yŏngan Province]. Seoul: Hanul, 1989.
Kŭnu [Friends of the Rose of Sharon]. Inaugural issue (May 10, 1929).
Kyŏngsŏng ilbo [Keijō nippō; Seoul Daily] (Seoul, September 1906 to October 1945)
Maeil sinbo [Daily News] (Seoul, August 1910 to November 1945)
Muhojŏngin (O Kiyŏng). "Ŭlmiltae sang ŭi ch'egongnyŏ: Yŏryu t'usa Kang Churyong hoegyŏn'gi" [The woman-in-the-sky on top of the Ŭlmiltae: An interview with Woman Fighter Kang Churyong]. *Tonggwang* 23 (July 1931): 40–42.
National Institute of Korean History (Kuksa P'yŏnch'an Wiwŏnhoe). Korean History Database. db.history.go.kr.
O Kiyŏng. "P'yŏngyang komu chaengŭi chinsang" [The real story of the Pyongyang rubber dispute]. Nos. 1–7. *Dong-A ilbo*, September 4–7 and 8–11, 1930.

——. "P'yŏngyang komu kongjang chaengŭi chŏnjŏk" [The battle site of the Pyongyang rubber dispute]. *Pyŏlgŏn'gon* 33 (October 1930): 56–59.
——. "P'yŏngyang p'oktong sakŏn hoego" [Reminiscing about the Pyongyang riot]. *Tonggwang* 25 (September 1931): 10–12.
Paektusan. "P'yŏngyang P'yŏngwŏn komu chikkong p'aŏp ŭi hyŏngmyŏngjŏk t'ujaengsŏng kwa kŭ ŭi kyohun" [Revolutionary militancy and the lessons of the Pyongyang P'yŏngwŏn rubber worker strike]. *T'aep'yŏngyang rodongja* 2, nos. 6–7 (June–July 1931). In Pak and Yi, *T'aep'yŏngyang rodongja*, 2:232–37.
Pak Hwan and Yi Sangil, eds. *T'aep'yŏngyang rodongja* [Pacific Workers]. Vol. 1 (1930) and vol. 2 (1931–32). Seoul: Kukhak Yŏn'guwŏn, 1998.
Pyŏlgŏn'gon [Another World] (Seoul, November 1926 to August 1934)
Samch'ŏlli [Three thousand *li*] (Seoul, June 1929 to January 1942)
Seoul National University. *Sŏuldae kugwan sinmun palch'we charyo: Chosŏn kwan'gye* [Seoul National University newspaper scrap material: on Chosŏn (Korea)]. Year unknown. Held at Seoul National University Library. Online access available through National Institute of Korean History's Korean History Database.
Tonggwang [Eastern Light] (Seoul, May 1926 to January 1933)
Yŏngjin, ed. *Ilcheha Chosŏn kwan'gye sinmun charyo chipsŏng* [A collection of newspaper articles on Korea during the colonial period]. Vols. 1–6. Seoul, n.p.

Korean- and Japanese-Language Sources

Contained in this section are primary and secondary source materials published in the Korean or Japanese languages. Author names follow the East Asian convention of the given name following the surname.

An Chaesŏng. *Ch'ŏnggye, nae ch'ŏngch'un: Ch'ŏnggye P'ibok nojo ŭi pinnanŭn kiŏk* [Ch'ŏnggye, my youth: A shining memory of the Ch'ŏnggye Garment Union]. P'aju: Tolbegae, 2007.
——. *Iröbŏrin Han'guk hyŏndaesa: P'i wa sunsu ŭi sidae rŭl saragan hangil tongnip undongga 19-in ŭi iyagi* [The Korean modern history that we have lost: The stories of nineteen anti-Japanese independence movement activists who lived through an era of blood and pureness]. Seoul: Inmun Sŏwŏn, 2015.
——. *Kyŏngsŏng t'ŭroik'a* [The troika of Seoul]. Seoul: Sahoe P'yŏngnon, 2004.
An Chŏngnam. "Pusan chiyŏk yŏsŏng nodong undong esŏ nat'anan yŏsŏng munje e kwanhan yŏn'gu" [A study on women's issues in the women's labor movement in the Pusan area]. MA thesis, Keimyung (Kyemyŏng) University, 1992.
An Chongu. "Chobang chaengŭi 1" [Labor disputes at Chobang 1]. *Nodong kongnon* 2, no. 8 (1972): 114–23.
——. "Chobang chaengŭi 2" [Labor disputes at Chobang 2]. *Nodong kongnon* 2, no. 9 (1972): 156–66.
An Sŭnghyŏn, ed. *Ilche kangjŏmgi Han'guk nodong sosŏlsŏn* [A collection of Korean labor novels from the colonial period]. 3 vols. Seoul: Pogosa, 1995.
An T'aejŏng. *Chosŏn Nodong Chohap Chŏn'guk P'yŏngŭihoe* [The National Council of Korean Trade Unions]. Seoul: Hyŏnjang esŏ Mirae rŭl, 2002.
Angkko, Kang Hyemin, Cho Namjun, Song Kiyŏk, Wŏn Hyejin, Yu Myŏngja, Chu Homin, et al. *Sŏm kwa sŏm ŭl itta 2* [Connecting islands 2]. Seoul: Han'gyŏre Ch'ulp'an, 2015.

Asahi Pijŏnggyujik Chihoe [Asahi Irregular Workers' Local]. *Tŭlkkot kongdan e p'ida* [Wildflowers, blooming in a factory complex]. Taegu: Hant'ijae, 2017.
Bank of Korea [Han'guk Ŭnhaeng]. *Ilche sidae mit haebang ihu Han'guk ŭi hwap'ye* [Korean currency during the colonial period and postliberation]. Seoul: Bank of Korea, 2004.
Ch'a Sŏnghwan, Yu Kyŏngsun, Kim Muyong, Kim Wŏn, Hong Hyŏnyŏng, Kim T'aeil, and Yi Imha, eds. *1970-yŏndae minjung undong yŏn'gu* [A study of the 1970s minjung movement]. Seoul: KDF, 2005.
Chang Kwiyŏn. "Taegiŏp nojo ŭi pijŏnggyu nodongja paeje" [The exclusion of irregular workers in major enterprise unions]. *Kiŏk kwa chŏnmang* 21 (2009): 213–341.
Chang Kyusik. "1920-yŏndae kaejoron ŭi hwaksan kwa Kidokkyo sahoejuŭi ŭi suyong chŏngch'ak" [The spread of reconstruction theory in the 1920s and the introduction and consolidation of Christian socialism]. *Yŏksa munje yŏn'gu* 21 (2009): 111–34.
———. "'Chosŏn ŭi Kandi' Kodang Cho Mansik" [Kodang (pen name) Cho Mansik, the Gandhi of Korea]. *Naeil ŭl yŏnŭn yŏksa* 26 (December 2006): 84–97.
———. *Ilcheha Han'guk Kidokkyo minjokchuŭi yŏn'gu* [A study of Korean Christian nationalism in the colonial period]. Seoul: Hyean, 2001.
———. *Minjung kwa hamkke han Chosŏn ŭi Kandi: Cho Mansik ŭi minjok undong* [The Gandhi of Korea who stood by the people: The nationalist activism of Cho Mansik]. Seoul: Yŏksa Konggan, 2007.
———. "Mi kunjŏng ha Hŭngsadan kyeyŏl chisigin ŭi naengjŏn insik kwa kukka kŏnsŏl kusang" [The understanding of the Cold War and plans for state building among intellectuals affiliated with the Hŭngsadan under the US military occupation]. *Han'guk sasang sahak* 38 (August 2011): 245–84.
Chang Sŏkhong. *6.10 manse undong* [The June 10th *manse* movement]. Ch'ŏnan: Han'guk Tongnip Undongsa Yŏn'guso, 2009.
Chang Yŏngŭn. "Ajit'ŭ k'ip'ŏ wa hausŭ k'ip'ŏ: Yŏsŏng sahoejuŭija ŭi yŏnae wa ipchi" [Agit (agitpunkt)-keeper and house-keeper: Female socialists' love and place]. *Taedong munhwa yŏn'gu* 64 (2008): 186–213.
Chi Chuhyŏng. *Han'guk sinjayujuŭi ŭi kiwŏn kwa hyŏngsŏng* [The origins and the formation of neoliberalism in South Korea]. Seoul: Ch'aek Sesang, 2011.
Chi Sugŏl. "Singminji sidae sinmun charyo: Kim Pongu p'yŏn, *Ilcheha sahoe undongsa charyojip*" [Newspaper materials in the colonial period: A sourcebook for social movement history in the colonial period, edited by Kim Pongu]. *Yŏksa wa hyŏnsil* 2 (December 1989): 274–83.
Cho Sŏnhŭi. *Se yŏja* [Three women]. 2 vols. Seoul: Han'gyŏre Ch'ulp'an, 2017.
Cho Tonmun. *Pijŏnggyujik chuch'e hyŏngsŏng kwa chŏllyakchŏk sŏnt'aek* [Subject formation of irregular workers and their strategic choices]. Seoul: Maeil Nodong Nyusŭ, 2012.
Cho Yŏngnae. *Ŏnŭ ch'ŏngnyŏn nodongja ŭi sam kwa chugŭm: Chŏn T'aeil p'yŏngjŏn* [The life and death of a young worker: A critical biography of Chun Tae-il]. Seoul: Tolbegae, 1983.
Ch'oe Kyujin. "1930-yŏndae ch'o Chosŏn sahoejuŭijadŭl ŭi 'Polsyebik'i tang' kŏnsŏllon" [The theory of "Bolshevik Party" construction among Korean socialists in the early 1930s]. *Marŭk'ŭsŭjuŭi yŏn'gu* 5-1 (February 2008): 224–51.
———. *Chosŏn kongsandang chaegŏn undong* [The Korean Communist Party reconstruction movement]. Ch'ŏnan: Tongnip Kinyŏmgwan, 2009.

——. "K'ommyunisŭt'ŭ kŭrup' kwa T'aep'yŏngyang Nodong Chohap kyeyŏl ŭi nodong undong pangch'im" [A plan for the labor movement by the "Communist Group" and those affiliated with the Pacific Trade Union]. *Yŏksa yŏn'gu* 5 (October 1997): 113–61.

Chŏn Ponggwan. "P'yŏngyang Chunggugin paech'ŏk p'oktong sakŏn" [The Chinese exclusion riot in Pyongyang]. *Sindonga* 51, no. 2 (February 2008): 588–99. http://shindonga.donga.com/Library/3/02/13/107067/1.

Chŏn Sŏngho. *Han'guk yahak undongsa: Chayu rŭl hyanghan yŏjŏng 110-yŏn* [A history of the night school movement: A 110-year journey toward freedom]. Seoul: Hagisisŭp, 2009.

Chŏng Hogi. *Minju changjŏng 100-yŏn, Kwangju Chŏnnam chiyŏk sahoe undong yŏn'gu: Nodong undongsa* [A one-hundred-year journey toward democracy, a study of social movements in Kwangju and the South Chŏlla region: A history of the labor movement]. Yangp'yŏng: Hyumŏn K'ŏlch'yŏ Arirang, 2015.

Chŏng Misuk. "70-yŏndae yŏsŏng nodong undong ŭi hwalsŏnghwa e kwanhan kyŏnghŏm segyejŏk yŏn'gu: Sŏmyuŏp ŭl chungsim ŭro" [A study through life experiences regarding the energization of the female labor movement in the 1970s]. MA thesis, Ewha Womans University, 1993.

Chŏng Pyŏnguk. *Singminji puron yŏlchŏn: Mich'in saenggak i paetsok esŏ naonda* [The biographies of rebellious people in the colony: Crazy ideas come out of the belly]. Seoul: Yŏksa Pip'yŏngsa, 2013.

Chŏng Yonguk. "Ch'egongnyŏ Kang Churyong twi en 'sahoebu kija' O Kiyŏng issŏtta" [Behind Woman-in-the-Sky Kang Churyong existed "social-section reporter" O Kiyŏng]. *Han'gyŏre sinmun*, November 25, 2018.

Chŏng Yŏnsun. "1970-yŏndae nodong kyoyuk sarye yŏn'gu: K'ŭrisŭch'yan Ak'ademi sanŏp sahoe chunggan chiptan kyoyuk" [A Case Study on 1970s Labor Education: The Industrial Society Intermediary Group Education of the Christian Academy in Korea]. MA thesis, Seoul National University, 1998.

Chu Ikchong. "P'yŏngyang Chosŏnin kiŏpka ŭi kyŏngyŏng inyŏm" [The management ideology of Korean entrepreneurs in Pyongyang]. *Kyŏngje sahak* 19 (1995): 137–66.

——. "Singminjigi Chosŏn esŏ ŭi komu kongŏp ŭi chŏn'gae" [The development of the rubber industry in colonial Korea]. *Kyŏngje sahak* 22 (1997): 83–120.

——. "Singminjigi P'yŏngyang meriyasŭ chabon ŭi saengsan hamnihwa: 1920-yŏndae chungyŏp—1930-yŏndae rŭl chungsim ŭro" [Production rationalization by knitwear capital in Pyongyang in the colonial period: Focusing on the period from the mid-1920s to the 1930s]. *Kyŏngje sahak* 18 (1994): 91–128.

Chu Kyŏngmi. "80-yŏndae Pusan chiyŏk yŏsŏng undong e nat'anan chisigin hwaltongga ŭi yŏsŏng munje insik mit p'yŏngka e kwanhan yŏn'gu" [A study of the consciousness and assessments of women's issues among intellectual activists seen through the women's movement in the Pusan region during the 1980s]. *Yŏsŏng yŏn'gu* (Pusan Women's University) 5 (2003): 155–74.

FKCU (Federation of Korean Chemical Workers' Union; Chŏn'guk Hwahak Nodong Chohap Yŏnmaeng). *Hwahak nojo 20-yŏnsa* [A 20-year history of the Korean chemical workers' union]. Seoul: FKCU, 1986.

FKTU (Federation of Korean Trade Unions; Han'guk Nodong Chohap Ch'ongyŏnmaeng). *Han'guk Noch'ong 50-yŏnsa* [A 50-year history of the FKTU]. Seoul: FKTU, 2002.

——. *Han'guk Noch'ong saŏp pogo* [Report on activities of the FKTU]. Seoul: FKTU, 1962–67.

——. *Han'guk nodong chohap undongsa* [The history of the Korean trade union movement]. Seoul: FKTU, 1979.

Fujii Takeshi (Hujii Tak'esi). *P'asijŭm kwa che-3-segyejuŭi sai esŏ: Chokch'ŏnggye ŭi hyŏngsŏng kwa mollak ŭl t'onghae pon haebang 8-yŏnsa* [In between fascism and Third-World-ism: A history of the eight years following liberation seen through the formation and demise of the National Youth Corps]. Seoul: Yŏksa Pip'yŏngsa, 2012.

Ham Inhŭi. "Han'guk chŏnjaeng, kajok kŭrigo yŏsŏng ŭi tajungjŏk kŭndaesŏng" [The Korean War, families, and women's multilayered modernity]. *Sahoe wa iron* 9 (November 2006): 159–89.

Han Sanguk. "60-yŏndae Kanghwa chingmul nojo sakŏn kwa Kat'ollik Nodong Ch'ŏngnyŏnhoe" [The Kanghwa textile union incident in the 1960s and the JOC]. *Inch'ŏnhak yŏn'gu* 23 (August 2015): 127–73.

Han'guk Yŏsŏng Yŏn'guso (Korean Women's Studies Institute), ed. *Yŏsŏng nodongja wa imgŭm* [Women workers and their wages]. Seoul: Han'guk Yŏsŏng Yŏn'guso, 1991.

Hashimoto Tetsuya. "Entotsu otoko Tanabe Kiyoshi shōron" [A discussion on the chimney man Tanabe Kiyoshi]. *Kanajawa daigaku keizaigakubu ronshu* [Economic Review of Kanazawa University] 17, no. 2 (1997): 129–49. http://hdl.handle.net/2297/18303.

Hŏ Sohŭi, Kim Ŭnmin, Pak Chisŏn, and O Toyŏp. *Chongi pae rŭl chŏmnŭn sigan: Hanjin Chunggongŏp 3-yŏn ŭi kirok* [A time to fold paper ships: A record of three years at Hanjin Heavy Industries]. Seoul: Samch'ang, 2013.

Hŏ Yun. "Naengjŏn Asiajŏk chilsŏ wa 1950-yŏndae Han'guk ŭi yŏsŏng hyŏmo" [The Cold War Asian order and misogyny in 1950s South Korea]. *Yŏksa munje yŏn'gu* 35 (2016): 79–115.

Hong Hyŏnyŏng. "Tosi Sanŏp Sŏn'gyohoe wa 1970-yŏndae nodong undong" [Urban industrial missions and the 1970s labor movement]. In Ch'a Sŏnghwan et al., *1970-yŏndae minjung undong yŏn'gu*, 375–447.

Hong Ŭnnang. "P'aullo P'ŭreiri kyoyuk sasang kwa Han'guk minjung kyoyuk undong" [The educational philosophy of Paulo Freire and the people's education movement in South Korea]. In *Nodongja, chagi yŏksa rŭl malhada* [Workers telling their own stories], edited by Yŏksahak Yŏn'guso (Institute of Historical Studies), 350–400. Seoul: Sŏhae Munjip, 2005.

Hosoi Wakizō. *Jokō aishi* [The pitiful history of female factory workers]. Tokyo: Kaizōsha, 1925.

Hwang Chŏngmi. "Kajok, kukka, sahoe chaesaengsan" [Family, state, and social reproduction]. In *Kajok kwa ch'inmilsŏng ŭi sahoehak* [A sociology of family and intimacy], edited by Kim Hyegyŏng, 31–52. Seoul: Tasan, 2014.

Hwang Ŭinam. "Han'guk ŭi imgŭm chŏngch'aek" [Wage policies in Korea]. MA thesis, Sungkyunkwan University, 1964.

Im Chongmyŏng. "Chosŏn Minjok Ch'ŏngnyŏndan kwa Mi kunjŏng ŭi 'changnae Han'guk ŭi chido seryŏk' yangsŏng chŏngch'aek" [The Korean National Youth Corps and its connections with a policy to nurture the "future Korean leader" by the United States Army Military Government in Korea]. *Han'guksa yŏn'gu* 95 (December 1996): 179–211.

Im Songja. *Taehan Min'guk nodong undong ŭi posujŏk kiwŏn: 1945-yŏn haebang—1961-yŏn kkaji* [The conservative origins of the South Korean labor movement: From the 1945 liberation to 1961]. Seoul: Sŏnin, 2007.

Isogaya Sueji. *Uri ch'ŏngch'un ŭi Chosŏn: Ilcheha nodong undong ŭi kirok* [Korea in our youth: Records of the labor movement under the Japanese occupation]. Translated by Kim Kyeil. Seoul: Sagyejŏl, 1988. First published 1984 by Kage Shobō (Tokyo) as *Waga seishun no Chōsen*.

JOC and KDF (Han'guk Kat'ollik Nodong Ch'ŏngnyŏnhoe 50-yŏn ŭi Kirok Ch'ulp'an Wiwŏnhoe and Minjuhwa Undong Kinyŏm Saŏphoe; Committee for the Publication of a 50-year Record of the JOC Korea and the Korea Democracy Foundation). *Han'guk Kat'ollik Nodong Ch'ŏngnyŏnhoe 50-yŏn ŭi kirok* [A 50-year record of the JOC (Jeunesse Ouvrière Chrétienne) Korea]. Seoul: Korea Democracy Foundation, 2009.

Kang Insun. *Han'guk yŏsŏng nodongja undongsa 2* [The history of the Korean women workers' movement 2]. Seoul: Hanul, 2001.

Kang Man'gil and Sŏng Taegyŏng, eds. *Han'guk sahoejuŭi undong inmyŏng sajŏn* [Dictionary of people in the Korean socialist movement]. Seoul: Ch'angjak kwa Pip'yŏngsa, 1996.

KCTU (Korean Confederation of Trade Unions; Chŏn'guk Minju Nodong Chohap Ch'ongyŏnmaeng). *1970–2000 minju nojo t'ujaeng kwa t'anap ŭi yŏksa* [A history of the struggle of democratic unions and the repression of them, 1970–2000]. Seoul: Hyŏnjang esŏ Mirae rŭl, 2001.

Kim Chit'ae. *Munhangna chŏgori nŭn pi e chŏtchi anatta* [Rain could not wet his patterned gauze jacket]. Seoul: Sŏkp'il, 2003.

Kim Chuik Kwak Chaegyu Yŏlsa 1-jugi Ch'umo Saŏp Ch'ujin Wiwŏnhoe (Committee for the First-year Anniversary Commemoration Project for Martyrs Kim Chuik and Kwak Chaegyu). *85-ho k'ŭrein: Kim Chuik Kwak Chaegyu yŏlsa ch'umo charyojip* [Crane no. 85: A collection of materials related to the commemoration of martyrs Kim Chuik and Kwak Chaegyu]. Pusan: Hanjin Heavy Industries Union, 2004.

Kim Chun. "1950-yŏndae ch'ŏlto nojo ŭi chojik kwa hwaltong" [Organization and activities of the Railway Workers' Union in the 1950s]. In Yi Chonggu et al., *1950-yŏndae Han'guk nodongja ŭi saenghwal segye*, 207–45.

———. "1970-yŏndae yŏsŏng nodongja ŭi ilsang saenghwal kwa ŭisik: Irŭnba 'mobŏm kŭlloja' rŭl chungsim ŭro" [Everyday lives and consciousness of women workers in the 1970s: Focusing on the so-called model workers]. *Yŏksa yŏn'gu* 10 (June 2002): 53–99.

———. "Minju nojo undong kwa kyohoe" [The democratic labor movement and churches]. In *Nodong kwa palchŏn ŭi sahoehak* [Sociology of labor and development], edited by Han'guk Sanŏp Sahoe Hakhoe (Korean Industrial Sociological Association), 101–31. Seoul: Hanul, 2003.

Kim Chungyŏl. "P'yŏngyang komu kongjang p'aŏp" [Strikes at rubber factories in Pyongyang]. *Nodong kongnon* 5, no. 2 (March 1975): 107–16.

Kim Hyŏn'gyŏng and Kim Chuhŭi. "'(Yŏsŏng) nodongja' Kim Chinsuk e Taehan yŏsŏngjuŭijŏk tokhae" [A feminist reading of "(female) laborer" Kim Jin-Sook]. *P'eminijŭm yŏn'gu* 12, no. 2 (2012): 1–28.

Kim Hyŏnmi. "Han'guk nodong undong ŭi tamnon punsŏk ŭl t'onghae pon sŏngchŏk chaehyŏn ŭi chŏngch'ihak" [The politics of gender representation seen through a discourse analysis of the South Korean labor movement]. *Yŏllin chisŏng* 6 (1999): 128–48.

———."Han'guk ŭi kŭndaesŏng kwa yŏsŏng ŭi nodongkwŏn" [Modernity and women's labor rights in South Korea]. *Han'guk yŏsŏnghak* 16, no. 1 (June 2006): 37–64.

Kim Hyŏnsaeng. "Kang Kyŏngae ŭi 'Kando' ch'ehŏm kwa munhak t'eksŭt'ŭ ŭi yŏksasŏng" [Kang Kyŏngae's "Jiandao" experience and the historicity of literary texts]. *Han'guk sasang kwa munhwa* 69 (2013): 60–85.

Kim Jin-Sook (Kim Chinsuk). *Sogŭm kkot namu* [Salt flower tree]. Seoul: Humanit'asŭ, 2007.

———. "Yŏsŏnghak hyŏptong kwajŏng t'ŭkkang" [A special lecture at the Women's Studies Interdisciplinary Program]. Transcript. Seoul National University, September 27, 2017.

Kim Kyŏnghŭi. "Han'guk yŏsŏng nodong chohap undong ŭi ch'ulhyŏn: Nodong undong ŭi saeroun p'aerŏdaim ŭl hyanghayŏ" [The appearance of the Korean Women's Trade Union: Toward a new paradigm]. *Kyŏngje wa sahoe* 43 (Autumn 1999): 133–53.

Kim Kyŏngil. "1950-yŏndae Han'guk ŭi nodong undong esŏ taeanjŏk chŏnt'ong" [Alternative traditions in the labor movement of Korea during the 1950s]. In Yi Chonggu et al., *1950-yŏndae Han'guk nodongja ŭi saenghwal segye*, 246–98.

———. "1970-yŏndae minju nojo undong ŭi chaengchŏm: Yŏsŏng kwa chisik ŭi munje rŭl chungsim ŭro" [Issues in the democratic union movement in the 1970s: Focusing on the question of women and knowledge]. *Yŏksa pip'yŏng* 73 (Winter 2005): 152–82.

———. "Ch'ulse ŭi chisik, haebang ŭi chisik: 1970-yŏndae minju nodong undong kwa yŏsŏng nodongja" [Knowledge for career enhancement, knowledge of liberation: The 1970s democratic labor movement and female workers]. *Minju sahoe wa chŏngch'aek yŏn'gu* 9 (2006): 158–88.

———. *Han'guk kŭndae nodongsa wa nodong undong* [Korean modern labor history and labor movement]. Seoul: Munhak kwa Chisŏngsa, 2004.

———. *Han'guk nodong undongsa 2: Ilcheha ŭi nodong undong 1920–1945* [The history of the Korean labor movement 2: The labor movement under Japanese colonial rule, 1920–1945]. Seoul: Chisik Madang, 2004.

———. *Ilcheha nodong undongsa* [The history of the labor movement under Japanese colonial rule]. Seoul: Ch'angjak kwa Pip'yŏngsa, 1992.

———. *Yi Chaeyu: 1930-yŏndae Sŏul ŭi hyŏngmyŏng undong* [Yi Chaeyu: The revolutionary movement in Seoul in the 1930s]. Seoul: P'urŭn Yŏksa, 2007.

———. *Yŏsŏng ŭi kŭndae, kŭndae ŭi yŏsŏng* [The modernity of women, women of modernity]. Seoul: P'urŭn yŏksa, 2004.

Kim Muyong. "1970-yŏndae Tongil Pangjik nodong undong ŭi chohap minjujuŭi wa chendŏ chŏngch'i" [Union democracy and gender politics in the Tongil Pangjik labor movement of the 1970s]. In Ch'a Sŏnghwan et al., *1970-yŏndae minjung undong yŏn'gu*, 193–306.

Kim Nakchung. *Han'guk nodong undongsa: Haebang hu p'yŏn* [A history of the Korean labor movement: The postliberation period]. Seoul: Chŏngsa, 1982.

Kim Sangsuk. "Sinjayujuŭi sidae ŭi taeanjŏk nodong undong: Sahoe undong nodong chohap chuŭi kwanchŏm esŏ pon Chŏn'guk Yŏsŏng Nodong Chohap ŭi hwaltong kwa chŏnmang" [An alternative labor movement in the neoliberal era: Activities of the Korean Women's Trade Union and its prospects seen from the perspective of social movement unionism]. *Minjujuŭi wa inkwŏn* 17, no. 2 (2017): 199–236.

Kim Sangt'ae. "1920–1930-yŏndae Tonguhoe-Hŭngŏp Kurakpu yŏn'gu" [A study of the Tonguhoe and the Hŭngŏp Kurakpu in the 1920s and 1930s]. *Han'guk saron* (Seoul National University) 28 (1992): 209–62.

Kim Sŏksun. "Kat'ollik Nodong Chŏngnyŏnhoe (JOC) ka kŏrŏon kil" [A path that the JOC has walked on]. In *Kwangju Taegyogu sahoe undong tanch'e semina* [Seminar of social movement organizations in the Kwangju Archdiocese], edited by Kwangju Inkwŏn P'yŏnghwa Chaedan (Kwangju Human Rights and Peace Foundation) and Chŏnjugyo Kwangju Taegyogu Chŏngŭi P'yŏnghwa Wiwŏnhoe (Committee for Justice and Peace, Catholic Kwangju Archdiocese). Unpublished and unpaginated document, 2012.

Kim Sujin. *Sinyŏsŏng, kŭndae ŭi kwaing: Singminji Chosŏn ŭi sinyŏsŏng tamnon kwa chendŏ chŏngch'i, 1920–1934* [Excess of the modern: The New Woman in colonial Korea, 1920–1934]. Seoul: Somyŏng Ch'ulp'an, 2009.

Kim Sŭng. "Charyo sogae: 1950-yŏndae Chosŏn Pangjik Chusik Hoesa chaengŭi kwallyŏn munsŏ haeje" [Introducing documents: Annotated introduction of the documents related to the disputes at the Chosŏn Spinning and Weaving Corporation in the 1950s]. *Hangdo Pusan* 25 (2009): 377–410.

Kim T'aesu. *Kkot kach'i p'iŏ maehokk'e hara: Sinmun kwanggo ro pon kŭndae ŭi p'unggyŏng* [Blossom like flowers and enchant: Scenes of the modern seen through newspaper advertisements]. Seoul: Hwangso Chari, 2005.

Kim Wŏn. "1970-yŏndae Kat'ollik Nodong Chŏngnyŏnhoe wa nodong undong" [The JOC and the labor movement in the 1970s]. In Ch'a Sŏnghwan et al., *1970-yŏndae minjung undong yŏn'gu*, 307–73.

———. "1970-yŏndae minju nojo wa kyohoe tanch'e: Tosi Sanŏp Sŏn'gyohoe wa Chiose tamnon ŭi hyŏngsŏng kwa mosun" [The 1970s democratic unions and church organizations: The formation of the discourses of the urban industrial missions and the JOC and their contradictions]. *Sanŏp nodong yŏn'gu* 10, no. 1 (2004): 57–94.

———. *Yŏgong 1970: Kŭnyŏdŭl ŭi pan yŏksa* [Factory women, 1970: Their counterhistory]. Seoul: Imaejin, 2006.

Kim Wŏn, Kim Sangsuk, Kim Yŏngsŏn, Yu Kyŏngsun, Yi Kwangil, Yi Namhŭi, Yi Chaesŏng, and Im Songja. *Minju nojo, nohak yŏndae kŭrigo pyŏnhyŏk* [Democratic unions, the worker-student alliance, and revolutionary changes]. Sŏngnam: Han'gukhak Chungang Yŏn'guwŏn Ch'ulp'anbu, 2017.

Kim Yŏnggŭn. "Rodong kyegŭp ŭi ttal Kang Churyong nyŏsŏng" [Woman Kang Churyong, the daughter of the working class]. *Chosŏn nyŏsŏng* 8 (August 1959): 26–28.

Kim Yukhun. *Minju konghwaguk Taehan Min'guk ŭi t'ansaeng* [The birth of a democratic republic, the Republic of Korea]. Seoul: Hyumŏnisŭt'ŭ, 2012.

Kim Yunhwan. *Han'guk nodong undongsa 1: Ilcheha p'yŏn* [A history of the Korean labor movement 1: The colonial period]. Seoul: Chŏngsa, 1981.

Kim Yunjŏng. "1930-yŏndae ch'o Pŏm T'aep'yŏngyang Nodong Chohap kyeyŏl ŭi hyŏngmyŏngjŏk nodong chohap undong" [The revolutionary trade union movement in the early 1930s by those affiliated with the Pan-Pacific Trade Union]. *Yŏksa yŏn'gu* 6 (December 1998): 127–66.

Komu Nodongja Hyŏbŭihoe (Council of Rubber Workers). *Komu nodongja t'ujaeng charyojip* [A sourcebook of rubber worker struggle]. Pusan: Komu Nodongja Hyŏbŭihoe, 1995.

Korean Labor Institute (KLI). *2003–18 KLI pijŏnggyujik nodong t'onggye* [2003–18 KLI labor statistics on irregular employment]. Sejong-si: KLI, 2018.

KSEC (Korea Shipbuilding and Engineering Corporation; Taehan Chosŏn Kongsa) Union archive. Unpublished document collection. Also available in *Taehan Chosŏn Kongsa Nodong Chohap hwaltong* [Activities of the KSEC Union], edited by Sŏnggonghoe Taehakkyo Nodongsa Yŏn'guso. P'aju: Han'guk Haksul Chŏngbo, 2014.

Kwak Kŏnhong. "1930-yŏndae ch'oban Chosŏn Chilso Piryo kongjang nodongja chojik undong" [The movement to organize workers at the Korea Nitrogen Fertilizer factory in the early 1930s]. *Yŏksa yŏn'gu* 4 (October 1995): 35–86.

———. *Ilche ŭi nodong chŏngch'aek kwa Chosŏn nodongja, 1938–1945* [Japanese colonial labor policy and Korean workers, 1938–1945]. Seoul: Sinsŏwŏn, 2001.

Kwŏn Chin'gwan. "1970-yŏndae sanŏp sŏn'gyo hwaltong kwa t'ŭkching" [Activities and characteristics of the industrial mission in the 1970s]. In Yi Chonggu et al., *1960–70-yŏndae nodongja ŭi chagŏpchang munhwa wa chŏngch'esŏng*, 199–231.

Kyŏnghyang sinmun [Kyunghyang Daily News] (Seoul, October 1946 to present).

Lim Chai Sung (Im Ch'aesŏng). *Senji keizai to tetsudō un'ei: "Shokuminchi" Chōsen kara "bundan" Kankoku e no rekishiteki keiro o saguru*. [Wartime economy and management of railways: Examining the historical path from the Korea "colony" to "divided" South Korea]. Tokyo: Tokyo University Press, 2005.

Nakao Michiko. "1950–52-yŏn Chosŏn Pangjik chaengŭi: Hyŏndae Han'guk nosa kwan'gye ŭi sŭt'at'ŭ lain" [The labor dispute at Chosŏn Spinning and Weaving from 1950 to 1952: The starting line of the industrial relations of South Korea]. MA thesis, Korea University, 1990.

——. "1950-yŏndae Han'guk nodong undong ŭi pun'gichŏm: Chosŏn Pangjik chaengŭi yŏn'gu" [The turning point of the 1950s South Korean labor movement: A study of the Chosŏn Spinning and Weaving dispute]. *Yŏksa pip'yŏng* 14 (February 1991): 151–57.

Nam Hwasook (Nam Hwasuk). "1920-yŏndae yŏsŏng undong esŏ ŭi hyŏptong chŏnsŏnnon kwa Kŭnuhoe" [United-front theory and the Kŭnuhoe in the 1920s women's movement]. MA thesis, Seoul National University, 1989.

——. "Kŭnuhoe undong" [The Kŭnuhoe movement]. In *Han'guk yŏsŏngsa* [Korean women's history], edited by Han'guk Yŏsŏngsa Yŏn'guhoe Yŏsŏngsa Punkwa (Women's History Division, Korean Women's History Research Society), 146–77. Seoul: P'ulpit, 1992.

National Statistical Office (T'onggyech'ŏng). *Chinan 20-yŏn'gan koyong sajŏng ŭi pyŏnhwa* [Comprehensive time series report on the economically active population survey]. Seoul: National Statistical Office, 1994.

O Hana. *Hakch'ul: 80-yŏndae kongjang ŭro kan taehaksaengdŭl* [Students turned worker activists: College students who went into factories in the 1980s]. Seoul: Imaejin, 2010.

O Miil. "1910–1920-yŏndae kongŏp palchŏn tan'gye wa Chosŏnin chabon'ga ch'ŭng ŭi chonjae yangsang: P'yŏngyang chiyŏk ŭl chungsim ŭro" [The stages of industrial development in the 1910s and 1920s and the conditions of the Korean capitalist class]. *Han'guksa yŏn'gu* 87 (December 1994): 193–233.

——. "1910–1920-yŏndae P'yŏngyang chiyŏk minjok undong kwa Chosŏnin chabon'ga ch'ŭng" [The nationalist movement in the Pyongyang region in the 1910s and 1920s and the Korean capitalist class]. *Yŏksa pip'yŏng* 30 (February 1995): 269–304.

——. "1920-yŏndae mal—1930-yŏndae Pusan-Kyŏngnam chiyŏk tang chaegŏn mit hyŏngmyŏngjŏk nodong undong ŭi chŏn'gae wa p'aŏp t'ujaeng" [The development of the movement to reconstruct the party and the revolutionary labor movement in the Pusan–South Kyŏngsang region from the end of the 1920s to the 1930s and the struggle through strikes]. In *Han'guk kŭnhyŏndae chiyŏk undongsa* [The modern and contemporary history of regional movements in South Korea], edited by Yŏksa Munje Yŏn'guso (Institute for Korean Historical Studies), 95–188. Seoul: Yŏgang Ch'ulp'ansa, 1993.

——. *Han'guk kŭndae chabon'ga yŏn'gu* [A study of capitalists in modern Korea]. Seoul: Hanul, 2002.

——. *Kŭndae Han'guk ŭi chabon'gadŭl* [The capitalists in modern Korea]. Seoul: P'urŭn Yŏksa, 2015.

——. "Pak Chinhong." *Yŏksa pip'yŏng* 21 (November 1992): 288–95.

——. "P'yŏngyang chiyŏk Chosŏnin chabon'gadŭl ŭi chohap chojik kwa kongŏp paltal" [Cooperatives organized by Korean capitalists and the industrial development in the Pyongyang area]. *Han'guksa yŏn'gu* 137 (June 2007): 109–42.

O Miran and An Chin. *Minju changjŏng 100-yŏn, Kwangju Chŏnnam chiyŏk sahoe undong yŏn'gu: Yŏsŏng undong* [A one-hundred-year journey toward democracy, a study of social movements in Kwangju and the South Chŏlla region: The women's movement]. Yangp'yŏng: Hyumŏn K'ŏlch'yŏ Arirang, 2015.

Pae Sŏngman. "'Chobang sakŏn' ŭi chŏngch'ijŏk koch'al" [A political examination of the "Chobang incident"]. *Hangdo Pusan* 25 (2009): 179–211.

——. "Haebang hu Chosŏn Pangjik ŭi kyŏngyŏng kwa kŭ sŏnggyŏk" [The management of Chosŏn Spinning and Weaving after liberation and its characteristics]. *Chiyŏk kwa yŏksa* 9 (2001): 81–108.

Pak Chaehwa. "1930-yŏn Chosŏn Pangjik nodongjadŭl ŭi p'aŏp yŏn'gu" [A study of the 1930 strike by Chosŏn Spinning and Weaving workers]. MA thesis, Pusan Women's University, 1993.

Pak Ch'ansŭng. *Taehan Min'guk ŭn minju konghwaguk ida* [The Republic of Korea is a democratic republic]. Seoul: Tolbegae, 2013.

Pak Minna. *Kasi ch'ŏlmang wi ŭi nŏngk'ul changmi* [Rose vines over barbed wire]. Seoul: Chisik ŭi Nalgae, 2004.

Pak Sŏryŏn. *Ch'egongnyŏ Kang Churyong* [Woman-in-the-sky Kang Churyong]. Seoul: Han'gyŏre Ch'ulp'an, 2018.

Pak Sujŏng. *Sumgyŏjin Han'guk yŏsŏng ŭi yŏksa* [A hidden history of Korean women]. Seoul: Arŭmdaun Saramdŭl, 2004.

Pak Sŭngdon. "Han'guk komu kongŏp 50-yŏn sosa 1" [A short history of the fifty years of the Korean rubber industry 1]. *Komu kisul hyŏphoeji* [Elastomers and Composites] 4, no. 1 (1969): 8–11.

Pak Sunsŏp. "1920–30-yŏndae Chŏng Ch'ilsŏng ŭi sahoejuŭi undong kwa yŏsŏng haebangnon" [Chŏng Ch'ilsŏng's socialist activism and theory of women's liberation in the 1920s and 1930s]. *Yŏsŏng kwa yŏksa* 26 (2017): 245–69.

Pak Yŏnggi and Kim Chŏnghan. *Han'guk nodong undongsa 3: Migunjŏnggi ŭi nodong kwan'gye wa nodong undong, 1945–1948* [The history of the Korean labor movement 3: Industrial relations and the labor movement in the US military occupation period, 1945–48]. Seoul: Chisik Madang, 2004.

Pak Yongok. *Han'guk yŏsŏng hangil undongsa yŏn'gu* [A study of anticolonial activism among Korean women]. Seoul: Chisik Sanŏpsa, 1996.

Pak Yuhŭi. "Ttosuni, nakkwan kwa t'onghap ŭi kyŏngjejŏk yŏsŏng chuch'e" [Ttosuni, a female economic subject of optimism and integration]. In *Ttosuni: The Birth of Happiness*, edited by the Korean Film Archive, 12–17. Seoul: Korean Film Archive, 2013.

Ri Kiyŏng. *Wŏlhŭi*. In *1930-yŏndae hŭigoksŏn* [Selected playscripts from the 1930s], 19–106. Pyongyang: Munhak Yesul Ch'ulp'ansa, 2008. Originally serialized in *Chosŏn chi Kwang* 1–7 (1929).

Sin Chubaek. "'Minju konghwaje' ron kwa pi chabonjuŭi rŭl chihyanghan 'minjokchuŭi' undong chwap'a' (1919–45)" [The "left wing of the nationalist movement" that pursued democratic republicanism and noncapitalism, 1919–1945]. *Yŏksa wa hyŏnsil* 108 (June 2018): 91–140.

Sin Illyŏng. *Na ŭi inyŏn iyagi* [Tales of connections I have had]. Seoul: Chisik Kongjakso, 2016.

——. *Nodongpŏp kwa nodong undong* [Labor laws and the labor movement]. Seoul: Irwŏl Sŏgak, 1987.

Sin Wŏnch'ŏl. "Chŏnsi nomu tongwŏn kwa kŭ yusan: Koyong kwan'gye rŭl chungsim ŭro" [Wartime labor mobilization and its legacies: Focusing on the employment relations]. In Yi Chonggu et al., *1950-yŏndae Han'guk nodongja ŭi saenghwal segye*, 166–206.

——. "Kiŏp naebu nodong sijang ŭi hyŏngsŏng kwa chŏn'gae: Han'guk chosŏn sanŏp e kwanhan sarye yŏn'gu" [The formation and evolution of firm internal labor

markets: A case study of the shipbuilding industry in South Korea]. PhD diss., Seoul National University, 2001.
Sŏ Chiyŏng. *Kyŏngsŏng ŭi modŏn kŏl: Sobi, nodong, chendŏ ro pon singminji kŭndae* [Modern girls of Seoul: The colonial modern seen through consumerism, labor, and gender]. Seoul: Yŏiyŏn, 2013.
Sŏ Chŏngja, ed. *In'gan munje (oe)* [The human predicament and other writings]. P'aju: Pŏmusa, 2005.
Sŏ Chungsŏk. "Yi Sŭngman chŏngkwŏn ch'ogi ŭi ilminjuŭi wa p'asijŭm" [The ideology of One-people-ism and fascism during the early years of the Syngman Rhee regime]. In *1950-yŏndae Nambukhan ŭi sŏnt'aek kwa kulchŏl* [Choices and refractions of South and North Korea in the 1950s], edited by Yŏksa Munje Yŏn'guso (Institute for Korean Historical Studies), 17–71. Seoul: Yŏksa Pip'yŏngsa, 1998.
Sŏ Chunsŏk, ed. *Mising ŭn tolgo toragane* [The sewing machine is spinning and spinning]. Seoul: Sŏul Yŏksa P'yŏnch'anwŏn, 2016.
Sŏ Hyŏngsil. "Singminji sidae yŏsŏng nodong undong e kwanhan yŏn'gu: 1930-yŏndae chŏnban'gi komu chep'um chejoŏp kwa chesaŏp ŭl chungsim ŭro" [A study of the women's labor movement under Japanese colonial rule: Focusing on rubber products manufacturing and silk-reeling industries in the first half of the 1930s]. MA thesis, Ewha Womans University, 1989.
Sŏ Munsŏk. "1960-yŏndae taep'yojŏk kwisok kiŏpch'e, Chosŏn Pangjik Pusan kongjang ŭi mollak" [The decline of the Chosŏn Spinning and Weaving Pusan factory, a representative vested company in the 1960s]. *Kyŏngyŏng sahak* 26, no. 3 (September 2011): 333–60.
Song Chiyŏng. "1930-yŏn P'yŏngyang komu kongjang nodongjadŭl ŭi p'aŏp" [Strikes by rubber factory workers in Pyongyang in 1930] (1959). In *Pukhan hakkye ŭi 1920, 30-yŏndae minjok haebang undong yŏn'gu* [The study in North Korean academia of the movement for national liberation during the 1920s and 1930s], edited by Kim Kyŏngil, 235–53. Seoul: Ch'angjak kwa Pip'yŏngsa, 1989.
Song Chongnae, Yi Tŏkchae, Yi Uhyŏn, Chŏng Chuyŏn, and Kang Sinjun. *Han'guk nodong undongsa 4: Chŏngbu suripki ŭi nodong undong, 1948–1961* [The history of the Korean labor movement 4: The labor movement of the period of the founding of the state, 1948–1961]. Seoul: Chisik Madang, 2004.
Song Kiyŏk. "Arŭmdaun t'ujŏng: Kat'ollik Nodong Ch'ŏngnyŏnhoe" [Beautiful complaints: Young Catholic Workers]. https://iminju.tistory.com/717. Seoul: Korea Democracy Foundation, 2011.
Song Yŏng. *O Suhyang* [O Suhyang]. In *Ilche kangjŏmgi Han'guk nodong sosŏlsŏn* [A collection of Korean labor novels from the colonial period], vol. 2, edited by An Sŭnghyŏn, 111–51. Seoul: Pogosa, 1995. Originally serialized in *Chosun ilbo*, March 1–26, 1931.
Sŏnggonghoe Taehakkyo Nodongsa Yŏn'guso (Labor History Institute, Sungkonghoe University). *Han'guk sanŏp nodongja ŭi hyŏngsŏng kwa saenghwal segye yŏn'gu: Nodongsa ak'aibŭ kuch'uk kwa saenghwalsa yŏn'gu rŭl chungsim ŭro* [A study of the formation and the life worlds of industrial workers in South Korea: Focusing on the establishment of a labor history archive and life history study]. Oral history recordings and transcripts, 2002–5.
———, ed. *Chŏn'guk Ch'ŏlto Nodong Chohap hwaltong* [Activities of the National Railway Workers' Union]. 80 vols. Han'guk nodongsa charyo ch'ongsŏ [The Korean labor history collection] series. P'aju: Han'guk Haksul Chŏngbo, 2014.
———, ed. *Taehan Chosŏn Kongsa Nodong Chohap hwaltong* [Activities of the Korea Shipbuilding and Engineering Corporation (KSEC) Union]. 63 vols. Han'guk

nodongsa charyo ch'ongsŏ [The Korean labor history collection] series. P'aju: Han'guk Haksul Chŏngbo, 2014.
Sonobe Hiroyuki. "Zaicho Nihonjin no sanka shita kyosanshugi undo: 1930-nendai ni okeru" [The Communist movement in which Japanese in Korea participated: On the 1930s]. Chōsenshi kenkyūkai ronbunshū 26 (1989): 213-39.
T'ae Hyesuk and Im Okhŭi. Han'guk ŭi singminji kŭndae wa yŏsŏng konggan [Colonial modernity and female space in South Korea]. Seoul: Yŏsŏng Munhwa Iron Yŏn'guso, 2004.
T'ak Hŭijun. Han'guk ŭi imgŭm munje wa imgŭm chŏngch'aek [The wage question and wage policies in South Korea]. Seoul: Sŏnggyun'gwan Taehakkyo Nodong Munje Yŏn'guwŏn, 1966.
Yi Chŏkhyo. "Ch'ongdongwŏn" [Total mobilization]. In Ilche kangjŏmgi Han'guk nodong sosŏlsŏn [A collection of Korean labor novels from the colonial period], vol. 2, edited by An Sŭnghyŏn, 213-37. Seoul: Pogosa, 1995. Originally serialized in Pip'an 3-4, 5, and 6 (1931).
Yi Chonggu, Kang Namsik, Kwŏn Chin'gwan, Kim Kyŏnghŭi, Pak Haegwang, Im Kyuch'an, Chang Migyŏng, Chang Sangch'ŏl, and Han Honggu. 1960-70-yŏndae nodongja ŭi chagŏpchang munhwa wa chŏngch'esŏng [Workplace culture and worker identities in the 1960s and 1970s]. P'aju: Hanul, 2006
Yi Chonggu, Pak Chunyŏp, Kim Wŏn, Sin Wŏnch'ŏl, Kim Chun, Kim Kyŏngil, Kim Hyŏnsŏn, Yi Hŭiyŏng, and Kim Sunyŏng. 1950-yŏndae Han'guk nodongja ŭi saenghwal segye [The life worlds of Korean workers in the 1950s]. P'aju: Hanul, 2010.
Yi Chŏngok. "Ilcheha kongŏp nodong esŏ ŭi minjok kwa sŏng, 1910-1945" [Ethnicity and gender in industrial labor under Japanese colonial rule, 1910-1945]. PhD diss., Seoul National University, 1990.
Yi Chŏngsŏn. "Kŭndae Han'guk ŭi 'yŏsŏng' chuch'e: Kip'yo ŭi kakch'uk ŭl t'onghae pon Ilche sigi yŏsŏng kaenyŏm" ["Women" subjects in modern Korea: The concept of women under Japanese colonial rule seen through competing signifiers]. Kaenyŏm kwa sot'ong 19 (June 2017): 93-137.
Yi Chŏngŭn. "1950-yŏndae nodong chibae damnon kwa nodongja ŭi taeŭng" [The dominant discourse on labor and the response of workers in the 1950s]. Yŏksa pip'yŏng 83 (May 2008): 152-75.
Yi Ch'ungnyŏl. Kŭrim ŭro ingnŭn Han'guk kŭndae ŭi p'unggyŏng [Scenes of Korean modernity read through pictures]. P'aju: Kimyŏngsa, 2011.
Yi Chunsik. Chosŏn kongsandang sŏngnip kwa hwaltong [The founding and activities of the Korean Communist Party]. Ch'ŏnan: Tongnip Kinyŏmgwan, 2009.
Yi Horyong. Han'guk ŭi anak'ijŭm: Sasang p'yŏn [Anarchism in Korea: On thoughts]. P'aju: Chisik Sanŏpsa, 2001.
———. Han'guk ŭi anak'ijŭm: Undong p'yŏn [Anarchism in Korea: On the movement]. P'aju: Chisik Sanŏpsa, 2015.
Yi Hŭiyŏng. "1950-yŏndae yŏsŏng nodongja wa 'kongjang nodong' ŭi sahoejŏk ŭimi: Kwangju Chŏnnam Pangjik kusul sarye rŭl chungsim ŭro" [1950s female workers and the social meaning of "factory labor": Focusing on the oral testimonies of Chŏnnam Spinning and Weaving workers in Kwangju]. Sanŏp nodong yŏn'gu 14, no. 1 (2008): 165-206.
Yi Hyojae. "Ilcheha ŭi yŏsŏng nodong munje" [The female labor question during the colonial period]. In Han'guk nodong munje ŭi insik [Understanding the labor question in South Korea], edited by Kim Yunhwan, 131-79. Seoul: Tongnyŏk, 1983.

Yi Hyŏnju. "Ilcheha (Suyang) Tonguhoe ŭi minjok undong kwa Sin'ganhoe" [The nationalist movement of the (Suyang) Tonguhoe and the Sin'ganhoe under Japanese colonial rule]. *Chŏngsin munhwa yŏn'gu* 26, no. 3 (Autumn 2003): 185–209.
Yi Imha. "1970-yŏndae K'ŭrisŭch'yan Ak'ademi sakŏn yŏn'gu" [A study of the Christian Academy incident in the 1970s]. In Ch'a Sŏnghwan et al., *1970-yŏndae minjung undong yŏn'gu*, 525–607.
———. *Yŏsŏng, chŏnjaeng ŭl nŏmŏ irŏsŏda* [Women, rising up, putting the war behind]. Seoul: Sŏhae Munjip, 2004.
Yi Kihun. *Ch'ŏngnyŏn a ch'ŏngnyŏn a uri ch'ŏngnyŏn a* [Youth, youth, oh, our youth]. Seoul: Tolbegae, 2014.
Yi Kilsŏng, Kim Hansang, and Kong Yŏngmin. *Kim Sŭngho: Abŏji ŭi ŏlgul, Han'guk yŏnghwa ŭi ch'osang* [title in English: *Kim Seung-ho: Face of Father, Portrait of Korean Cinema*]. Seoul: Korean Film Archive, 2007.
Yi Kyŏngsŏk, Yi Ch'anggŭn, Yu Sŭngha, Hŭijŏng, Kim Sŏnghŭi, Ha Chonggang, Ma Yŏngsin, et al. *Sŏm kwa sŏm ŭl itta 1* [Connecting islands 1]. Seoul: Han'gyŏre Ch'ulp'an, 2014.
Yi Kyunyŏng. *Sin'ganhoe yŏn'gu* [A study of the Sin'ganhoe]. Seoul: Yŏksa Pip'yŏngsa, 1993.
Yi Okchi. *Han'guk yŏsŏng nodongja undongsa 1* [The history of the Korean women workers' movement 1]. Seoul: Hanul, 2001.
Yi Sanggyŏng. *Han'guk kŭndae yŏsŏng munhaksaron* [A study of the history of modern Korean women's literature]. Seoul: Somyŏng Ch'ulp'an, 2002.
———. *Im Sundŭk: Taeanjŏk yŏsŏng chuch'e rŭl hyanghayŏ* [Im Sundŭk: Toward an alternative feminist subject]. Seoul: Somyŏng Ch'ulp'an, 2009.
———. "Kang Kyŏngae munhak ŭi kukchejuŭi ŭi wŏnch'ŏn ŭrosŏ ŭi Manju ch'ehŏm" [Kang Kyŏngae's experience in Manchuria: The source of proletarian internationalism]. *Hyŏndae sosŏl yŏn'gu* 66 (2017): 337–82.
Yi Sangŭi. *Ilcheha Chosŏn ŭi nodong chŏngch'aek yŏn'gu* [A study of labor policies in colonial Korea]. Seoul: Hyean, 2006.
———. "Ilcheha Miguk yuhaksaeng ŭi chabonjuŭi kŭndaehwaron kwa nodonggwan" [Theories of capitalist modernization and views on labor among students who studied in the United States in the colonial period]. In *Cheguk ŭi kwŏllyŏk kwa singmin ŭi chisik* [The power of empire and colonial knowledge], edited by Ch'oe Kyujin, 411–56. Seoul: Sŏnin, 2015.
Yi Songhŭi. "Ilcheha Pusan chiyŏk pangjik kongjang komu kongjang yŏsŏng nodongjadŭl ŭi chaengŭi yŏn'gu" [A study of labor disputes by female workers in textile and rubber factories in the Pusan region in the colonial period]. *Ihwa sahak yŏn'gu* 30 (2003): 365–88.
Yi Suae, Han Sinae, Pak Namsun, and Song Kyŏngja. *Chŏnnam yŏsŏng 100-yŏn* [Women of South Chŏlla, a hundred years]. Seoul: Tajiri, 2004.
Yi Wŏnbo. *Han'guk nodong undongsa 5: Kyŏngje kaebalgi ŭi nodong undong, 1961– 1987* [The history of the labor movement in South Korea 5: The labor movement of the period of economic development, 1961–1987]. Seoul: Chisik Madang, 2004.
Yi Yunjŏng. "O-wŏl Kwangju hangjaeng ŭi Songbaekhoe undong e kwanhan yŏn'gu" [A study of the movement of the Songbaek Society in the May Kwangju struggle]. PhD diss., Chosun University, 2012.
Yokota Nobuko. *Kankoku no toshi kasō to rōdōsha: Rōdō no hiseikika o chūshin ni* [The urban substratum and workers in South Korea: Focusing on the irregularization of labor]. Tokyo: Mineruba Shobō, 2012.

Yu Kyŏngsun. *Arŭmdaun yŏndae: Tŭlpul chŏrŏm t'aorŭn 1985-yŏn Kuro tongmaeng p'aŏp* [A beautiful alliance: The 1985 Kuro solidarity strike that flared up like a wildfire]. Seoul: Meidei, 2007.

———. "Chendŏ kwan'gye esŏ pon 1970-yŏndae minju nojo ŭi yuhyŏngbyŏl t'ŭksŏng" [Characteristics of the 1970s democratic unions by type seen through gender relations]. *Kiŏk kwa chŏnmang* 36 (2017): 95–151.

———. "Ch'ŏnggye P'ibok Nodong Chohap ŭi hwaltong kwa tŭkching" [Activities and characteristics of the Ch'ŏnggye Garment Union]. In Ch'a Sŏnghwan et al., *1970-yŏndae minjung undong yŏn'gu*, 97–191.

———. "Haksaeng undonggadŭl ŭi nodong undong chamyŏ yangsang kwa yŏnghyang: 1970-yŏndae rŭl chungsim ŭro" [Student activists' participation in the labor movement and its effect: Focusing on the 1970s]. *Kiŏk kwa chŏnmang* 29 (2013): 52–96.

———, ed. *Na, yŏsŏng nodongja 1: 1970–80-yŏndae minju nojo wa hamkke han sam ŭl malhanda* [I, a female worker 1: Speaking of my life spent in democratic unions in the 1970s and 1980s]. Seoul: Kŭrinbi, 2011.

———, ed. *Na, yŏsŏng nodongja 2: 2000-yŏndae onŭl pijŏnggyujik sam ŭl malhanda* [I, a female worker 2: Speaking of the irregular worker's life today in the 2000s]. Seoul: Kŭrinbi, 2011.

———. "Nodong chohap ŭi chidoryŏk kwa chendŏ chŏngch'i: Ch'ŏnggye P'ibok Nojo ŭi yŏsŏng chidoryŏk hyŏngsŏng sido wa chwajŏl" [Leadership and gender politics in trade unions: The attempt and failure to establish female leadership in the Ch'ŏnggye Garment Union]. *Yŏksa munje yŏn'gu* 38 (October 2017): 407–48.

Yun Chŏngnan. "Singminji sidae chesa kongjang yŏgongdŭl ŭi kŭndaejŏgin chaa ŭisik sŏngjang kwa nodong chaengŭi ŭi pyŏnhwa kwajŏng: 1920–1930-yŏndae chŏnban'gi rŭl chungsim ŭro" [The growth of modern self-consciousness among silk-reeling factory female workers and the changes in their labor disputes in the colonial period: Focusing on the 1920s and the first half of the 1930s]. *Tamnon 201 9*, no. 2 (2006): 37–76.

Yun Kyŏngno. *105-in sakŏn kwa Sinminhoe yŏn'gu* [A study of the 105-person incident and the Sinminhoe]. Seoul: Ilchisa, 1990.

English-Language Sources

This section contains primary and secondary source materials written in English.

Anderson, Benedict. *The Age of Globalization: Anarchists and the Anticolonial Imagination*. London: Verso, 2005.

Barraclough, Ruth. *Factory Girl Literature: Sexuality, Violence and Representation in Industrialising Korea*. Berkeley: University of California Press, 2012.

———. "Red Love and Betrayal in the Making of North Korea: Comrade Hŏ Jŏng-suk." *History Workshop Journal* 77 (Spring 2014): 86–102.

Chakrabarty, Dipesh. *Rethinking Working-Class History: Bengal 1890–1940*. Princeton, NJ: Princeton University Press, 1989.

Cheon, Jung-Hwan (Chŏn Chŏnghwan). "Untimely Death and Martyrdom after May 1980: Suicide in the South Korean Democracy Movement Seen through the Case of Pak Sŭnghŭi." In Kim et al., *Beyond Death*, 231–59.

Cho, Wha Soon (Cho Hwasun). *Let the Weak Be Strong: A Woman's Struggle for Justice*. Bloomington, IN: Meyer-Stone, 1988.

Chun, Jennifer Jihye. "Legal Liminality: The Gender and Labour Politics of Organizing South Korea's Irregular Workforce." *Third World Quarterly* 30, no. 3 (2009): 535–50.
——. *Organizing at the Margins: The Symbolic Politics of Labor in South Korea and the United States*. Ithaca, NY: Cornell University Press, 2009.
Chun, Soonok (Chŏn Sunok). *They Are Not Machines: Korean Women Workers and Their Fight for Democratic Trade Union in the 1970s*. Aldershot, UK: Ashgate, 2003.
Cumings, Bruce. *Korea's Place in the Sun: A Modern History*. New York: W. W. Norton, 2005.
Eckert, Carter J. *Offspring of Empire: The Koch'ang Kims and the Colonial Origins of Korean Capitalism, 1876–1945*. Seattle: University of Washington Press, 1991.
Frader, Laura Levine. *Breadwinners and Citizens: Gender in the Making of the French Social Model*. Durham, NC: Duke University Press, 2008.
Glickman, Lawrence B. *A Living Wage: American Workers and the Making of Consumer Society*. Ithaca, NY: Cornell University Press, 1997.
Gordon, Andrew. *The Evolution of Labor Relations in Japan: Heavy Industry, 1853–1955*. Cambridge, MA: Harvard University Press, 1985.
Hein, Laura E. *Fueling Growth: The Energy Revolution and Economic Policy in Postwar Japan*. Cambridge, MA: Council on East Asian Studies, Harvard University, 1990.
Hwang, Dongyoun. *Anarchism in Korea: Independence, Transnationalism, and the Question of National Development, 1919–1984*. Albany: State University of New York Press, 2016.
Jung, Byung Wook (Chŏng Pyŏnguk). "Migrant Labor and Massacres: A Comparison of the 1923 Massacre of Koreans and Chinese during the Great Kando Earthquake and the 1931 Anti-Chinese Riots and Massacre of Chinese in Colonial Korea." *Cross-Currents: East Asian History and Culture Review* 22 (March 2017): 30–53. http://cross-currents.berkeley.edu/e-journal/issue-22/jung.
Jung-Kim, Jennifer. "Gender and Modernity in Colonial Korea." PhD diss., University of California Los Angeles, 2005.
Kessler-Harris, Alice. *In Pursuit of Equity: Women, Men, and the Quest for Economic Citizenship in 20th-Century America*. New York: Oxford University Press, 2001.
——. *A Woman's Wage: Historical Meanings and Social Consequences*. 2nd ed. Lexington: University Press of Kentucky, 2014.
Kim, Charles R., Jungwon Kim, Hwasook Nam, and Serk-Bae Suh, eds. *Beyond Death: The Politics of Suicide and Martyrdom in Korea*. Seattle: University of Washington Press, 2019.
Kim, Janice C. H. *To Live to Work: Factory Women in Colonial Korea, 1910–1945*. Stanford, CA: Stanford University Press, 2009.
Kim, Seung-Kyung. *Class Struggle or Family Struggle? The Lives of Women Factory Workers in South Korea*. Cambridge: Cambridge University Press, 1997.
Kim, Sun-Chul. "The Construction of Martyrdom and Self-Immolation in South Korea." In Kim et al., *Beyond Death*, 202–30.
Konishi, Sho. *Anarchist Modernity: Cooperatism and Japanese-Russian Intellectual Relations in Modern Japan*. Cambridge, MA: Harvard University Asia Center, 2013.
Koo, Hagen. *Korean Workers: The Culture and Politics of Class Formation*. Ithaca, NY: Cornell University Press, 2001.
Koo, Hagen, Keong-il Kim (Kim Kyŏngil), and Jun Kim (Kim Chun), eds. *Modern Korean Labor: A Sourcebook*. Sŏngnam: Academy of Korean Studies, 2015.
Kwon, Nayoung Aimee. *Intimate Empire: Collaboration and Colonial Modernity in Korea and Japan*. Durham, NC: Duke University Press, 2015.
Land, Hilary. "The Family Wage." *Feminist Review* 6 (1980): 55–77.

Lee, Namhee. *The Making of Minjung: Democracy and the Politics of Representation in South Korea*. Ithaca, NY: Cornell University Press, 2007.
Lee, Yoonkyung. "Sky Protest: New Forms of Labour Resistance in Neo-Liberal Korea." *Journal of Contemporary Asia* 45, no. 3 (2015): 443–64. doi: 10.1080/00472336.2015.1012647.
Mackie, Vera. *Creating Socialist Women in Japan: Gender, Labor, and Activism, 1900–1937*. Cambridge: Cambridge University Press, 1997.
Moon, Seungsook. *Militarized Modernity and Gendered Citizenship in South Korea*. Durham, NC: Duke University Press, 2005.
Nam, Hwasook. *Building Ships, Building a Nation: Korea's Democratic Unionism under Park Chung Hee*. Seattle: University of Washington Press, 2009.
——. "Narratives of Women Workers in South Korea's Minju Union Movement of the 1970s." *Review of Korean Studies* 12, no. 4 (December 2009): 13–36.
——. "Reading Chun Tae-il: Making Sense of a Worker Self-Immolation in 1970s South Korea." In Kim et al., *Beyond Death*, 167–201.
——. "Shin In-ryung" [Sin Illyŏng]. In *Intellectuals in Dark Years*, edited by Henry Em, Youngju Ryu, and John Duncan. Ann Arbor: University of Michigan Press, forthcoming.
——. "Shipyard Women and the Politics of Gender: A Case Study of the KSEC Yard in South Korea." In *Gender and Labor in Korea and Japan: Sexing Class*, edited by Elyssa Faison and Ruth Barraclough, 78–102. London: Routledge, 2009.
Notar, Ernest J. "Japan's Wartime Labor Policy: A Search for Method." *Journal of Asian Studies* 44, no. 2 (February 1985): 311–28.
O, Won-chol (O Wŏnchŏl). *The Korea Story: President Park Jung-hee's Leadership and the Korean Industrial Revolution*. Seoul: Wisdom Tree, 2009.
Ogle, George E. *South Korea: Dissent within the Economic Miracle*. London: Zed, 1990.
Park, Albert L. *Building a Heaven on Earth: Religion, Activism, and Protest in Japanese Occupied Korea*. Honolulu: University of Hawai'i Press, 2015.
Park, Soon-Won. "Colonial Industrial Growth and the Emergence of the Korean Working Class." In *Colonial Modernity in Korea*, edited by Gi-Wook Shin and Michael Edson Robinson, 128–60. Cambridge, MA: Harvard University Asia Center, 1999.
Park, Sunyoung. *The Proletarian Wave: Literature and Leftist Culture in Colonial Korea, 1910–1945*. Cambridge, MA: Harvard University Asia Center, 2015.
Parr, Joy. *The Gender of Breadwinners: Women, Men, and Change in Two Industrial Towns, 1880–1950*. Toronto: University of Toronto Press, 1990.
Perry, Samuel. *Recasting Red Culture in Proletarian Japan: Childhood, Korea, and the Historical Avant-Garde*. Honolulu: University of Hawai'i Press, 2014.
Robinson, Michael E. *Cultural Nationalism in Colonial Korea, 1920–1925*. Seattle: University of Washington Press, 1988.
Saguchi, Kazurō. "The Historical Significance of the Industrial Patriotic Association: Labor Relations in the Total-war State." In *Total War and "Modernization,"* edited by Yasushi Yamanouchi, J. Victor Koschmann, and Ryuichi Narita, 261–87. Ithaca, NY: Cornell University Press, 1998.
Self, Robert O. *All in the Family: The Realignment of American Democracy since the 1960s*. New York: Hill & Wang, 2012.
Song, Jiyeoun. *Inequality in the Workplace: Labor Market Reform in Japan and Korea*. Ithaca, NY: Cornell University Press, 2014.
Spencer, Robert. *Yogong: Factory Girl*. Seoul: RAS, 1988.
Standing, Guy. "Global Feminization through Flexible Labor: A Theme Revisited." *World Development* 27 (1999): 583–602.

Weinbaum, Alys Eve, ed. *The Modern Girl around the World: Consumption, Modernity, and Globalization*. Durham, NC: Duke University Press, 2008.

Yi Chongnae. "Damage Compensation Claims and Provisional Attachment: The Context and Problems." Paper presented at "'Sky Protest' and 'Hope Bus': The South Korean Labor Movement Confronts Neoliberal Restructuring" workshop, University of Washington, April 17, 2017.

Yokota, Nobuko. "A New Attempt at Organizing Irregular Workers in Korea: Examining the Activities of the Korean Women's Trade Union." *Korean Journal of Sociology* 48, no. 6 (December 2014): 73–93.

Yoo, Theodore Jun. *The Politics of Gender in Colonial Korea: Education, Labor, and Health, 1910–1945*. Berkeley: University of California Press, 2008.

Yu-Lee, Jiwoon. "Expressive Struggles: Neoliberal Temporalities and the Social Reproduction of Feminized Labor in South Korea." PhD diss., University of Washington, 2018.

Index

Page numbers in italics refer to figures.

Alinsky, Saul, 135, 233n96, 234n98
An Chaehong, 98
An Ch'angho, 33, 70, 97, 198n104, 198nn100–101, 199n108, 200n113
An Chongu, 85–86, 93–94, 102–7, 220n35, 221n50
An Hosang, 97
anarchist movement, 21, 27, 33, 76, 193n49, 196n79, 215n60, 216nn65–66; bourgeois nationalists and, 79–81, 98–99; trade unions and, 78–79
anarcho-communists, 78–80, 196n79, 215n62, 216n76
anarcho-syndicalists, 78–80, 98–99, 196n79, 196n82, 215n60, 215n62
anticommunism, 9, 93, 173, 190n10, 236n117; colonial period, 37, 41, 54–55, 82–83; in right-wing labor organizing, 93–99
April Revolution of 1960, 86, 105, 111
arrests, 16–17, 75, 82, 103, 208n53, 208n57, 218n10, 236n117. *See also* prison conditions
asa tongmaeng, 66. *See also* hunger strikes
Asian Christian Council, 135
Asian financial crisis (1997–98), 10, 157, 168, 183

Bolsheviks, 193n49, 202n5
bourgeois nationalist movement, 9, 14, 27–28, 30; anarchists and, 80–81, 98–99; equality and, 98–99; rural areas and, 76–78; socialists and, 49–51, 76, 215n50; *suyang* and, 33–35; US occupation and, 97. *See also* Protestant nationalist movement

capitalist class system, 27–28, 41, 80–82, 160, 205. *See also* Christian capitalist elite
capitalist development, 19–22, 34, 81, 99, 106, 129. *See also* nation-building
Cardijn, Joseph, 131
Ch'a Kwangho, 246n80, 248n100
Chang Chaebong, 95, 100, 222n65
Chang Hyŏnja, 138, 234n107

chemical industry workers, 42, 121, 154, 192n34, 194n58
Cheonggye Garment Workers' Union, 130, 132–33, 138, 141, 143–44, 230n59, 232n78, 236n116, 237n132
"chimney man" incidents, 15, 45, 82–83, 190n15, 191n17
Cho Chisong, 234n101
Cho Mansik, 35–36, 78, 189n2, 200n113, 200n116
Cho Pongam, 201n4
Cho Pyŏngok, 97, 199n108, 221n52, 222n53
Cho Sinsŏng, 37, 50, 206n37
Cho Wha Soon, 239n150
Cho Yŏngnae, 129–30, 172
Cho Yŏngok, 9, 37–38, 41–43, 45, 49–51, 53–56, 58, 73
Chobang labor dispute (1951–52), 9–10, 55, 85–86, 99–105, 224n91, 224n93; legacies of, 105–10; women's activism in, 86, 90, 104–5
Chobang textile factory: history of labor activism, 87–99, 102, 218n17; Rhee and, 223n84; sale of, 105–6, 222n63, 223n69; scholarship on, 222n61. *See also* Chobang labor dispute; Chosŏn Spinning and Weaving
Ch'oe Sunyŏng, 138, 149, 234n107, 236n116
Ch'oe Yongdŏk, 17–18, 41–43, 68, 75–76, 81, 192n33
Chokchŏng (National Youth Corps), 97, 99
Chŏn Chinhan, 95–96, 99, 102–7
Chŏndogyo, 49, 77, 199n107
Chŏng Ch'ilsŏng, 47–48, 50, 204n29, 206n37
Chŏng Chongmyŏng, 48, 204n25, 206n37, 209n64, 213n23
Chŏng Hojong, 94–95, 100–101, 105, 222n65
Chŏng Hyangja, 127–28, 136, 149, 161
Chŏng Insuk, 132–33
Chŏng Pisŏk, *Chayu puin*, 114, 225n3
Chŏng Talhŏn, 39–45, 49, 52, 73, 75, 201nn3–4, 216n73
Chŏn'guk Nohyŏp, 225n1

267

INDEX

Chongyŏn Spinning (Chongyŏn Pangjŏk; Kanegafuchi Spinning; Kanebō), 55, 88, 232n86

Chŏnnam Silk Reeling, 136, 149, 161

Chŏnnam Spinning and Weaving (Chŏnnam Pangjik), 108, 134, 233n86

Chŏnp'yŏng (National Council of Korean Labor Unions), 55, 92–93, 97, 99, 130, 219nn25–26, 220n37, 221n50, 224n103, 226n13

Chōsen Chisso, 40, 42

Chosŏn Heavy Industries, 94, 220n35. See also Korea Shipbuilding and Engineering Corporation

Chosŏn Nodong Kongjehoe (Korean Workers Mutual Aid Association), 27, 78

Chosŏn Silk, 55, 101

Chosŏn (Chōsen) Spinning and Weaving (Chosŏn Pangjik; Chobang; Chōbō), 9–10, 55, 74–75, 85, 88, 197n84, 223n84. See also Chobang labor dispute

Christian Academy, 131, 137–40, 146, 148–49, 233n96, 234n98, 234n107, 235n111, 235nn114–16, 239n151

Christian capitalist elite, 32–37, 57, 68, 97, 198n100. See also Protestant nationalist movement

Christian feminists, 49. See also feminism

Christian labor activism, 131–37. See also Christian Academy; JOC Korea; UIM

Christian reform movement, 199n110

Christian Rural Research Association, 78, 200n116

Christian Social Action Council, 233n96

Christian socialism, 27, 33, 35–36, 78, 135, 200n116

Chu Kilja, 143–44

Chu Sejuk, 48–49, 202n4, 210n65

Chu Yohan, 34–35, 193n46, 199n105, 199n108, 213n29

Chu Yŏngha, 40

Chu Yosŏp, 20, 193n46

Chun Doo-Hwan, 152

Chun Tae-il: biography of, 129–30, 172; labor activism, 234n104; as male hero, 162; suicide protest, 113, 128–32, 136–37, 141, 156

Chungnakhoe, 89

citizen subjects, 99, 115–16, 198n99

class consciousness, 145; gendered, 113, 138; in literature, 210n74; of women workers, 2, 13, 51–56, 62, 74, 84, 162, 189n3, 196n78, 238m133

class ideologies, 4–7, 24, 48–56, 76, 239n150. See also capitalist class system; communism; Marxism-Leninism; red union movement; socialist labor activism

Cold War, 4, 96

colonial era labor movement, 4, 7, 9, 12–84; militancy, 16–17, 26, 64–70, 73, 75–76, 113; Pyongyang area and, 20–21. See also Pyongyang rubber strikes

colonial government, Japanese: anticommunist persecution, 82–83; assimilation policies, 91; bourgeois nationalists and, 31; control over anticolonial and leftist forces, 37; nationalist movement and, 34

Comintern, 27, 73, 81, 190n10, 202n5, 205n35

communism, 21, 81; international solidarity, 43–44; mass demonstrations, 40; use of term, 196n80. See also Korean Communist Party; red union movement

Communist University of the Toilers of the East, 40

consciousness: new forms of, 4, 9–10; small-group method and, 132–33, 135–36. See also class consciousness; gender consciousness; small-group method

Constitution of South Korea, 96, 98

contingent workers, 8, 11, 167–69, 183, 243n56. See also irregular workers

Control Data, 128, 138, 141, 143, 145–49, 230n61, 238n144, 239n151

Cook, Alice, 227n34

cooperative movement, 77–78, 80, 215n52, 215n54, 217n79, 222n57. See also industrial cooperatives; worker-owned factory cooperatives

Cornell University, Industrial Research Institute, 227n34

Cort and Cor-Tec union, 246–47n85

Council of Korean Women Workers' Associations, 161, 164, 242n30, 242n40. See also Korean Women Workers' Association

Council of Rubber Workers, 156, 159

damage compensation and provisional attachment, 177, 245n75

Danish cooperative system, 77, 215n52

democracy movement, 3, 129–30, 135, 140–41, 151–52, 160–63, 187. See also *minju* union movement

Densan wage structure, 118–19, 226n20

discrimination: class-based, 126–27; ethnic, 88, 117; gender-based, 10, 50–51, 145–50, 184–85, 235n109

dismissals, 16–17, 24, 29, 76, 89–90, 102, 105, 164, 175–76, 224n97, 225n1, 237n130, 238n144. See also layoffs

Dong-A ilbo (Tonga ilbo; East Asia Daily), 17, 24, 28, 77, 189n4; on global competition, 197n83; on labor issues, 29–30, 34, 36–37, 76, 103; on militant factory women, 63, 65–68, 75–76; on red unions, 43, *44*; on rubber industry strikes, 75, 200n117; "Woman-in-the-Sky" article, 1–2, *2*, 13, 15; on worker-owned factories, 80–81
downsizing, 158–59, 176, 240n13

economy, 33–34, 101, 108, 112. *See also* neoliberalism
education, 73–74, 127, 142, 171, 190n12, 230n58, 236n125. *See also* Christian Academy; labor night schools; small-group method; student movement
E-Land/Homeplus, 182, 247n86
electronics industry, 111–12, 140, 182–83, 236n119, 247n87
enlightenment *(kyemong)*, 49–50, 57, 77
equality *(kyun)* ideology, 98–99, 115–16, 126, 198n104
exceptional leaders, 68, 74, 174–75
export-industry factories, 10; capital flight, 157–58; income, 240n17; women workers, 111–12, 125–26. *See also* manufacturing sector

factories: closure of, 159, 238n144; working conditions, 63–64, 128–29, 197n89, 214n41. *See also* export-industry factories; manufacturing sector
Factory Complex (2015), 165
Factory New Village Movement, 141
factory self-management movement, 92–96
faith-based social movements, 77
family: company-as-family ideology, 236n121; women's wages and, 28–30, 64, 108–9, 116–17. *See also* male breadwinner ideal; married women workers
farmers, 15, 27, 53, 217n79, 224n98. *See also* rural areas
fascism, 96–97
Federation of Korean Trade Unions (FKTU), 107, 112–13, 121–23, 140–41, 154, 227n29, 227n34, 228n35, 229n45, 243n49
Federation of Women Workers' Trade Unions, 243n49
feminism, 46, 48–51, 137–50, 204nn28–29, 205n30. *See also* women's liberation movement
feminization of labor, 184, 243n56
fine system, 29, 88

free or "red love," 56, 209n64
Freire, Paulo, 135, 233n96, 234nn98–99

gender consciousness, 113, 138–39, 145, 238n145, 239n151
gender equality, 133–34, 137–50
gender ideologies and discourses, 4–7, 186–87, 210n65; citizenship and, 99; Confucian, 108; conventional trope of helpless factory girls, 2–3, 37–38, 43, 52–53, 65, 67, 71, 207n48; family and women's wages, 28–30, 64, 108–9, 116–17 (*see also* male breadwinner ideal); labor market transformation and, 184–85; middle-class womanhood and, 124–25; patriarchal, 53, 114, 116, 213n27; relationship between "new women" and *yŏgong*, 46–51; rubber industry strikes and, 24; slang terms, 230nn55–56 (see also *kongsuni*); socialist, 51–56; union-busting and, 143; wartime, 91. *See also* feminism
gendered power relations in labor movement, 11, 111–12, 117, 151, 160, 181–82, 237nn130–32. *See also* trade union movement
general strikes, 26, 42, 72, 93, 197n83, 243n49; Chŏnp'yŏng-organized, 93; literary representations of, 58
good wife ideal, 64, 204n22
Great Workers' Struggle (1987), 5, 10, 123, 151, 153–54, 161–62, 176, 243n53

hakch'ul, 153, 162, 239n5, 241n24. *See also* worker-student/intellectual alliance
Ham Sanghun, 77
Han Myŏnghŭi, 138, 145, 149, 238n144
Han Myŏngsuk, 137, 140, 235n116
Han Sunim, 236n116
Hanjin Heavy Industries Union, 7–8, 141, 174–82. *See also* Korea Shipbuilding and Engineering Corporation
Hanjin Subic yard, 176–77, 245n73
Heavy and Chemical Industrialization (HCI) drive, 126, 165, 170
heavy-industry workforce, 154, 168, 170–86, 243n53; male dominance in, 153, 181–82
Herring, John, 227n34
high-altitude sit-ins, 1–3; in 1990s, 185–86; by irregular workers, 182–83; longest, 247n85, 248n100; solidarity with, 179–81, 246n80. *See also* "chimney man" incidents; Kang Churyong; Kim Jin-Sook
Hŏ Chŏngsuk, 48–50, 190n11, 201–2n4, 204n25, 205n31, 206n35, 209n64, 210n65, 213n20, 213n23

Hŏ Kyun, 54–56, 92
Hope Bus caravans, 179–81, *180*, 185, 246n80, 247n87
Hosoi Wakizō, *The Pitiful History of Female Factory Workers*, 71
housekeeper role, 56, 209n63
Housemaid (1960), 124–25, 229n48
housemaids, 108, 124–26, 197n84, 206n37
humanism, 32–33
hunger strikes, 18, 24, 60, 65–67, 70; criticism of, 52–53; by irregular workers, 182–83; by Kang Churyong, 16, 43, 71–72; by Kim Jin-Sook, 174–76, 244n69; in textile industry, 90
Hŭngŏp Kurakpu, 32–33, 198n100
Hŭngsadan movement, 97, 198n100
Hwang Sindŏk, 48–49, 204n29
Hwang Yira, 178
hyŏnjang t'usin, 161–62
Hyundai Motors, 183, 185, 246n80, 247nn88–89

ilminjuŭi (one people-ism), 97
Ilsin Spinning and Weaving, 134
Incheon UIM, 135, 233n96, 234n98, 234n101, 239n150
industrial cooperatives, 79, 81, 196n82, 216n69. *See also* cooperative movement; worker-owned factory cooperatives
industrial democracy, 106–7
industrial relations system, 10, 86, 91–92, 111–12, 115–18, 199n105
industrial warriors, 96, 113, 154, 158, 165
industrialization, 3, 9, 20, 48, 72, 109, 124, 126, 191n17
inflation, 101
International Confederation of Free Trade Unions (ICFTU), 121, 228n35
International Labor Organization (ILO), 121, 243n56
irregular workers, 151, 154–55, 166, 176–79, 181–85, 248nn96–97; categories of, 248n91; definition of, 183–84; labor movement and, 176–77, 247nn86–88. *See also* contingent workers
Island of Shadows (2014), 174
Isogaya Sueji, 203nn17–18

Japan: communist groups, 43–44, 82; end of colonial government in Korea, 4 (*see also* colonial government); Kŭnuhoe chapters in, 51; labor disputes, 65–66, 226n13 (*see also* "chimney man" incidents); labor relations, 90–91, 118–20; Labor-Farmer Party, 15; socialist feminism in, 48; union movement, 121
JOC Korea, 131–37, 139, 142, 156, 231nn69–70, 232n71, 232n73, 232n80, 233n96
June 10 Manse movement (1926), 40
June 1987 Struggle, 5, 153, 161, 173

Kagawa Toyohiko, 33
Kanebō. *See* Chongyŏn Spinning
Kang Churyong: arrests, 16–17, 75, 82; biography, 23, 30, 72–73, 194n61; communist union organizing and, 37–45, 53, 73–75; death of, 74–75, 82–83, 194n62; high-altitude sit-in, 1–3, *2*, 6–9, 11–18, 37, 43–45, 60, 73–74, 83, 183; hunger strikes, 16, 43, 71–72; media representations of, 63–70, 214n29; memories of, 62, 82, 113, 155, 185–86, 248nn101–2; oratory skills, 176
Kang Ilmae, 85–86, 95, 100–107, 224n91
Kang Kyŏngae, 56, 72; *The Human Predicament*, 57–59; "Replying to Older Brother's Letter," 59, 84; *Salt*, 210n75
Kang Wŏnyong, 137, 139
Kidok Sinuhoe, 199n109
Kim. *See* "Miss Kim"
Kim Chit'ae, 95, 100–101, 220n41, 222n65, 223n69
Kim Choi, 202n4, 210n65
Kim Chuhong, 107
Kim Chuik, 245n75; suicide protest, 177–78
Kim Ch'wisŏn, 17–18, 66, 68–69, 75–76, 192n33
Kim Dae-Jung, 129, 247n89
Kim Jin-Sook: biography, 170–72; high-altitude sit-in, 7–8, 10–11, 84, 174–81, *177*, 183, 185–86, 244n69, 246n83, 248n102; Hope Bus caravans and, 179–81, *180*, 185, 247n87; hunger strikes, 174–76, 244n69; Kang Churyong and, 155; oratory skills, 176, 245n71; *Salt Flower Tree*, 176; union activism, 172–82
Kim Myŏngsi, 202n4, 213n20, 214n38
Kim Namchŏn, 56; "Factory Fraternity," 57; "Factory Newspaper," 57
Kim Sŏngsu, 28
Kim Soyŏn, 247n87
Kim T'aejun, 208n57
Kim Tongwŏn, 31, 35–36, 57, 97, 194n60, 197n94, 198n96, 198n101, 200n112, 200n119, 221n52
Kiryung Electronics, 182–83, 247n87
kisaeng courtesans, 57–58

Kisuhoe (Society of Worker Flagbearers for Women's Liberation), 137–49, 234n107
kkŏl, 45–47, 203n21, 204n25
knitwear industry, 19–20, 24, 197n83
Kollontai, Alexandra, 204n25, 209n64
komusin, 7, 19, 29, 59, 192n40
kongdan, 126–27
kongdori, 127, 230n55
kongjang kasinae, 108, 125
kongsuni, 3, 113, 125, 127–28, 149, 154, 165–66, 230n55, 230n61
Korea Shipbuilding and Engineering Corporation (KSEC, later, Hanjin Heavy Industries), 7–8, 94, 115, 121, 154, 168, 170–86. *See also* Hanjin Heavy Industries Union; Subic Bay Freeport Zone, Philippines
Korea Student Christian Federation (KSCF), 233n96
Korea-Japan Normalization Treaty, 121
Korean Communist Party, 40, 53, 196n80, 201n3, 202n6, 207n49, 208n54, 208n57
Korean Confederation of Trade Unions (KCTU), 154, 156, 167, 169–70, 175–76, 181, 184, 231n67, 243n49, 244n57, 244n66, 245n71, 245n75
Korean Contingent Worker Center (KCWC), 183–84
Korean labor history, 7–8, 163–64, 189n3. *See also* memory politics
Korean Public Service and Transport Workers' Union, 167
Korean Railway, 119–20
Korean Textile Workers' Union, 228n40
Korean War, 85, 87, 94. *See also* United States
Korean Women Workers' Association (KWWA), 138, 161, 166
Korean Women's Association United (KWAU), 166
Korean Women's Trade Union (KWTU), 166–67, 243nn49–50
Korean Workers Mutual Aid Association. *See* Chosŏn Nodong Kongjehoe
Kropotkin, Peter, 33, 78, 196n79
KTX, 182, 247n86
kŭlloja, 90–91, 96, 99, 117
k'ŭnagi (k'ŭnaegi), 29, 47, 69, 108
Kungmindang (peoples' party), 98
Kŭnu (journal), 47, 49–50
Kŭnuhoe (Rose of Sharon Society), 14, 206nn35–38; anticolonial student activism and, 54; founding of, 201n123; literary representations of, 57–58; membership, 205n33, 206n40; red union movement and, 41, 47–51; rubber industry strikes and, 34, 36–37, 201nn122–23; socialist feminism and, 205n31; textile industry and, 89
Kuro Industrial Complex, 126, 128, 146, 153, 160
Kwangju Massacre, 150, 152, 161
kwinong campaign, 77
kwisok chaesan. See vested properties
Kwŏn Migyŏng, 128, 155–56, 158–59
Kwŏn Osŏl, 201n3
Kyŏngbang. *See* Kyŏngsŏng Spinning and Weaving
Kyŏngsŏng RS Association, 54
Kyŏngsŏng Spinning and Weaving (Kyŏngsŏng Pangjik; Kyŏngbang), 28, 30, 48, 55, 197n83, 224n101

labor activism: marginalization of women workers, 109–10, 116, 154–55, 163; statistics on, 240n7; strategies, 218n18 (*see also* high-altitude sit-ins; hunger strikes; militant activism; strikes). *See also* Chobang labor dispute; Great Workers' Struggle (1987); June 1987 Struggle; *minju* union movement; Pyongyang rubber strikes; red union movement; *yŏgong* activism
labor control regimes, 144–45, 158–59, 241n22
labor laws, 10, 76, 106, 111–12, 115, 128–29, 184; Chobang dispute and, 106–7; passed in 1950s, 86
labor market transformation, 184–85. *See also* neoliberalism
labor night schools, 127, 131, 136, 139, 142, 172, 201n125, 230n59, 234n98, 239n5
labor rights, 5, 106, 115–16
labor supply, 244n59
labor-capital cooperation, 33–34, 87, 92, 96–99, 214n48
land reform, 200n116, 215n52
Law on the Disposition of Vested Properties, 95
layoffs, 244n69, 246n83, 247nn88–89. *See also* dismissals
leftist labor organizing, 27, 93. *See also* communism; red union movement; socialist labor activism
liberal feminism, 48, 205n30
Liberal Party, 223n70
literacy, 42, 232n71
livelihood wage, 10, 112, 118–24, 226n14, 226n18, 226n20, 227nn28–29. *See also* male breadwinner ideal

Madame Freedom (1956), 114
male breadwinner ideal, 10, 29–30, 108, 110, 112; demise of, 168–69; union-busting and, 143; women's wages and, 114–24. *See also* livelihood wage
Manchuria, 72, 193n47
manufacturing sector: female-dominated firms, 141–42; irregular women workers, 182–83; number of workers in, 125–26; rates of employment in, 229n49. *See also* export-industry factories
March First Movement, 31, 35, 78, 198n96
married women workers, 64, 69; discrimination against, 147; irregular work, 184; seasonal employment and, 21–22
martyrdom. *See* suicide protests
Marufuto (Hwandae) Rubber, 89, 212n16
Marxism-Leninism, 21, 27, 193n49, 196n80
Masan Free Export Zone, 126, 160
masses *(taejung)*, 126, 153
media: bourgeois nationalist, 62–63, 67, 109; coverage of suicide protests, 128; gender discourses, 29–30, 62–70, 160; on sweatshop working conditions, 128–29. See also *specific newspapers and journals*
Media Ethics Committee, 230n55
memory politics, 8, 10–11, 185–86; Kang Churyong and, 62, 82, 113, 155, 185–86, 248nn101–2; *minju* movement and, 154, 160–70, 186, 231n67, 239n3; oral histories and, 163–64; "single spark" narrative, 130, 137; of *yŏgong* activism, 130, 137, 165–66, 185–87
menstruation leave, 146, 148
militant activism, 2–3, 8–9, 13, 15, 90; colonial era, 16–17, 26, 64–70, 73, 75–76, 113; irregular workers and, 182; labor laws and, 106–7; in mid-1980s, 153 (*see also* Great Workers' Struggle); in twenty-first century, 169–70. *See also* strikes
minimum wage, 123, 228n41
Ministry of Commerce and Industry, 100–101, 103, 106, 223n71
minju (democratic) union movement, 3, 5, 7, 112–13, 127; beginning of, 130, 136–37; collapse of, 152–53; criticism of, 151, 161–63; high-altitude sit-ins, 185; JOC members in, 136; male leadership, 154; scholarship on, 236n118; small group method and, 132, 135; use of term "*minju*," 140–41; women's leadership in, 3, 7, 238n133; women's liberation and, 137–50; women's movement and, 238n145. *See also* memory politics

"Miss Kim," 231n69, 234n104; suicide protest, 113, 131, 134–37, 156
modern girl figure, 45–46, 64, 203nn19–22, 204n23, 204n25
modernization and modernity: Christian elite and, 20–21; desirability of, 46; nationalist version of, 68; women industrial workers and, 3–7
Moon Jae-in (Mun Chaein), 8, 185, 246n85
Movement for General Mobilization of the National Spirit, 91
Movement to Promote Chosŏn Native Goods, 33
Muhojŏngin. *See* O Kiyŏng
multinational corporations, 238n144
Mutual Aid (Kongje) Rubber, 70, 76, 78–82
mutual aid theory, 78, 196n79
Myŏng Tŏksang, 31

Nangmyŏn incident, 100, 223n69
National Assembly, 86, 95, 101–4. *See also* labor laws
National Council of Korean Labor Unions. *See* Chŏnp'yŏng
National Institute of Korean History, 63, 211n4
National Railway Workers' Union, 107, 115, 121
National Security Law, 142–43, 247n87
nationalist ideologies, 4, 199n107. *See also* bourgeois nationalist movement; Protestant nationalist movement
nation-building, 96–99; colonial era, 165–66; Park Chung Hee and, 87, 112, 123, 125–29, 165, 170; women industrial workers and, 3–7. *See also* capitalist development; industrialization; modernization and modernity
neoliberalism, 10–11, 151, 154, 156–57, 166–69. *See also* economy
New Village Movement, 126, 141, 229n52
new woman figure, 14, 45–51, 55, 64, 72, 203nn20–21, 204n23, 207n44
night schools, 230n59. *See also* labor night schools
North Korean spy rings, 140, 173, 224n103
Northwest Black Friends Society, 27, 79–80, 216n76
Northwest Youth Corps, 93, 220n35, 220n37

O Kiyŏng (Muhojŏngin), 13, 16–18, 25–26, 34, 36, 65, 80, 97, 190n14, 193n47, 199n105, 200n117, 211n18, 222n54

O Wŏnchŏl, 126, 165
O Yunsŏn, 35–36
Oak Electronics, 140, 236n119
old-style woman figure, 46, 204n22
oral history projects, 163–64
organized labor movement, 1–11; colonial era, 12–84; developmental era (1960s to 1980s), 10, 111–50, 243n53; postcolonial period (1945 to 1950s), 4, 9–10, 85–110; postdevelopmental period (post-1987), 10–11, 151–87. *See also* gendered power relations in labor movement; labor activism; trade union movement
ŏyong (pro-company stance), 134, 141

Pae Minsu, 200n116
Pae Sŏngnyong, 205n35
paehu (behind-the-scenes agitators), 29, 37–39, 43, 68, 75, 89–90, 142–43, 201n1
Paek Kwangun (Ch'ae Ch'an), 23
Pak Chinhong, 54, 74, 202n9, 208n55, 208n57, 209n58, 209n63
Pak Chŏngae, 202n4
Pak Chŏngt'ae, 102, 224n89
Pak Hŏnyŏng, 52–53, 208n57
Pak Sŭngguk, "Restart," 58
Pak Sunhŭi (Chobang), 55, 89, 213n21
Pak Sunhŭi (Wŏnp'ung), 131, 133, 138, 148–49, 162, 234n107, 236n116, 239n3
Pak T'aeyŏn, 138, 235n115
Pak Wansik, 217n86
Pak Wŏnhŭi, 48, 50
Pak Yŏngje, 173, 178–79, 244n64
Pando Trading union, 136, 138, 236n116, 237n128
Pang Yongsŏk, 237n130
Pan-Pacific Trade Union Secretariat. *See* T'aero Secretariat
Park Chung Hee: anticommunism, 236n117; assassination of, 152; Christian Academy and, 140; democracy movement against, 135; martial law, 141; nation-building and development, 87, 112, 123, 125–29, 165, 170; rural revitalization and, 229n52; union-busting, 142–44; wage cuts, 121–22; *yŏgong* and, 165
paternalism, 63–64, 68, 81, 165
patriotic units, 90–91, 120, 141. *See also* wartime mobilization
patriotism, 96, 227n25
payment in kind, 101
Peace Market garment district, 128–30, 132–33, 232n78

Peace Rubber factory, 76, 79–81, 129, 216n73
pijŏnggyujik (nonstandard employment), 154–55, 166–69, 184, 243n57. *See also* irregular workers
"pity" discourse, 29, 52–53, 63, 71, 207n48
police, 103, 173, 179; colonial, 17, 25–26, 37. *See also* arrests; state repression
poverty, 29, 33–34, 67, 76, 171; rates of, 211n15
precarious labor, 11, 167, 169. See also *pijŏnggyujik*
prison conditions, 55, 74–75, 82–83, 190n11, 209n60, 214n40
Profintern (Red International of Labor Unions), 40, 73, 81, 202n5, 217n79
prostitution, 107–8, 114, 224n97, 226n11. *See also* sex workers
Protestant nationalist movement, 14, 20–21, 30–31, 198n104; ideology, 31–37; social reform and, 81; turn to the countryside, 76–78. *See also* bourgeois nationalist movement; Christian capitalist elite
Provisional Government of Korea, 98
puin, use of term, 207n44
punyŏ, 116–17
Pusan: demonstrations in, 86; export industries, 126; rubber industry, 21, 25, 89, 144, 195n68; shoe industry in 1990s, 7, 10–11, 154–60, 168–69, 186
Pusan Regional Federation of Trade Unions, 85
P'yŏngwŏn Rubber strike (1931), 9, 13, 15–18, 25–27, 37, 52, 59–60; communist cells and, 42–43; militancy of female strikers, 71; outcome, 75–76; wage cuts and, 2, 29–30, 70; worker-owned factories and, 80. *See also* Kang Churyong
Pyongyang: as capital of North Korea, 83; Christian nationalists in, 32–33; colonial-era economic and social conditions, 18–23, 196n78. *See also* Pyongyang rubber industry; Pyongyang rubber strikes
Pyongyang Labor Alliance, 25, 27, 30, 191n23
Pyongyang rubber industry, 7, 9, 11, 18–23, 35, 192n38; communist organizing and, 55; literary representations of, 56–60; male technicians, 25–26; number of employees in, 22, 194n60; red union organizing in, 49–51; seasonal employment, 21–22, 28–29. *See also* P'yŏngwŏn Rubber strike

INDEX

Pyongyang Rubber Industry Employers' Association, 25
Pyongyang rubber strikes, 12–18, 23–28, 57, 65, 195n68; 1930 strike, 29, 57, 72–73, 75, 200n117; female leadership, 89. See also P'yŏngwŏn Rubber strike
Pyongyang Rubber Workers' Association, 23, 25, 72
Pyongyang Society for the Promotion of Chosŏn Native Goods, 35, 200n114
pyŏnhyŏk, 161

radical writers, 9, 56–60, 71
rape, 64, 144, 241. See also sexual violence
red scare, 29, 68. See also paehu
red union movement, 83–84; communist organizing, 9, 27, 52–53; female self-worth and, 60; Japanese workers in, 203nn17–18; "new women" and yŏgong activists, 46–51; Pyongyang rubber workers and, 39–45; revolutionary propaganda, 42, 214n28; sexism in, 56; strikes and, 89; students and, 51–56. See also communism; socialist labor activism
red-baiting of labor activists, 142–43, 173
Rhee, Syngman, 32, 87–88, 96–97, 111, 198n100, 221n50, 223n69; Chobang dispute and, 99–106, 223n84, 224n91; end of regime (see April Revolution of 1960); Taehan Noch'ong and, 224n87; women's issues and, 226n11
Ri Kiyŏng, 56; Wŏlhŭi, 57, 210n74
right-wing labor organizing, 93–99
RS (reading societies), 53–54, 208n57
rubber shoe industry, 7, 9, 11, 18–23; costs, 195nn70–71; domestic demand, 19, 21; number of employees in, 192n34; youth labor, 193n52. See also Pusan, rubber industry; P'yŏngwŏn Rubber strike; Pyongyang rubber industry; Pyongyang rubber strikes; Seoul, rubber industry
rural areas: Christian nationalism and, 76–78; rural-urban gap and, 229n52; socialist organizing and, 50. See also tenant farmers
rural-to-urban migration, 126, 229n51, 244n59

Samhwa Rubber, 241n22
Samsung Pharmaceutical, 141, 148, 237n131, 238n145
Samwŏrhoe (the March Society), 204n29
Sanpō. See wartime mobilization

"save-the-company corps" (kusadae), 144, 154, 159, 240n11
seasonal employment, 21–22, 28–29
Sech'ang Rubber, 70, 80, 203n16
self-government movement, 199n107
Seoul, 10; export industries, 126, 153; minju unions in, 149; population growth, 229n54; Protestant Christian nationalists in, 32–35; rubber industry, 19, 21, 24–25, 195n68
Seoul Female Student Movement (Kŭnuhoe incident), 54
service sector, 182, 241n28. See also housemaids
sex workers, 107–8, 230n57. See also prostitution
sexual division of labor, 22, 112, 170–71
sexual exploitation, 64, 69, 75
sexual harassment, 47, 64, 148–49, 171, 175, 181, 197n89, 230n57; protests against, 128, 144–45
sexual morality, 56, 64, 69, 209n63, 230n57; free or "red love," 56, 209n64. See also free or "red love"
sexual violence: against factory women, 117, 142, 144–45, 148–49, 159, 182, 241n25; against housemaids, 126; in villages, 58. See also rape
sexualization of factory girls, 47, 127
shipbuilding union workers, 6–8, 121–22
shoe industry in Pusan (1990s), 7, 10–11, 154–60, 168–69, 186
Signetics Korea, 140, 236n119
silk-reeling industry, 214n41, 233n86
Simdo Textile union, 134, 233n91
Sin Illyŏng, 137, 140, 149, 234n98, 234n107, 235nn115–16
Sin'ganhoe (New Korea Society), 14, 199n108, 200n119, 201n122, 205n29, 214n37; anarchists and, 79, 216n65; anticolonial student activism and, 54; Chobang strike and, 88; communists in, 190n10; literary representations of, 58; rubber industry strikes and, 34–37; rural cooperative movement and, 77
Sinhŭng coal mine strike, 26
Sinminhoe (New People's Association), 31–32
sit-ins: in factories, 16. See also high-altitude sit-ins
small-group method, 132–33, 135–36, 142, 166
social Darwinism, 32, 196n79
social hierarchy, 4–5, 64, 84, 117, 126–27, 143–45, 235n109
socialist feminism, 48–51, 204n28, 205n31

socialist labor activism, 13, 26–27, 33–34, 193n49; equality and, 98–99; male ideologues and, 71; transnational, 43–45. See also red union movement
Society for the Promotion of Chosŏn Native Goods, 36
solidarity strikes, 13, 16, 22, 24–25, 89, 145; gender and, 186; Hope Bus caravans, 179–81, *180,* 185, 246n80; irregular workers and, 176; Kisuhoe and, 234n107; precarious labor and, 169–70; in Pyongyang rubber industry, 191n23; worker-student alliance and, 152–53, 162
Song Wŏndo, 220n35
Song Yŏng, 56, 210n71; *O Suhyang,* 57–58, 202n12, 210n74
South Korean Workers' Party, 94, 100, 208n57
Special Law Regarding National Security, 141, 147
speedups, 128, 155–56, 158–59, 241n22
Star Chemical, 246n80, 246n85, 248n100
starvation, 67, 126
state repression, 27, 112, 152, 179; of anarchists, 216n66; anticommunist, 37, 41, 54–55, 173, 190n10, 236n117; suicide and, 246n85. See also arrests; violence
strike demands, 4, 17, 21, 24–25, 29–30, 62, 88, 197n87, 214n41, 226n13; end of violence, 159; gender-specific, 75, 117 (*see also* women's issues). See also livelihood wage; wage levels
strikebreakers, 16–17, 25, 65
strikes: in 1930s textile industry, 88–90; colonial era, 13, 26, 195n67; numbers of, 211n10, 219n26, 219n29; rubber industry, 22–28, 42; in shipbuilding industry, 177; against wage cuts, 13, 15–16, 24–25; women janitors, 181–82. See also Great Workers' Struggle (1987); militant activism; solidarity strikes
student movement, 51–56. See also *hakch'ul;* worker-student/intellectual alliance
subcontracting firms, 237nn128–29, 241n23
Subic Bay Freeport Zone, Philippines, 176–77, 245n73
suicide protests, 113, 128–32, 134–37, 141, 155–56, 177–78, 245n75
Sŭng Togyŏng, 80
suyang (self-cultivation): bourgeois nationalists and, 33–35, 77; feminists and, 49
Suyang Tongmaenghoe, 198n101

Suyang Tonguhoe, 32–35, 70, 97, 190n5, 198nn100–101, 199n105, 199nn107–9, 200n113
sweatshop workers, 128–30, 171

Taebong, 155, 240n13
taegongjuŭi, 198n104
Taehan Noch'ong (Federation of Korean Trade Unions), 93–96, 98–99, 102–5, 107–9, 115, 121, 220n34, 220n37, 220nn34–35, 223n70, 224n87, 225n1, 226n13, 227n29
Taehan Spinning and Weaving, 225n1
T'aero Secretariat, 40–41, 43, 52, 75, 202n12, 203nn16–17, 208n53, 214n38
Taeyang Rubber, 240n13, 241n24
Tanabe Kiyoshi, 15, 82–83, 190n15
temporary workers, 168. See also irregular workers
tenant farmers, 27, 53. See also farmers; rural areas
textile industry: communist organizing in, 55; Japanese white-collar workers, 88; labor disputes, 86–90, 225n1; literary representations of, 58–59; national union, 116, 123; strikes, 7, 65, 74–75, 88–90, 134–35, 219n29; women workers, 22, 88, 111–12. See also Chobang labor dispute; Chobang textile factory
Tonggwang (Eastern Light), 13, 16–18, 34, 47, 63, 65, 71–72, 74, 190n5
Tongil Spinning and Weaving (Tongil Pangjik) union, 136, 138, 141, 143–45, 236n125
torture, 31, 55, 74, 82, 140, 142, 173, 201n3, 214n40, 241n25
Tosi Sanŏp Sŏn'gyohoe. See UIM
Tōyōbō (Tongyang Pangjŏk), 88, 234n100
trade union movement, 5–11; anarchists and, 78–79; contract coverage, 225n10; female leaders, 173–75 (see also *minju* union movement; *yŏgong* activism); institutionalization of, 110; leftist national trade union federation, 92; male leadership, 89–90, 109–12, 115–17, 132, 143–44, 154, 160, 162–63, 169, 237n132; membership rates, 184, 248n97. See also Chŏnp'yŏng; red union movement
Ttosuni (1963), 229n47
t'usa, 70, 131–32, 213n29

UIM (urban industrial mission), 131, 135–36, 139, 142, 231n69, 233nn95–96, 234n101, 238n144, 239n150
unemployment, 222n67, 244n59

union-busting campaigns, 134–35, 142–44, 158–59, 236n119, 237n130
United States, 4, 32, 96, 114, 221n52; occupation, 87, 94, 97, 226n11
United States Army Military Government in Korea (USAMGIK), 92, 97, 199n105, 221nn52–53

vested properties, 92, 95, 100, 106, 220n41, 222n54, 223n71, 233n86
violence: anti-Chinese, 193n47; against labor activists, 103–4, 142, 173, 241n25, 244n64 (see also torture); between left- and right-wing activists, 94; in rubber shoe industry, 158–60; verbal, 146, 155–56. See also Kwangju Massacre; militant activism; sexual violence

wage levels, 23–24, 28–30; cuts, 70, 88, 121–22, 197n83–197n84, 197n89. See also livelihood wage; women's wages
war widows, 114, 225n2
warriors, 221n48. See also industrial warriors; t'usa
wartime mobilization, 9, 90–92, 120, 219nn22–24; Sanpō policies, 90–91, 93, 96, 117–20, 218n21, 227nn24–25
woman-in-the-sky moments, 1–2, 2, 8, 13, 15, 45, 185–86, 190n14. See also Kang Churyong; Kim Jin-Sook
women comrades (yŏdongji), 107
women industrial workers: agency and capacity of, 6, 37–38, 43, 61–70, 90, 102–9, 186–87; demographics, 229n45, 229n50; employment by sector, 194nn57–58; empowerment of, 114, 211n6; leftist discourse on, 51–56; numbers of, 241n28; positive views of, 224n101; respect for, 10, 52, 64, 68–70; terms for, 207n44; young single women, 22, 69, 228n41, 238n141. See also married women workers; yŏgong activism
women's issues, 46, 48, 117, 148, 205n30, 206n38, 209n62, 236n116
women's liberation movement, 9, 137–50. See also feminism
women's wages, 148, 184, 197n84, 228n43; fine system and, 29, 88; male breadwinner ideal and, 122–24 (see also male breadwinner ideal); in rubber industry, 23–24, 28–30; seasonal employment and, 21–22, 28–29; textile industry, 228nn40–41

Wŏnp'ung Wool union, 136, 138, 141, 144, 148, 232n77, 236n116, 236n125, 237nn129–30, 239n151
Wŏnsan general strike, 26
work bureaus, 79–80, 196n82, 216n69
worker-owned factory cooperatives, 62, 76–82, 95–96
worker-student/intellectual alliance, 10, 113, 129–30, 152–53, 161–62, 239n5. See also hakch'ul
working-class women: as breadwinners, 226n12 (see also women's wages); leftist journals and, 47; social bias against, 7 (see also discrimination; gender ideologies and discourses). See also service sector; sex workers; women industrial workers; yŏgong activism

Yamakawa Kikue, 48, 205n29, 226n13
YH Trading union, 138, 141, 236n116
Yi Chaeyu, 53, 55, 208n57, 209n62–209n63, 214n40
Yi Chŏkhyo, 31, 57, 210n67
Yi Chŏlsun, 151, 160–61, 166, 186, 189n5, 230n55
Yi Ch'ŏnggak, 138, 149, 234n107
Yi Chonghŭi, 54, 208n55, 209n58
Yi Chŏnghŭi, 139
Yi Chŏngsik, 173, 244n64
Yi Chuha, 41, 45, 203n16
Yi Haenam, 231n70
Yi Hyojae, 248n98
Yi Hyŏn'gyŏng, 48–50, 204n29, 205n31
Yi Kwangsu, 198n101, 199n108, 199n197
Yi Kwansul, 208n57
Yi Kyŏngsim, 234n107
Yi Kyŏngsŏn, 54, 208n54
Yi Oesŏn, 103–4, 223n82
Yi Pŏmsŏk, 97, 99
Yi Pukmyŏng, 56, 191n17
Yi Sangok, 94, 102, 223n82, 224n89
Yi Sosŏn, 132
Yi Sukhŭi, 132–33, 138
Yi Sun'gŭm, 54, 74, 208n54, 209n63
Yi Taewi, 33, 76, 97, 199n105, 199n109, 221n52, 222n53
Yi Yŏngsun, 138, 145–46, 149, 234n107
YMCA, 33, 35–36, 77, 172
yŏgong activism, 1–11; classed and gendered discourses on, 1–5, 7, 46–47, 61–71, 108–9, 125, 218n17 (see also gender ideologies and discourses); film portrayals of, 124–25, 165,

229n47; literary representations of, 56–60, 210n71; socialist "new women" and, 45–51; subjectivities of, 70–75, 84; use of term, 207n44. *See also* Chobang labor dispute; gender consciousness; memory politics; militant activism; *minju* union movement; Pyongyang rubber industry; strikes; women industrial workers
yŏgong t'usa, 52, 70, 113

yŏjangbu, 13, 68, 213n23
yŏjikkong, 47, 63, 207n44, 211n3
Yŏngdŭngp'o UIM, 135, 233n96
yŏsa, 68–70, 90, 213n25
yŏt'usa, 2, 13, 52, 68, 213nn19–21
Yu Oksun, 138, 145, 238n139
Yu Sunhŭi, 55, 209n58
Yusin constitution, 140–41
YWCA, 136

CPSIA information can be obtained
at www.ICGtesting.com
Printed in the USA
LVHW091912120521
687241LV00005B/34/J